North Korea and the
Science of Provocation

North Korea and the Science of Provocation

Fifty Years of Conflict-Making

Robert Daniel Wallace

McFarland & Company, Inc., Publishers
Jefferson, North Carolina

LIBRARY OF CONGRESS CATALOGUING-IN-PUBLICATION DATA

Names: Wallace, Robert Daniel, author.
Title: North Korea and the science of provocation : fifty years of conflict-making / Robert Daniel Wallace.
Description: Jefferson, North Carolina : McFarland & Company, Inc., Publishers, 2016 | Includes bibliographical references and index.
Identifiers: LCCN 2015047846 | ISBN 9780786499694 (softcover : acid free paper) ♾
Subjects: LCSH: Korea (North)—Foreign relations. | Threats—Korea (North)—History. | Military policy—Korea (North)—Decision making. | National security—Korea (North)—Decision making. | Crises—Political aspects—Korea (North)—History. | Korea (North)—Foreign relations—Case studies. | Korea (North)—Social conditions. | Korea (North)—Politics and government.
Classification: LCC DS935.65 .W35 2016 | DDC 327.5193—dc23
LC record available at http://lccn.loc.gov/2015047846

BRITISH LIBRARY CATALOGUING DATA ARE AVAILABLE

ISBN (print) 978-0-7864-9969-4
ISBN (ebook) 978-1-4766-2314-6

© 2016 Robert Daniel Wallace. All rights reserved

No part of this book may be reproduced or transmitted in any form or by any means, electronic or mechanical, including photocopying or recording, or by any information storage and retrieval system, without permission in writing from the publisher.

On the cover: a North Korean soldier looking through binoculars across the Demilitarized Zone, © 2015 EdStock/iStock

Printed in the United States of America

McFarland & Company, Inc., Publishers
  Box 611, Jefferson, North Carolina 28640
  www.mcfarlandpub.com

Table of Contents

List of Figures	vii
List of Tables	viii
List of Acronyms	ix
Preface	1
Introduction	9
1. North Korea's Hostile Foreign Policy Actions (1948–1961)	19
2. Introduction and First Case (North Korea Emerges)	35
3. The Arduous March: North Korea's Great Famine	72
4. Regime Succession and Case Comparisons	103
5. Hostile Foreign Policy Event Analysis	142
6. Comparisons and Conclusions	176
Appendix A. Azar's Event Categories	185
Appendix B. Korean Conflict Dataset	187
Appendix C. Map of the Korean Peninsula	195
Chapter Notes	197
Bibliography	205
Index	251

List of Figures

2.1	DPRK Military Expenditures 1960–1970	43
2.2	Hostile Foreign Policy Activities 1960–1970	45
2.3	Composite Index of National Capacity Scores 1960–1970	51
2.4	North Korea's Budget Allocations 1961–1971	54
2.5	Daily Food Availability (calories per person)	56
2.6	Timeline: North Korean and U.S.–ROK Events 1963–1971	71
3.1	Hostile Foreign Policy Activities 1990–2000	76
3.2	North Korea GDP Change Year-on-Year 1970–1999	87
3.3	International Food Aid to North Korea 1995–2000	89
3.4	Child Mortality Rate Comparisons	90
3.5	Timeline: North Korea's Great Famine 1993–1999	101
4.1	DPRK Hostile Foreign Policy Activities 2000–2011	106
4.2	DPRK Conflict Level and ROK–U.S. Military Exercises	132
4.3	Timeline: The Succession	138
4.4	DPRK Hostile Foreign Policy Levels Compared	139
5.1	Event Data Sources	151
5.2	DPRK Hostile Foreign Policy Activities 1960–2011	154
5.3	Significant Variable Comparisons	173

List of Tables

2.1	Structured Analysis Results: North Korea Emerges (1963–1969)	67
3.1	Riots and Coup Attempts (1992–1999)	85
3.2	Structured Analysis Results: The Great Famine (1993–1999)	97
4.1	U.S.–ROK Military Exercises (2008–2011)	131
4.2	Structured Analysis Results: Regime Succession (2008–2011)	136
4.3	Case Study Comparisons	139
5.1	Azar's Conflict and Cooperation Scale	148
5.2	Quarterly Hostile Intensity Scoring	153
5.3	Data Adjustments and Quarterly Estimate Examples	153
5.4	Descriptive Statistics for all Variables (1960–2011)	168
5.5	Statistical Analysis Results: All Models	170
6.1	Case Study and Statistical Analysis Comparison	176

List of Abbreviations

2ID	Second Infantry Division (U.S.)
BOK	Bank of Korea (South Korea)
CINC	Composite Index of National Capabilities
CINCPAC	Commander in Chief Pacific (U.S.)
CNTS	Cross National Time Series
COW	Correlates of War Project
CPX	Command post exercise
DMZ	Demilitarized Zone
DON	Dimensions of Nations Project
DPRK	Democratic People's Republic of Korea (North Korea)
DVAR	Dependent variable
FOIA	Freedom of Information Act
FTX	Field training exercise
GDP	Gross domestic product
HFP	Hostile foreign policy
IAEA	International Atomic Energy Agency
ICBM	Intercontinental Ballistic Missile Program
IMR	Infant mortality rates
IVAR	Independent variable
JCS	Joint Chiefs of Staff (U.S.)
KATUSA	Korean Augmentee to the United States Army
KEDO	Korea Peninsula Energy Development Organization
KIA	Killed in action
KIS	Kim Il-sung ("father" of North Korea)
KJI	Kim Jong-il (son of KIS)
KJU	Kim Jong-un (son of KJI and grandson of KIS)

KPA	Korean People's Army (North Korea)
KR-FE	KEY RESOLVE—FOAL EAGLE (military exercises)
KWP	Korea Worker's Party (North Korea)
MAC	Military Armistice Commission (in Korea)
MDL	Military Demarcation Line
MID	Militarized interstate dispute
MND	Ministry of National Defense (South Korea)
MPS	Ministry of Public Security (North Korea)
NDC	National Defense Commission (North Korea)
NKAF	North Korean Air Force
NLL	Northern Limit Line
NPT	Nuclear Non-Proliferation Treaty
NVA	North Vietnamese Army
PRC	People's Republic of China (China)
PSI	Proliferation Security Initiative
ROK	Republic of Korea (South Korea)
RSOI	Reception, Staging and Onward Integration
SCA	Strategic conflict avoidance
SOFA	Status of Forces Agreements
SPA	Supreme People's Assembly (North Korea)
UFG	ULCHI FREEDOM GUARDIAN
UN	United Nations
UNC	United Nations Command (in Korea)
UNCURK	UN Commission on the Unification and Rehabilitation of Korea
UNSC	United Nations Security Council
U.S.	United States
USFK	United States Forces Korea
WGI	World Governance Indicators
WIA	Wounded in Action
WMD	Weapons of Mass Destruction

Preface

Over the years, North Korea has shown a surprisingly consistent foreign policy, focused on national sovereignty and ensuring that the ruling Kim family remains in power. As a means to this end, the Kim regimes have historically relied on both internal oppression and external provocations. As a result, North Korea continues to be influential within the international political environment and rarely has such a poor country garnered the level of international attention from a military, political and social perspective. The Democratic People's Republic of Korea (or DPRK, North Korea's formal name) has also consistently threatened both its neighbors and the West with conventional military power, nuclear weapons development, and cyber-attacks while maintaining strict control over its borders and population. At the same time, the DPRK remains relatively opaque to the international community with rare glimpses of life in the "Hermit Kingdom" only surfacing through defectors or the occasional visitor from the outside. North Korea's development and acquisition of sophisticated conventional weapons and nuclear technology has further complicated relations within the region, and while the probability of a catastrophic event or war remains low, the possibility remains. By examining these aspects of North Korea and its foreign policy activities, this book provides insight to the unique security dilemma the DPRK presents to both East Asia and the international community.

The Kim regimes' actions over the past six decades have included hostile military and diplomatic foreign policy actions that have threatened to destabilize East Asia. These activities tend to confound most observers and seem inconsistent with parallel DPRK efforts to obtain international assistance and peacefully engage its neighbors. The scope and timing of these events are almost always surprising, and the West has consistently attempted (and failed) to implement policies to influence this reclusive state. Both policymakers and political analysts frequently contend that North Korea's actions are often impossible to predict and that the lack of available data makes systematic research of the Kim regimes' actions difficult, if not impossible.

This research takes an alternative approach and argues that *information is available* that can help to understand North Korea's political and military (foreign policy) activities. This study examines North Korean "hostile" (or conflict-focused) military activities and foreign policy actions directed at its neighbors and the international community by presenting a detailed analysis of three case studies and "event" (or incident) data. To support this effort, conflict activity levels are compared to political, social, and economic indicators present in North Korea to determine the relationship between internal characteristics and external conflict activities and influencers. These findings are viewed through the lens of diversionary theory, the idea that leaders use external conflict to "divert" domestic attention, as a possible explanation for North Korea's political and military activities.

Although the overall focus of this book is North Korea, this research also provides a useful demonstration of how both political science and historical analysis can be blended to provide useful observations on state activities. This research demonstrates the usefulness of these methods to examine other closed states and their conflict actions. By examining the actions of an isolated DPRK and providing a template for conflict scholarship in general, this study provides an original perspective on the intricate relationships between state-level activities. North Korea is a difficult nation to understand and its international activities consistently seem to threaten international peace and stability. This book is a useful addition to scholarship focused on shedding more light on this reclusive nation and the Kim regimes' interactions with the rest of the world.

Narushige Michishita (2009) notes that North Korea's use of military force remains its "single most important policy tool in the foreseeable future." In fact, North Korea has historically used both diplomatic threats and armed force to advance its own political, socio-economic, and military agendas. These have included assassination attempts against South Korean political leaders, terrorist-style bombings, kidnapping of civilians, border clashes with ROK and U.S. troops, missile tests, and most recently, the development of nuclear weapons. Unfortunately, the closed nature of North Korea's government and society makes efforts to understand and explain these activities difficult. The DPRK is a rare exception among modern states where the government insinuates itself throughout society, maintaining significant control over its population. While North Korean–produced information is often either unreliable or impossible to obtain, data and methods do exist that have the potential to explain why the Democratic People's Republic of Korea chooses foreign policy actions ranging from cooperation to the use of military force. This book seeks to explain North Korea's foreign policy behavior, focusing on its use of force in relation to the domestic and international conditions encountered by the Kim regimes.

Although conceived as a socialist state, North Korea has developed into an oppressive dictatorship with a large military possessing both conventional and nuclear capabilities. As Cho (2009, 1) observes, "North Korea presents a dual challenge as a newly-nuclear global rogue state and, at the same time, a traditional regional security problem." The tense relationship between North Korea and its neighbors has resulted in continuous efforts by South Korea (and its main ally, the U.S.) to attain the military capacity needed to deter the North from hostile military activity. Despite the potential for positive change in the DPRK after the death of Kim Jong-il in 2011, the "new Kim regime" led by his son (Kim Jong-un) has continued North Korea's historic trends of external conflict and internal oppression.

North Korea routinely initiates both localized and international "provocations," often considered both inexplicable and unprovoked by the outside world, with regional and global implications. Pyongyang's efforts to maintain control over its population, aggressive defense posture, military buildup and repositioning of forces, routine clashes along its borders, nuclear proliferation and provocative statements all cause concern for its neighbors and the international community. Kongdan Oh (2000, 185) observes,

> The basic problem is that the principles that the Kim regime pursues ... are incompatible with the principles of the dominant Western states. Threatened by this incompatibility, the Kim regime resorts to harsh totalitarian measures ... while pursuing a policy of military strength and state-sponsored crime to carve out a place in a post-cold war environment that is becoming increasingly hostile to oppressive regimes.

This "incompatibility" results in an environment of consistent tension within East Asia and an ongoing security dilemma for regional actors (including the United States). These tense international conditions, North Korea's domestic challenges, and the DPRK's hostile foreign policy activity all form the basis for this research effort.

The closed nature of North Korea makes the ruling Kim regime extremely difficult to study. One of the primary goals of this research is to provide an example of how scholars and policymakers can use available information to examine the characteristics of North Korean conflict behavior. This research examines individual North Korea activities (qualitative data) and their characteristics (quantitative outputs) to shed light on the potential causes of DPRK-initiated conflict. While examining interstate conflict is commonplace in international relations scholarship, few studies attempt this type of analysis involving North Korea. For example, there is a vast array of important scholarship on theoretical approaches to the causes of interstate conflict and state interactions to include scholarship by Waltz (1954; 1979); Wendt (1992); Bueno de Mesquita and Lalman (1992); Putnam (1988); and Morgan and Bickers (1992). Domestic causes of interstate conflict research has also been explored by a number of authors such as Peceny and Beer (2003), Lai and Slater (2006), Sobek (2007), Bell (2009), Li, James, and Drury (2009), Pickering and Kisangani (2005, 2007, 2009, 2010), and Bak and Palmer (2011).

While those research efforts influenced this book, most generally omit analysis of conflict activities in Korea and East Asia. This research on North Korea seeks to enhance and build upon the techniques of these previous projects to examine the relationships between internal conditions and external uses of force. Unfortunately, most current scholarship on the DPRK focuses solely on the current threat posed by the DPRK and outputs often include short term, time-sensitive policy recommendations, or historical views of North Korean activities. Notable past research efforts include assessments by academic and government sources, which often provide important analyses of North Korean society, politics, and provocative actions. This includes research by scholars such as Cha (2012), Hassig and Oh (2009), Martin (2006), and Cumings (2005), who all provide excellent qualitative accounts of North Korea from a political, societal and historical perspective. Yet only a few scholars have attempted to systematically analyze the Kim regimes' activities using available conflict information. Additionally, only a handful of cross-national research efforts attempt to analyze North Korean political and military activity using modern social science methods. There have been some generalized studies on authoritarian conflict behavior that have (to a limited extent) included North Korea (Lai and Slater 2006; Kisangani and Pickering 2007).

There are two important studies worth mentioning and both directly influenced this book. The first, and most significant, is Narushige Michishita's (2003; 2009) dissertation and expanded case studies on North Korea's diplomatic history and use of military force. Michishita (2009) examined eight cases of key events, from armed conflict to nuclear testing, on the Korean peninsula from 1966 to 2008. These case studies included: (1) conflict along the DMZ from 1966 to 1968; (2) the seizure of the USS *Pueblo*; (3) West (Yellow) Sea naval incidents from 1973 to 1976; (4) the 1976 Panmunjom Axe Murder incident; (5) nuclear threats and diplomacy from 1993 to 1994; (6) missile firings; (7) DMZ incidents and other Armistice violations (1993–2002); and (8) nuclear testing (2002–2008). While Michishita's research provides an excellent basis for this project, he uses only qualitative (case study) methods to analyze North Korean conflict behavior. The use of a mixed-method approach (using quantitative and qualitative analysis) might have provided more support for his conclusions.¹ Michishita (2009, 1–3) uses a structured qualitative method (using a fixed set of questions to examine for each case) and concluded that North Korea's diplomatic-military activities were rational, based on political objectives, and focused on deterrence (Michishita 2009, 1–3). In his examination of North Korean activity Michishita (2009, 3) concludes that "none of North Korea's major military-diplomatic actions have been primarily caused by domestic factors … the contention that North Korea tends to undertake military actions when it faces a hostile international environment is not true."

While these statements imply that internal and external factors are not primarily influential in North Korea's decisions to use force, Michishita does admit that on several occasions, diversionary considerations were influential in Kim regimes' decisions to use force for the establishment and consolidation of power. In several passages, he mentions the linkage between North Korea's initiation of conflict activities and domestic concerns of the Kim regimes. For example, he acknowledges that the DMZ and the USS *Pueblo* incidents in the 1960s were possibly intended to strengthen Kim Il-sung's status both at home and abroad (Michishita 2009, 31, 50). Michishita (2009, 92) also notes that North Korea's 1976 Axe Murder Incident helped bolster the position of Kim Jong-il as the future leader of the regime. Additionally, he identifies partial associations between North Korea's nuclear threats in 1994, missile testing and proliferation activities, West (Yellow) Sea naval clashes and efforts by the Kim regimes to maintain power (Michishita 2009, 114, 135, 160). Finally, Michishita (2009, 186) observes that North Korea's nuclear test in 2006 was "extensively used for domestic propaganda purposes. After the nuclear test, words of celebration appeared in every corner of the nation." This analysis, along with observations by other scholars and policy practitioners, provides the background for new research (such as this project) to examine the relationships between North Korea's domestic conditions and external conflict behavior.

The second research effort, which influenced this study to a limited extent, is Sung-chul Jung's (2012) analysis of North and South Korean conflict behaviors. Jung (2012) examines the relationship between internal conditions and external conflict using a mixed-methods approach to analyze the applicability of diversionary theory and other explanations of conflict. Jung's (2012) study includes two case studies, one on South Korea's deployment of troops in support of American forces in Vietnam during the 1960s and the North Korean nuclear crisis in the 1990s. Additionally, Jung (2012, 168–169) adds a quantitative cross-national analysis to the case studies and concludes that there is a complicated relationship between domestic unrest and interstate conflict. Jung (2012, 168–169) notes that his quantitative analysis showed that the presence of a "rising power, the territory target, and the hegemony target" all contribute to a relationship between interstate conflict and domestic unrest. Jung (2012, 169) also states, "political leaders are motivated by domestic unrest to initiate military aggression but also constrained by foreign conditions."

These two studies provide an important, although limited, foundation for the examination of internal conditions and ongoing conflict between the Koreas. Although there have been a few other studies that include data on conflict involving the Koreas,[2] none have used a mixed-method approach (using qualitative and quantitative analysis)[3] focused solely on the relationship between North Korean hostile actions and internal conditions. While these same methods have been used extensively to study Western nations, this research provides an example of how to analyze a politically and socially closed nation and demonstrates the importance of using social science methods to analyze similar regimes. In political science terms, this is a "single-country longitudinal study" and provides an in-depth analysis of DPRK-initiated hostile foreign policy on the Korean peninsula from 1960 to 2011. Although there are merits to comparing the Korean situation with other authoritarian states (as in cross-sectional studies), the focus of this research seeks to conduct a thorough analysis of DPRK-initiated diplomatic or armed conflict and to identify and explain relationships in Korean-specific cases. While the findings may offer limited generalizability (comparability to other states), the methods have broad applications in the analysis of other "limited-information" states. This study provides an example of how to gather and analyze data on an authoritarian state with limited outside access: the North Korean regime remains arguably the most closed garrison state that exists today. Additionally, this research is both relevant to the "real world" and makes a "specific contribution" to existing literature: conditions which political scientists such as King, Keohane, and Verba (1996, 15) have identified for useful academic scholarship.

This research effort also strives to apply methods that include the "best practices" from both historians and political scientists as both fields have much to offer to the study of conflict. While historical narratives often lack comparability and breadth, political science research is often too focused on methodologies, theoretical discussions, and quantitative analysis techniques that overlook the advantages of in-depth studies of particular events. This research provides the advantage of using both detailed examinations of specific cases and comparisons across time of the relationships between North Korea's conflict events and external factors. Levy (1997, 33) notes the benefits of using both political science and historical methods and states, "The worst abuse of each discipline is to ignore the other. History is too important to leave to the historians, and theory is too important to leave to the theorists." This research blends two academic approaches in an effort to address a significant gap in current scholarship on DPRK conflict behavior.

From my own perspective as the author, this book was inspired by a personal and professional relationship with the Koreas. Almost thirty years before I came to South Korea, my father worked directly with ROK ground troops deployed to Vietnam. As a U.S. Army helicopter pilot, he provided air-mobile support to South Korean combat units in Vietnam during military engagements such as Operation Kil Tong Hong in 1967. A few years later, I lived with my family in the Philippines while my father coordinated logistical support for U.S. troops in Vietnam. Three decades later, I found myself in South Korea as an intelligence officer with the U.S. Army and was quickly introduced to the tensions that existed on the peninsula. My experiences included tactical deployments, war scenario exercises, late nights in operation centers, "no-notice" emergency meetings and briefings, and numerous other military activities that ranged from the tactical to the strategic level.

During my next military assignment, I taught Reserve Officer Training Corps (ROTC) classes at Kansas State University. This assignment afforded the opportunity to begin my graduate studies, and scholars such as Dale Herspring, Emizet Kisangani, and Jeff Pickering served as mentors and friends during my tenure in Kansas. These same individuals were instrumental in my decision to return to Kansas to teach at the Command and General Staff College at Fort Leavenworth and to pursue doctoral studies. After returning to Kansas (and with the financial help provided by the GI Bill), I began KSU's Security Studies program, a joint effort between KSU's history department, political science faculty and Fort Leavenworth. Professors Herspring, Pickering, and Kisangani, along with my other Ph.D. committee members (David Graff, Andrew Long, and Kristin Mulready-Stone), were my guides throughout the process. Many other faculty members at Kansas State, including Sabri Ciftci and David Stone, also helped me navigate between the worlds of political science and history and to understand the tremendous advantages of using both disciplines to examine the behavior of states, such as North Korea.

In 2012, I was selected as a research fellow at the Center for Strategic Intelligence Research (CSIR) at the National Intelligence University in Washington, D.C. This experience provided the time and support to finish the background research for this project. I am grateful to the exceptional individuals at CSIR: Cathryn Thurston for accepting me as a fellow and creating an atmosphere which allowed for serious academic work; Mike Petersen for his positive attitude, guidance and advice; Katherine Pujanauski and Kris Inman for their exceptional technical assistance; and Kathy Culclasure who always seemed to have an answer for anything else that I had questions about. Additionally, the other academic fellows in the program, Andy Salamone and Kevin Wirth, sat in adjacent cubicles and were constant sources of both inspiration and distraction (both of which were sorely needed at times). A number of other unnamed military professionals were extremely helpful, and without their support for both this project and other adventures throughout my career, none of this would have been possible. While the individuals listed above were all instrumental in my efforts to research and analyze conflict activities between the Koreas, this work is mine alone to include any flaws in analysis or omissions of fact.

Those closest to me have provided overwhelming support and the inspiration to continue my research efforts. My parents fostered an atmosphere at home that provided not only love, but also everything needed to be successful, and I am thankful for all they have done. Additionally, my wife and children, who inspire me daily, have tolerated years of work at night and on weekends, a necessary inconvenience (among many) required for this research. Finally, my service in the U.S. Army has provided a series of incredible experiences, as both a scholar and a military officer, that have helped me to understand the complexities surrounding conflict between states such as the two Koreas. I am humbled by this opportunity and hope to contribute, in a small way, to a better understanding of the tension that currently exists in a place that I know well.[4]

Introduction

This book examines the following question: "What is the historic relationship between the domestic conditions in Korea and the Kim regime's propensity to engage in diplomatic and military activities considered 'hostile' by the international community?" Scholars have often argued there is a linkage between domestic conditions and external conflict. Diversionary theory is one way in which this concept has been explored and provides a potential explanation for the continued state of tension between North Korea and its neighbors. In this book, diversionary theory is used to test the proposition that internal conditions can help explain North Korea's external foreign policy behaviors.

Diversionary Theory: An Explanation for DPRK Actions?

As a "middle-range" concept in international relations, diversionary theory argues that in times of crisis, leaders may choose international conflict to shift the population's attention away from domestic issues. In other words, domestic leaders identify an external threat (or actor) and engage in hostile actions to distract the nation's attention from internal troubles. As a result, according to diversionary theory, this external threat helps to alleviate focus on the domestic strife and ensure the leader's position in power.

Diversionary foreign policies provide advantages for leaders including the potential shift of public attention towards international issues and demonstrate the domestic "leader's capacity for strong leadership" (Hagan 1986, 293). Other benefits of diversionary activities include increased domestic support, justification of a societal oppression (such as martial law), distraction of public attention from issues that cause domestic dissatisfaction, and increased support to the regime due to "an in-group/out-group effect" (Sobek 2007, 31). Thus, leaders may have tangible incentives to divert public attention from domestic problems.

Anecdotes are plentiful on the use of external force to address domestic tensions and prominent individuals such as Machiavelli, Shakespeare and Jean Bodin have noted the unifying potential of foreign policy actions that include diversion. Machiavelli (1882 [1513], 73) referred to diversionary behavior when he observed "the present king of Spain ... attacked Granada ... [and] kept the nobles of the Castile occupied with this enterprise, and, their minds being thus engaged by war, they gave no attention to the innovations introduced by the king, who thereby acquired a reputation and an influence over the nobles without their being aware of it." In *King Henry IV*, Shakespeare (1823 [1600], 295) comments, "Be it thy course to busy giddy minds with foreign quarrels; that action, hence borne out, may waste the memory of former days." Additionally, Bodin (1955 [1606], 168) stated, "The best way of preserving a state, and guaranteeing it against sedition, rebellion and civil war is to keep the subjects in amity one with another, and to this end, to find an enemy against whom they can make common cause."

One of the more recent stories of diversion involves the Russo-Japanese War (1904–1905) which may have begun because of the domestic repercussions of the Russian Revolution. Russia allegedly needed a "short victorious war to stem the tide of revolution" (Walder 1974, 56). More recently, scholars have argued that cases of diversion included the 1982 Falklands War, the 1991 and 2003 U.S. invasions of Iraq, U.S. missile attacks against terrorist targets in Afghanistan and Sudan in 1998, and the conflict between Russia and Georgia in 2008 (Oakes 2006, 442; Kisangani and Pickering 2009, 485; Oreskes 1990, A21; Milbank 2002, A1; Purdum 1998, A1; Filippov 2010, 1844).[1] In the case of North Korea, examining this concept of diversion may help clarify why Pyongyang chooses to use diplomatic threats and military force in some instances and not in others.

The Research Approach: Mixed Social Science Methods

This book uses mixed social science methods (quantitative and qualitative analysis) and a multidisciplinary approach (political science and history scholars' techniques) to analyze North Korean conflict. The research acknowledges that historians and political scientists study conflict often through vastly different approaches. The historian generally uses an inductive approach by analyzing events and facts, which helps to determine the root causes of the conflict, the interconnectedness of key actors, and the overall impacts of these actions.

Historians are less inclined to attempt to make predictions of future activity and more likely to provide evidence to help prepare for the future (Gaddis 1997, 84).

Political scientists approach the study of conflict using deductive techniques in hopes of both identifying current and future patterns of activity. They formulate and test theories on the relationships between events or conditions and attempt to provide simple ("parsimonious") and generalizable explanations as to why conflict occurs (Kellstedt and Whitten 2009, 4). Although historians and political scientists approach the study of conflict from different methodological perspectives, both fields generally agree that tension between nations remains an enduring characteristic of interstate activity and a crucial focus for study. The unpredictable nature of seemingly unstable states, such as North Korea, makes the analysis and prediction of conflict activities events a critical task.

The Relationship: Internal Conditions and External Actions

Considering the importance of attempts to understand North Korean conflict activities, this research suggests there is an identifiable relationship between North Korea's domestic conditions and its external conflict activities. To be more precise, this research initially proposes that as domestic conditions within the DPRK deteriorate (such as food shortages, economic crises, political instability), the incidence of North Korean-initiated conflict activities potentially increases. This study uses a quantitative analysis of North Korean event data collected from both U.S. and Korean sources from 1960 through 2011 and a qualitative analysis of three case studies to explore this concept. The text begins by exploring the argument that North Korea uses diplomatic pronouncements, political maneuvering, and military force to achieve its policy objectives and these events are dependent on internal conditions faced by the Kim regimes. The concept of diversionary theory is examined as a possible explanation for why the Kim regimes have historically chosen to engage in these types of activities, presumably to address domestic concerns.

Although the link between internal (domestic) conditions and international actions by authoritarian states is often difficult to identify, most scholars acknowledge that internal factors influence external policy activities. North Korea's foreign policy actions might also be susceptible to domestic influence, similar to Western democracies, or Pyongyang might be "exempt" from these types of influences due to its seemingly total control of North Korean society. At the same time, North Korea's interactions with other states range from conflictual to cooperative relationships. For example, the DPRK does have trade relations with other nations, demonstrated by the considerable effort the Kim regime has made to establish Chinese and South Korean special economic zones (Lankov 2011). Domestic concerns and foreign policy are inextricably linked to national efforts to maintain internal and external security. Foreign policy is also a tool used by states to maintain conditions that are supportive of the regime in power and is exercised through political, diplomatic, and military power (Sarkesian et al. 2008, 4). Foreign policy activities (policies) encompass a continuum of state actions ranging from cooperation to conflict and the following descriptions help clarify these concepts.

Hostile Foreign Policy Actions (The Dependent Variable)

DPRK's actions which potentially lead to state-level conflict are a significant concern for the international community. Pyongyang (at least on the surface) consistently reminds the world of its willingness to risk war to achieve foreign policy objectives. These "hostile foreign policy" (or HFP) actions have historically included activities such as diplomatic threats, military infiltration into South Korea, naval clashes, and the development and testing of nuclear weapons. Hostile foreign policy actions are one of the ways North Korea interacts with other states and, for this study, constitute what political scientists call the "dependent variable." From a political science perspective, Kellstadt and Whitten (2009, 7) note that theories are often conceived in terms of causal relationships between variables (such as the relationship between internal conditions and HFP), which must be observable and include "any entity that can take on different values" (Trochim 2005). In other words, a theory describes the link between the individual variables and is a "reasoned and precise speculation about the answer to a research question, including a statement about why the proposed answer is correct" (King, Keohane and Verba 1994, 19). These variables are related to the research question and are the "building blocks" of theories.

In this research, variables are categorized according to their function: the dependent variable (HFP) is the output of a particular event is caused or influenced by a single or a number of independent variables (internal or external conditions). Additionally, in this study, control variables are considered and provide alternate explanations for events not associated with the independent variables. Finally, hypotheses are presented in an attempt to describe the relationship between these variables and to predict future activities. Thus the overall intent of this research is to determine the relationship between North Korea's HFP activities and other variables (such as the conditions faced by the regime) to identify relationships as described above.

Clearly describing the concepts in this study is an important, yet challenging task. For example, simply defining the concept of *foreign policy* can be difficult—in fact, many studies of international relations and foreign policy activities omit definitions of this concept entirely. Rochester (2008, 21) notes, "Trying to define foreign policy is reminiscent of the judge in the obscenity case who said, 'I can't define it, but I know it when I see it.' We all sort of know what is meant by the term." Yet defining this term and others used in this study terms terms helps to shape the overall discussion of HFP. For international relations scholars studying state interactions, the term "foreign" generally denotes actions and entities that are focused or exist outside the state and the term "policy" represents a wide range of activities including "specific decisions (to sign a weapons treaty, for example) and general guidelines (to support human rights, for example)" (Kaarbo et al., 2002, 4). These actions can range from military activities to diplomatic communication between nations (in a cooperative or threatening manner).

Foreign policy also constitutes an underlying philosophy of action states use to pursue their own best interests. Rochester (2008, 21) defines foreign policy as "a set of priorities and guides for action that underlies a country's behavior toward other states and includes both the basic goals a national government seeks to pursue in the world and the instruments used to achieve those goals." Others have expanded this definition to the subject of this study. For example, Miroslav Nincic (1975, 624) defines hostile foreign policy as "emanating from bearers of official authority in each nation and directed toward other nations in the international system ... [and] ... a set of behaviors characterized by negative affect and/or the desire to impose deprivations." Additionally, given this discussion and the unique characteristics of North Korea, the idea of *hostile* foreign policy consists of interactions or "events" involving two states. In this context, events are defined as "Any overt input and/or output of the type 'who does what to and/or with whom and when,' ... [with] ramifications for the behavior of an international actor or actors and [is publicly] recorded" (Azar et al. 1982, 374).

Based on the discussion above on the scope of foreign policy actions, this research defines hostile foreign policy (HFP) activity as

> Domestic or international actions by governments or government-sanctioned entities intended to negatively influence or detrimentally affect a target state through diplomatic, social, economic, or military activities ranging from provocative statements to hostile acts in support of national or regime goals.

This statement focuses on both domestic and international measures and the effects of those activities on target states. These actions are undertaken by governments or entities that are supported by the governments (either overtly or covertly) including foreign policy actions (events) by diplomats, economic organizations (domestic or international), and military actions that can have internal or external characteristics. These types of actions can include localized land-based military exercises or show of force operations in international waters. This study focuses on North Korea's international actions conducted against other states with the intent of detrimental effects. Although examining the conflict and cooperation actions of states at the same time can provide a more comprehensive view of DPRK interstate activities, this research focuses solely on the study of North Korean-generated conflict. This includes a range of actions from armed conflict to public declarations or incidents in which North Korea simply chose not to cooperate with the international community. These HFP actions encompass the elements of the DPRK's national power to include diplomatic activities, economic choices with domestic or international effects and military actions ranging from maneuvers and exercises to combat activities against external states. This study examines North Korea's use of these activities to support the overarching objectives of the Kim regime to remain in power and maintain DPRK sovereignty.

The definition of HFP shown above allows for the full scope of North Korea's policy actions to be studied. For example, HFP activities not only include military activities, but also involve North Korea's routine use of diplomacy and aggressive policy announcements. For example, the case of a North Korean diplomat stating that the DPRK would turn Seoul into a "sea of fire" (a veiled threat of nuclear attack) is an example of a HFP action (Financial Times 1994). Public announcements by the DPRK, such as its annual "New Year's Statement," often include threats against both the U.S. and South Korea and are also considered HFP actions. This annual message, broadcast in North Korea and internationally via national television and print media, is somewhat similar to the United States' yearly "State of the Union" address. It is intended for both domestic and international audiences and outlines key areas of progress and concern. For example, the 2011 message "warned the South's [ROK] government to stop what it called 'north-targeted moves' and a 'smear campaign' against it [DPRK]" (Ramstad 2011).

Economic activity that fits the category of "hostile foreign policy" is often directed against joint (North-South) economic ventures, such as the Kaesong Industrial Complex near the western border of North and South Korea and the Mount Kumgang Tourist Area on the east coast of the DPRK. A recent incident involving this resort demonstrates the complexities of North-South relations. In 2008, North Korean guards killed a South Korean tourist for "trespassing in a military-controlled area" near Mount Kumgang (Chosun Ilbo 2011a). After South Korea responded by ceasing tours, North Korea began unsuccessfully soliciting business in other nations (including China, Japan, and the U.S.) to provide assistance in restarting tours in the area (Chosun Ilbo 2011b). In August 2011, the Kim regime seized all ROK assets at Mount Kumgang and closed down operations with South Korea at that mountain resort (Chosun Ilbo 2011a; 2011b). While North Korea's actions are partially inspired by its own economic objectives, the killing of the South Korean tourist became an international incident that triggered the closure of this resort and both negative actions and denouncements by North Korea.

Finally, the most visible signs of the Kim regime's HFP activities are its military actions. These range from clashes between naval vessels and border incidents to missile testing and the DPRK's nuclear program activities. Concurrently, there seem to be limits to the Kim regime's hostile foreign policy activities, as the resumption of a second Korean war would most likely spell the end of the regime (and North Korea as a sovereign state). War on the Korean peninsula would result in catastrophic effects, and most scholars agree that the Kim regime would not survive a large-scale conflict with South Korea and the U.S. Instead, the Kim regime's focus consistently remains on efforts to remain an independent state and in firm control of all aspects of North Korean society.

Domestic Conditions (The Independent Variables)

This research argues that, while many factors impact North Korea's foreign policy, internal conditions are potentially the most significant influencers of hostile actions. The internal characteristics of North Korean society, while intensely controlled by the Kim regime, remain linked to its political, social, or economic conditions. Thus, if these internal conditions change (deteriorate), the subsequent effects will negatively impact the Kim regime's ability to govern and control North Korean society. In fact, many scholars discuss this idea in terms of domestic challenges faced by a ruling regime. Dassel and Reinhardt (1999, 57) use the term "domestic strife," defined as "the contestation of political institutions, or conflict over the basic rules governing political competition" while discussing diversionary activity and link this concept to external conflict behavior. Davies (2002, 682) uses several variables to measure domestic strife including riots, armed attacks, protests, and political strikes. Fordham (2005, 141) refers to "domestic economic and political conditions" as influential in the actions of U.S. rivals to avoid conflict. Fordham's (2005, 143) research examines domestic political difficulties to include U.S. economic conditions (unemployment, inflation, GDP growth) and rival states' economic performance, using energy consumption as a proxy for economic growth. The concept of domestic conditions for this study is generally represented as the conditions within a state (North Korea, in this case) that have effects on its society from a political, economic, or social perspective. In this book, both positive and negative domestic conditions are examined to test whether diversionary theory explains North Korean activities.

For North Korea, political conditions that fall into this category (of domestic conditions) include regime stability and the control of DPRK society. Ake (1975, 273) defines political stability as "the extent that members of society restrict themselves to the behavior patterns that fall within the limits imposed by political roles expectations. Any act that deviates from these limits is an instance of political instability." Gates et al. (2006, 907) add that it requires "institutional consistency" and that both autocracies and democracies have inherent characteristics that "self-enforce" political stability. Political stability is often difficult to measure, but this study uses measures of state capacity and political violence to determine the ability of the North Korea government to remain in control of its population. These include Kaufmann's (2009) World Governance Indicators (WGI) project, which measures political violence, and the Correlates of War (COW) Project's Composite Indicator of National Capabilities (CINC) index (COW 2011). These measures will be discussed in detail later in this study.

Internal stability is also determined by the economic conditions that exist within a state. This study uses information on North Korea's GDP (gross domestic product) and trade levels to measure economic stability. These measures potentially help identify the strength (or weakness) of the DPRK's economy and how much the Kim regime depends on external support for its domestic material needs. Finally, indicators of social stability include how the elites and masses view leadership and government (overall satisfaction levels). This follows Kisangani and Pickering's (2007, 285) discussion of elite unrest in terms of "government crises and purges" and mass unrest as characterized by "general strikes, riots, and anti-government demonstrations" in their analysis of the effects of diversionary military activities. Social stability is also influenced by food, medical and energy shortages, health care capabilities and the number of North Korean citizens who flee the country (defectors). These factors are potential indicators of the ability of the DPRK to provide the basic necessities for its citizens.

These three categories (political, economic, and social factors) form the basis for this study's concept of the conditions which possibly cause diversionary behavior and are referred to as "domestic difficulties." For this study, domestic difficulties are defined as:

The actual or perceived political, economic, or social conditions that negatively affect North Korean society including conditions that interfere with or enable the Kim regime's ability to govern and maintain control over the DPRK population.

The definition is focused on the idea that internal conditions which impede the government's control over North Korean society may result in diversionary behavior and conflict with other states. Conversely, it also implies that conditions which favor domestic stability should result in decreased levels of external conflict.

Purpose and Organization

This study examines the relationship between North Korea's hostile foreign policy activities and its domestic conditions. It also seeks to identify the causal relationships between these two variables in order to test the relevance of diversionary theory as an explanation. This research assumes that North Korea remains susceptible to the domestic pressures that potentially cause attempts to divert popular attention through aggressive foreign policies. By using a structured empirical (qualitative and quantitative) analytical approach, this study also examines linkages between specific conditions and North Korean-initiated conflict actions. The next chapter in this book explores the history of conflict on the Korean peninsula to set the stage for the case study analyses. The subsequent three chapters include the individual case studies of conflict during three key periods in North Korea's history: prosperity and tension (1966–1972), the famine period (1993–1999), and regime succession (2008–2011). The following chapter presents a quantitative analysis of Korean conflict between 1960 and 2011 is used to complement the case study findings. The book concludes with a comparison of the quantitative and qualitative ("mixed-method") results, discusses policy implications, and presents recommendations for further research. The international community seeks stability and prosperity for East Asia and a better understanding of the determinants of North Korean activities can be a valuable contribution to this end. This text strives to bring added coherence to conflict study research on both North Korea and other closed states.

CHAPTER 1

North Korea's Hostile Foreign Policy Actions (1948–1961)

This chapter provides an overview of North Korea's hostile foreign policy activities from the founding of North Korea in 1948 through 1961, a year in which Kim Il-sung sat firmly in control of the DPRK. The modern history of North Korea includes the peninsula's opening to the west (late 1800s), Japanese colonial rule (1910–1945), the formation of two Korean states (1948), the Korean War (1950–1953) and recovery and political consolidation by DPRK leader Kim Il-sung (through the early 1960s). There is a large amount of useful scholarship on unified Korea from its early relationship with the West in the 1800s through the formation of two Korean states in 1948 (see endnote for some useful reading suggestions for those periods).[1] Although an understanding of the modern background of the Koreas is essential for any analysis of the peninsula, the following summary focuses on North Korea's rise as a sovereign state and its HFP activities through 1961. This section provides the background for both the case studies of North Korea's conflict activities and the quantitative analysis presented later in the text.

The Early Years

North Korea declared itself an independent socialist state on September 9, 1948, and the "only legitimate government on the peninsula" (Eckert 1990, 343). Prior to the 1940s, Korea had existed as a generally unified state for over a thousand years since Korea's Silla era (dating back to the year 668).[2] Korea remained intact through its opening to the West in the 1800s and during over 40 years of Japanese occupation in the 1900s. At the end of World War II, Japanese occupation troops left Korea, and the U.S. and Soviet Union jointly controlled the peninsula. Military forces from those nations took control of the peninsula (the Russians in the northern half and the Americans occupied the south). This resulted in competition between communist and Western democratic concepts on the peninsula. Unsurprisingly, the Americans and Soviets guided the development of the two Koreas based on different ideological views of state governance.

After World War II, Soviet objectives in the region focused on ensuring that the USSR had influence "at least equal to the United States" (CIA 1946, 1). From the U.S. perspective, Soviet actions in Korea demonstrated an intent to secure "all of Korea as a satellite" (CIA 1947a, 1). In 1947, CIA analysts commented that the Soviets had, since Japan's surrender, conducted subversion operations against the South, consolidated power and assumed control of North Korea (CIA 1947b, 1). The CIA identified a number of actions by the Soviets including the construction of a "military-political machine under Soviet auspices ... strengthening of the South Korean Communist Party ... [by] infiltrating its members into key positions in the administrative and policy organization of South Korea (CIA 1947b, 2). From Stalin's perspective, his objectives in Korea included a focus on regional security, as well as global influence. The Soviets were determined that any future Korea would not be "turned into a staging ground for future aggression against the USSR" and that Russia must participate in any trusteeship of the peninsula (Weathersby 1993, quoting Russian archival sources, 11–12).

By the end of 1945, both the United States and Soviet Union had designated leaders for each of the Korean zones. Syngman Rhee, a 72-year-old U.S.-educated Korean, was the American choice to govern, while the Soviets selected Kim Il-sung, a 33-year-old war hero, to eventually assume control of the DPRK (with Stalin's support). Although Rhee was officially elected by the South's National Assembly in July 1948 (Finley 1984, 50), he had established widespread support from the U.S. In October 1945, Rhee (along with another conservative, Kim Ku) were living abroad and, with U.S. support, returned to Seoul. Both men were introduced by General Hodge (the U.S. forces commander on the peninsula) to the southern Koreans. The Soviets installed Kim, a Korean hero in the war against the Japanese, as the communist party leader in October 1945 (Finley 1984, 49).[3] Within a few months of their arrival, both Rhee and Kim were "the dominant political figures in the two zones" (Cumings 2005, 195). Between 1946 and 1948, Kim and his former soldiers established the Korean People's Army and control over the People's Provisional Committee, which was the primary source for civilian governance and administration in the North (Suh 1988, 68–69). Kim was aided by a core group of supporters who had fought with him as partisans against the Japanese in Manchuria (Suh 1988, 68–69).

The early years of Kim's rule in North Korea were turbulent and filled

1. North Korea's Hostile Foreign Policy Actions (1948–1961) 21

with "factious rivalry inside the North Korean leadership" (Lankov 2002b, 60) and it took years for him to establish firm control over the entire government (Vreland and Shinn 1976, 35). To those in the North, Kim represented the promise of progress and recovery after decades of Japanese rule, which bled the peninsula of both resources and its heritage through attempts to assimilate the Koreans into Japanese culture. Prior to and during the annexation period (1905–1945) Japan viewed Korea as a resource to fuel its growing need for raw materials and as a colony that could serve as a reservoir of cheap labor and industrial goods. Although the Japanese Meiji government is credited with improving Korea's infrastructure through the building of ports, roads and schools, this came at a high price as Japanese officials also established "a 'legalized' system of racial discrimination against Koreans, making them second-class citizens in their own country" (Cumings 2005, 148). For example, during the 1930s, Japan enacted a number of measures in Korea including mandatory worshiping at Shinto shrines, use of Japanese language in all public places, pressure to adopt Japanese family names and cessation of Korean language newspapers (Choe 1997, 315).

Decades of rule by an external power (Japan) had left the Koreans with little experience with self-governance, resulting in the U.S. and Soviet Union advocating that Korea be governed under "trustee status" until it could rule itself (FRUS 1943, 869). Thus, the government and foreign policy of Korea (and subsequently North Korea in 1948) were not initially determined by the Korean people, but again under the aegis of more foreign occupiers (now the Soviets and Americans). North Korea's government and subsequent foreign policy actions were rooted in the tutelage of the Soviets and their pressure to form a socialist state that would ally itself with the communist world. This appealed to the ruling faction in North Korea (led by Kim Il-sung) who hoped this new government would help the DPRK embark on a

> path of modernity modeled on the Soviet Union, in the postcolonial context of a newly independent country: a specifically non-capitalist, anticolonial modernity that would propel Korea from the status of a backward subjugated nation into the forefront of social, cultural and technical progress [Armstrong 2003, 2–3].

With Soviet help, North Korea hoped to become a model socialist state, an active part of a communist alliance with the USSR and both a political and economic power. From the Soviet perspective, Korea was important to its regional security objectives. Yet Stalin had concerns that were at a much higher priority, such as the recovery from the devastating effects of World War II.[4] Additionally, while the Soviets were influential in the formation of a socialist government in the North, Stalin did not directly support communist activities and subversion in the South until early 1950 (Weathersby 1993, 24). In fact, it was the domestic Korean communists (in both the North and the South) who instigated destabilization activities occurring in the South in the late 1940s in hopes of eventual reunification (Weathersby 1993, 23–24). At the same time, between 1946 and 1950, the Soviets provided an estimated $546 million in total aid to North Korea (Kim 1970, 241). With that aid, the Soviets provided the "necessary protection, a womb within which a socialist state could incubate until it was strong enough to stand alone" (Cumings 1990, 436–437).

Ideologically, Kim Il-sung and his followers were also influenced by Mao Zedong's Chinese Communist Party and many within Kim's inner circle had been active in China's revolution (Armstrong 2003, 2). While China would soon become more influential in the Korean situation, Mao's priorities in the late 1940s were focused on defeating the Chinese Nationalists and establishing the People's Republic of China.[5] Nevertheless, support from communist allies strengthened the DPRK in its efforts to become a viable state, and this supported the Kim regime's pursuit of reunification through the destabilization of the South. During this period, South Korea was ripe for turmoil and instability. A large number of refugees returned to South Korea in the weeks that followed the Japanese defeat in 1945, including 400,000 from the North and over one million from Japan (Millett 2005, 59). Additionally, between 1945 and 1947, there were thousands of guerrilla fighters operating in the South in a bloody "rural peasant protest" against historic landlord-tenant disparities (Cumings 2005, 243–245). The overarching political situation on the peninsula was tenuous and hostile foreign policy actions became the vehicle for eventual reunification.

Both North and South Korea considered the division of the peninsula by external powers an unnatural state of affairs and reunification was always a foreign policy priority for both states. For example, Kim Il-sung (2001, 127) expressed his ongoing support for reunification in 1948 by stating, "Our Party's stand on the establishment of a unified democratic government remains the same as ever. Our Party holds that a supreme legislative body for all Korea should be elected by secret ballot on the principle of universal, equal, and direct suffrage." In the South, Syngman Rhee's administration also pursued this goal throughout his rule from 1948 to 1960 (Lankov 2008). Additionally, during the late 1940s, the DPRK initiated a number of hostile foreign policy actions with the intent to set the stage for reunification. These included North Korean military operations in the Ongjin peninsula (June and August 1949), protests to the UN over its presence in Korea (Oct 1949), border skirmishes (throughout 1949), and the DPRK shelling of the border town of Kaesong (May 1950) (Finley 1984, 53). By mid–1949, the majority of foreign troops had been withdrawn from their post-war occupation. The Soviets withdrew their forces in December

1948 and the Americans removed their troops in June 1949 (Suh 1988, 62; Cumings 1990, 163). Yet the peninsula was far from stable. In the South (including the southern island of Cheju), there were several groups of pro–North Korean insurgents (numbering between 500 and 1,000 individuals) who were conducting unconventional military operations (Millett 2005, 180–181).

In fact, a 1949 U.S. intelligence assessment predicted an invasion of South Korea by communist forces sometime after the withdrawal of American forces causing a "collapse of the US-supported South Korea" (CIA 1949, 1). Additionally that same year, both Kim and Rhee sought support from the Soviets and the U.S. respectively for "a major assault on the other side"—Kim received approval and support from both Mao and Stalin while Rhee was promised U.S. assistance "only if South Korea were attacked without provocation" (Cumings 2005, 253–254). By 1950, the entire peninsula was on the verge of war.

War Between the Koreas

For the two Koreas, the war from 1950 to 1953 was the most devastating event these states have ever experienced. There is extensive literature on the background of the conflict and some of the scholarship remains contested, such as an ongoing disagreement among historians (and between the governments of North and South Korea) on who instigated combat operations. Traditional accounts of the war include Appleman (1961), Fehrenbach (1963), Ridgeway (1967), Blair (1987) MacDonald (1987), and Yup (1999) who view the war as an unprovoked North Korean attack. More balanced (sometimes referred to as "revisionist") views include Cumings (1990; 2005), Stueck (2002) and Chen (2011). These scholars base their assessments on an extensive variety of sources, including Russian and Chinese archival materials and note that both North and South Korea were involved in the onset of hostilities. More recent and "revisionist" analyses tend to portray the war in the context of both the inter-Korean and international dynamics.[6]

The North Koreans consistently blame the war on the United States (KCNA 2012b) while the South Korean government's official stance is that the attack was an "unprovoked full-scale invasion of the South" (ROK 2012). These views contrast with archival evidence, which supports the view that Kim Il-sung initiated combat operations after gaining approval from both Mao and Stalin to reunite the peninsula by force (Zubok 2007, 79–80; CWIHP 1949; Stueck 2002, 75–76; Cumings 2005, 253). It is also important to note that South Korea and the Rhee government also wanted to reunify Korea (by force if necessary), although North Korea was much more prepared for war (Armstrong 2003, 236).

The first engagements (generally thought to be on the South Korean-held Ongjin peninsula) might actually have been in response to ROK artillery fire (Cumings 1990, 575–577). However, the North Koreans had spent months preparing for war and by the middle of 1950, the Kim regime was prepared to invade. In fact, a telegram from Soviet diplomat Grigory Tunkin to the USSR foreign ministry sent in September 1949 described Kim's plans to invade South Korea including initial combat operations on the Ongjin peninsula (CWIHP 1949). The Truman administration received a number of conflicting warnings from its intelligence apparatus predicting either DPRK aggression (CIA 1949) or a reliance on propaganda and guerrilla actions to foment instability in the south (CIA 1950). In any case, the ROK and U.S. military forces were caught unawares by the beginning of the war on June 25, 1950. Within four days of the initial attack, Kim's soldiers had taken Seoul and within six weeks had pushed ROK forces (and recently arrived UN troops composed primarily of U.S. soldiers) to a perimeter around the southeastern port of Pusan (Appleman 1961, 35; Ridgeway 1967, 29–30). The United States' deployment of U.S. forces to support the South was not anticipated by communist leaders as Mao had previously boasted that "there is no need to be afraid.... The Americans will not enter a third world war for such a small territory" (Shtykov, 1950). In December 1950, Kim Il-sung admitted, "the American intervention was an unexpected turn of events" in a speech before the DPRK's Central Committee (Suh 1988, 122). U.S. President Harry Truman considered the conflict as part of a larger attempt by Communists to expand their sphere of influence (NYT 1950) and based his intervention decision on efforts to contain perceived Soviet expansionism (Truman 1950). Although the U.S. did not publicly refer to Soviet involvement at the onset of the war, the administration (including President Truman) believed that Stalin was supporting the North Koreans (Truman 1950). By the end of summer, the two Koreas were in heavy combat and both the U.S. and USSR suddenly found themselves in a "hot" Cold War.

Three months after conflict began, an amphibious counterattack by UN forces (led by U.S. General George MacArthur) on the west coast port of Inchon resulted in the recapture of Seoul. These actions turned the war in favor of the ROK and UN (Fehrenbach 1963, 240–253). Throughout September and early October 1950, UN forces pushed Kim's troops northward to the border with China and the brink of total capitulation. Around the same time, Mao's government attempted to publicly warn the Americans that if they crossed the 38th parallel, China would intervene in the war (Stueck 2002, 89) although the Americans dismissed this as a "bluff" (MacDonald 1987, 52–56). As late as October 12, 1950, the U.S. intelligence community, while acknowledging that Chinese intervention was a possibility, noted, "there are no convincing indications of an actual Chinese Communist intention to resort to full-scale intervention in Korea" (Smith 1950, 1). As the U.S. and ROK forces approached the Sino-Korean border, they began to encounter small units of Chinese soldiers and by the end of October 1950, they realized that Mao had sent over 180,000 Chinese "volunteers" over the border to save the North Koreans (Cohen 1988, 54). By mid–November, more than 300,000 Chinese forces were fighting against the UN troops (Appleman 1961, 767). Had it not been for the intervention of Chinese communist forces in mid–October, Kim's forces would have been pushed out of North Korea and most likely defeated. A full-scale UN retreat followed and by early January 1951, United Nations forces were again pushed out of Seoul to defensive positions 40 miles south of the capital (U.S. Army 2009, 239–240). Although the UN recaptured Seoul in March 1951, fighting from that point on through the end of the war stagnated (Eckert 1990, 345). The war dragged on until peace was negotiated in 1953 after a two-year stalemate in roughly the same area that had been the previous partition line: the 38th parallel. Admittedly, this summary of the conflict overlooks both the combat actions and complex negotiations that occurred between 1951 and 1953.[7]

The overall cost of the war was horrendous. Most of the Korean national infrastructure was destroyed, the division on the peninsula was further solidified, and horrific casualties were borne, mostly by the Koreans and Chinese. UN and ROK losses included 776,000 total casualties (killed and wounded) with South Koreans accounting for 80 percent of the total (ROK Government 2012a). The South Korean government (2012a) lists ROK losses as 137,000 killed and 621,000 injured as well as over 39,000 U.S. dead and 137,000 injured. Additionally, an estimated 600,000 North Koreans and 700,000–900,000 Chinese were killed or wounded (Spence 1990, 530). Approximately ten percent of the civilian population (roughly three million people) of both the North and South Korea were casualties and five million became refugees because of this conflict (Oberdorfer 1997, 9–10). As Eckert (1990, 345–346) notes,

> Those who experienced the war know that such numbers [as shown above] do not even begin to convey a sense of what it was like ... the terror of alien armies and incendiary bombing; the separation of families, often to be permanent; the frantic flight to refugee camps up and down the peninsula ... [leaving] scars on an entire generation of survivors, a legacy of fear and insecurity that continues even now to affect the two Koreas....

To the North Koreans, the war was a necessary vehicle to eliminate the division of their ancient land and culture; the Kim regime considered it the most efficient solution to the division of the peninsula. War with the South was considered "inevitable" in light of Syngman Rhee's stated intention "to march North" to unite the Koreas (Suh 1988, 112).

To the rest of the world, Korea was a test of Truman's doctrine of containment and the first instance of armed conflict directly between the major Cold War foes (the U.S., China, and the Soviet Union). In May 1947, Truman declared "I believe that it must be the policy of the United States to support free peoples who are resisting attempted subjugation by armed minorities or by outside pressure" in an appeal to the U.S. Congress to support aid to Greece and Turkey in their own efforts in engaging destabilizing forces (Truman 1947a, 4). Truman's policy was tested throughout the Cold War period including during the Korean conflict. The stalemate at the end of the Korean War was an ominous foreshadow of the Cold War itself: a continual struggle between the communists and the West, often ending with maintenance of the status quo. By 1953, war had wrecked both sides of the 38th Parallel and solidified Korea as a permanently divided peninsula.

Recovery and Kim's Ascendance

The war itself had left North Korea's infrastructure and industrial capacity in tatters.[8] An eyewitness account notes that there was "complete devastation between the Yalu River and the capital [Pyongyang] … [there were] no more cities in North Korea" (Cumings 2005, 297–298).[9] In the aftermath of the war, North Korea sought economic assistance from the Soviet Union, China, and other states for recovery efforts. Immediately after the signing of the Korean Armistice, the DPRK gained commitments from the Soviets for support (FBIS 1953). By 1954, Kim had garnered pledges of aid including $250 million from the Soviets (intended for both heavy industry and defense projects), $350 million from China (providing transportation and agricultural equipment and raw materials), and $250 million from other communist states for reconstruction projects (CIA 1954). Other aid from the Soviets and Chinese included providing necessities (such as fuel) at "artificially low prices" or in exchange for inferior North Korean-produced goods that "would otherwise have been unsaleable on the international market" (Lankov 2002b, 63).

Additionally, technical assistance was essential for North Korea's rebuilding and included help from not only the Soviet Union, but also from other Eastern Bloc nations. For example, Poland and Romania provided assistance with transportation and construction power; Czechoslovakia assisted with tool production; engineering support came from East Germany; and help with forestry came from Bulgaria (CIA 1957a, 18). Finally, thousands of Chinese soldiers (Chinese People's Volunteers) remained in North Korea after the end of the war and provided needed labor for rebuilding damaged infrastructure. The Chinese maintained troops in North Korea until 1958, both to support recovery and to deter perceived external threats from the U.S. (Martin 2006, 92). The support provided by the 300,000 Chinese troops that stayed behind most likely "saved the North Korean regime from total collapse" and reportedly fixed railways, repaired 1,300 bridges, constructed over 200,000 square meters of buildings (in Pyongyang alone), and created 313,000 miles of embankments for flood control (Kim R. 1968a, 715).[10] North Korea's recovery was dependent on these types of assistance and by the mid–1950s, the DPRK showed signs of stability and even prosperity.

Although the war in Korea was devastating for the DPRK, it did serve to unify competing North Korean communist factions against a common enemy (Nam 1974, 138). Prior to the Korean War, there were four primary communist factions in Korea. These included the Domestic faction (underground rebels in Korea during the Japanese occupation); the Yanan[11] (communists who left Korea for China in the 1920s and returned); Soviet Koreans (who were born and grew up in Russia and arrived with the occupation forces); and the Guerrilla faction (who had fought the Japanese in Manchuria and had fled to the Soviet Union in the late 1930s, eventually returning to Korea in 1945) (Lankov 2002b, 78–80). Although Kim was from the Guerrilla faction, the other members of this group did not have the same influence as Kim and were generally marginalized in the late 1940s (Lankov 2002b, 84–85). However, the relationship between Kim and this faction did allow them to rise to prominence in the Korean communist leadership and eventually assume control (led by Kim) of the North Korean government (Lankov 2002, 86–87). In any case, after the Japanese surrender, these four groups united themselves into a single organization, the North Korean Communist Party (Lankov 2002b, 80–81), which was solidified during the Korean War period.

Kim Il-sung's goals in the aftermath of the Korean War were focused on national recovery and efforts to strengthen his position as leader of the DPRK (Suh 1988, 139). Kim was able to garner significant international assistance throughout the 1950s and successfully rebuilt the North's industrial base. Yet his political status was far from secure and without the unifying influence of a common enemy, dissent among the competing Korean communist factions emerged once again. Kim's faction strengthened its hold on power immediately following the end of the Korean War through a series of purges. These began with the trial and conviction of twelve members of the South Korean Workers Party, and along with a series of other actions in the mid–1950s, effectively eliminated the influence of the "domestic communists" from the south (Nam 1974,

92–93; Szalontai 2005, 85–86). Lankov (2002a, 90) notes that "The faction's leaders were put on show trial as 'U.S. spies' and then shot, while most of their fellow activists were removed from the Party." The Soviet Koreans diminished in influence during the 1950s and while many simply returned to the USSR, others were purged by Kim's group (Suh 1988, 156; Nam 1974, 139). Additionally, high ranking party members associated with the Yanan (Chinese Korean) faction criticized Kim during the plenum meeting in August 1956. They accused Kim of "being an adherent of outdated Stalinist methods and personally responsible for numerous 'distortions of the socialist legality' and a headlong rush toward heavy industrialization. These accusations were in tune with the general mood of the time" Lankov (2002a, 90). This resulted in another series of purges and members of the Yanan party were "demoted and castigated" (Lankov 2002a, 90; Paige 1963, 19–23; Nam 1974, 139).

During this same time, Kim and his faction were reacting to the wave of "de-Stalinization" that was sweeping through the communist world (Kim I. 1962a, 37). Kim's post-war efforts to collectivize North Korea's agriculture, the focus on rapid industrialization in accordance with the Stalinist model and the DPRK's continued "wartime mobilizations" were in conflict with Moscow's evolving and more open approach to foreign policy (Shimotomai 2011, 124). In fact, Shimotomai (2011, 125) contends that Kim was "simply copying" failed Stalinist policies. Domestic criticism of Kim and his policies also occurred, especially in 1956, as party leaders faulted Kim for "lack of party democracy, the cult of personality … and flawed economic policies" (Person 2006, 29). Khrushchev's February 1956 speech attacking the "legend" of Stalin was also seen (from Pyongyang's view) as a political attack against North Korea's leader (Kiyosaki 1976, 52). Kim's "cult" status also worried Moscow and caused the Soviet ambassador to pressure the North Korean leader to separate his political duties as Chairman of the Korean Workers Party and head of the government (Shimotomai 2011, 125). While Kim complied with the request from Moscow (Shimotomai 2011, 125), this was indicative of North Korea's efforts to maintain its relationship with both Moscow and Beijing, neither of which he could afford to ignore. Khrushchev's (1959) "Peaceful Coexistence" approach to dealings with the West was a significant change for communist foreign policy efforts and both Kim and Mao had their doubts about the new Soviet policies. Khrushchev's more liberal approach towards the West was most likely influential in an increase in Chinese aid to the DPRK, thus decreasing Kim's dependence on Moscow for support (Kiyosaki 1976, 52).

North Korea's response to Soviet political changes was similar to China and focused on decreasing its dependence on external states for assistance. Kim's policies included the idea of self-sufficiency as a societal goal as part of

North Korea's national ideology of "juche."[12] Although the North Korean concept of juche has evolved over the years, it generally refers to the supremacy of Koreans as the masters of their own destiny and the importance of independence and national self-reliance. Ironically, self-reliance as a concept was something that Japan also focused on during its expansionist period through the end of World War II.[13] In December 1955, Kim (1955a) introduced the concept of juche by emphasizing the importance of an independent ideological and economic path for North Korea:

> It is important in our work to grasp revolutionary truth, Marxist-Leninist truth, and apply it correctly to the actual conditions of our country. There can be no set principle that we must follow the Soviet pattern. Some advocate the Soviet way and others the Chinese, but it is not high time to work out our own?

The North did not go as far as severing diplomatic ties with either China or the Soviet Union (as other parts of his 1955 speech praised both nations), but this nationalist ideal was a guiding principle for both domestic and international foreign policy actions. Interestingly, the juche "campaign" announced in 1955 and another speech (four years later) coincided with national food shortages—and at least one scholar (Shimotomai 2011, 131) argues that in this case, Kim was potentially attempting to divert public focus towards the negative influences of the USSR and China.[14] Additionally, Kim's consolidation of power and ascension to ruler of North Korea from 1945 to 1960 was strikingly similar to Stalin's rise from 1924 to 1936 (Lankov 2002b, 78). Nam (1974, 140–141) commented,

> In the road leading to his final victory, Kim showed himself a thoroughgoing Machiavellian. He displayed remarkable skill in balancing the contending forces by mergers, making timely alliances with individuals or groups and changing such alliances when their usefulness was at an end.

In any case, Kim eventually consolidated power and then sought to expand his influence beyond the borders of the DPRK. At the end of the 1950s and North Korea's recovery from the war, the Kim regime began to pursue significant hostile foreign policy activities aimed at its two key foes: South Korea and the United States.

Early Hostile Foreign Policy Actions

The North's initial approach to foreign diplomacy was cautious and often characterized by secrecy and suspicion, even in dealings with its own communist allies (Szarvas 1955). The Hungarian attaché in Pyongyang noted that in the North Korean government "there is a certain incomprehensible secret-mongering aimed at covering up mistakes and difficulties, not just toward the diplomatic corps but toward the Korean people too. Of course, this manifests itself much more sharply toward the diplomatic corps" (Szarvas 1955). Yet from the very beginning, the Kim regime did establish diplomatic relations with other communist states including the Soviet Union, most of its satellite states, and the People's Republic of China (Koh 1984, 11). These relations were instrumental in the post-war period and helped North Korea work towards achieving its policy goals, which included a "national cohesiveness centered on Kim Il-sung," rebuilding of the industrial base, and balanced diplomatic relations with both Beijing and Moscow (Kiyosaki 1976, 48). Another foreign policy goal was security from external attack, and the presence of thousands of Chinese troops helped mitigate threats from the U.S. and South Korea (Martin 2006, 114).

North Korea's foreign policy interactions during the mid–1950s often focused on the aftermath of the Korean War and were characterized by diplomatic interactions between the DPRK and the United Nations. There were few, if any, instances of significant military confrontations until around 1958. Up until that time, North Korea routinely criticized the United States and the "puppet regime" of Syngman Rhee (KINU 2011), but the rhetoric rarely involved militarized actions. Subsequent events, initiated by both South Korea and the United States, triggered a resurgence in military hostilities on the peninsula.

During this same period, the U.S. and the Eisenhower administration had embraced the use of nuclear weapons as an option not only in dealing with the Soviet Union, but also in localized conflicts in which American interests were threatened (Gaddis 2005, 146–148). Eisenhower's "New Look" strategy was intended to establish dominance (lost under Truman) in the Cold War without endangering the U.S. economy (Dockrill 1996, 2).[15] Eisenhower sought to reduce the size of the U.S. military (in hopes of strengthening the economy) while relying heavily upon the capabilities provided by lower cost military options, such as nuclear weapons, to counterbalance threats posed by the Soviets and other communist states. Although the U.S. and South Korea had signed a mutual defense treaty[16] following the Korean War, Eisenhower's foreign policy was focused on maintaining security commitments on the peninsula with fewer conventional forces (Stueck 2009, 584). This was part of Eisenhower's "New Look" strategy to reduce overall conventional troop levels. Eisenhower's long term plan was to reduce "army divisions from 21 to 14, navy ships from 1,200 to 1,030, and air force wings from 143 to 137" through troop withdrawals in Korea and cuts to military support units in the U.S. and Europe (Stueck 2009, 584).

United States troop levels in South Korea had been decreasing since the end of the Korean War. When the Armistice was signed in July 1953, the U.S. had 326,000 troops deployed to Korea—this was reduced to 225,000 in 1954, and by 1957 there were only 71,000 U.S. troops remaining (DoD 2012a). Concurrently, the North continued to rebuild and strengthen its forces with help from both the Soviets (providing weapons and equipment) and the Chinese (supplying manpower). In February 1958, the North Korean army (without the Chinese forces) was estimated to contain between 300,000 and 400,000 troops, 1,000 tanks, and 500–1,000 Russian-built aircraft compared to 600,000 ROK troops in the South (Trumbull 1958a). Trumbull (1953a) estimated that were 350,000 Chinese military troops in North Korea although he also noted that China had announced that these troops would soon be moved back across the Yalu into Manchuria. Regardless of the status of these units, Mao retained the ability to rapidly move troops into North Korea to assist with military operations based on China's shared border with the DPRK. During this time, the North Koreans were also increasing their military capabilities, including obtaining advanced jet aircraft (in violation of the Armistice Agreement), and there were rumors of deployed nuclear-capable rockets and artillery systems in the DPRK (Hailey 1956). For the South Koreans, the U.S. agreed to support a South Korean army with up to 720,000 soldiers (20 divisions), but the U.S. "did not agree to provide the Korean forces with the latest US equipment" which would violate the Armistice Agreement (Callow 1995, 12–13).

However, the increased military capabilities spurred concerns in the U.S. over the South's ability to defend itself against a North Korean attack (Hailey 1956). Eisenhower responded in June 1957 and announced that the U.S. would deploy nuclear capable bomber aircraft to South Korea to bolster defense capabilities in response to perceived violations of the Armistice Agreement by the DPRK (Raymond 1957). U.S.-financed modernization came after a "reinterpretation" of the Armistice Agreement by the U.S. Department of Defense and State Department based on violations by the DPRK and fears that the ROK would be outmatched by the DPRK in a conventional military conflict (Raymond 1957; Callow 1995, 13–14). North Korea's immediate response was that these deployments also violated existing agreements and called for a withdrawal of all foreign troops from Korean soil (NYT 1957a). Additionally, the seeming disparity between ROK military capabilities and North Korea's modernized forces resulted in South Korea's President Rhee appealing to Eisenhower for additional military assistance.

Rhee (1957) agreed to reduce South Korean troop levels in exchange for additional military modernization assistance, stating it was necessary to "counterbalance the unfair buildup of Communist military strength in the northern part of our country which has been taking place since the day the Armistice Agreement was signed." Rhee also agreed to reduce South Korean troop levels by 60,000 to address Washington's economic concerns on sustaining the ROK's large army financed by U.S. aid (Raymond 1958). In return, Eisenhower agreed to modernize the South Korean forces and in August 1957, he authorized the deployment to South Korea of two nuclear-capable systems: surface-to-surface missiles ("Honest Johns") and 280mm howitzers (NSC 1957). The U.S. had previously deployed the Honest John systems to Okinawa with the intent to deter aggression in the region (NYT 1955a) and in January 1958, U.S. nuclear weapons systems began arriving in South Korea (controlled and manned by the U.S. Army) (Finley 1984, 108). This was followed in December 1959 by the U.S. deployment of Matador nuclear cruise missiles that could range all of North Korea (Jackson 2005, 65; Stars and Stripes 1958).

Immediately after nuclear weapons were deployed to South Korea, North Korea's hostile military actions began to increase significantly. The first notable incident occurred just two weeks after the public announcement of the Honest John deployments. North Korean agents hijacked a South Korean airliner and forced it to land in Pyongyang (Finley 1984, 108). North Korea released the passengers and crew in March 1958, minus six DPRK agents that had been on board, and kept the DC-3 aircraft in Pyongyang (Finley 1984, 108). During this same time, although the Chinese declared that all of their troops had returned to Manchuria (and that there were no foreign troops in North Korea), the U.S. announced that it would continue to maintain two ground divisions in the South (Trumbull 1958a). All of these incidents resulted in significantly increased tensions on the peninsula.

Other hostile military incidents in 1958 and 1959 include North Korea's shoot down of a U.S. Sabre jet which had flown over the DMZ; five DPRK armed infiltration attempts (resulting in the deaths of at least two North Koreans); MiG jet fighter attacks against a U.S. Navy reconnaissance plane; and increased fortifications along the DMZ on the North Korean side (Finley 1984, 108–109). North Korean military activities during this time (from a South Korean and U.S. perspective) are well-documented, although South Korean military actions against the DPRK, which may have preceded or even instigated these events, are rarely mentioned in publicly available sources. This is an inherent weakness of analyses of activities on the Korean peninsula at this time: North Korean military actions are often reported at length, but through the lens of the U.S. and its allies, while ROK and U.S. military activities involving the DPRK often are overlooked in media and other reporting. During this same time, North Korea also denounced both the United Nations and the ROK–U.S. alliance through diplomatic pronouncements. These included charges that the U.S.

violated the Armistice Agreement, appeals for the removal of foreign troops, and claims that the UN activities in South Korea and within the international community were inappropriate and unlawful (KINU 2011, 20–21; NYT 1957a).

Surprisingly, there was a marked decrease in North Korea's hostile foreign policy military activities in 1960 and 1961, possibly influenced by political turbulence within South Korea. During this time, South Korea's Syngman Rhee was removed from power in April 1960 due to civil unrest and opposition to his government. Additionally, a South Korean coup d'état by ROK General Park Chung-hee on May 16, 1961, most likely influenced the North's efforts to maintain stability on the peninsula, since DPRK was unprepared to effectively "exploit" the unrest in the South (CIA 1961c, 5). The Kim regime denounced the coup as orchestrated and controlled by the U.S. (DPRK 1961) but had little reaction otherwise.

Also during this time, the DPRK signed mutual defense treaties with the Soviet Union (on July 6, 1961) and China (July 11, 1961) (Nam 1974, 130). The negotiations for these agreements may have dampened Kim Il-sung's proclivity to raise tensions on the peninsula to assure Khrushchev and Mao that conflict between the Koreas was not imminent. This was an example of Kim's unique ability to balance between the two benefactors who were essential to support his efforts to maintain a sovereign North Korean regime. These events helped solidify Kim Il-sung's grip on power in North Korea by demonstrating that the DPRK could actively engage its political and military foes (South Korea and the United States). Alternatively, these incidents also showed that North Korea was becoming an influential and potentially destabilizing part of the security regime of northeast Asia.

Evidence of Diversion?

Linkages between hostile foreign policy activities and diversionary intentions were not apparent, at least on the surface. During the late 1950s, although North Korea was recovering from the devastation of the Korean War, it had made significant progress as a society to establish stability and basic services. In fact, many in the South noted that at that time, the North Koreans enjoyed a higher quality of life due to both foreign aid and Kim's success at recovery (Nam 1974, 130). Kuark (1963, 63) conducted a detailed study of North Korea's economy during the 1950s and concluded that even if "one makes allowance for Communist propaganda and window-dressing ... it appears indisputable ... that North Korea has made greater economic strides during the post-war period as a whole than has South Korea." Diversion might have been a consideration for Kim in his diplomatic rhetoric, but the incidence and timing of DPRK hostile military actions (or lack thereof) often seemed to be related to external events, such as the atomic weapons deployments by the United States in 1958 and the coup d'état in South Korea led by a former ROK general in 1961.[17]

However, diversion may have played a role in other policy behaviors by the Kim regime, such as the initiation of his concept of juche and its focus on independence and self-sufficiency (Shimotomai 2011, 131). Evidence points to diversionary activity as a logical policy option for the Kim regime. Kim's efforts to chart an independent course for Korea, despite his country's reliance on an immense amount of aid from both China and the Soviet Union, most likely appealed to nationalist attitudes in the North. Additionally, the maintenance of a "wartime stance" against the U.S. and South Korea probably united the North Koreans either through fear or patriotism against a common foe. The atmosphere in North Korea during the reconstruction period was ripe for diversionary activities as Kim Il-sung sought to unify popular attitudes against the U.S., enhance his ability to eliminate rivals, and crack down on public dissent.[18] Additionally, during this period, North Korea did experience food shortages beginning in 1954 (Lee 2003, 8) and considerable economic turmoil associated with recovery from the devastation of the Korean War. Yet the most significant hostile foreign policy activities began at the end of the reconstruction period (in 1958), and coincided with tensions associated with external threats. Thus, during this period, diversion might have been a factor, but other influences, such as the rising external threat, and the regime's desire to remain in power, played a larger role in the DPRK's reactions to security concerns.

The preceding discussion has outlined the historical background of the Kim Il-sung regime and the historic relationship between internal factors and external conflict activity. The next three chapters include case studies which examine relationships between North Korea's hostile foreign policy actions and influential domestic and international factors.

CHAPTER 2

Introduction and First Case (North Korea Emerges)

This chapter includes an overview of the case study method used and is followed by the first case study on North Korea's conflict activities during the 1960s. Case study selection for this study adheres to techniques described by a number of qualitative methods theorists to include King, Keohane, and Verba (1994), Seawright and Gerring (2008) and George (1979). King, Keohane, and Verba (1994) stated that cases should be chosen to avoid selection bias concerns[1] and vary on the dependent variable (hostile foreign policy). Seawright and Gerring (2008, 296) note that case study selection should have "useful variation on the dimensions of theoretical interest" and should include a sample that represents the larger population.

For example, in his qualitative analysis of Korean "military-diplomatic campaigns" Michishita (2010, 4) based his selection of Korean cases on two criteria: sustained use of force or threat for at least a year and a major crisis in which the U.S.–ROK defense condition level (DEFCON) was increased significantly. Although these criteria yielded important cases (mentioned previously), his research omitted significant domestic crises associated with "shocks" (such as famine) to the North Korean system from a domestic or international perspective. The case selection strategy for this project provides a selection of cases that cover a number of distinctive periods of conflict (and limited cooperation) in North Korea's history based on "shocks" to either the domestic or international political systems associated with the DPRK.

Goertz and Diehl (1995, 31) noted that a significant change in the pattern of international conflict might require a "large shock" to occur. They identified this condition as a "political shock" and defined it as "a dramatic change in the international system or its subsystems that fundamentally alters the processes, relationships, and expectations that drive nation-state interactions" (Goertz and Diehl 1995, 35). While Goertz and Diehl studied this concept in relation to enduring rivalries, this same concept applies to the analysis of states such as North Korea. In this research, this view of political shocks is expanded to include domestic (as well as international) events that have significantly affected the political and security status quo. In this research, the concept of "political shocks" is used to identify North Korean cases that have significantly affected the political and security status quo within East Asia. The case selection strategy identified two cases (famine in the 1990s and the succession efforts in the 2000s) in North Korea's history based on "shocks" to the domestic and international political environment associated with the Kim regimes. Additionally, a third case (North Korea's rise to power) is examined—this case includes a period of relative political stability for North Korea and provides depth to the discussion. The final case demonstrates the difference between the independent and dependent variables in periods of domestic stability and instability for the DPRK and conforms to the case selection concept of "useful variation" (Seawright and Gerring 2008, 296). The cases are listed chronologically below and a synopsis of each follows:

Case 1—North Korea Emerges (1963–1969). This period saw North Korea's rise as a stable communist state with political and economic links to both the Soviets and Chinese. Additionally, the Kim regime did not hesitate to use force as a means for diplomacy, which changed the regional balance of power and increased both international tensions and reactions (both military and diplomatic) from the U.S. and ROK. Although this was a time of relative prosperity for the DPRK, it did experience the beginnings of economic difficulties that would become amplified in the decades that followed. This case also adds considerable depth to the research by expanding the overall temporal framework of the study. Additionally, the inclusion of the Kim regime's actions and relative stability during the 1960s allows for useful comparison and contrast with the other two cases of "political shocks" to the DPRK regime.

Case 2—The Great Famine (1993–1999). This internal shock resulted in the deaths of 5–10 percent of the population and caused the first-ever North Korean appeals for international humanitarian assistance. During this time, North Korea weathered the death of its founder, Kim Il-sung, and succession to Kim's son, Kim Jong-il, and a nuclear standoff with the United States and South Korea. This period fit the criteria of a "political shock" as North Korea assumed a new role within the region—as an aid recipient that posed a significant military threat to neighboring states.

Case 3—Regime Succession (2008–2011). This period included efforts to secure the succession to a new Kim regime and was accompanied by nuclear tests, missile development and unprecedented naval battles and artillery attacks against South Korea. This final period firmly established North Korea's newest role and "political shock" to the region: the DPRK became one (maybe the only) state which had a demonstrated nuclear capability and was concurrently dependent on international economic assistance to survive.

This case selection strategy has also incorporated the "diverse case method" and represents cases that include "maximum variance along relevant dimensions" (Seawright and Gerring 2008, 300). To ensure case comparability, the concept of "unit homogeneity, equivalence, and cross-case validity" (Gerring 2005, 183) also influenced the selection process. Based on these criteria,[2] selected cases include periods of international[3] hostilities (all cases), peace (the last year of case 1), external aid intervention (case 2), and internal tension (all cases) based on conditions facing the Kim regimes. Admittedly, these cases include different events, but the most effective method to analyze North Korea's activities is to encompass a broad historical spectrum as demonstrated by Michishita (2009). This also leverages the advantages of the blending of both international relations qualitative methods and "history-centric" views (Levy 1997; Gaddis 1997; Kennedy-Pipe 2000) of hostile foreign policy actions by North Korea.

Each case is examined using a structured, focused comparison method (frequently used by political scientists) based on the idea that North Korea's domestic conditions are related to external conflict levels. This examination technique requires developing a set of questions and applying these in the same manner to each case. This allows for a "systematic comparison and culmination of the findings of the cases possible ... and deals with only certain aspects of the historical cases examined" (George and Bennett 2005, 67). The questions are focused on both internal and external conditions experienced by North Korea to examine whether or not causal relationships exist between conditions faced by the Kim regime and external conflict. This method is "structured" for comparison and "focused" to limit the examination to important aspects of each case. Jung (2012, 90–91) used a similar technique in his study of both Koreas and it provides a logical and systematic method to examine each of the cases. Additionally, Jung (2012, 90–91) adapts a technique (the "hoop test") developed by Van Evera (1997, 29–31) to measure the validity of his theories. He notes that if the concept successfully passes the tests (by answering the questions or passing through the "hoops"), then the "confidence in the validity of a given hypothesis" is increased (Jung 2012, 91). Admittedly, this is not a perfect measure, but given the subjective nature of qualitative analysis, it does provide a means to compare each case. For this study, the following questions were developed and focus on the effects of internal and external conditions faced by the regime:

Measuring the level of conflict (dependent variable):
1. What was the level of hostile foreign policy (HFP) during the case study?

Effects of internal conditions (independent variables):
2. Was political instability associated with heightened HFP activities?
3. Were economic difficulties associated with increased HFP?
4. Was social instability associated with periods of increased HFP?

Effects of external conditions (independent variables):
5. Were UN Security Council resolutions against the DPRK associated with increased HFP?
6. Were ROK leadership changes associated with increased HFP?
7. Were U.S. leadership changes associated with increased HFP?
8. Were ROK/US strategic-level military exercises associated with DPRK hostile actions?
9. Was the presence of a conservative ROK government associated with increased HFP?

These questions represent the overall research design and will examine the linkage between the dependent variable (hostile foreign policy) to the independent variables (the internal and external conditions faced by the DPRK).

Measuring Hostile Foreign Policy (The Dependent Variable)

To support the case study analysis, this research effort required the construction of a database of events that includes reported instances of hostile foreign policy activities. The sources for the events were open press and government reports from the U.S., South Korea, and North Korea.[4] This database provides the basis to analyze North Korea's hostile foreign policy events. In the case study introductions, the level of conflict for each case is compared to the overall average levels (based on the HFP activities levels, as noted in Appendix B) throughout the study period. This allows for an initial examination of the intensity levels in relation to the independent variables. More details on how the database was constructed are available in Chapter 5 and the data is provided in Appendix B.

The Effects of Internal and External Conditions (Independent Variables)

If the concept of diversionary theory applies to North Korea in a particular case, the internal conditions present in North Korea should affect the levels of diplomatic and military conflict. This is tested by analyzing the political, social, and economic stability of North Korea in each of the case studies. For these case comparisons, the concept of "political difficulties" indicates the overall political control exercised by the North Korean regime and the government's ability to remain intact. The second condition, "economic problems," is measured by using historical cases of economic difficulties for North Korean citizens as indicated by the expansion or contraction of the economy. Finally, "social instability" indicates the ability of North Korea to meet its citizens' basic needs and includes the availability of food, energy, and shelter using historic events, refugee testimonies and United Nations reports on overall food availability in the DPRK.

An alternate view of the causes of conflict on the Korean peninsula is that external influences are the primary driver of DPRK conflict activity. This second argument contends that North Korea's actions are based on exogenous influences such as international sanctions, external elections, and U.S./ROK military exercises. Potential external influencers include the presence of UN resolutions and sanctions,[5] the presence of presidential elections (or succession) in the U.S. and ROK, and strategic-level U.S.–ROK military exercises (such as "TEAM SPIRIT" or its equivalent). From 1976 to 1993, the U.S. and ROK conducted TEAM SPIRIT strategic military exercises to improve joint and combined operations capabilities and to exercise U.S. reinforcement of South Korea in the event of war with North Korea (Yoon 2003, 98). The ROK and U.S. also conducted other strategic exercises and relevant ones will be discussed in each case study.

Methodological Concerns

Research on closed states such as North Korea often requires a refined approach based on the availability of data. The dearth of reliable information on the DPRK activities has influenced both the selection of cases and variables, yet an effort has been made to conform to commonly used social science academic practices. Cases and variables for this research were chosen based on theoretical concepts (diversion) and operationalized using generally accepted standards for qualitative analysis (Seawright and Gerring 2008; Gerring 2001). Analytical methods commonly used by social scientists to examine authoritarian states have been incorporated when possible. Additionally, scholars often use many of the same variables as this study (economic factors, military capabilities, election cycles, political stability, and societal factors) to conduct research on diversion. In fact, similar techniques have been used to study diversion and other interstate conflicts by Kisangani and Pickering (2005), Bell

(2009), Tir (2010), Leeds and Davis (1997), Crescenzi, Enterline, and Long (2008), D'Orazio (2012) and Jung (2012). Thus, these case study methods, selection techniques, and variables are among the best (and perhaps the only) options available to support a comprehensive analysis of the Kim regimes' foreign policy choices. To support this research, the following three case studies are analyzed to examine the potential relationships between the conditions faced by North Korea and its external conflict activities.

The First Case Study: North Korea Emerges (1963–1969)

The rest of this chapter analyzes the relationship between DPRK-initiated hostile foreign policy and the conditions faced by the regime between 1963 and 1969. The same structured, focused questions identified above are used identify factors that have potentially influenced the DPRK's engagement in military and diplomatic HFP activities. The case study begins with a discussion of North Korea's initial success as an emerging communist state followed by an examination of the Kim regime's decision to increase the level of hostilities on the peninsula. Next, the case is "tested" using qualitative tests (the questions) mentioned above. These questions examine North Korea's internal conditions (political, economic, and social), external influences (UN resolutions, South Korean elections, and ROK–U.S. military exercises), and the relevance of diversionary theory to the case. The chapter concludes with a summary of the test results and a discussion of the relationships between the independent variables (questions), the dependent variable (hostile foreign policy), and the concept of diversion. Finally, a timeline (Figure 2.6) is provided at the end of the chapter to provide a historical perspective on the events described in the analysis.

North Korea Emerges and Then Risks War

The 1960s were the "Golden Age" for North Korea compared to later, much more difficult times. While the economy was not performing to its full potential, the DPRK experienced a standard of living higher than many of its neighbors, including South Korea and China. North Korea provided free education and health care and literacy rates rose significantly. Kim Il-sung had gained international notoriety as his government navigated a political and economic path between both the PRC and USSR. By the early 1960s, North Korea had successfully emerged from the devastation of the Korean War and firmly established itself as a stable communist state.

North Korea demonstrated its unique international position by maintaining active diplomatic relations with both the Chinese and Soviets. Through 1962, despite the Sino-Soviet split, the DPRK was able to remain relatively neutral in the disagreements between the Soviets and Chinese. One of the most significant outward signs of this neutral stance was Kim's agreement to mutual defense treaties in 1961 with its "fraternal Socialist allies"—both Moscow and Beijing (Scalapino 1963). But the DPRK soon began to "lean" towards China because of fundamental disagreements over Soviet ideological shifts and differences in how to approach the West, especially the U.S. (Kiyosaki 1976, 55). Both North Korea and China considered the U.S. an obstacle to their reunification policies and "favored the adoption of a tough posture toward the United States rather than an attitude of conciliation" (Kiyosaki 1976, 55). Additionally, Chinese concessions to the North Koreans on border negotiations and disagreements over arms sales with the Soviets pushed Kim into closer alignment with Beijing (Westad 2007, 164; Shimotomai 2011, 139). These actions resulted in a reduction of both financial and technical support from Moscow (Koh 1976, 126). Strained relations followed in 1963 and 1964 with the Soviets and North Koreans experiencing a number of economic disputes. In fact, the Soviet Ambassador to North Korea mentioned a noticeable change in his communications with DPRK diplomats, stating, "I am noticing as of late that all responsible Korean officials, beginning with the highest leadership, have turned into meteorologists. They cannot find any other topic for discussion except for weather" (Moskovsky 1963).

Khrushchev's removal from power in October 1964 provided the opportunity for the North Koreans to improve relations with Moscow without having to face the former communist leader directly (Kiyosaki 1976, 62). In 1964, North Korea chose to distance itself from Mao and engage the Soviets due primarily to the economic consequences of poor relations with Moscow. The loss of Soviet military aid forced Kim to divert precious resources (both labor and materials) to North Korea's defense industry, and China's aid was always insufficient to fill DPRK needs (Kun 1967, 48–49). Soviet diplomats also noted that North Korea became uncomfortable with "the negative consequences of their orientation only towards China" including Beijing's alleged use of the DPRK to split the "international communist movement" (Borunkov and Gorovoi 1965). Finally, the Kim regime changed its stance on the "main enemy" of international communism. Rather than maintaining that "modern revisionism" (a key aspect of Soviet post–Stalin Soviet policies) was the most serious threat to the worldwide communist movement, Kim began to focus on imperialism (and the U.S.) as the biggest international danger and called for unified action from socialist states (Kun 1967, 56–57).

Relations between the North Koreans and Soviets immediately began to thaw and were enhanced by the reestablishment of Russian military support, evidenced by Moscow's agreement to supply air defense systems to the DPRK in May 1965 (Kuznetsov 1965). Kim had been asking for these systems at least as early as 1962 (Moskovsky 1962). Additionally, after a series of coordination visits between the North Koreans and Soviets, both signed formal economic agreements in June 1966 providing long-term support for DPRK industrial projects and trade (RFE 1966). This event formally marked North Korea's political shift back towards the Soviets. During this time, North Korea's emergence as an active political and military player within the Communist Bloc forever changed the relative balance of power within the region.

In the early 1960s, Kim's national focus shifted from efforts to improve the DPRK's economy towards prioritized support to the military, which signaled a change in foreign policy emphasis from "peaceful unification" to a more aggressive policy of "Korean revolution" in the South (Kim H. 1977, 208). Kim Il-sung (1961 137, 148) declared in 1961 that South Korea's

> broad masses of the people came to realize ... that without the peaceful reunification of the country they could not free themselves from poverty, complete lack of rights, and colonial slavery.... The only way for the South Korean people to completely free themselves from their present tragic situations is to drive out the U.S. army, overthrow the fascist dictatorship and reunify the country peacefully.

Kim supported armed conflict against the Americans—to both drive them from the peninsula and pave the way for "peaceful reunification" with the South. This policy of revolution in the South was often referred to as a "national salvation struggle" or "national liberation war" and was Kim's main theme beginning in September 1961 (Kim H. 1977, 211). Additionally, "it became clear that the North Korean regime had changed its tactics for national unification" by efforts to blend both political and military measures to destabilize the ROK (Kim H. 1977, 212–213). As a result, North Korea's military expenditures increased exponentially during this period. From 1960 to 1966, defense spending accounted for 4.3 percent of the DPRK's total budget—this number rose to 30 percent of total spending from 1967 to 1970 (Vreeland and Shin 1976, 37).

During this time, North Korea's national slogan became "A Gun in One Hand and a Hammer or a Sickle in the Other!" (DPRK 2001, 228). In a 1965 speech, Kim argued that the U.S. used aid to oppress and "plunder" South Korea, and that "U.S. imperialism is the real ruler in South Korea" (KIS 1965, 240–241). Kim Il-sung (1965b, 240–241) noted that South Korea used U.S. aid as a substantial part of its national budget and that the

Figure 2.1 DPRK Military Expenditures 1960–1970 (in Millions)

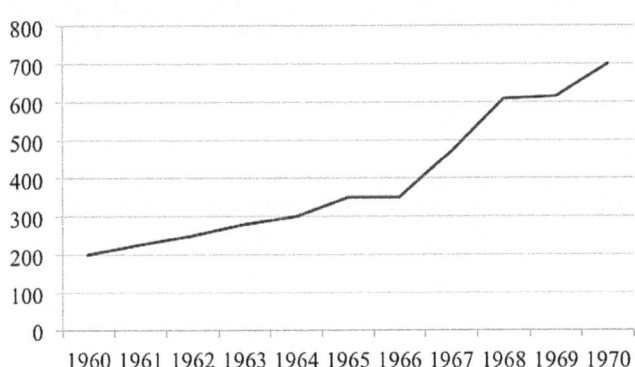

Source: CINC 2012

[Americans controlled] 45–50 percent of South Korea's financial budget and 30 percent of its banking funds, and monopolize 70 to 80 percent of its raw materials supply and 80 percent of its import trade. Today the South Korean economy is tied up entirely to the United States; the financial and economic organizations and enterprises in South Korea are in a situation where they will have to stop operations the moment US imperialist "aid" is cut off.

In fact, U.S. economic and military aid to South Korea in the early 1960s actually declined (from $529 million in 1960 to $309 million in 1965), and averaged about $438 million per year (USAID 1998, 55–56). Additionally, South Korea's GDP rose from $2 billion (USD) to over $7 billion per year during the case study period (World databank 2012).

Kim also charged that the United States needed to occupy South Korea "as the logistical base for the occupation of the whole of Korea, as a bridgehead for hostile activities against the Soviet Union and the People's Republic of China … [and] as an important strategic point for world domination" (KIS 1965, 244). North Korea viewed the United States as the biggest obstacle for eventual reunification of the Korean peninsula. Both North and South Korea considered the division of the peninsula by external powers an unnatural state of affairs and reunification was always a foreign policy priority for both states. To address this issue, the DPRK actively began to pursue foreign policies directed at destabilizing the South and straining U.S.–ROK relations in hopes of the removal of U.S. forces from the peninsula. Yet there were other influential factors that swayed the Kim regime's decision to pursue increased hostile foreign policy activities.

Beginning in the mid–1960s, North Korea's military activities changed the overall security environment between the Koreas from an uneasy peace to an atmosphere of military confrontation. While Kim Il-sung sought to destabilize the peninsula and set the conditions for reunification, South Korea's Park Chung-hee strove not only to counter North Korea's actions, but to achieve security through economic growth.[6] As a result, tensions were high on the peninsula as military confrontations on both sides of the DMZ resulted in hundreds of casualties—cross-border incursions became commonplace. For example in 1966, there were many instances of DPRK military attacks including bombings of a U.S. barracks, seizure of an American reconnaissance naval vessel (USS *Pueblo*), a direct attack against the South Korean president's residence, the shooting down of a U.S. Navy reconnaissance aircraft, and hundreds of smaller confrontations. In fact, between 1965 and 1971, there were over 2,000 total casualties associated with North-South conflict (Finley 1984, 220). These included 1,129 ROK casualties (including 203 civilians), 270 U.S. servicemembers (including 83 sailors from the USS *Pueblo* that were later repatriated) and 815 North Korean soldiers killed, captured or wounded (Finley 1984, 119, 128, 130 and 220).

Why did North Korea pursue intense levels of hostile foreign policy actions during this period of seemingly low levels of domestic distress? On the surface, Kim had little to gain by war with the South and the continuous stream of provocations that occurred could have brought the U.S. (and potentially China) into another Korean War. Yet heightened levels of conflict did occur. The following questions help analyze the internal and external conditions that were present during this period of both prosperity and conflict for the DPRK.

Hostile Foreign Policy Activity Analysis

As noted above, a list of questions are used to determine the potential relationship between conditions faced by the Kim regime, diversionary theory, and the incidence of hostile foreign policy activities. These "tests" of the case study constitute the structured, focused method to examine this case (Levy 1989, 284; George and Bennett 2005, 67; George 1979) and allow for comparisons with the other cases in this study. The following questions provide for a nuanced examination of the Kim regime and its environment during this period.

What was the level of hostile foreign policy activities during this period?

This case involves North Korea's emergence as a viable communist state and included the Kim regime's shift towards a more militant foreign policy towards South Korea and the U.S. The events during this period were also the most intense levels of interstate conflict experienced on the peninsula since the Korean War. Figure 2.2 shows the level of conflict in 1960–1970, as recorded

2. Introduction and First Case (North Korea Emerges) 45

in the event database (Appendix B) and scored using Edward Azar's (1993) intensity scale. Additionally, the figure below shows the overall average intensity levels for the study period (1960–2011). See Chapter 5 for additional information on Azar's (1993) scale and hostility score calculations.

Figure 2.2 Hostile Foreign Policy Activities 1960–1970

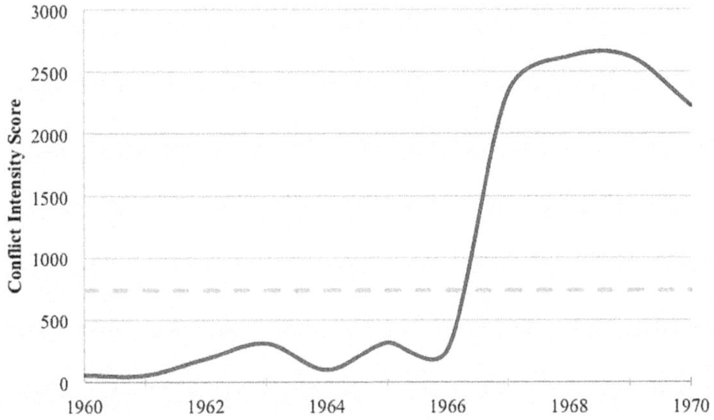

Sources: Chapter 5 and the Korea Conflict Database (Appendix B)

As shown in Figure 2.2, the conflict intensity levels during the first case study period (1963–1969) were 66 percent higher than historic norms during the entire study timeframe (1960–2011). Conflict intensity scores for the case study period (1963–1969) averaged 1222 per year while the scores for 1960–2011 were an average of 735 annually (Appendix B). Additionally, when compared to the rest of the decade, the end of the 1960s was characterized by a noticeable increase in DPRK hostile foreign policy actions. To help explain why this surge in HFP activities occurred, the following paragraphs examine the most significant categories of events during the case study.

DMZ Confrontations. Beginning in 1966, clashes along the DMZ between North Korean and ROK–U.S. troops occurred regularly, and these were often brutal and intense engagements. The following narrative of an ambush of U.S. and ROK troops was typical of many of these firefights:

> In the predawn darkness on 2 November [1966], while the American president slept near Seoul under heavy guard, a KPA [North Korean People's Army] squad tracked an eight-man patrol from Company A, 1–23 Infantry. The northerners, probably from the 17th Foot Reconnaissance Brigade, paralleled the oblivious American soldiers. Once the U.S. element reached a point about a kilometer south of the DMZ proper, the North Koreans estimated that the Americans had

relaxed their vigilance. The Communist soldiers swung in ahead of the plodding American file, assumed hasty ambush positions, and engaged the Americans with hand grenades and submachine guns.

The U.S. squad disintegrated under a hail of bullets and grenade fragments. Despite later wishful stories of heroics, six Americans and a KATUSA [Korean soldier augmentee] went down almost instantly. A seventh American survived by playing dead. The KPA troops pumped a few more bursts into some of the corpses, plunged in a bayonet here and there, and disappeared into the night. One northerner might have been wounded in the one-sided fight. The sole American survivor ran for his life as soon as the attackers pulled out [Bolger 1991, 37–39].

These types of infantry engagements occurred repeatedly along the DMZ and those attributed to the North Koreans are well documented. Yet those initiated by ROK forces were rarely recorded in publicly available literature, except for fleeting references in U.S. intelligence memorandums (FRUS 1966b). In fact, the ROK media was controlled by the South Korean government until the 1990s (Park 2009, 3) and the U.S. had no interest in having the tensions in Korea portrayed as being related to South Korean military activities (FRUS 1967a). During this case study period, other more intense incidents also occurred, to include an attempt to kill South Korean President Park, the seizure of a U.S. naval intelligence ship and the downing of a U.S. reconnaissance aircraft.

The Blue House Raid. In January 1968, the North Koreans crossed the DMZ during a commando operation intended to "destroy the 'Blue House' presidential mansion, and key members of the ROK government, most importantly, the ROK president" (EUSA 1968a). The operation began on 18 January 1968 as the DPRK team, dressed as South Korean soldiers, cut through the fence in the 2ID sector in the DMZ. The team encountered and detained four ROK civilian woodcutters—the North Koreans held the civilians for five hours, provided them with propaganda items, "praised North Korean dictator Kim Il-sung, and boasted that Korea would be reunified in 1968," and threatened retaliation if the woodcutters reported their presence (EUSA 1968b). In fact, one of the agents gave the civilians a watch to compensate for the "loss of a day's work" and released them (EUSA 1968b). The civilians informed the ROK police and pursuit of the DPRK infiltrators began. After engagements with the ROK Army and national police, the South Koreans stopped the commandos a mere 800 meters from the Blue House and firefights continued until 31 January (EUSA 1968b; NYT 1968b). In the end, twenty-seven North Koreans were killed (one was captured and two were never found), thirty-eight South Koreans died and sixty-four were wounded (EUSA 1968b).[7]

USS *Pueblo* Seizure. One week after the North Korean raiders infiltrated into South Korea, the DPRK seized a U.S. intelligence ship, the USS *Pueblo*, and towed it to North Korea's east coast port of Wonsan (CIA 1966b, 1).[8] This ship was the U.S. Navy's first seaborne electronic surveillance vessel used on a mission against the North Koreans (HASC 1969, 1620). Some analysts within the U.S. government considered the mission risky—the U.S. National Security Agency (NSA) stated that the North Korean regime possibly posed a danger to the *Pueblo* mission, although this was not brought to the attention of senior leaders or the crew prior to departure from Japan on 11 January 1968 (HASC 1969, 1623). Additionally, the USS *Pueblo* was never informed about the Blue House incident that occurred during its mission; the Seventh Fleet intelligence officers assumed that information would flow to the crew via routine intelligence reports (Armbrister 2004, 33). Nevertheless, the signals surveillance ship began its scheduled 17-day intelligence mission (Gallery 1970, 153–154). On 23 January 1968, the *Pueblo* was fired upon by the North Koreans and subsequently boarded. One U.S. servicemember died and the North Koreans detained the remaining eighty-two crewmembers (U.S. Embassy 1968a; FRUS 1968b; Bolger 1991, 65). Six hours later, the *Pueblo* found itself docked at the DPRK port of Wonsan (Mobley 2003, 41).[9]

The timing of the USS *Pueblo* seizure might seem illogical as North Korea had managed to conduct two extremely serious attacks against both the U.S. and ROK in the span of a few days. Yet, these incidents were consistent with the Kim regime's strategic goals. The CIA assessed that the seizure of the USS *Pueblo* was, among other things, a sort of "insurance policy" against ROK retaliation for the Blue House attack (CIA 1969a, 5). The CIA notes that

> As the U.S. became even more heavily engaged in Vietnam, Kim evidently decided that he could stage more risky provocations with relative impunity. The Blue House raid and the seizure of the *Pueblo* followed. The North Koreans clearly calculated that their possession of the *Pueblo* and its crew would exert an additional powerful deterrent against retaliatory action. Pyongyang took pains to draw attention to its leverage by threatening to try to punish the *Pueblo* crews [CIA 1969a, 4–5].

Additionally, Bolger (1991, 69) notes the timing of the Blue House raid and *Pueblo* seizure in relation to events in Southeast Asia: in Vietnam, the NVA attacks against Khe Sanh and the Tet Offensive also occurred during January 1968. Thus the Blue House and USS *Pueblo* attacks might have been Kim Il-sung's contribution to the overall communist fight against the U.S. and its allies, such as the South Korean regime (U.S. Embassy 1968a). As the U.S. Ambassador noted,

> NK leadership may well have felt that they could make no greater contribution to Communist cause and to their own purposes in Korea than to take bold actions designed to reduce support in ROK for augmented or even continued participation in Vietnam, to take advantage of current political difficulties of and to further

reduce public confidence in Park government, and to shake mutual confidence between U.S. and ROK. Bold action could also, of course, create a diversion in Korean peninsula and force U.S. to divert military resources from Vietnam effort and stimulate additional domestic and overseas pressures against U.S. Asian policy [U.S. Embassy 1968a].

In any case, these actions had wide-ranging effects on the ROK–U.S. alliance. When South Koreans compared the U.S. responses to North Korea's attack on the Blue House and to the capture of the USS *Pueblo*, they noticed a significant difference. The U.S.-led United Nations Command's reaction to the Blue House raid was to call for a Military Armistice Committee meeting to criticize the incident, while the USS *Pueblo* seizure resulted in a U.S. protest to the UN Security Council (FRUS 1968a) and active military measures in response to the seizure. After the capture of the *Pueblo* and its crew, the U.S. deployed a naval carrier task group to the area, led by the USS *Enterprise* and supported by the Seventh Fleet. The U.S. also moved the Fifth Air Force from bases in Japan to Osan (South Korea), called up over 14,000 Air Force and Navy reservists, and deployed almost 200 aircraft to South Korea and Japan as a show of force (Bolger 1991, 71–72; EUSA 1968a, 6). This overwhelming U.S. reaction to the *Pueblo* crisis and seemingly lower priority given to the Blue House attacks resulted in negative reactions by the South Korean public and its leaders. Bolger (1991, 70) notes that many in the South "urged Park to 'go north'—with or without the Americans." There were reports of student demonstrations at the U.S. embassy in Seoul that had to be dispersed by U.S. soldiers firing weapons into the air as the South Koreans felt "that the United States was far more concerned over the humiliating loss of the *Pueblo*" than an attack against a sitting head of state (NYT 1968c). From South Korea's view, the ROK fully supported the United States as a reliable ally, as demonstrated by the deployment of over 48,000 South Korean troops to fight in Vietnam. Thus the perceived lack of action by the U.S. was alarming to the Park regime.

While the North Koreans stated that the seizure of the *Pueblo* was in response to "a provocative act directed at gathering intelligence" (Romanian Embassy 1968a), the U.S. perspective was that the motivation for the seizure of the USS *Pueblo* was, among other things, also related to an effort to "harass the US in its conduct of the [Vietnam] war" (FRUS 1968c). The United States presented the *Pueblo* situation as a complaint to the UN Security Council, but no action resulted (UN 1968a). In discussions, the USSR noted that the captain himself (who was in North Korean captivity) admitted to entering the territorial waters of the DPRK and that the UN Security Council did not have the jurisdiction to act on matters involving territorial water violations (UN 1968a). Yet in diplomatic communications between the Soviet embassy and the North

Koreans, the Soviets made it clear that they did not support DPRK efforts to "to hasten reunification through the use of force" (Romanian Embassy 1968b). Additionally, the official UN Security Council record included no mention Blue House attacks in relation to the *Pueblo* incident (UN 1968a). In any case, the North Koreans released the USS *Pueblo* crew in December 1968.

EC-121 Shootdown. In 1969, a mere four months after the release of the *Pueblo* crew, two NKAF MiGs shot down a U.S. Air Force EC-121 reconnaissance aircraft, killing all thirty-one crewmembers (ROK MND 1986, 76; Beecher 1969a). The U.S. intelligence aircraft had been conducting signals surveillance and mapping North Korea's recently modernized east coast air defense shield and radar sites (Mobley 2003, 99). For months, the U.S. had conducted similar intelligence missions without incident and while North Korea had often scrambled aircraft in response (and previously attacked a U.S. RB-47 on a similar mission four years earlier), there had been no current indications that the DPRK would undertake a lethal engagement (Mobley 2003, 100–103).

In response to the EC-121 incident, North Korea accused the U.S. of violating its airspace both in its domestic press and in Armistice Commission negotiations that occurred five days after the downing (NYT 1969; CINCPAC 1970, 134). The immediate U.S. reaction was to activate a task force of warships to deploy to the area, including six aircraft carriers and a battleship (Zagoria and Zagoria 1979, 38–39). While the shootdown resulted in a three-week cessation of reconnaissance flights and a flurry of U.S. government meetings, the final response from the Nixon administration was to conduct a naval show of force with several aircraft carriers, publicly denounce the attack, and resume flights (Mobley 2003, 139; Bolger 1991, 101–107). The U.S. considered more violent military responses, but none were undertaken (Mobley 2003, 139). The lack of military retaliation by the Nixon administration was seen by North Korea as proof that the U.S. was a "paper tiger" and that the North Koreans "had nothing to fear" from the Americans (Kim I. 1975, 312). Nixon considered an immediate air strike as a response, but was dissuaded by a number of factors. These included logistical problems (few U.S. forces were in the area that were capable of an effective strike), recommendations by aides to find a diplomatic solution, similarities with U.S. actions in the Gulf of Tonkin in 1964 (which also included airstrikes against targets in North Vietnam) and a widened American commitment to Vietnam (Beecher 1969b).

By the end of April 1969, the U.S. began moving its "show of force" naval fleet (Task Force 71) out of Korean waters (Lydons 1969). In an effort to decrease tensions, the Soviets made an effort to distance themselves from responsibility for the incident, provided on-site assistance to the U.S. naval effort to find survivors, and offered condolences for the loss of personnel

(CINCPAC 1970, 139).[10] This incident and the others described above demonstrate the intense level of conflict that occurred during this period. These types of spectacular events and the constant air of tension brought the peninsula closer to all-out conflict than at any other time since the Korean War.

WAS POLITICAL INSTABILITY ASSOCIATED WITH HEIGHTENED HFP ACTIVITIES?

Political instability during this period was low as Kim Il-sung reaffirmed his position as leader of the DPRK throughout the mid–1960s. He did this through non-violent purges of the North Korean leadership structure, active participation in domestic activities, highly visible international foreign policy actions (such as the re-establishment of diplomatic and economic ties with the USSR) and increased engagement with developing nations. Kim conducted a significant number of political purges during the 1960s based on policy failures and disagreements, in contrast to past party demotions which were associated with power struggles (Nam 1974, 146–147). These actions included the removal of civilian party officials who were supporters of Chinese ideology (in 1966), others who opposed the "hawkish" strategy towards reunification (in 1967) and several military generals in 1968 after the attack against the South Korean presidential residence (DVO 1967; Nam 1974, 146–147). The North Korean leader also remained engaged with the public and used "on-the-spot guidance" visits to industrial sites, farms, and military units. These visits were intended to portray Kim as a "young and energetic leader" and were an attempt to inspire and sustain the North's expanding economic progress by focusing on the individual worksites and citizens (Suh 1988, 163–164).

The DPRK's national capacity expanded throughout the 1960s as measured by the Correlates of War CINC (Composite Indicator of National Capabilities) index (CINC 2011). The CINC index provides a composite score based on defense personnel levels, military spending, population, iron and steel production and energy consumption (CINC 2011). In this study, the CINC index is used to measure the overall political stability of the Kim regime. Increased capacity has historically provided North Korea an enhanced ability to maintain control over its population and thus increases the overall stability of the North Korean government.[11] Figure 2.3 shows the overall CINC scores for North Korea during the 1960s compared to South Korea's during the same period.

As shown in Figure 2.3, North Korea improved its national capacity levels throughout the decade. North Korean gains in national capabilities were largely due to increases in defense spending beginning in 1966, and expanded industrial capacity due to increases in iron and steel production and energy consumption throughout the decade (CINC 2011). Fluctuations in 1965 were most likely related to stagnated military spending during that period, and defense spending rose significantly beginning in 1966 (CINC 2011). This gradual increase in overall capacity during the 1960s provided Kim with the means to both maintain power and pursue hostile foreign policy activities.[12]

Figure 2.3 Composite Index of National Capacity Scores 1960–1970

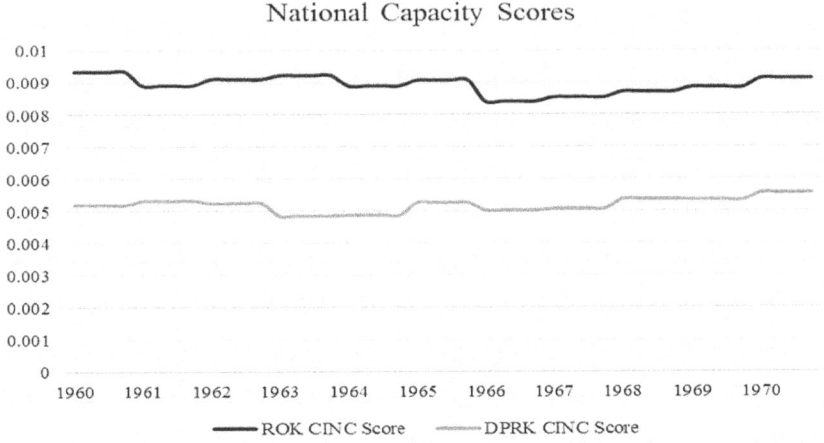

Source: CINC 2011

Kim also sought to secure North Korea's place in the international community through active political engagement with the Soviet Union. North Korea never completely severed its diplomatic contacts with the Soviets in the early 1960s and with the departure of Khrushchev in 1964, began efforts to improve their relationship with the USSR (Shimotomai 2011, 139–140). In fact, trade between the Soviets and North Koreans remained relatively steady despite tense relations (between 1961 and 1964) and ranged from $156 to $170 million per year (Carter 1972, 114–115). Relations began to improve and, in 1965, the Soviets and North Koreans agreed to resume military and economic cooperation. That same year, the USSR provided 150 million rubles (about 75 million U.S. dollars at that time) in military equipment—in fact, after personally thanking the Soviet Ambassador for the aid, Kim immediately asked for more military assistance (Kuznetsov 1965). The Kim regime needed Soviet capital to finance both its economic and military goals (Koh 1969, 953). In 1966 due to the Sino-Soviet split, the DPRK made efforts to change the nature of its dealings with the PRC, primarily due to economic factors.

To appease the Soviets, North Korea began to change its relationship with the PRC by stopping cultural exchanges, limiting diplomatic contacts, and ceasing both the publication of Chinese written materials and the radio broadcast of Bejing's news programs (Soviet Embassy 1966). Kim Il-sung was quoted in private conversations as referring to Mao's Cultural Revolution as "incredible madness" and also made similar statements in closed KWP (Korea Workers' Party) meetings (DVO 1967). Kim understood that maintaining a productive relationship with the Soviet Union was essential to achieving his own foreign policy goals and was willing to dampen relations with the PRC to ensure Soviet aid remained intact. This was a delicate "balancing act" by Kim between the powerful Soviets, who installed Kim as leader of the DPRK in 1948 and provided critical financial support, and the resurgent Chinese, who had saved North Korea from annihilation during the Korean War. Kim's efforts served to solidify his political power and stance in both the DPRK and the international community.[13]

Finally, North Korea pursued international relations with less powerful states, such as those associated with the Non-Aligned Movement (NAM), an international forum for developing nations. The NAM was initially established in 1955 in Indonesia and included 29 developing nations with the overall goal of "resisting the pressures of the major powers, maintaining their independence and opposing colonialism and neo-colonialism, especially western domination" (NAM 2012). For example, between 1964 and 1967, Kim hosted visits by the leaders of a number of states such as Mali, the Congo, and Mauritania (Suh 1988, 224). These were intended to establish Kim Il-sung as a recognized international leader and bolstered his standing in the eyes of his own people. This helped reinforce and sustain Kim's national persona; as Nam (1974, 147) observed, "the basic characteristics of the North Korean leadership—namely, the absolutism of Kim Il-song and the pervasive influence of his former partisans from Manchuria—remained the same." Throughout this period, Kim Il-sung was clearly in control of North Korea and its domestic and international activities. Thus during this case study, there was little overall political instability. Domestic conditions allowed the Kim regime to pursue its foreign policy goals without significant resistance from the DPRK citizens or the ruling elite.

Were Economic Difficulties Associated with Increased HFP?

North Korea's economy performed well during the first half of the 1960s, and despite the signs of a downturn in the latter half of the decade, this was a time of relative economic stability. This period began with North Korea's economy showing indications of strength and robust expansion, yet in 1966, the

DPRK's successes began to demonstrate the limits of command-directed economic systems. Nevertheless, North Korea's economy did perform well enough for Kim to commit significant resources to the defense sector and support "military adventurism" beginning in the mid–1960s.

North Korea's official industrial growth statistics were impressive and Kim Il-sung stated that between 1957 and 1970, North Korea's industrial production increased at a rate of 19.1 percent per year (Kim 1972, 412). In 1957 alone, the North Koreans reported that industrial output had increased by 44 percent and that grain production (in excess of requirements) was 12 percent (DPRK 2001, 203). North Korea's GDP per person grew steadily throughout the 1960s, rising 77 percent (from $1,104 per person to $1,954) between 1960 and 1970 with economic growth rates ranging from -1.0 to 12 percent per year (Maddison 2008).[14] Additionally, North Korea's trade levels almost doubled during the decade, increasing from $320 million per year in 1960 to $710 million per year in 1970 (COW 2011). Yet there is little doubt that this economic growth was directly related to external aid.

The Kim regime was often able to obtain aid based on the competition between the Soviets and Chinese and those states' efforts to establish strong alliances and shape the development of fledgling communist states such as the DPRK. Prybyla (1964, 468–469) notes that Sino-Soviet support to the communist regimes in Vietnam and Korea included loans, grants, industrial goods and equipment, training, and workers. Park (1984, 277) calculates that the Soviet Union and the PRC provided the majority of economic aid to North Korea (until the early 1970s) compared to other communist states and the rest of the world. From 1945 to 1980, total economic aid delivered to North Korea was $2.76 billion (1984 rates), with the Soviets providing the majority (57.7 percent) followed by China (30.5 percent) (Park 1984, 275). At least on paper, North Korea's economy was robust enough to support the redirection of funds in support of increased defense spending.

Yet Eberstadt (2007, 29–31) notes that while the DPRK's reported per capita income steadily rose throughout the 1960s, "there is no reason to invest any great confidence in official DPRK claims about per capita national income or national output" due to inconsistencies in reporting methods and data. Additionally, North Korea experienced significant problems during this time with "unbalanced growth" (over-allocation of resources to heavy industry), inconsistent levels of assistance from the Soviet Union and China, poor harvests and production difficulties due to poor economic planning (Lee 1993, 13). By 1966, North Korea realized that its national goals were not being met, and Kim Il-sung commented, "industry and agriculture are not balanced" and called for "general equilibrium" in the North's economic plan (KIS 1965, 256, 274). These difficulties resulted in an extension of its ongoing economic plan by three years to 1970 and beginning at this time, North Korea ceased to report "detailed economic statistics to the outside world" (Lee 1993, 13).

During the latter half of the 1960s, North Korea's command economy began to demonstrate signs of distress. Per capita income was reportedly double that of the South, although one analyst observed that a "North Korean has to work five or six times as long as a South Korean to earn enough money to buy a comparable item" (Trumbull 1967, 14). Further, the Kim regime's economic priorities had shifted from domestic production to military defense. This shift was possibly due to the "military coup d'état" in South Korea in 1961 and the characteristics of the ROK leaders, who focused on economic and military strength. As a result, the North switched its economic focus in the 1960s towards defense and away from development, reportedly setting back the North Korean economy "at least 10 years" (Trumbull 1967, 14). By the mid–1960s, economic development slowed for North Korea as the result of the "diversion of resources to military modernization," changes in aid from China and the Soviets, and "unrealistic economic planning" (CIA NIE 1972, 9–10). During the latter half of the 1960s, North Korea was spending 30 percent of its national income on defense (Axen and Matern 1967).

Figure 2.4 North Korea's Budget Allocations 1961–1971

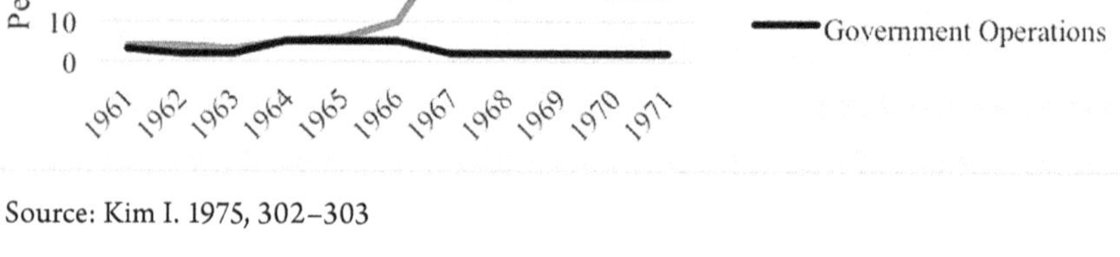

Source: Kim I. 1975, 302–303

*Socio-Cultural Expenses were costs associated with North Korea's own "cultural revolution" and emphasis on public (and political) education and other efforts to improve DPRK society (Kim I. 1975, 288).

As shown in Figure 2.4, economic expenses (which were costs associated with domestic production) decreased significantly beginning in 1966 and military spending jumped 20 percent between 1966 and 1967 (Kim I. 1975, 288). By 1967, North Korea had only achieved 57 percent of its goals under its economic development plan initiated in 1960 (Trumbull 1967, 14).[15] In discussions with the Soviets, Kim Il-sung admitted that while industrial and agricultural production was meeting target goals, domestic construction was lagging behind other sectors (Soviet Embassy 1968). Energy production deficits were negatively affecting metal and chemical production (both were running at 50 percent as a result) and drought in the winter of 1967 and spring of 1968 cut wheat and barley production in half (Soviet Embassy 1968). During this same time, there was a significant increase in North Korea's HFP activities. Between 1966 and 1967, North Korea's hostile foreign policy events increased nine-fold (from a score of 264 to 2328)[16] in intensity. Through the end of the decade, HFP activities remained at their highest levels since the Korean War.

These economic difficulties resulted in efforts by the Kim regime to invigorate the DPRK's domestic economy through increased contacts with the international community for economic assistance. By the 1970s, North Korea began to purchase "turn-key" plants from both Japan and the West to increase industrial capabilities; these purchases and continued economic distress resulted in high external debt and marked the beginning of a sustained financial downturn (Savada 1993, 41). Chung (1972, 527) describes North Korea's economic experiences during the 1960s as a "decade of mixed achievements and failures. For the first time since the inception of the North Korean regime, it experienced setbacks and slowdowns throughout the economy, a far cry from the days of unparalleled growth during the 1950's." North Korea's economy did support Kim's efforts at sustained military activities against the South in the latter half of the decade; yet this reallocation of resources, as mentioned above, came at a high price. Overall, there was economic progress during this period and relative economic stability, but when difficulties did occur, there was also an increase in HFP activities.

Was social instability associated with periods of increased HFP?

Social instability during this period was low and unrelated to HFP activities. By most accounts, North Korea was able to provide for citizen needs. Also during this time (in comparison to the ROK), the North Korean public enjoyed better access to advanced medicine, higher levels of employment, and an overall quality of life that outpaced the South. During the 1960s, North Koreans reportedly benefited from heavily subsidized food rations and housing, free healthcare, an eight-hour workday, equal opportunity for both sexes, and no taxes (LOC 2007; Barrett 2011, 53; Fukushima 1975, 221, 245–246). One defector commented that, in comparison to more modern times,

> even though it was difficult to have an easy and comfortable lifestyle, at least the rations came regularly—never delayed ...There were actually goods made in North Korea that you could buy in the stores—clothing, material, underwear, candy [Martin 2006, 121].

The DPRK also made significant progress in other basic necessities. By 1963, 71 percent of its population had electricity and in 1970, nearly all citizens had access to power (Cha 2012, 24). In addition, the DPRK instituted compulsory primary education in 1956 and by the mid–1960s, the DPRK had twice as many university students as the ROK (Kim I. 1975, 290–291). Food availability, which would become a devastating problem in the 1990s, remained steady throughout the period except for a slight decrease in 1968, most likely due to weather effects. This was probably due to flooding associated with monsoon rains in 1967 (Soviet Embassy 1968) which potentially affected harvest levels in 1968. Although DPRK food availability was higher than China, it remained just above 2000 kcal per person (per day) and failed to demonstrate progress similar to the ROK during the period (as shown in Figure 2.5).

Figure 2.5 Daily Food Availability (calories per person)

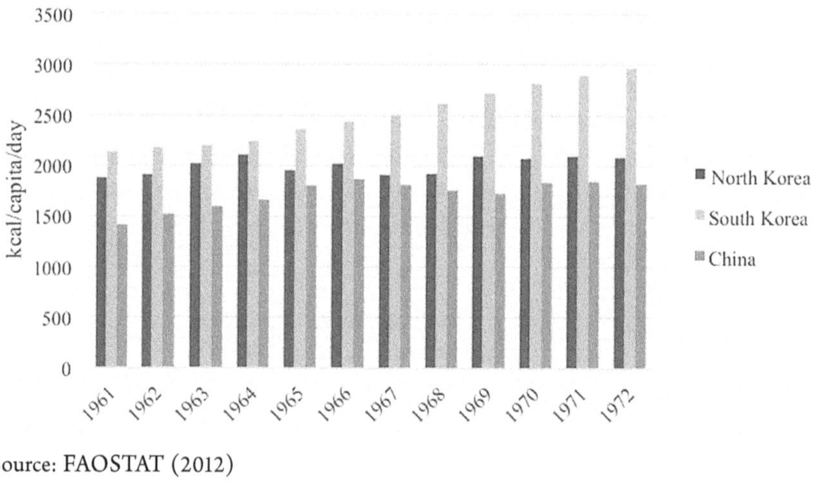

Source: FAOSTAT (2012)

Another measure of social stability, the numbers of those who chose to flee North Korea (in the Korea case, these are generally referred to as "defectors"), provides a proxy measure of the level of satisfaction citizens feel towards their society (more defectors potentially indicates higher levels of dissatisfaction). While defections from North Korea to the South most likely happened during this period, they were most likely limited to only a handful each year and exact numbers are not available.[17] But those that were reported included a spectacular escape in 1967 by a North Korean journalist (who was later found to be a North Korean agent) through the Joint Security Area at Panmunjom and the defection of a North Korean air force pilot and his MiG-15 in 1970 (NYT 1967; UNC 2012).

Alternatively, North Korea did experience an influx of repatriated Koreans who returned from Japan and other locations during the early 1960s. Approximately 1.4 million ethnic Koreans returned to both the DPRK and ROK immediately after the end of World War II in 1945. Yet more than 600,000 remained in Japan after the war, despite being denied Japanese citizenship and facing severe discrimination (Creamer 2003, 14; Morris-Suzuki 2006, 305). For those willing to return to the DPRK, North Korea offered free education, health care, jobs, and housing (Morris-Suzuki 2005, 372). As Morris-Suzuki (2005, 372) notes, the Koreans in Japan were

> [barred] by law from all forms of public sector employment, including teaching in public schools and even the most menial local government jobs, while careers in large companies were in effect closed, not by law but by entrenched tradition. The very limited welfare that they could obtain was not a right but a "gift" bestowed by administrative discretion.... Now, suddenly they were presented with the offer of cheap housing, guaranteed jobs and free welfare in [the DPRK] where they would be full citizens. Pictures published by North Korea at the height of the repatriation movement contrasted the spotless new apartments promised to returnees with the squalor of their slum dwellings in Japan.

Comparatively, the South Koreans reportedly offered "practically no assistance" for returnees from Japan (Foster-Carter 1978, 147, quoting DeVos and Wetherall 1974, 15). As many as 75,000 ethnic Koreans were repatriated from 1959 to 1962 as part of the Calcutta Agreement between the DPRK and Japanese government (Mitchell 1967, 154; Creamer 2003, 23–24).[18] The number of returnees slowed significantly by the mid–1960s and stopped completely between 1967 and 1971 due in part to Japanese government efforts to limit the activities of the Chosen Soren, a pro–North Korean group of ethnic Koreans in Japan (Foster-Carter 1978, 148). The Chosen Soren was founded in 1955 by "overseas citizens of the DPRK" living in Japan and fully supported both Kim Il-sung and North Korea's policy for eventual reunification (Creamer 2003, 2). Despite willing repatriation to their ancestral home, most of the returnees found life in North Korea difficult and often were persecuted in the DPRK as "distrusted as outsiders": thousands of these repatriated Korean citizens "vanished into prison camps, and of these, many were never heard from again" (Morris-Suzuki 2005, 259).

In fact, North Korea solidified itself as a police state during this period. This was based on efforts that began immediately after Kim Il-sung rose to power. Kim followed Stalin's example and in 1946, the DPRK formed the Ministry of People's Security (MPS) to provide internal security and protect the borders (Martin 2004, 60; Hyun 2004, 7). The MPS assumed the security duties of the departing Japanese military forces. While this organization went through some changes, namely subordination to the Department of Internal Affairs in the 1950s and subsequent re-emergence as an independent bureau in 1962, the MPS was tasked with internal security and policing throughout most of the 1960s (Hyun 2004, 10–12). Beginning in 1958, the Kim regime began efforts to classify all North Korean citizens based on political loyalty and between 1967 and 1970, the population was divided into three overarching classes with fifty-one subordinate designations (Hassig and Oh 2009, 198; KINU 2011b, 149). There were three primary class designations: the "core," wavering or "basic," and hostile or "complex" classes (Hassig and Oh 2009, 198; KINU 2011b, 219–221). The core class (28 percent of the population) included those loyal to the regime, the wavering or basic class (45 percent) consisted of those not in the core class, generally workers and low-level technicians, and the hostile or complex class (27 percent) were "branded enemies, impure elements, and reactionaries" (KINU 2011b, 219–221).[19] As part of this campaign, North Korea designated thousands as sectarians or anti-revolutionaries—these individuals were either executed "or sent to remote sites" (Gause 2012, 104). During the 1960s, the MPS reportedly sent 70,000 individuals to political prison camps and executed more than 6,000 North Korean citizens (KINU 2011b, 149).

While the Kim regime did provide for the welfare of North Korean citizens during this period, it was repressive and continued to refine its control over DPRK society. The DPRK's quality of life had a price, which included consistent pressure by the Kim regime to increase efficiency and production and prepare for "inevitable" war with the South. During the 1960s, North Korea provided food for its citizens on par with other East Asian states and DPRK citizens did receive the education and healthcare benefits promised by the Kim regime. Nevertheless, it was a bland and repressive atmosphere as choices for the consumer were limited, and as one analyst observes, "Everything is uniform. There is no poverty, but no prosperity either" (Trumbull 1967, 14). During this period, North Korean society was stable and Kim Il-sung's extensive control allowed him to pursue domestic and internal policy goals. Consequently, there was no direct relationship found between social instability and the level of HFP activities.

2. Introduction and First Case (North Korea Emerges) 59

Were UN Security Council resolutions against the DPRK associated with increased HFP?

From 1963 to 1969, there was periodic discussion in both the UN Security Council and General Assembly on the future of the peninsula. After 1953 and throughout the 1960s, the United Nations General Assembly participated in an annual "ritual" of debating the future of the Koreas (Koh 1995, 31–32). These included the consideration of five topics on the Korean issue: invitations for both Koreas to participate in the discussion, the annual UN Commission on the Unification and Rehabilitation of Korea (UNCURK) report, the disbanding of the UNCURK, withdrawal of foreign military forces from the peninsula and the ending of discussion of the Korean question (Pak 2000, 52–53). North Korea objected to these debates in the UN General Assembly and demanded that "all parties" participate, including the DPRK (Kim H. 1977, 224–225). As Kim H. (1977, 225) notes, "the North Korean regime still utilized the world forum [UN] for its cause. Thus every year, the [DPRK] transmitted its unification formula to the United Nations." This was the same proposal that the DPRK consistently used in discussions with the ROK and included the removal of U.S. forces, reduction of armed forces to 100,000 on each side of the DMZ, an international conference to discuss solutions, and direct DPRK–ROK negotiations (Kim 1977, 225). As a result, North Korea ensured that the Korea question was consistently submitted the United Nations for debate, despite little hope of action on the issue.

In 1969 and 1970, UN supporters of North Korea submitted a draft resolution (which failed to pass) calling for the expulsion of foreign troops from the peninsula and the dissolution of the UNCURK (Koh 1995, 31). The UN established this organization in 1950 (and disbanded it in 1973) with the purpose of oversight of "relief and rehabilitation in Korea, as determined by the [General] Assembly in accordance with the [UN] Economic and Social Council" (Pak 2000, 7). The UNCURK issued a yearly report (which was put before the General Assembly for approval) which detailed not only economic and political progress in South Korea, but also North Korean "provocations" and issues surrounding reunification (Pak 2000, 55). While these discussions occurred yearly, there were also at least two General Assembly resolutions that passed on the Korean issue, such as Resolutions 2516 and 2668 (enacted 1969 and 1970), both reaffirming UN objectives to establish a unified, democratic and peaceful Korea (UN 1969; UN 1970). Both North and South Korea viewed reunification as something that had to occur under either a communist or democratic system, but not both, thus stifling any hope of a negotiated solution under the guise of the United Nations. Thus the effects of UN Security Council resolutions on hostilities are difficult to measure (because there were no actual UNCR resolutions passed), yet the UN's forum allowed for debate on issues surrounding the ongoing division between the Koreas. Thus there was no discernible relationship between these UN activities and the levels of North Korean hostile foreign policy actions.

Were ROK leadership changes associated with increased North Korean hostile foreign policy activities?

During this period, another external influence, national elections, was associated with HFP activities. After assuming control of South Korea by coup in 1961, Park Chung-hee shed his military uniform, ran for president in national elections, and narrowly won the presidency in South Korea in both 1963 and 1967 (Savada and Shaw 1990, 39). Park ran for election in 1963 after pressure from the Kennedy administration to transition his government to a representative democracy (FRUS 1961b; Oberdorfer 1997, 32). Park then pushed through constitutional change allowing for a third term and narrowly won against his liberal political foe, Kim Dae-jung, in 1971 (Durdin 1972).

Few North Korean incidents of note occurred around the time of Park's election in 1963, but an intense spike in DPRK hostile foreign policy activity coincided with Park's reelection bid in 1967 (see Figure 2.2). North Korea's activities during Park's campaign and election demonstrated a significant shift towards military action against the ROK and U.S. forces in South Korea. In fact, North Korean activity began in earnest in March 1967. By mid-year, the U.S. government reported over 300 DMZ incidents (ranging from non-violent confrontations to firefights)—a six-fold jump compared to previous years—and significant increases in the infiltration of DPRK agents focused on guerrilla and sabotage missions in South Korea (CIA NIE 1967, 2). Additionally, between Park's party nomination in February 1967 and his election three months later, military incidents included infiltration attempts, ambushes, the sinking of a DPRK naval vessel, and a six-hour small arms and artillery engagement between dozens of troops on both sides of the DMZ (Finley 1984, UNC 2012). Non-military hostile actions by the North Koreans included pronouncements against U.S. actions in Vietnam, South Korean activities, and DMZ incidents. Thus during this period, the reelection of South Korea's Park Chung-hee in 1967 did occur in conjunction with a significant increase in conflict on the peninsula.

Were U.S. leadership changes associated with increased North Korean hostile foreign policy activities?

North Korea's hostile foreign policy activity levels varied during the U.S. election periods, but showed noticeable increases during the 1968 presidential election. The U.S. administration underwent three leadership changes during the case study period: Lyndon B. Johnson's assumption of the presidency after President Kennedy's assassination in 1963; Johnson's election in 1964; and Richard Nixon's election as U.S. president in 1968. The assumption of command by Vice President Johnson as the U.S. leader in November 1963 occurred at a time when conflict between the Koreas was at a relatively low level (see Figure 2.2). There were a few military confrontations between North Korea and U.S.–ROK forces in 1963. These military confrontations during 1963 occurred primarily between May and August and included the downing of a U.S. helicopter and the capture of its crew, the shootdown of a small U.S. transport plane (killing six), and the deaths of three U.S. soldiers in a DMZ firefight (Finley 1984, 113). South Korea's CIA chief attributed these attacks as North Korean responses to the killing of nine DPRK agents in South Korea (Finley 1984, 113). In fact, there was no detectable relationship between Johnson's assumption of the presidency of the United States and hostile foreign policy actions on the peninsula. Overall, there was little change in North Korean activities during Lyndon Johnson's campaign and subsequent election in 1964.

Four years later, conflict on the Korean peninsula was at unprecedented levels. North Korea's actions between the U.S. political party conventions in August 1968 and national elections in November included at least 12 firefights along the DMZ with a total of 30 U.S. and ROK casualties (killed and wounded) and 31 North Korean casualties (Bolger 1991, 138–139; ROK MND 1986, 107–108). Other hostile foreign policy actions included diplomatic pronouncements criticizing U.S. policy in Laos and Okinawa and negative statements concerning U.S. actions along the DMZ. There was little mention of the U.S. presidential contenders (Nixon and Humphrey) in North Korea's press until after Nixon won by a slim margin. After that, the DPRK government described him as a "notorious war maniac" who would continue "pursuing vicious and shame-less aggression" (NYT 1968a). In retrospect, Kim Il-sung might have felt that the Democrats and Humphrey could offer a "better deal" for the Communists than Richard Nixon—similar views were held by the Soviets and North Vietnamese (Small 2004, 526).

The increased HFP activity during the final months of the Nixon's presidential election campaign in 1968 might have been related to DPRK efforts to demonstrate that instability on the peninsula required the attention of both the ROK and U.S. governments. While this was not an effort to open a "second front" for the Vietnam War against the United States (FRUS 1966b; Borunkov 1966), Kim hoped to weaken the resolve of the South Korean's government and its decision to send troops overseas while a significant threat existed on the Korean peninsula (Porter 1966). The spike in HFP might have been North

Korea's contribution to the international communists' struggle against "imperialist" nations. As the North Korean ambassador to the USSR noted, "keeping tensions high along the demarcation line is a kind of help for the Vietnamese people, because it is distracting a part of the US forces from Vietnam" (Podgorny 1967). During this time, North Korean hostile foreign policy actions aimed to disparage U.S. operations against communist forces in Vietnam and to negatively affect the ROK–U.S. alliance.

Nixon's 1968 election win came at the height of increased hostilities between the DPRK and the ROK–U.S. alliance and at the same time, North Korea still held the 82-member crew of the USS *Pueblo*. In fact, the 1968 election might have spurred North Korea to release the USS *Pueblo*'s crew prior to Nixon's assumption of office in January 1969 (Mobley 2003, 88). During negotiations, the outgoing Johnson administration emphasized to the North Koreans that they would not get a better "deal" from Nixon and the U.S. offered to sign a letter that included a "qualified" apology (Mobley 2003, 88–89). The U.S. signed the statement and the crewmembers of the USS *Pueblo* were released by North Korea on December 23, 1968 (Lerner 2002, 212–214). Evidence examined in this case makes it difficult to determine if North Korea's increased hostilities during the late 1960s were associated with U.S. presidential elections. But there was an undeniable increase in DPRK hostile actions during the 1968 U.S. campaign and general election compared to previous changes in U.S. leadership.

Were ROK and U.S. strategic-level military exercises associated with increased hostile foreign policy activities?

ROK and U.S. strategic military exercises sometimes coincided with changes in North Korea's hostile foreign policy activities. During some exercises, DPRK activity increased and while others occurred, HFP remained unchanged. The DPRK often framed its responses in the context of the threat posed by the United States and its regional alliances. The United States maintained a substantial presence in East Asia, not only in Korea, but also with military bases spread throughout Japan. United States troop levels in Korea during this time averaged between 50,000 and 60,000 personnel while the U.S. assigned more than 80,000 servicemembers annually to Japan and Okinawa (U.S. DOD 2011c). The American regional posture included robust air, naval and nuclear-capable forces. Between 1966 and 1970, U.S. forces included between 80 and 120 combat aircraft, including F-5 jet fighters and at least two squadrons of advanced F-4s; the ROK's aircraft inventory included 11 squadrons with a mix of Korean War-era F-86s and the more modern F-5s (Beecher 1970). While there was a limited U.S. naval presence on the Korean peninsula itself, the U.S.

stationed its powerful Seventh Fleet in nearby Japan. U.S. ships from its base at Yokosuka were used in efforts to limit rising tensions between China and Taiwan between 1955 and 1958 (Whiting 2001, 108), routinely patrolling the Taiwan Strait (Marolda 2012, 84). The U.S. Navy was also active as a deterrent to Vietnamese activity and instability in Laos and South Vietnam (1961) and in transporting Marines to deployments to Thailand (1962). After the South Vietnam Gulf of Tonkin incident (1964), the Seventh Fleet became an active combatant in Southeast Asia (Marolda 2012).

The U.S. maintained an established regional military presence, conducting both command post and field training events with ROK forces throughout the period. A number of small-scale annual military exercises occurred each year. These included both command post exercises (CPXs) focused on training headquarters, field training exercises (FTXs) and deployments of ROK–U.S. troops to on-peninsula locations to exercise combined war plans. For example in 1962, U.S. and ROK defense forces participated in seven exercises (four CPXs, three FTXs and one amphibious landing exercise) (CINCPAC 1963, 136). But, more importantly the late 1960s saw an increase in the number and scope of larger, strategic-level exercises based on the "defense of South Korea" (from the U.S. and ROK perspective). The most significant of these was an ROK–U.S. CPX, dubbed "FOCUS LENS," which began in 1968 and was conducted throughout this period, being designed to test plans for the defense of Korea (CINCPAC 1970, 158).

The FOCUS LENS exercise, scheduled for March 1968, was postponed due to the Blue House attacks and *Pueblo* crisis but occurred in October 1968. The exercise was scenario-driven and "based on a general attack from the north" (Finley 1968, 125; CINCPAC 1969, 151).[21] This was followed in March 1969 by an exercise designated "FOCUS RETINA," which included 7,000 total troops and the paradrop of a brigade of soldiers from the U.S.-based 82nd Airborne Division to "scatter a mythical aggressor" near the Han river (Bolger 1991, 99–101 and CINCPAC 1970, 158). During this exercise, the U.S. moved 2,500 troops from U.S. stateside bases to Korea (8,500 miles) in 31 hours (Finley 1984, 129). This was a clear demonstration of the U.S. ability to respond in the event of hostilities with the North. Ironically, this worried the South Koreans as well, as it signaled that the U.S. was testing its ability to support the ROK during hostilities using means that did not require a permanent troop presence on the Korean peninsula (Shabecoff 1969). In 1969, the FOCUS LENS exercise occurred in October (and each fall thereafter) and all headquarters at the division level (and air force and naval equivalents) took part (CINCPAC 1970, 158). These types of exercises raised tensions on the Korean peninsula and the consistent North Korean reaction was to declare that the peninsula was on the "brink of war" (NYT 1967c). In published speeches, Kim Il-sung denounced these exercises and others conducted by the U.S. and its regional allies (KIS 1976, 96 and 272).

The levels of North Korean hostilities during these exercises were mixed with increases in hostile foreign policy actions generally during October of each year (especially in 1968 and 1969), but no increases (compared to adjacent months) in the months of February and March (KINU 2011; Finley 1984; UNC 2012). Thus, there was an increase in hostilities for some but not all of the strategic exercises during this period. Another key relationship identified was that the North Korean downing of an EC-121 U.S. intelligence aircraft in April 1969 was possibly a response to the FOCUS RETINA exercise, based on the timing of the incident and North Korean rhetoric at the time (Zangoria and Zangoria 1979, 9–34 to 9–35). While these strategic exercises did raise tensions between the North and South throughout this period, ROK–U.S. joint military operations in Vietnam were much more influential in North Korean decisions to use force on the Korean peninsula. These exercises and the continued presence of American troops in Korea were a stark reminder to the Kim regime of the continued military alliance between the United States and ROK. At the same time, there were changes in DPRK hostile foreign policy activities during at least some of these exercise periods.

Was the presence of a conservative ROK government associated with increased HFP?

Park Chung-hee's conservative and staunch anti-communist foreign policy most likely increased the level of North Korean hostile foreign policy events during this period. While future ROK administrations (to include those in the 2000s) generally shunned direct military responses to DPRK actions, the Park administration was, at least in the 1960s, determined to respond directly to North Korean security threats. In the early 1960s, Park first acquired the means to increase its defensive posture (through economic success) and then sought to actively counter the DPRK's hostile actions throughout the decade. Yet while the Park administration had tense relationship with the DPRK throughout this period, it did not pursue the same political objectives in regards to North Korea as previous leaders, such as Syngman Rhee. The 1950s slogan of Rhee's party, "March North and Unify!," was replaced by the Park regime's call in the early 1960s for "Unification after Construction" (Kim H. 1977, 176, 197).

There were charges of U.S. involvement in the 1961 coup which brought Park to power. Although the Soviets argued that the U.S. may have instigated the coup (NYT 1961), Joungwon Kim (1975a, 226) noted that the initial reaction by the U.S. was to demand a return to the previous "lawful government authorities" rather than to support the new government. Kim (1975a) referenced statements made by the Chief of the UN Command's public statement that called "upon all military personnel in his Command to support the duly recognized Government of the ROK headed by Prime Minister Chang Myon [and he] expects that the Chiefs of the Korean Armed Forces will use their authority and influence to see that control is immediately turned back to the government authorities and that order is restored in the armed forces" (FRUS 1961).

Park Chung-hee's assumption of power in 1961 solidified South Korea's emphasis on priorities other than reunification. Park's initial efforts were focused on "national reconstruction" which rested on policies (or "the prerequisites") of economic progress and anti-communism (Kim H. 2004, 71). His prioritized goals for South Korea in the 1960s included economic prosperity, followed by national security, efforts to reconstruct "genuine democracy," and finally, reunification (Kim, YJ 2011, 98). Park gradually established control over the ROK and by 1965, he was "firmly anti–Communist ... [and] in a position of unchallenged authority in Seoul and appears to have the support, or at least acquiescence, of a majority of the population" (CIA NIE 1967, 5). It was at this same time that defense spending on both sides of the DMZ began to increase substantially, followed by a significant rise in military activities and tensions. Compared to North Korea's more technologically advanced but smaller military (370,000 troops), South Korea maintained a much larger force of 600,000 personnel (CINC 2012). While the DPRK had mutual defense treaties with both the USSR and China, the U.S. presence on the peninsula (and defense treaty with the ROK) ensured that any conflict between the Koreas would quickly involve both sides of the ongoing Cold War conflict.

South Korea's efforts soon began to achieve economic success. By the 1970s, industrial production was reportedly growing 25 percent annually (Savada and Shaw 1990, 143). The CIA reported that by 1965, it was actually South Korea's economy that was stronger compared to the DPRK (CIA NIE 1967, 4). In fact, between 1961 and 1965, South Korea's GDP averaged $3.2 billion per year and grew at an average annual rate of 5.9 percent (World dataBank 2012). Additionally, economic and military aid provided by the United States, which was approximately $400–$450 million per year (USG 1998, 56), enabled the Park regime to effectively counter North Korean military activities. This U.S. aid was a response to developments on the peninsula, such as infiltrations and armed incursions by the DPRK. These military actions were potentially intended to "test the effectiveness and reaction of South Korean forces deployed along the DMZ as well as to undermine troop morale" (FRUS 1966b).

In October 1966, the North Koreans began more intense operations and conducted seven "surprise attacks" against South Korean forces (FRUS 1966b). Despite U.S. objections, ROK troops responded by crossing the DMZ and killing or wounding as many as 30 North Koreans (FRUS 1966c and CIA NIE 1967, 2). The UN Commander, U.S. General Charles Bonesteel, heard rumors concerning a planned ROK response (a retaliatory combat raid) and met with the ROK Minister of National Defense in efforts to dissuade this action (Sarantakes 2000, 441). Bonesteel reminded him that an attack against North Korea "could have severe and unintended political and diplomatic impact on the pending visit of President Lyndon B. Johnson to the peninsula and a scheduled UN General Assembly debate on Korea" (Sarantakes 2000, 441).

The United Nations Command considered this an Armistice violation, while the South Korean generals felt that the raid was justified and that the U.S. "paid too little attention to ROK casualties" (Bolger 1991, 36). The South Korean position was articulated by Park Chung-hee in 1967 as he stated,

> Whenever the North Koreans violate the military demarcation line ... all the United Nations Command has done so far is to table the complaint at Panmunjom, where the North Koreans categorically deny it. For the last 14 years, the United Nations Command has abided by the armistice while the North Korean side has ignored it ... whenever the North Koreans violate the armistice they must be made to pay by retaliation [FRUS 1967a].

This raid and other ROK activities that followed were disconcerting to U.S. leaders who reminded Park that "such actions undercut the ROK's position at the UN, provided fodder for North Korean propaganda, undercut General Bonesteel's authority, and jeopardized U.S. Congressional support for military assistance to Korea" (FRUS 1967a).[22] The Park government considered North Korea's actions along the DMZ as a direct threat to South Korea's security while the U.S., with its increasing commitment to Vietnam, had no interest in heightened tensions and military clashes with the DPRK (Hungarian Embassy 1967). Throughout the 1960s, the conservative Park government continued these types of activities to counter North Korea's increased level of military confrontations, possibly resulting in heightened levels of DPRK hostile actions.

Case Study Summary and Conclusions

Throughout the 1960s, Kim Il-sung solidified his grip on power over North Korean society, built the DPRK's economy, enhanced its military capabilities and established a legitimate and stable communist state. North Korea's foreign policy activities evolved from an emphasis on diplomatic solutions to the division of Korea to active military measures intended to cause the downfall of the Park government. Kim's efforts to destabilize South Korea failed and the Park government remained intact. Nevertheless, the hostile actions by the North Koreans provide clear examples of the DPRK's future patterns of relations with the rest of the international community. They also demonstrated the Kim regime's unique ability to conduct sustained provocations, with little regard to the potential reactions by either South Korea or the U.S.

Table 2.1 Structured Analysis Results: North Korea Emerges (1963–1969)

Category	Question	Test Result	Details
Hostile Foreign Policy (Dependent Variable)	1. What was the level of hostile foreign policy during the case study?	High	Conflict scores were higher than historical averages and averaged 1222 each year.[23]
Internal Conditions (Independent Variables)	2. Was political instability associated with heightened HFP activities?	No	There was low political instability during this period.
	3. Were economic difficulties associated with increased HFP?	No	Although there was an increase in the DPRK HFP as economic conditions changed, in general, the DPRK experienced economic stability during this period.
	4. Was social instability associated with periods of increased HFP?	No	Social instability during this period was low and unrelated to HFP activities.
External Conditions (Independent Variables)	5. Were UN Security Council resolutions against the DPRK associated with increased HFP?	n/a	UN Security Council resolutions were not enacted during this period.
	6. Were ROK leadership changes associated with increased HFP actions?	Yes	National elections during this period were associated with HFP activities.
	7. Were US leadership changes associated with increased HFP actions?	Yes	Activity levels varied during the election periods, but did increase during the 1968 U.S. election.
	8. Were ROK/US strategic-level military exercises associated with DPRK hostile actions?	Yes	Activities did increase during some exercises, but not during others.
	9. Was a conservative ROK government associated with increased HFP?	Yes	Park's foreign policy influenced North Korea's HFP incidents.

Table 2.1 (above) provides a summary of the relationship between the incidence of hostile foreign policy activities, conditions faced by the Kim regime, and alternate explanations. This period saw significantly higher levels of North Korean HFP activities compared to historical averages (see Figure 2.2). In fact, the conflict levels between the Koreas in the 1960s were at the highest level found during the research period (1960 to 2011). Additionally, although there was evidence of an increase in hostilities in conjunction with a slowing of the North Korean economy, this was an overall period of economic stability. The heightened levels of HFP activities, in the absence of significant domestic distress, do not support the contention that diversionary activity occurred. Thus, while the Kim regime pursued activities focused on uniting the population against an external foe, these actions are not consistent with the diversionary theory argument. Alternatively, the case does provide support to the idea that external influences, such as ROK elections and the conservative anti-communist nature of the Park administration, were related to increases in DPRK hostilities.

The relationship between hostile activities and South Korea's conservative administration was as expected. As the Park administration pursued an increasingly harder line towards the DPRK, especially during the latter half of the 1960s, tensions on the peninsula increased. Additionally, North Korea garnered significant support from the Communist Bloc because of Cold War alliances and the overall foreign policy objectives of both Moscow and Beijing. These Cold War relationships provided the Kim regime with the military and economic support to pursue North Korea's policy goals. Yet there are important relationships that were not found; for example, North Korean hostile foreign policy activities did not increase consistently with strategic military exercises[24] and U.S. leadership changes had little effect on DPRK hostile activity levels. Yet, the Kim regime did use hostile foreign policy events and external threats in attempts to solidify domestic support for national priorities. To a limited extent, the DPRK also might have potentially attempted to divert public attention away from economic difficulties during this period. This is consistent with Lerner's (2010) contention that North Korean actions during the mid–1960s were linked to diversionary behavior. Through an in-depth analysis of the diplomatic communications records of communist embassies in Pyongyang, Lerner (2010, 44–45) argues that the Kim regime was focused on furthering the concept of juche while simultaneously using a constant state of tension to "further his political agenda at home."[25]

The Kim regime decided to shift tactics in the mid–1960s towards more violent actions against South Korea and the U.S. based on a variety of factors. These included DPRK concerns about its economy, the Kim regime view that

South Korea was ready for revolution, opportunities afforded by U.S. involvement in Vietnam, and the evolving regional security situation faced by North Korea. The Kim regime was also dealing with the effects of dedicating nearly one-third of its national income to defense programs, its desire to be a viable and influential communist state, and the need for continued economic and military aid from its allies. By the mid–1960s, economic and political conditions in the South had stabilized and the possibility of an ROK revolution (in support of the communists) seemed to be slipping away. Thus, the pursuit of external "adventures" by the Kim regime was a logical response to support reunification efforts and bolster its position at home (Michishita 2010, 31).

The Kim regime followed a political course similar to the Soviets. The DPRK embraced both ideological and practical means to vilify threats to the North's communist system and maintain Kim Il-sung's grip on power over the DPRK. For example, Kennan's (1946) "Long Telegram" proposed that the Soviets made full use of Marxist-Leninist ideology "because it offered them an external threat in capitalism that could be used to validate their repressive regime" (Lerner 2010, 47). The Kim regime similarly focused on the sustained threat of war with the ROK–U.S. alliance to keep the DPRK population both on edge and under control (Hungarian Embassy 1963; NYT 1967c). Thus, the North Korean regime was able to use the specter of a rising threat posed by South Korea as the impetus to rally the North Korean population. Additionally, the sustained focus on the U.S. as the enemy of the Korean people (KIS 1972, 198) and references to the rise of Japanese militarism (Romanian Embassy 1971) were clear attempts by the Kim regime to keep North Korea's citizens focused on external threats.

The existence of a successful South Korean government was disconcerting to the Kim regime: Park Chung-hee was enjoying economic progress and international political prestige. South Korea's success reflected negatively on the DPRK's claim of establishing a "legitimate" socialist system (Kim I. 1975, 287). Thus, North Korea's efforts to destabilize the South hinged on heightened guerrilla warfare and attacks against the perceived core of South Korea's success: the ROK President. The DPRK hoped that the 1968 Blue House raid, if successful, would "reduce South Korea to leaderless chaos, and thus set in motion a social revolution that would pave the way for unification under his regime" (Martin 2006, 127). While North Korea's attacks against the South failed to cause the instability sought by the Kim regime, they did prove that the Johnson and Nixon administrations were unwilling to respond in kind to provocations against the ROK–U.S. military alliance. The lack of an American military response to both the USS *Pueblo* capture and EC-121 downing and the U.S. ability to block ROK retaliation for the Blue House raid set a precedent for future reactions to similar DPRK activities: U.S. reactions to North Korean attacks would primarily involve diplomacy, rather than military retaliation.

North Korea's other behaviors were based on Kim's desire to maintain power and reactions to international conditions, which supports the arguments surrounding external influences as the influences for DPRK HFP activities. The Kim regime maintained domestic tension by using the threat of a U.S. and South Korean invasion to maintain the public's focus on regime goals (CIA 1969a, 8; Zagoria and Zagoria 1979, 49). Additional efforts to malign increasing ties between Japan and South Korea (Romanian Embassy 1971) also served similar purposes in attempts to keep the North Korean population focused on external threats. Whether or not the Kim regime was actually successful in distracting DPRK citizens from internal concerns is difficult to determine, but in any case, there is substantial evidence (as discussed above) that the North Korean leaders did intend to use external threats in an effort to affect domestic attitudes.

Finally, one of the most significant findings in examining this case is that while lower levels of hostilities were expected during this period (because of relative domestic stability), high levels of HFP occurred. This lends support to arguments against the diversionary hypothesis (which hinges on domestic distress) in this case. Yet at the same time, efforts to focus public attention on external threats did occur in tandem with North Korea's establishment of a police state (as discussed above). These policies allowed the Kim regime to continue to pursue foreign policy goals with public support (at least on the surface).

Thus while the overarching characteristics of North Korea during this time do not support the idea of diversion as a primary cause, a more nuanced examination reveals that some evidence of diversion-style behavior is present. During this case study, there was clear evidence that the Kim regime used diversionary behavior throughout the period to support a constant air of "wartime readiness" and mobilization of the population against external threats to sustain its grip on power. Domestic conditions during this case study were generally stable, arguably the best during the entire study period (1960–2011). Finally, this period also saw the DPRK's use of brinksmanship tactics and the Kim regime's realization that provocative actions usually resulted in muted responses from the ROK and U.S. In the future, these responses often became economic concessions, as evidenced in the next case study.

Figure 2.6 Timeline: North Korean and U.S.–ROK Events 1963–1971

North Korean Events		ROK–U.S. Events
DPRK begins to "lean" towards China Soviet-DPRK relations deteriorate	1963	U.S. President Kennedy assassinated Johnson becomes U.S. President
Soviet-DPRK relations improve	1964	Johnson elected as U.S. President
DPRK obtains military aid from USSR	1965	U.S. deploys combat troops to Vietnam
DPRK military activities increase President Johnson visits ROK	1966	ROK deploys troops to Vietnam
DPRK spends 30 percent of budget on defense	1967	ROK President Park reelected
Intense combat along the DMZ DPRK commandos attack ROK Blue House USS *Pueblo* and crew seized by DPRK USS *Pueblo* crew released	1968	U.S. commitment to Vietnam peaks Nixon elected U.S. president
U.S. intelligence aircraft shot down by DPRK	1969	U.S.–ROK FOCUS RETINA exercise
Large-scale military exercises Tensions along DMZ increase	1970	Large-scale military exercises U.S. withdraws 20,000 troops from ROK
	1971	ROK withdraws troops from Vietnam ROK President Park reelected

CHAPTER 3

The Arduous March: North Korea's Great Famine

This chapter analyzes the relationship between the conditions (internal and external) North Korea experienced from 1993 to 1999 and hostile foreign policy levels. During this time, the Kim regimes endured one of the most catastrophic events in recent history: famine resulting in nearly 2.5 million deaths (11 percent of North Korea's population) (Natsios 1999, 7–8). Diversionary theory suggests that leaders seek external uses of force to distract public attention from domestic distress (such as famine). The low levels of overall conflict during this case study and the presence of significant domestic distress stand in contrast to the predictions made by this concept. Yet, this period did include conflict activities initiated by the North Korean government such as events surrounding its nuclear and missile programs. These were both potential attempts to gain concessions from the international community and, to a lesser extent, distract its citizens from the hardships caused by food shortages. Alternatively, this case study provides support for the idea that external conditions were more influential in the Kim regimes' activities. This case study shows that events such as ROK elections and strategic military exercises influenced North Korea's propensity to conduct hostile foreign policy (HFP) activities.

This case was selected based on the overall "political shock" (Goertz and Diehl 1995, 31) of the famine years, and their profound impact on both North Korea's socialist society and its relationship with the international community. Aside from the extreme death toll, the famine caused DPRK citizens to become disillusioned with their government and allowed international aid organizations unprecedented domestic access to the most closed society on the planet (Natsios 1999, 9). In fact, "The food aid program is visible evidence of the failure of juche, the governing state ideology; it has undermined state propaganda about the outside capitalist world; and it has accelerated the privatization of the economy" (Natsios (1999, 9). Additionally, this period saw North Korea firmly established as a nation that had an emerging nuclear program and, ironically, remained dependent on international aid to address its food shortages. The following sections include a synopsis of the crisis, the same structured questions as in the previous case study, and conclude with a comparative analysis of the results and timeline (Figure 3.5) for reference.

The Great Famine

Prior to the 1990s, North Korea experienced a number of food shortages, but these did not fundamentally change the DPRK's societal structure or its relationship with external actors. North Korea's previous food shortages were associated with external influences or natural disasters including scarcities in 1945 (attributed to coordination problems after the end of Japanese rule); post–Korean War effects in 1954; and problems with food availability from 1970 to 1973 due to poor weather, increased spending based on military confrontations, and industrial underperformance (Lee 2003, 8). The famine in the 1990s had longer-lasting effects and established North Korea's chronic dependence on external assistance to feed its citizens. Through the 1980s, North Korea fed its citizens through a combination of domestic production and imports of food and other products (such as fuel) at discounted prices to support its agricultural industry. Prior to the 1990s, the Soviets were North Korea's most important trading partner, followed by China, and both provided fuel and fertilizer to the DPRK at a substantially reduced rate to support food production (Noland 2000, 97–99; Bennett 1998, 3).

Yet North Korea's focus on large state farms and centralized decision-making historically influenced the incidence and severity of food shortages (Noland, Robinson and Wang 2001, 73). These choices, along with antiquated agricultural practices, corruption, and conflicting policies, all contributed to the poor harvests of the 1990s. Noland (2003, 4) observes,

> [in 1987] the North Koreans initiated a number of at times conflicting policies in the agricultural sector, including the expansion of state farms, tolerance of private garden plots, expansion of grain-sown areas, transformation of crop composition in favor of high-yield items, maximization of industrial inputs subject to availability, and the intensification of double-cropping and dense planting. Continuous cropping led to soil depletion, and the overuse of chemical fertilizers contributed to acidification of the soil and eventually a reduction in yields. As yields declined, hillsides were denuded to bring more and more marginal land into production. This contributed to soil erosion, river silting, and ultimately, catastrophic flooding.

Press reports from 1994 began to mention strain on the Kim regime as Pyongyang's official radio broadcast stated, "in parts of the country people go hungry" (Noland 2000, 13). Prior to the famine period, the DPRK government's Public Distribution System (PDS), a food allocation system used by North Korea to ration foodstuffs, supplied food to approximately sixty percent of the population with all others receiving rations through alternate methods (Haggard and Noland 2011a, 48; Natsios 2000, 96).[1] Using the PDS, the North Korean government purchases food from collective farms and redistributes it to all citizens (Apte and Mokdad 1998, 1315). Prior to 1995, the system was structured to divide the population into ten levels, based on work type and productivity, and afterwards, it was restructured to a three-tiered system based on age (Bennett 1999, 9). One of the key indicators of problems with food availability in North Korea was changes to this system, which reportedly began to falter in the late 1980s (Lee 2005, 5). Refugee surveys indicate that by 1993, less than 20 percent of the population could depend on the PDS and the Kim regime as their primary supplier of food (Haggard and Noland 2011a, 48). As Haggard and Noland (2011a, 48) note,

> As the PDS broke down, people were forced to turn to foraging and the nascent markets for sustenance. Such coping responses included rearing livestock, growing kitchen gardens, and collecting wild foods like edible grasses, acorns, tree bark, and sea algae.

In 1994, Chinese analysts warned that North Korea was headed for severe food shortages (Eberstadt 1997, 233).[2] As DPRK refugees began to flee across the Sino-Korean border looking for food, North Korea began to reach out to its neighbors and other organizations for aid (KBSM 1998; Lee 2003, 142; Kristof 1996). The North quietly requested food aid from Japan in the fall of 1994 and again in January 1995 (Haggard and Noland 2011a, 137). It also began requesting aid from non-governmental organizations such as World Vision International (WVI) (Noland, Robinson and Wang 2001, 750). Although North Korea had unsuccessfully sought 500,000 metric tons of food aid from South Korea in the early 1990s (Woo-Cumings 2002, 21), this was first time the DPRK solicited and received help from the wider international community.

Unsurprisingly, severe flooding in 1995 compounded the situation and North Korea could not compensate for crop losses that year. The DPRK leadership consistently stated that natural disasters caused the famine (KCNA 1996c), while refugees often blamed the DPRK leadership for the shortages (Natsios 2001, 127). In fact, 60 percent of North Korea refugees surveyed from 1997 to 1999 attributed the famine to North Korean leaders, economic lapses, priority given to the military (only 25 percent considered natural disasters as the primary cause) (Natsios 2001, 219). Although natural events certainly played a role in the food shortages, the proximate causes were the North Korean economic system and other structural problems (Cumings 2005, 443–444; Haggard and Noland 2007, 209; Lee 2003, 313). As Natsios (2001, 177) observes, "even without flooding, North Korea would have entered the mid–1990s with a substantial food deficit."

The crisis was one of the worst famines in the 20th century, with the most severe stages lasting from 1996 to 1997. The DPRK famine was "the century's fifth great totalitarian famine," and ranked alongside the Soviet Ukraine (1930–1933), China (1958–1962), Ethiopia (1984–1985) and Cambodia (1975) (Natsios 2001, 49–54). Ironically, the famine in the Ukraine under Stalin's rule and severe food shortages from 1958 to 1962 during China's "Great Leap Forward" period were the also the result of political choices and institutional failures, rather than natural disasters (Bernstein 1984). Similar to the Kim regime, both Stalin and Mao relied on grain procurements and redistributions to deal with the crisis, which often exacerbated the shortages (Bernstein 1984, 369–370). The famine in the 1990s had longer-lasting effects as it established North Korea's chronic dependence on external assistance to feed its citizens. This period, often referred to by North Koreans as the "Arduous March,"[3] was undoubtedly the most traumatic time for the DPRK since the Korean War.

Hostilities During the Famine Period

The following section includes the same set of structured questions introduced in the first case study. These are again used to identify linkages and determine the influence of diversionary behavior. These questions and an analysis of the case study results follow.

What was the level of hostile foreign policy activities during this period?

When compared to historic norms, overall DPRK hostility levels were low during the famine period. Yet a number of significant events (described below) characterized this decade as North Korea pursued two primary, yet distinctive, foreign policy goals during this period. The first was a sustained effort to gain international assistance, to include humanitarian aid (food and medicine), energy aid (heavy fuel oil), developmental grants and loans, and a variety of other external assistance. The DPRK had little experience in these efforts, but sought to quickly obtain and use aid to avoid economic and social collapse. The second was to maintain domestic stability through efforts to ensure the Kim regime (Kim Jong-il after the death of his father in July 1994) and its supporters remained in power. These two goals were often at odds with each other; for example, the influx of international aid workers had the potentially destabilizing effect of exposing the secretive North Korean society to the international community (Smith 1999; Natsios 2001, 217–236). Additionally, the DPRK's pursuit of security objectives, which often resulted in hostile foreign policy actions, typically made the international community reluctant to provide aid. Despite this, North Korea was able to obtain an almost continuous stream of aid throughout the crisis period and between 1994 and 1999, the DPRK received over 3.7 million tons of food aid through the World Food Program and $370 million in fuel subsidies from KEDO (UN FAIS 2012; KEDO 2001). At the same time, the Kim regime was also engaging in a moderate number of hostile military and diplomatic activities.

Figure 3.1 shows the levels of hostile foreign policy actions that occurred during the famine period. In comparison to the average conflict levels during the 1960s, the occurrence of hostile foreign policy incidents during the famine period was almost 50 percent lower.[4]

Figure 3.1 Hostile Foreign Policy Activities 1990–2000

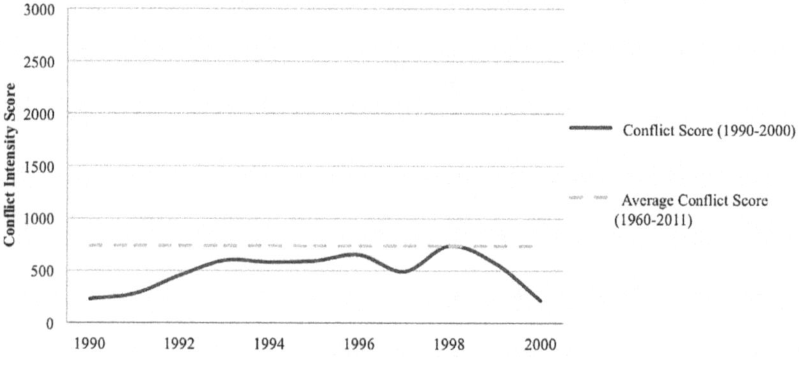

Source: Chapter 5 and Korea Conflict Database (Appendix B)

North Korea's famine seemed to dampen the overall incidence of hostile foreign policy activities compared to the rest of the period examined in this study. Additionally, the Taepodong missile crisis period in 1998 (discussed below) was the only time hostility incidents reached the average historical levels for the study period (see Figure 3.1). In fact, overall conflict intensity scores during this period were 18 percent lower than historical norms for the entire study period.[5] Yet significant incidents did occur, including efforts to develop nuclear weapons and missile systems, infiltration activities, and naval engagements.

The Nuclear Crisis. The onset of the initial phase of the famine in the 1990s coincided with enhanced North Korean efforts to develop its nuclear capabilities. North Korea's nuclear energy program had been around since at least the mid–1950s, when the Soviets began providing technical support, and in the 1960s, the USSR helped North Korea build its first reactor at Yongbyon (CIA 1982). The program evolved into dedicated efforts to develop a nuclear bomb in the 1980s (Oberdorfer 2001, 252–254). From a security standpoint, obtaining nuclear weapons was a key priority for Pyongyang and was consistent with Kim's concept of national self-reliance. North Korea's quest for nuclear weapons was not surprising as nuclear weapons had been present in South Korea and controlled by the U.S. since 1958. Balancing against this threat was an unfulfilled goal for the Kim regime (Yun 2005, 14–15). These U.S. weapons included the 280mm nuclear cannons and Honest John nuclear capable missiles manned by the U.S. Army and the addition (in 1959) of a U.S. Air Force Matador cruise missile squadron (Jackson 2005, 65; Oberdorfer 2001, 257). In 1977, U.S. presidential candidate Jimmy Carter announced that the U.S. had stationed over 700 of these weapons on the peninsula (the actual figure from classified U.S. government sources was 683 weapons) (Oberdorfer 2001, 89). North Korea's response was the acquisition of nuclear weapons, which provided the Kim regime a means to support its national goal of continued state sovereignty (Oberdorfer 2001, 89). The international community became concerned in 1993 as the DPRK announced its intention to withdraw from the Non-Proliferation Treaty (NPT). Subsequent negotiations with the International Atomic Energy Agency (IAEA) and the West also increased tensions on the peninsula, leading to a number of military and diplomatic hostile actions by the DPRK.

In the early 1990s, the U.S. and other members of the international community began to pursue efforts to denuclearize the peninsula and dissuade Pyongyang from developing nuclear weapons. This included proposals for the removal of all nuclear weapons from South Korea, offers to cease strategic-level ROK–U.S. military exercises, and a U.S. diplomatic exchange (the first since the Korean War) with the DPRK in New York in January 1992 (Mazarr 1995, 94–95). Although North Korea had joined the Non-Proliferation Treaty in 1985, it declined to allow inspectors to visit its facilities, citing the presence of U.S. nuclear weapons in the ROK (Spector 1992, 28). When the U.S. removed its nuclear weapons from the peninsula in 1992,[6] the Kim regime signed additional IAEA agreements but "continued to find excuses to delay and restrict inspection" (Nye 1992, 1295). The following two years included failed attempts to inspect the DPRK facilities, IAEA demands for more access, a restart of U.S.–ROK military exercises, and threats by North Korea to withdraw from the NPT (Mazarr 1995, 95–96).[7]

Former U.S. President Jimmy Carter helped ease the mounting crisis by traveling to Pyongyang in June 1994 for negotiations and providing "what turned out to be a successful exit ramp to allow the North Koreans to give in to the substance of American demands" (Wit 2004, 243). In late 1994, North Korea agreed to halt its nuclear program in exchange for a number of international aid concessions, to include the annual delivery of fuel and food aid and developmental assistance to build two light water nuclear reactors in the DPRK (KEDO 2012). This arrangement, dubbed the "Agreed Framework," was an official agreement between North Korea and the United States—yet it was not a standard treaty and was not ratified by the U.S. Congress. The Agreed Framework was a formal set of pledges intended to increase cooperation on the nuclear issue (Cha and Kang 2003, 136; U.S. State Department 1994). Under the Framework, North Korea agreed to dismantle its graphite-moderated reactors, freeze its nuclear weapons program and remain part of the NPT, and allow IAEA inspectors to monitor its progress (Agreed Framework 1994).

The U.S. pledged to provide a light water reactor "project" (which included two nuclear power generating reactors), 500,000 tons annually of heavy oil for energy use, normalization of political and economic ties, and assurances that it would not attack the DPRK with nuclear weapons (Agreed Framework 1994). While this agreement eventually broke down in 2002 and became defunct, annual deliveries of heavy fuel oil did occur (over $400 million) between 1995 and 2002 (Manyin and Nikitin 2010, 2) and about one-third of the reactor project was completed (KEDO 2005, 6). The Agreed Framework encountered insurmountable problems in 2002, when the implementing organization (KEDO) suspended oil shipments and work on the nuclear plants. This was in reaction to reports that North Korea had begun enriching uranium (essential for nuclear weapons production) in violation of the Framework agreements. In early 2003, North Korea expelled IAEA inspectors, withdrew from the NPT, and resumed reprocessing activities at its Yongbyon nuclear facility (KEDO 2012; Breen 2004, 38). Throughout the famine period, the Agreed Framework did provide two needed advantages to the DPRK: a "free" source of energy supplies (heavy fuel oil shipments) and, just as importantly, decreased tensions with the U.S. and its allies. As a result, the groundwork was laid for future negotiations and tensions regarding nuclear concerns eased.

Missile Development and Testing. North Korea's continued efforts to develop missile technology during this period remained an ongoing concern for the international community. These missiles were seen as a provocative aspect of North Korea's overall military efforts because they provided the DPRK a long-range "first strike" and retaliatory capability. For the DPRK, the missiles provided both a source of income as exportable weapons and an asymmetric capability to balance against the military power of both South Korea and the United States. North Korea's ballistic missile efforts have been part of its overall defense program since the 1960s when the Soviet Union provided FROG (Free Rocket Over Ground) surface to surface missile systems (Yun 2004, 122; Samore 2004a, 63). In the late 1960s, the USSR refused to provide upgrades or additional assistance for the program and the Kim regime turned to China for cooperation and assistance, establishing an extensive set of technology and exchange agreements (Bermudez 2001, 239). In the 1970s, North Korea pursued its own program, spurred by South Korean efforts to develop short-range surface-to-surface missiles (Pinkston 2008, 15; Bermudez 2001, 240). In 1976, while China and the Soviets declined to sell newer systems to North Korea, the Kim regime arranged to procure Scud-B (short range ballistic missiles) from Egypt, which had acquired these from the Soviets (Worden 2008, 257–258). North Korea reverse-engineered these systems, renaming them as "Hwasong-5" missiles, and conducted their first test launches in 1984 (Yun 2004, 124–125).[8]

Over the next few years, North Korea improved upon its Scud missile platform and began working on an advanced version capable of carrying a nuclear warhead. The Scud-D (also called the Nodong missile) was test-launched in May 1993 and subsequently deployed throughout North Korea (Yomiuri Shimbun 1993; Kyodo News 1995). To counter this emerging threat, the U.S. deployed Patriot anti-missile systems to South Korea in 1994 (Shin 1994). North Korea's development of long-range Nodong missile (able to reach targets up to 1500 kilometers) resulted in protests from Tokyo and requests to also deploy the Patriot systems to Japan (Yomiuri Shimbun 1993).

After the Nodong missile tests and the 1994 Agreed Framework accords were concluded, North Korea's missile program became a key issue for U.S. diplomats (Michishita 2010, 118–119). Low-level negotiations occurred throughout 1995, followed by official talks in April 1996. Those talks were interrupted by preparations for an additional Nodong test in 1997, but were restarted the following year. The North Koreans canceled this launch as part of the negotiations process (Michishita 2009, 119). The negotiations were again delayed by the U.S. due to another pending missile launch of a new, even more advanced DPRK missile (Michishita 2010, 118–123). This time, talks stalled due to North Korea's most ambitious missile project to date: the Taepodong-1 (Samore 2004a, 75). This missile system had been in production at the same time as the Nodong missiles and provided the DPRK an intermediate-range ballistic (IRBM) capability that was nuclear payload-capable and could range up to 1,500 kilometers (Worden 1999, 258). Concurrently, the Taepodong-2 was also being developed as an ICBM (inter-continental ballistic missile) with a range of up to 12,000 kilometers, which was long enough to target the United States (Worden 2009, 258; Bermudez 2001, 276). That same year, North Korea caused significant concern in the region as it test-launched the Taepodong-1 in a trajectory over Japan (eventually landing in the Pacific Ocean) (Nihon Keizai Shimbun 1998; Cumings 2005, 502). The Taepodong-1 system could range further than North Korea's previous systems and potentially target all of South Korea and Japan and U.S. forces stationed at those locations (Bermudez 2001, 276).

In 1999, the U.S. government determined that both the nuclear and missile technology capabilities of the North Koreans threatened the stability of the region. The U.S. subsequently pursued intense diplomatic discussions to secure agreements with the Kim regime to curtail both efforts in exchange for international aid (Perry 1999; Cumings 2005, 502–503). After further negotiations and after preparing to test launch its other new missile, the longer-range Taepodong-2,[9] North Korea announced in September 1999 that it would freeze missile development and testing (Michishita 123–125). This lasted through the end of the famine period and was reaffirmed by North Korea in 2001 (Worden 2009, 258).

Infiltration Activities and Naval Engagements. Other types of HFP actions, such as reconnaissance and infiltration operations against South Korea, did occur during this period albeit at lower levels than during the 1960s.[10] North Korean special operations troops continued to conduct missions intended to both destabilize South Korea and gather intelligence information.[11] South Korea and its allies detected many infiltration incidents occurring during the famine period, although North Korea sought to keep these out of the public's view (Bermudez 1997, 159). In the late 1980s, infiltration operations into the ROK "decreased dramatically" based on high-level negotiations resulting in a 1992 agreement on non-aggression and reconciliation (Bermudez 1997, 159). At the same time, the levels of hostile foreign policy activities, based on the nuclear issue and missile development and tests, were at significantly higher levels. Yet North Korea's sporadic infiltration activities did continue to support the Kim regime through intelligence information and destabilizing activities aimed at South Korea and the U.S. The North Koreans considered strategic reconnaissance and other special operations missions in South Korea as an essential part of the overall security strategy to survive and eventually reunify the two Koreas (Hodge 2003). In fact, the DPRK's special forces, which constituted fifteen percent of North Korea's overall ground troop structure, were fully capable of conducting these types of operations and had constructed elaborate training facilities in the DPRK, such as an eight kilometer long underground mockup of Seoul for "reality training" (Chosun Ilbo 1994; Martin 2004,

539; Yonhap News 1994a). Refugees reported other training included kidnapping techniques, methods to destroy ships from within, ways to destroy telecommunications systems, and how to bomb institutions (Martin 2004, 540).

The most significant infiltration events during this period were primarily associated with naval activity beginning in 1995 and continued throughout the period. Over the previous decades, North Korea routinely conducted infiltration operations against the ROK via sea routes, due to the porous nature of South Korea's coastlines—the activities in the 1990s were typical of previous patterns. These included agent infiltrations via water near the Imjin River (north of Seoul) and near Cheju, a South Korean island just south of the peninsula (Bermudez 1997, 160; Fischer 2007, 12).[12] These operations also included the 1996 grounding of a North Korean spy submarine on the East coast near Kangnung (South Korea) on a mission to recover a three-person DPRK reconnaissance team (Bermudez 1997, 163). After a local taxi driver spotted the submarine, localized chaos ensued as the South Korean military mobilized over 40,000 soldiers and chased DPRK agents who had left the vessel (Witter 1996; Fischer 2007, 13). The incident resulted in the deaths of all but one of the infiltrators and 17 South Koreans (Koh 1997, 2). After significant international pressure on North Korea, the Kim regime "expressed regret" over the incident, which negatively affected the DPRK's ongoing efforts to obtain international aid (Bermudez 1997, 165; Myers 1996).[13]

During the following years, additional incidents occurred, including DPRK agent operations in Seoul and other naval activities. In November 1997, South Korea's Agency for National Security Planning (NSP) announced the detection of a spy ring involving a number of individuals including a professor at Seoul National University (Kristoff 1997c; Yonhap News 1997c).[14] One of the key missions of these agents was "to recruit leading members of South Korean society including scholars and politicians" (O 1997). This was followed by the June 1998 discovery of another submarine that was grounded and entangled in fishing nets near Sokcho (approximately 40 kilometers south of the DMZ on South Korea's east coast) (KBS 1998). All nine crewmembers were found dead of apparent suicide (Oh 1999, 100). In December 1998, the South Korean navy sank a DPRK infiltration vessel (semi-submersible high-speed boat) with at least six persons on board, all suspected of committing suicide prior to capture (Lee 1998). In March 1999, North Korea's spy efforts against Japan led to a naval clash between DPRK infiltration ships and "a small armada" of Japanese military vessels (*Daily Telegraph* 1999; Fischer 2007, 18). This was the first time the Japanese had fired on naval vessels since World War II (*Daily Telegraph*, 1999). Ironically, these incidents occurred while North Korea was desperately seeking international assistance—the Kim regime continued to solicit food aid from the international community while concurrently continuing a program of aggressive hostile foreign policy targeting other states.

Finally, a nine-day naval battle occurred in June 1999 involving North Korean and ROK vessels along the Northern Limit Line (NLL) (Fischer 2007, 18–19; Van Dyke 2003). This incident occurred along the disputed NLL in the waters just to the west of the Koreas. This incident, often referred to as the "First Battle of Yeonpyeong," was the first of two significant naval engagements between the ROK and DPRK in the region between 1999 and 2002. Naval tensions began to rise in early June 1999 when North Korea started to aggressively enforce the 12-mile nautical boundary claimed by the DPRK (KCNA 1999b; ICG 2010, 6). The incident culminated with an exchange of fire that left up to 30 DPRK sailors dead, one North Korea torpedo boat destroyed (with four others damaged), five ROK vessels damaged, and nine South Korean sailors wounded (Van Dyke 2003, 143; Whymant and Watts, 1999).[15] The second clash occurred in June 2002 when DPRK boats opened fire on South Korean vessels near the NLL, the maritime extension of the Military Demarcation Line (MDL) and the official boundary between North and South Korea.[16] This second incident resulted in the deaths of six South Korean sailors, the sinking of an ROK speed boat and severe damage to a North Korean ship (CSIS 2010).

While the level of hostile foreign policy during this period was significantly lower than during the other two case studies, the events noted above caused tensions on the peninsula to rise significantly. Many of these were based on Kim regime efforts to increase political stability, and some (such as the nuclear program and missile launches) were directly tied to Kim regime efforts to divert public attention while concurrently seeking international food and energy aid. These linkages are discussed further in the sections below.

Was political instability associated with heightened HFP activities?

Direct links between instability and external HFP actions were difficult to identify. However, there was a significant level of political turmoil during this period as the DPRK faced a leadership power transition from Kim Il-Sung (father) to Kim Jong-il (son). In fact, when the DPRK power transition occurred in 1994, there was a marked decrease in North Korean hostile foreign policy activities (see Appendix B). In July 1994, Kim Il-sung[17] died of an apparent heart attack, reportedly after inspecting a collective farm (Oberdorfer 2001, 339). While there was some suspicion in the open press of foul play because of the timing of the elder Kim's death (which occurred just prior to the next round of negotiations), the U.S. and South Korean governments concluded that there was no credible evidence of extraordinary circumstances (Wit 2004, 256). This event had wide-ranging effects and North Korea officially mourned his death for three years (Suh 199, 13).

As Natsios (2001, 127) observes, "In any country, the death of the sitting head of state would be disruptive and perhaps destabilizing; in North Korea, given the cult of personality surrounding the *Great Leader*, it was an apocalyptic event [emphasis in the original]."[18] Kim Il-sung was the founding father of the North Korean state, appointed and sponsored by the Soviets during their post–World War II occupation of the DPRK. After spending the 1930s as a communist guerrilla fighter against the Japanese in Manchuria and much of the 1940s training in Soviet camps, Kim returned to Korea in September 1945 to a hero's welcome (Eckert and Lee 1990, 341). Kim was instrumental in the early formation of the DPRK and by early 1948, after a purge of older communists, he established firm control of the North Korean Workers Party (Buzo 2002, 56). In September 1948, the Democratic People's Republic of Korea announced itself as an independent nation, with Kim Il-sung as its leader. Kim led North Korea for over 45 years: through war with the South and rebuilding (supported by both the Soviets and the PRC); challenges to his authority in the late 1950s; industrial and social achievements and an "undeclared war" with South Korea and the U.S. in the 1960s; limited reconciliation with the ROK in the 1970s; and the beginnings of economic stagnation in the 1980s.

Kim's death was a national shock to the North Koreans, who had depended on his regime for over four decades, and resulted in a national outpouring of grief, both genuine and instigated by the government (Lintner 2005, 84). Although the younger Kim (Jong-il) had been groomed to succeed his father and the international community was well aware of the planned succession, his father's death was seen as a threat to both the peace process and political stability in the DPRK (Wit 2004, 257). In fact, South Korea took a much harder line towards North Korea in the wake of the elder Kim's death, including forbidding ROK citizens from attending the funeral in Pyongyang, crackdowns on student dissidents, and the release of archival documents which allegedly proved "beyond a shadow of a doubt the Great Leader's responsibility for starting the Korean War" (Wit 2004, 261). Yet, due to the careful preparation and the strong Stalinist institutions which had been established in North Korea, the succession from father to son brought few structural changes to the DPRK.

The roots of this transition can be traced to the early 1970s. Beginning in 1971, Kim's son was promoted through positions of increasing power in the KWP and in September 1973, Kim Jong-il was "formally anointed as his father's successor" during a secret KWP politburo meeting (Savada 1994, 169 and Oh 1988, 6). Although most of Kim Il-sung's faction supported the choice of the younger Kim to succeed the "Great Leader," there were some who considered the "monarchist" transition of DPRK power as inappropriate and there were obvious questions of the younger Kim's credibility (Cha and Sohn 2012, 49). Kim Jong-il did attempt to establish his bona fides as a capable "revolutionary" successor. He was reported to have engineered a number of hostile incidents, including the 1974 Poplar Tree ("Axe Murder") incident in which two U.S. officers were killed by North Koreans during a tree-trimming dispute along the DMZ; an assassination attempt against the South's president during a visit to Canada in 1983; another presidential assassination attempt in 1983 in Rangoon in which a bomb killed 17 senior ROK officials; the 1986 bombing of South Korea's Kimpo airport; and the downing of Korean Airlines flight 857 in which 115 passengers and crew died after North Korean agents planted a bomb on the flight (Becker 2005, 154–155). After officially assuming control of the DPRK, Kim Jong-il sought to continue his father's legacy and the "essential structure of North Korea's self-proclaimed 'Juche system' is being preserved much as it has existed for nearly half a century" (Quinones 2003, 13). The intent of the Kim Jong-il regime was a continuation of previous economic and political policies, despite inherent flaws and shortcomings.

Although a tremendous outpouring of grief occurred following the death of Kim Il-sung, the reaction of most North Koreans to the onset of the famine and reductions in government rations was muted. The food distribution system (the PDS), which had existed for decades, faltered and in some areas stopped completely, resulting in a cessation of government-supplied food rations (Lee 2005, 6–11). Protests did occur, but they were uncoordinated and resulted in severe government responses. As Noland (1997, 106) observes, North Korea has "no institutions capable of channeling mass discontent into effective political action." The penalties in North Korea for protesting government actions or violating national policies were harsh and often resulted in individuals and their families being sent to prison camps or executed.[19] Additionally, the social characteristics of closed societies, such as North Korea, often limit the tendency for actions that stray outside of the norms of expected conduct (Triandis 2001). Thus, the North Koreans were probably limited in their responses to social distress due to both societal (government) and cultural constraints. Yet, the famine period was an unprecedented situation for the North Koreans and there were sporadic reports of riots and other actions during the famine period. Riots and protests during the famine period were significantly higher than during the other two cases. During the 1960s, there were no instances of protests found and the only significant protests during the 2000s were associated with the DPRK's 2009 currency reform (KINU 2011b, 542). Table 3.1 lists reported incidents in the 1990s.

Table 3.1 Riots and Coup Attempts (1992–1999)

July 1992	Riots occurred in several North Korean cities over monetary policy adjustments and food availability (Kyodo News 1992).
August 1992	North Korea reportedly executed 18 military officers, including generals, involved in a coup attempt against Kim Il-sung and Kim Jong-il (The Age 1993; Lim 1993).
March 1993	DPRK State Security Department detected and prevented a coup attempt by officers of the KPA's 7th Infantry Division (Bermudez 1997, 158).
April 1993	Large scale riots associated with food shortages and unrest occurred in Sinuiju near the Yalu River estuary involving 40,000 individuals. Approximately 30,000 North Korean troops suppressed the riots, making 3,000 arrests. (Cho 1993; KBS Radio 1993; Chon 1993).
Autumn 1995	The Korean People's Army's (KPA) 6th Corps (Hamhung Province) was purged and reorganized "under circumstances suggesting disarray in the ranks" (Oberdofer 1997, 375). Reports surfaced that the 6th Corps had been planning a coup (Natsios 2001, 217).
February 1996	Approximately 200 students protested in Chonjin over food embezzlement by party cadres (No and Choe 1996).
March 1996	In Yanggang Province, 800 North Korean forestry workers missed work in protest of the suspension of food rations. (Chungang Ilbo 1996a).
October 1996	At least 200 North Korean soldiers from the KPA 6th Corps in Najin-Sonbong (North Hamhung Province) participated in a "massive riot" over food rations and labor conditions. The North Koreans execute approximately 120 soldiers as a result (Chungang Ilbo 1996b).
March 1999	Statues of Kim Il-sung are vandalized throughout North Korea (Korea Times 1999a).[20]
October 1999	Riots occurred in coal mining areas near Onsong, North Hamgyong province. These were suppressed by a North Korean "special espionage unit" (Chi 1999).

The 1992 coup attempt (listed above) was, at least on the surface, the most serious challenge to the Kim regime. Defectors reported that during the incident, a group of DPRK generals planned to use their troops to occupy key government buildings in Pyongyang and attempt to arrest both Kim Il-sung and Kim Jong-il. The plot failed when one of the officers informed regime authorities (*The Age* 1993; Lim 1993). Other rumors also surfaced of localized food riots (Snyder 2000, 528), although the frequency and circumstances are unknown. Yet these occurrences in North Korea (ten incidents between 1992 and 1999) are low in comparison to the number of strikes and protests that occur in South Korea each year, which can number in the hundreds.[21] Food riots and other forms of protest certainly occurred in North Korea, but not at levels that seriously challenged the overall ability of the Kim regime to remain in power: the governmental apparatus was too strong and North Korea's civil society was much too weak (Bennett 1994, 4). North Korea's overall reaction to the famine situation was fundamentally different than other societies. Bennett (1994, 4) compared reactions in Africa to famine to those of North Korea and observed,

> In contrast to famine in Africa, where state disintegration and a weakening of civil society are often the norm, North Korea is characterized by stability, cen-

trality and civil order. Social control permeates all aspects of society; there is no "civil society" association which is not state run, and information is closely guarded. The current [DPRK] humanitarian crisis has emerged in a fully mature Stalinist polity in which the notion of "humanitarian space" is alien.

The average North Korean family most likely focused on basic survival during the famine, rather than efforts to challenge the government (Cha 2004). Thus during this period, the Kim regimes retained enough control over North Korean society to ensure the DPRK government remained intact and politically stable. While the Kim regimes might have used hostile foreign policy to distract the public's attention, there was no evidence of an increase in HFP due to political instability.

Were Economic Difficulties Associated with Increased HFP?

There is some evidence of a link between North Korea's economic difficulties and its hostile foreign policy activities during this period. The DPRK used its nuclear program to both threaten the international community and seek external aid and concessions. For example, North Korea's announcement that it intended to withdraw from the NPT in 1993 and declaration of its intent (in a crisis) to use nuclear weapons against Seoul in 1994[22] both occurred at the beginning of the famine period. For the DPRK, the limits of its centrally controlled economy became painfully apparent as North Korea's emphasis on "self-reliance," failure to establish trade relations with the international community, "promotion of state-owned heavy industries," disproportional emphasis on defense spending, and weather conditions all served to cause severe economic stress (Nanto 2008, 6).

Despite the emergence of increased economic ties with South Korea just prior to the famine in the early 1990s, the DPRK economy during the years prior to the famine was characterized by significant trade deficits with its neighbors. Between 1990 and 1991, North Korea's total trade decreased 44 percent from $4.7 billion to $2.6 billion (Nozoe 1997, 26). North Korea's most significant trading partner through 1990 remained the USSR (56 percent of total trade) followed by China (11 percent); after the fall of the Soviet Union, DPRK-China trade increased to approximately 25–30 percent of total trade (Nozoe 1997, 26), yet the overall level of North Korean trade was substantially lower than in previous years.

Thus by the early 1990s, North Korea's economy was in severe trouble. The loss of Soviet support coupled with changes in its relationship with China demonstrated the inherent weaknesses in the DPRK's economic system and external political ties. North Korea's industrial capacity faltered because of the loss of economic support and trade after the "demise of the Soviet Union, and a subsequent collapse in the energy regime necessary to sustain industry" (Woo-Cumings 2002, 21). At the beginning of the famine period, GDP levels plunged, shrinking an average of 13 percent each year between 1992 and 1997 (Maddison 2008). Figure 3.2 shows the historic levels of North Korea's GDP.

Figure 3.2 North Korea GDP Change Year-on-Year 1970–1999

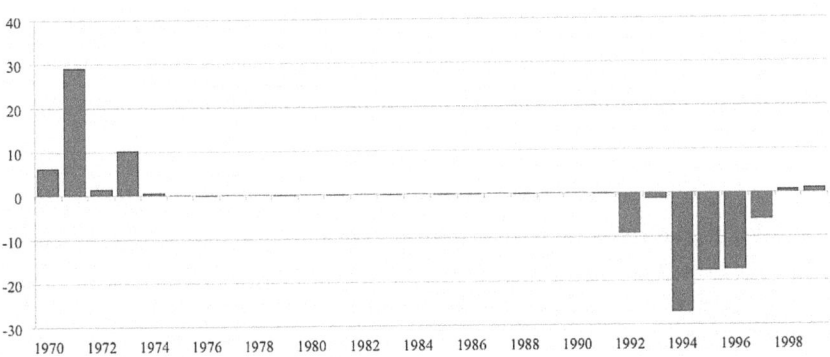

Source: Maddison 2008

Figure 3.2 shows exactly how dire the economic circumstances were during the famine years. The contraction of the DPRK's economy had resounding effects throughout North Korean society and the Kim regime sought alternate means to obtain needed international aid. As a result, North Korea also made efforts to enhance its missile capabilities (partly in an effort to influence aid negotiations), and a number of launches and tests occurred during the worst years of the famine beginning in 1996. The missile launches (especially the Taepodong-1) came at a time when North Korea was suffering from the effects of both the famine and economic catastrophe. The DPRK used its missile program as part of the aid negotiation process, eventually agreeing to a test ban in exchange for international food and fuel support (Michishita 123–125). These events served to provide a means for the DPRK to obtain external assistance and were potentially also focused on diversion. North Korea's official news announcement (KCNA 1998d) demonstrated the domestic perceptions Pyongyang hoped to reinforce by stating that the DPRK had "set up a new milestone in the building of a strong and prosperous socialist country … [signifying] … the strength of the DPRK, independent in politics, self-sufficient in the economy and self-reliant in national defense." The missile development program and launches were primarily focused on forcing external states to provide needed economic support, but also helped to maintain an air of tension between the Koreas to support that end.

Yet, despite the presence of some diversionary-type behaviors, a comparison of the level of economic difficulties (which were high) and the overall level of HFP activities provides limited support to the idea of diversion during this period. The severe economic distress experienced by North Korea should have spurred high levels of conflict actions, as predicted by diversionary theory. Conflict actions did occur during this period, but not in the manner predicted, and were mostly focused on efforts to secure aid for the regime.

Was social instability associated with periods of increased HFP?

Social instability, caused by the lack of food and incidence of starvation, was extremely high throughout the famine period. Yet there was not a corresponding increase (compared to historic averages) in overall hostile foreign policy activity levels, as diversionary theory would suggest. In the previous section on economic stability, research findings suggest that the nuclear program and missile tests occurred at both the beginning and peak of the famine. In the case of social instability (which was present throughout the entire case study period), the linkage between specific conditions, such as food shortages and rising mortality rates, and heightened levels of HFP actions was much more difficult to detect.

Food shortages were rampant in certain parts of the country, and access to sustenance often depended upon party affiliation and geographic location. During the famine, members of North Korea's "core class" (classified as loyal supporters) and Pyongyang residents fared much better compared to the "hostile class" (under suspicion by the DPRK government) and those who lived in the urbanized areas of the eastern provinces (Cumings 2005, 443; Hassig and Oh 2009, 203; Haggard and Noland 2007, 51–52).[23] Visitors to Pyongyang saw few indications of the chaos that existed in the countryside (Yonhap 1996c), especially the northeastern area, which was the first to lose food shipments from the PDS in 1993 (Natsios 1999, 105). In fact, Natsios (2000, 105–106) argued that North Korea's northeastern provinces were "triaged" (denied aid) by the Kim regime to ensure adequate food was available in Pyongyang. Yet this was not initially apparent to aid workers (whose movements were carefully monitored and controlled by the North Korean authorities), who were often shown extreme cases of famine in some areas and barred entry to others (Haggard and Noland 2007, 89).

Prior to 1995, North Korea did not receive international aid from the UN and other donors in a formalized method, although China and the Soviets habitually provided commodity support (at reduced prices). Beginning in 1995, North Korea obtained massive amounts of public and private international assistance (Haggard and Noland 2011a, 55). Figure 3.3 shows the levels and donor distribution of international food assistance recorded by the UN World Food Program between 1995 and 2000.

Figure 3.3 International Food Aid to North Korea 1995–2000

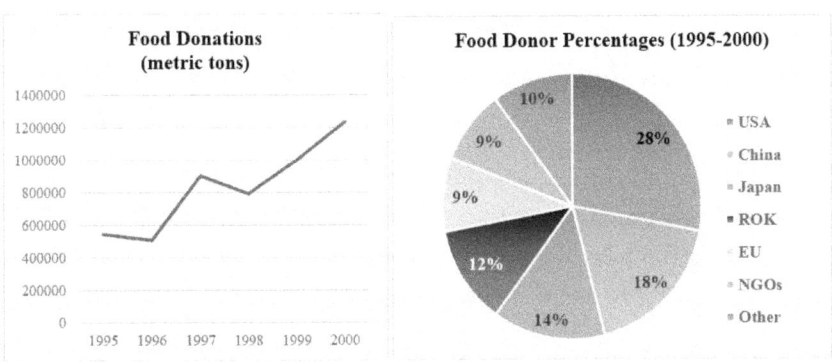

Source: UN FAIS 2012

As shown in Figure 3.3, food aid to North Korea generally increased throughout the famine period and between 1995 and 2000, with four nations (the U.S., China, Japan, and ROK) providing 72 percent of the total aid (UN FAIS 2012).

Child mortality rates, another indicator of social distress, increased significantly during the crisis and were 170 percent higher in 1996 than in 1990 (UN IGME 2012). Changes in longevity information also demonstrated the severity of the crisis. A North Korean child born in 1991 could expect to live to age 70 (comparable to most modern states), while a child born just 5 years later could only expect to live to age 64 (World dataBank 2012; Goodkind and West 2001, 226). Additionally, the effects of malnutrition were widespread. In fact, a 1997 World Food Program survey of almost 4,000 children indicated that 16.5 percent were "wasted" (underweight for their height) and 38.2 percent were "stunted" (not tall enough for their age), both of which are signs of chronic malnutrition (Katona-Apte and Mokdad 1998, 1317). Figure 3.4 shows child mortality rates on the Korean peninsula during the crisis period.

Figure 3.4 Child Mortality Rate Comparisons

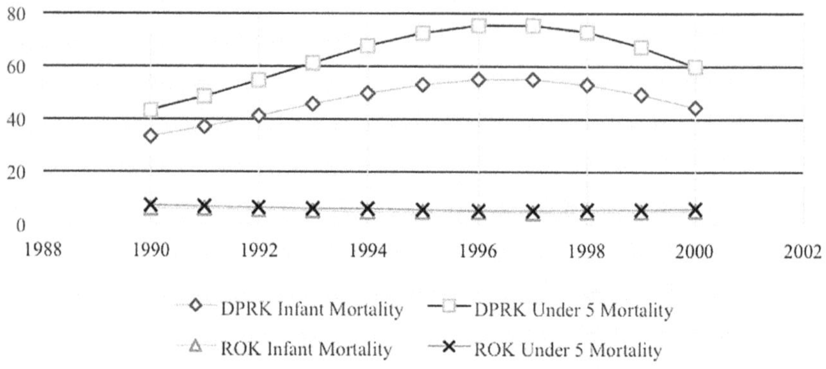

◇ DPRK Infant Mortality   □ DPRK Under 5 Mortality
△ ROK Infant Mortality   ✕ ROK Under 5 Mortality

Source: UN Inter-agency Group for Child Mortality Estimation (IGME) (2012)

A number of other surveys identified the long-term effects of North Korea's lack of food. For example, during the height of the famine, the average DPRK seven-year-old was 22 pounds lighter and 8 inches shorter than South Korea children at the same age (Eberstadt 2000, 875–876). While these domestic conditions demonstrated that North Korean social structures were under significant stress, none of these conditions seriously challenged the Kim regime. In fact, at least one assessment (Kaufman 2010) indicated that overall societal stability actually increased during this period.[24] This was possibly due to factors such as the citizens' focus on obtaining the basic needs for survival (rather than challenging the regime), the ability of the Kim regime to maintain the support of the military, international aid and the control exercised by the DPRK government over its people. As Oh and Hassig (2000, 145) note, "Arguably, no government in the twentieth century has succeeded in exercising as much control over its people as has the Kim government." Overall, despite the shock of famine and its effects, North Korean society "muddled through"[25] and the regime remained under stress but intact.

As with food shortages, evidence of direct linkages between social instability and hostile foreign policy are difficult to determine. The social effects of the crisis undoubtedly affected the Kim regimes' choices to engage in HFP activities, and the North Korean leaders did pursue diversionary activities during this period (as identified throughout this chapter). Thus while direct evidence of increased HFP due to domestic distress was limited, the social crisis caused by the famine probably resulted in some hostile actions by the Kim regimes in efforts to force international concessions.

3. *The Arduous March*   91

WERE UN SECURITY COUNCIL RESOLUTIONS AGAINST
THE DPRK ASSOCIATED WITH INCREASED HFP?

The sole UN Security Council resolution enacted on North Korea at the beginning of this case study was in reaction the DPRK's abandonment of an international security regime. When North Korea announced its withdrawal from the Non-Proliferation Treaty (NPT) in March 1993, the UN responded with Security Council Resolution 825, which rebuked the DPRK and called for it to return to the NPT (UN 1993; Lee and Choi 2009, 29).[26] Political rhetoric dominated hostile foreign policy events during that period and these incidents were at levels consistent with previous periods (Appendix B). Thus, the research found that the UN Security Council resolutions were unrelated to DPRK activities during this period.

However, other sanctions imposed unilaterally by the U.S. and other states did seem to affect DPRK activities and Pyongyang's efforts to blame its difficulties on the international community. International community responses to North Korean provocative actions ranged from strongly worded denouncements to economic sanctions. Sanctions are defined as "deliberate, government-inspired withdrawal, or threat of withdrawal, of customary trade or financial relations" (Hufbauer 1990, 2). Despite the debate on the effectiveness of sanctions regimes (Hufbauer 1990), these have become common foreign policy responses to North Korea's actions. For states concerned about DPRK activities, sanctions provided a diplomatic option with little risk (compared to military solutions) and gave policymakers the satisfaction that, at the very least, "something was being done" in response to North Korean activity. The United States has a long history of enacting sanctions against the Kim regime, dating back to 1950, based on the DPRK's actions as a communist government and other perceived threats to U.S. interests in the region. During the famine period, at least 17 U.S. sanctions were in place including limits on almost all types of economic interaction. This had the overall effect of minimizing United States trade and foreign aid to the DPRK (except for humanitarian aid approved by U.S. leaders), and blockage of any arms transfers or sales (Rennack 2011). Additionally, the U.S. froze assets for certain DPRK businesses and individuals associated with missile technology and weapons transfers (Rennack 2011, 21–22). South Korea and Japan also imposed limitations on economic contact, often based on hostile foreign policy actions, such as the 1998 Taepodong-1 missile launch over Japan (Fischer 2007, 17; Lee and Choi 2009).

North Korea's reactions to sanctions and the United Nation's NPT withdrawal resolution followed previous diplomatic patterns: forceful denouncements and rhetorical public statements by the Kim regime, followed by protests and threats. In fact, the DPRK called the Security Council action a "declaration of war" (AFP 1993a). This allowed the Kim regime to reinforce the perception of an external threat, which was "a classic tool for suppressing dissent, demanding sacrifices, and consolidating power" (Wit 2004, 37).[27] North Korea was persuaded back to the negotiating table in June 1993, followed by a year's worth of negotiations and the Agreed Framework accords in October 1994. Other linkages between U.S. sanctions, most of which were in place long before the 1990s (USITC 1998), were not evident on the surface, but they certainly sustained the levels of hostility between the U.S. and the DPRK (KCNA 1995a; KCNA 1996a; KCNA 1996b). Thus while UN resolutions were not directly linked to increases in North Korean HFP activities, the ongoing U.S. unilateral sanctions allowed the Kim regime to continue to blame external actors for its internal challenges.

Were ROK leadership changes associated with increased North Korean hostile foreign policy activities?

An examination of ROK national election periods indicated that increased HPF activities were present during South Korean presidential elections. During this period, South Korean politics were still emerging from a legacy of authoritarian rule. After a long history of authoritarian rule and public dissatisfaction, South Korea's government revised its constitution in 1987 to allow for direct democratic elections. In 1987, former ROK Army general Roh Tae-woo was the first democratically elected South Korean leader followed by Kim Young-sam's election in 1993 which solidified the democratic electoral process for the ROK.[28] In 1992, South Korea staged its second democratic election and Kim Young-sam emerged as the ROK's first non-military head of state in over 30 years. This was followed by the 1997 election of Kim Dae-jung and continued democratic presidential elections of South Korean civilians.

Kim Young-sam's 1992 presidential campaign elicited negative responses from North Korea, including a "freezing of relations" in November 1992 ahead of the national elections in December (Lee 1992). During this same time, negotiations were ongoing in an effort to establish an "inter-Korean treaty" but were halted due to a number of key events. These included North Korean protests against pending ROK–U.S. military exercises (the most significant being TEAM SPIRIT), Seoul's discovery of an underground 400-member DPRK spy ring, and the ongoing tensions associated with North Korea's nuclear efforts (Fischer 2007, 11; Breen 1992; Lee 1992). The spy scandal and allegations that North Korea used its "propaganda machine" and operatives to influence the election in favor of former dissident Kim Dae-jung[29] may have tipped the balance in conservative Kim Young-sam's favor (Lee 1992; Breen 1992). When Kim

Young-sam was elected with 41 percent of the popular vote (versus Kim Dae-jung's 33 percent), North Korea denounced the elections and accused the U.S. of manipulating the election (Lee 1992). Additionally, hostile foreign policy activities during early 1993 (when Kim Young-sam assumed office) were at higher levels than the adjacent time periods (the years prior and afterwards, see Figure 3.1), but they remained at levels lower than historic norms. Thus, there was a potential relationship between the 1992 ROK election and DPRK hostile activities.

South Korea's next presidential campaign occurred in 1997, when former dissident Kim Dae-jung faced the incumbent party led by establishment candidate and former Prime Minister Lee Hoi Chang.[30] North Korea again used public statements to criticize the ruling party and sitting President Kim Young-sam (KCNA 1997; Lee 1992; Breen 1992). North Korea focused its propaganda attacks on the Kim Young-sam government, which was both accused of corruption and blamed for South Korea's financial crisis (Kristof 1997b). At this time, the North Korean famine was at its worst and South Korea was struggling with both the Asian financial crisis and efforts to comply with International Monetary Fund (IMF) lending requirements. The Asian financial crisis, which lasted from May 1997 to February 1998, was triggered by a loss of confidence by international investors in Asian currencies and stocks (Nanto 1998). In October 1997, the value of South Korea's won dropped significantly and Seoul applied for International Monetary Fund (IMF) assistance, eventually receiving $57 billion in bailout support. Throughout 1997, South Korean government officials were reluctant to provide additional funds to alleviate the DPRK famine while the ROK itself was experiencing its own domestic crisis and receiving financial aid from the IMF (Korea Times 1998a).[31]

Aside from North Korean rhetoric criticizing the sitting ROK government and media outlets, the DPRK had little else to say about the election.[32] Additionally during 1997, North Korea's tendency for provocative actions was most likely limited because of the pending presidential election and the DPRK's crucial need for humanitarian aid. In December 1997, Kim Dae-jung was declared the winner with 40 percent of the popular vote. The Kim Jong-il regime's response was predictably positive[33] as it officially "expressed hopes for improved relations with South Korea under President-elect Kim Dae-Jung" (Japan Economic Newswire 1997).

DPRK actions in 1992 were a visible, but ultimately unfruitful, attempt to influence elections in the North's favor. North Korea's HFP activities in 1997, although at a lower level than during the 1992 elections (see Figure 3.1), were also indicative of its intent to influence the South Korean presidential election. North Korea's actions provide support to the argument that North Korea increased (or intended to increase) its HFP activities in conjunction with ROK leadership changes.

Were U.S. leadership changes associated with increased North Korean hostile foreign policy activities?

A U.S. presidential election occurred during the North Korean famine period in 1996, with Bill Clinton seeking to retain his incumbent status as president. North Korea's hostility levels during the campaign and in the months that followed were at consistent levels indicating little relationship with this U.S. leadership change. Two years prior to the election, the Clinton administration successfully navigated a nuclear crisis with North Korea and signed the Agreed Framework (Manyin and Nikitin 2010, 2). During Clinton's campaign, famine in North Korea was well underway after crop losses occurred partially due to monsoon flooding in July and August 1995 and early 1996. In response, the Clinton administration took a number of steps to support North Korea and to ease tensions—these included the unilateral provision of $2 million and removal of the DPRK from the U.S. "terrorist states" list. While the Clinton administration stated that these actions were intended to support continued DPRK participation in the Agreed Framework, South Korean media charged the U.S. intended to avoid conflict with the DPRK prior to the national elections that year (Yu 1996; Hanguk Ilbo 1996). North Korea's public rhetoric was relatively quiet during this period, and the regime refrained from criticizing both the South Korean and U.S. leaders (Kim K. 1996).

While there was no evidence that North Korea actively supported the reelection of Bill Clinton, it did take note of his opponent. Conservative Robert Dole was the challenger and publicly advocated a more hawkish stance towards North Korea compared to the Clinton administration. The DPRK indirectly criticized Dole's views by stating, "Amidst presidential election campaign in the United States, some forces are trying to improve their image by slandering the DPRK" (AFP 1996). Clinton's potential reelection was much more consistent with North Korean goals of continued aid and support from the West. Pyongyang's government radio station briefly acknowledged Clinton's reelection win in November 1996 by simply stating, "Analysts feel that even though Clinton has been reelected, he will be faced with grave challenges in domestic and foreign affairs" (DPRK 1996a). Considering their history of tersely worded diplomatic pronouncements condemning the U.S. and its actions, this was a relatively benign statement for the North Koreans.

The most significant hostile foreign policy event during the U.S. election period was the grounding of a North Korean spy submarine attempting to insert agents on the eastern coast of the ROK in September 1996, causing South

Korea to withdraw its support to KEDO. This event was followed by the murder of a South Korean diplomat in Vladivostok, Russia, attributed to North Korean agents following a DPRK threat of "retaliation" for South Korea's actions during the submarine incident (Fischer 2007, 13). While North Korea apologized for the submarine incident, expressing "deep regret" (Myers 1996), this incident was indicative of the ongoing clandestine efforts by the DPRK in South Korea and the ROK considered this an "armed provocation" (Yonhap News 1996d). Although North Korea certainly did not intend to allow one of its submarines to be detected by the ROK,[34] this incident was another example of North Korea's efforts to maintain an aggressive military posture while concurrently seeking international aid. Despite this incident and others that occurred during the famine, no clear relationship was found between North Korea's hostile foreign policy actions and the U.S. presidential election.

Were ROK/U.S. strategic-level military exercises associated with increased hostile foreign policy activities?

Partial support was found for a linkage between DPRK activities and strategic military exercises during the famine period. North Korea's threat to withdraw from the NPT, one of the most significant North Korean HFP acts during this period, was most likely in reaction to the restart of the 1993 U.S.–ROK TEAM SPIRIT military exercises (Michishita 2010, 93). These exercises had been suspended in 1992 for two primary reasons: to bring North Korea into multilateral negotiations and convince the DPRK to allow IAEA inspections (Michishita 2010, 93). Beginning in 1976, the U.S. and ROK jointly conducted this event to exercise assistance to South Korea in the event of war with North Korea. Although TEAM SPIRIT was held in 1993, between 1994 and 1996, it was scheduled, then cancelled each year (Yoon 2003, 98) and has not been held since. Other ROK–U.S. strategic-level exercises focused on similar tasks continued each year during the famine period (including ULCHI FOCUS LENS and FOAL EAGLE) although those events were not at the overall scale and scope of TEAM SPIRIT (Yoon 2003, 99).

The North Korean leaders welcomed the suspension of TEAM SPIRIT, but denounced the other ROK–U.S. annual exercises as "the second TEAM SPIRIT" and an attempt to "stifle" the DPRK (KCNA 1995a; KCNA 1999a). In reality, although the other two biannual exercises were at a smaller scale than TEAM SPIRIT, the ROK and U.S. also used those other exercises to rehearse the defense of the Korean peninsula against a North Korean attack. Yet when examining the levels of hostile foreign policy during the exercise periods, little difference was found between the hostility levels during exercise periods and other times during the case study (see Appendix B). As noted above, at least one significant North Korean event (the NPT withdrawal threat) occurred in reaction to the ROK–U.S. military exercises. Yet during other periods, the levels of hostilities generally did not vary in relation to those external events.

Was the Presence of a Conservative ROK Government Associated with Increased HFP?

Although the presence of a conservative ROK leader was associated with increased HFP activities in the 1960s, South Korea's government type had little effect on conflict levels during the famine period. Two markedly different ROK administrations ruled during the famine period: the conservative Kim Young-sam administration (1993–1998) and the more liberal Kim Dae-jung administration (1998–2003). Based on the DPRK's preference for Kim Dae-jung, both during the 1993 and 1998 elections (Lee 1992; Breen 1992; KCNA 1997), hostility levels were expected to be lower during the Kim Dae-jung presidency, beginning in 1998. As one of his first official acts, Kim Dae-jung announced his "Sunshine Policy," a foreign policy strategy aimed at enhanced engagement with North Korea, which eventually led to a North-South summit in 2000 (Kim, D. 1998). Kim Dae-jung (1998) stated the three key principles of his Sunshine Policy in his inaugural address: "First, we will never tolerate armed provocation of any kind. Second, we do not have any intention to harm or absorb North Korea. Third, we will actively push reconciliation and cooperation between the South and North beginning with those areas which can be most easily agreed upon."

Yet despite the election of an ROK leader that seemed more open to negotiation with the DPRK, the levels of HFP between 1998 and 1999 were similar to the 1993–1997 timeframe (Appendix B). Although the pre–1998 period includes a number of significant events, such as the nuclear crisis and several infiltration incidents, North Korea continued to conduct HFP actions after Kim Dae-Jung was elected. These include North Korea's missile program development and testing, nuclear program actions (fuel reprocessing), and continued infiltration operations (Fischer 2007; KINU 2012). After analyzing actions across both administrations, North Korean hostile foreign policy activities did not change with the arrival of a more liberal ROK president.

Summary and Case Study Conclusions

In October 2000, the Kim regime publicly declared that the "Arduous March" had ended (Kwon and Chung 2012, 173). International food aid helped the DPRK endure this crisis, supported up to one-third of North Korea's population (8 million people), and resulted in lasting effects on North Korean society (Haggard and Noland 2007, 90). Kim Jong-il's efforts to pursue "emergency management" measures, which involved the acceptance of international food aid, shifted the population's focus away from ideology and towards solutions to the famine (McEachern 2010, 74). Because of this change, ideology now became one of many guiding factors for decisions made by the regime, rather than the sole focus of internal and foreign policies (McEachern 2010, 74).

North Korea's famine seemed to provide a perfect opportunity for diversion by the DPRK government. The domestic distress caused by economic and social instability should have spurred the Kim regimes to engage in diversionary behaviors and heightened levels of hostile foreign policy against its neighbors (Gelpi 1997, 256; Miller 1995). As discussed previously, while the overall levels of DPRK hostile foreign policy activities were below historic norms (see Figure 3.1) during the famine period, Pyongyang did strive to use conflict activities to force international concessions, scapegoat external states and, to a limited extent, distract North Korea's domestic audience.

In many respects, North Korea's pursuit of self-reliance limited its own capacity to reach out for assistance (either through purchase or international aid) (Haggard and Noland 2007, 23) and when food shortages occurred, the DPRK could not rely on Cold War mechanisms to respond. During the famine, North Korea did use hostile foreign policy actions to alleviate the insecurity effects of the food shortages and to ensure the Kim regimes remained in power, although the overall HFP levels were at historic lows. The following table shows the results of this analysis.

Table 3.2 Structured Analysis Results: The Great Famine (1993–1999)

Category	Question	Test Result	Details
Dependent Variable (HFP)	1. What was the level of hostile foreign policy during the case study?	Low	Conflict scores were lower than historic norms and averaged 601 per year.[35]
Internal Conditions (Independent Variables)	2. Was political instability associated with heightened HFP activities?	No	Instability occurred but no links to HFP were found.
	3. Were economic difficulties associated with increased HFP?	No	While nuclear provocations and missile launches did occur, linkages between economic and HFP events were limited.
	4. Was social instability	No	Although social insta-

Category	Question	Test Result	Details
	associated with periods of increased HFP?		bility was present throughout, there was no identifiable link between social instability and external conflict.
External Conditions (Independent Variables)	5. Were UN Security Council resolutions against the DPRK associated with increased HFP?	No	Although the UN enacted a resolution, there was no relationship to conflict.
	6. Were ROK leadership changes associated with increased HFP actions?	Yes	The DPRK increased HFP actions in a direct effort to affect the elections.
	7. Were US leadership changes associated with increased HFP actions?	No	Although the DPRK commented on the campaign, there was no evidence it attempted to pursue HFP to influence the outcome.
	8. Were ROK/US strategic-level military exercises associated with DPRK hostile actions?	Yes	In at least one instance (NPT withdrawal), there was a direct link between HFP and military exercises.
	9. Was the presence of a conservative ROK government associated with increased HFP?	No	Conflict was consistent across South Korea's conservative and liberal governments.

As shown in Table 3.2, no relationships were found between internal conditions (political, economic, and social difficulties) and hostile foreign policy activities. Thus, while diversionary theory would predict that increases in HFP actions would have occurred due to the high levels of domestic distress, none were present. The Kim regime's actions did include the use of threats of nuclear retaliation and its missile program to gain economic concessions, although these actions were related to the DPRK's need for economic support. Social instability occurred throughout the famine period and the Kim regime weathered the death of Kim Il-sung intact without substantial threats to Kim Jong-il's assumption of power (aside from sporadic rioting). The relationship between North Korea's HFP activities and both ROK leadership changes and strategic military exercises supports the external influence argument. It is possible that these two findings result from North Korea's efforts to increase international tensions to force economic concessions and obtain needed food support in response to the famine period. Thus, the increase in hostilities may relate to the political shock created by the famine, rather than the ROK administration elections.

Throughout the famine period, Pyongyang's efforts at nuclear and ballistic missile development did help to distract North Korean citizens, while concurrently presenting the international community with a security crisis. However, there was no corresponding increase in the overall levels of HFP. North Korea's efforts to develop nuclear weapons were also related to efforts to obtain the security advantages of becoming a member of the "nuclear club."[36] Domestically, this also provided the Kim regime with both an apparent deterrent from external attack and a rallying point for DPRK citizens. In discussing the development of nuclear weapons, North Korea's official news outlet stated

> It is only too natural that we took a self-defensive measure some time ago to deter a war beforehand and defend peace and security in face of the worst situation ... the outbreak of war ... on the Korean peninsula [KCNA 1996a].

The nuclear crisis and its resolution also provided Kim Jong-il with "his own myth of national rescue" as North Korea's internal propaganda credited the 1994 Agreed Framework breakthrough solely to the "Dear Leader's" negotiation skills (Myers 2010, 51). From a practical standpoint, nuclear weapons provided Kim Jong-il with a means for the DPRK to maintain its international standing (Demick 2010, 66). The nuclear crisis negotiations, which caused the temporary U.S. resumption of its TEAM SPIRIT exercise in 1993, also enabled Kim Jong-il (with his father's blessing) to issue a national order to "alert the entire North Korean armed forces for any eventuality and to put the entire nation and the people on a semi-war footing" (Suh 1993, 61; Yonhap News Agency 2003, 992). Domestically, the Kim regime fostered a sense of tension and hatred (based on the actions of the U.S. and its allies) resulting in an atmosphere of national emergency. As Michishita (2009, 115) notes, "North Korea's nuclear diplomacy might have worked to divert people's attention away from domestic difficulties," such as internal instability over food shortages and political unrest. The crisis also helped to maintain the Kim regime's grip on power domestically and was most likely intended to help bolster public support for the regime. While diversion was not the only purpose of the Kim regime's endeavors to develop nuclear capabilities, it was one among many results of that effort.

In May 1993, after the launch of its Nodong missile, "North Korea showed its first signs of using missiles as a diplomatic tool" (Michishita 2009, 118). While the Nodong program was likely focused on pressuring the U.S. and South Koreans during the nuclear negotiations, the DPRK intended the Taepodong program to influence both domestic and international audiences. Despite the apparent failure of the 1998 Taepodong-1 missile to achieve orbit (Pinkston 2008, 25), the event became a source of national pride, with a launch video appearing on North Korean and international television repeatedly during the weeks that followed.[37] The Taepodong-1 launch "worked as a catalyst, giving new momentum" to the ongoing missile and nuclear talks between the U.S. and North Korea (Michishita 2010, 123). Thus, North Korea was able to use this event, like so many of its other foreign policy actions, for several purposes, namely creating international pressure for negotiations and domestic diversion during the famine period.

North Korea's other military activities, such as its infiltration operations, were also indirectly linked to domestic concerns. The DPRK's ongoing efforts to maintain its military posture sent a clear sign to its military establishment that the Kim regime valued their defense efforts. Intensified defense training events (such as the Winter Training Cycle exercises in 1996–1997), military weapons displays and parades, and the Songun (military first) policy were all efforts to increase military morale in hopes of improved domestic stability (Yonhap 1997a; Yonhap 1997b). The historic role and integration of the military in North Korean society, referred to by Kim Il-sung as an "instrument of socialism" (Vreeland 1976, 316), made the sustainment of that institution critical to the survival of the regime. Thus, the Kim regime's efforts to placate the military during the famine enabled the DPRK to maintain social and political control over the state.

The June 1999 naval Battle of Yeonpyong was the most aggressive conventional military action undertaken by the North Koreans during this period. This was another example of the Kim regime dealing with multiple concerns through a single provocative event. After the clash, North Korea stated,

> As a result of the [South Koreans'] reckless provocation, our People's Army soldiers' lives were threatened gravely, a warship of our side was sunk, and three other warships were damaged severely.... The enemy's armed provocation in the West Sea did not expand into a full-scale war entirely because of our People's Army soldiers' extreme patience and self-restraint [KCBN 1999].

In this case, North Korea publicized this event as an unwarranted provocation, which helped reinforce the national position that external forces continued to cause economic and social problems within the DPRK. The Kim regime repeatedly issued public statements claiming, "war might break out at any time" (KCNA 1999c). This incident, along with ongoing military activities on both sides of the DMZ, helped reinforce the constant state of political crisis that the Kim regime sought to foster during the famine period. This sense of national emergency and continued military conflict with both the U.S. and ROK helped maintain Kim Jong-il's position as undisputed leader of the DPRK and usher in his era of Songun policies (Michishita 2010, 160).

Thus, these types of efforts to unify the public's support for the Kim Jong-il regime were present during the famine. Other measures the Kim regime used to survive the domestic crisis (not explored in this study) included the DPRK's adroit control of the media, maintenance of secure borders, and its willingness to accept international aid. These measures helped ensure the Kim regime remained in power. The Kim regime also engaged in ongoing hostile foreign policy activities while simultaneously seeking economic and humanitarian assistance for its people. This type of dual-track diplomacy worked well for the Kim regime and it was able to survive the Arduous March intact. The DPRK secured future guarantees of economic and developmental aid, which also supported the Kim regime's grip on power. North Korea did this while retaining its ability to continue to threaten regional and international stability, a characteristic that provided distinct advantages both from a security and negotiation standpoint. This threat to the international community served to ensure that North Korea continued to portray itself as a "strong" independent state to both domestic and international audiences. As Noland (2000, 10) stated, "The threat that North Korea poses is its sole asset. It is unlikely to negotiate away this asset very easily." Hostile foreign policy activities and diversionary-type behaviors, while not the only measures the DPRK used to deal with the catastrophic effects of the famine period, were both necessary for the Kim regime's survival during this crisis.

Figure 3.5 Timeline: North Korea's Great Famine 1993–1999

North Korean Events		ROK–U.S. Events
DPRK withdraws from the NPT Nuclear crisis Signs of pending famine appear	1993	Kim Young-sam elected ROK President
Death of Kim Il-sung Kim Jong-il becomes DPRK leader	1994	UN Security Council Resolution 825 enacted
PDS breaks down Harvest lost due to flooding	1995	Food aid provided to DPRK
Sever famine begins DPRK publicly acknowledges famine North Korean sub grounded on ROK coast	1996	International aid workers present throughout DPRK
Large-scale population movements	1997	U.S. President Bill Clinton reelected
Famine eases	1998	Kim Dae-jung elected ROK President

North Korean Events		ROK–U.S. Events
Taepodong-1 missile launch		Japan, ROK and U.S. impose sanctions
Famine ends	**1999**	Food aid drops temporarily
		Food aid returns to previous levels
Battle of Yeonpyeong naval clash between the Koreas		

CHAPTER 4

Regime Succession and Case Comparisons

This final case study examines the conditions North Korea experienced between 2008 and 2011 and its use of hostile foreign policy activities. This case includes efforts by the DPRK to set the stage for the second communist "dynastic" succession from Kim Jong-il to Kim Jong-un, continued internal economic distress, and a number of provocative events such as North Korea's second nuclear test. Under these circumstances, diversionary theory predicts that the internal distress surrounding the succession to a new Kim regime and chronic economic difficulties should spur increased external conflict behavior. The research finds support for a connection between economic conditions and the onset of a period of hostilities between the Koreas and the overall levels of HFP activities during the study period. Additionally, there is substantial support for the external conditions argument as UN resolutions and military exercises were found to be related to increases in DPRK hostile foreign policy activities.

This case was chosen using the same method as the famine study, using Goertz and Diehl's (1995, 31) concept of "political shocks." North Korea's domestic conditions had wide-ranging effects on the international system based on the emergence of Kim Jong-un and other events surrounding the Kim regime's succession. North Korea's concerns over the succession were related to increased HFP actions during this period, which included nuclear tests, missile firings, and direct clashes with South Korea. The following sections include an overview of the case, explore the same set of focused questions, and conclude with a summary, analysis of the results and a timeline of events.

The Kim Regime Endures

North Korea's experiences during the 2000s were filled with events just as dramatic as those described in the two previous case studies, yet demonstrated significant continuity with the past. After over 50 years of rule, the Kim family still retained power and remained firmly in control of most aspects of North Korea's society. Additionally, after withstanding the 1990s famine period intact, the Kim regime continued to both seek aid and conduct provocative actions, to the dismay of the international community. Hostile foreign activities included events such as nuclear weapons and missile tests, which significantly raised international tensions and spurred United Nations sanctions.

During this time, the DPRK attained unofficial membership in the international "nuclear club" due to its weapons research program and nuclear weapons tests in 2006 and 2009. It also (again) withdrew from the Non-Proliferation Treaty, which was a clear sign that North Korea not only had nuclear weapons technology, but was willing to share it with other states. Additionally, North Korea conducted a series of short and long-range missile tests that began with Silkworm missiles fired from coastal batteries followed by longer-range missile tests, using systems such as the Taeopodong-2 that had "the theoretical capacity to reach the continental U.S." (Fischer 2007, 32). These missile firings, the first in five years, ended North Korea's 1999 missile test moratorium. This test ban was agreed upon during negotiations on energy aid and details surrounding the international community's provision of two light water nuclear reactors (Fischer 2007, 25; Kimball 2012). North Korea also engaged in conventional attacks in the Yellow Sea against ROK military and civilian targets, the first incidents of their kind since the Korean War (Hom and Thompson 2010; Klinger 2010). These events indicated that North Korea's security relationship with both the region and the international community had entered a new and much more dangerous phase.

While North Korea's economy continued to flounder and the DPRK struggled in many areas, demonstrated by a continued inability to feed its people, regime succession issues came to the forefront. During this period, North Korea's leadership dealt with preparations for its second transition of power from father to son, as Kim Jong-il's failing health spurred plans for the next Kim generation to assume control of the DPRK. After Kim Jong-il's death in December 2011, his son took control of the DPRK and the transition to Kim Jong-un went relatively smoothly (at least from the international community's perspective). Moreover, the new Kim regime remained focused on the same primary goal of retaining power, regardless of the domestic or international implications. Between 2008 and 2011, the DPRK solidified its process of succession to the next Kim family member, maintained enough control over domestic conditions to ensure the regime remained intact, and continued to use hostile foreign policy actions against external states.

Structured Questions and Analysis

In this final case, the same structured, focused questions are used to examine the potential relationship between the DPRK's conditions and hostile foreign policy activities, and whether diversionary theory helps explain these actions. The following sections focus on North Korea's most recent succession period between Kim Jong-il and his son, Kim Jong-un.

What was the level of hostile foreign policy activities during this period?

Hostile foreign policy activity levels during this period were at levels not seen since the first case study and demonstrate that the Kim regimes chose HFP as a means to achieve national policy goals. In fact, these levels, along with the severe levels of domestic distress that occurred during this period, should be an indicator of North Korea's use of diversion as a tool for governance. The Kim-Jong-il regime entered the millennium politically intact and in firm control of civil society, despite the devastating effects of the famine of the 1990s. Yet the DPRK government also relied upon external aid to sustain itself and remained vulnerable to the restrictions and conditions imposed by donor states. At the end of the famine period, North Korea desperately required both food and energy to "meet the minimum survival requirements of its population" (Noland 2000, 335). However, North Korea did manage to maintain a robust military force that was capable, at the very least, of defending the DPRK from external attack and was not reluctant to conduct limited military engagements against South Korean forces.

During the case study period, the North Koreans had over 800 ballistic missiles (600 SCUDs and 200 medium range Nodong systems) with capabilities to range as far as Japan (Bell 2006, 7). The North Koreans also possessed a significant unconventional war capability with 20 brigades of special operations troops that would be most likely be employed in a wartime scenario (Samore 2004; Bell 2008, 16). These numbers might seem extreme and North Korea's ability to sustain these units (considering its constant resource challenges) certainly could be disputed. Nevertheless, by the mid–2000s, KPA artillery and missile units were in position to directly fire upon areas along the DMZ and the northern areas of Seoul. USFK Commander General B.B. Bell (2008, 16) testified before the U.S. Senate stating,

> North Korea also maintains the world's largest special operations force (SOF), with over 80,000 in its ranks. Tough, well trained, and profoundly loyal, these

forces are capable of conducting strategic reconnaissance and asymmetric attacks against a range of critical civilian and military targets. Among the best resourced in its military, North Korean special operations forces provide an asymmetric enabler to North Korea in crisis, provocation, or war.

North Korean air and naval forces, while severely limited in capability and extremely outdated, remained focused primarily on defensive missions. The DPRK navy remained dedicated to coastal defense, but was often used near the maritime border to react to and sometimes engage South Korean naval and Chinese and ROK fishing vessels. The North Korean navy includes over 1,000 ships with 430 surface combatants and about 60 submarines with the latter sometimes used to support infiltration operations (Worden 2008, 253–254). As of 2008, the NKAF was primarily focused on air defense and included approximately 1,600 aircraft (including 780 fighters), mostly Soviet-made antiquated first- and second-generation planes (MiG-15s through MiG-21s) although it did have a limited number of more advanced aircraft (MiG-23s, MiG-29s and Su-25s) (Worden 2008, 252). North Korea's air and naval forces actively patrolled its borders and occasionally engaged in cross-border actions aimed at South Korea and the United States. Thus, while the DPRK continued to require international assistance, it concurrently posed a threat to regional security. Figure 4.1 shows the level of DPRK hostilities during the 2000s, to include the case study period.

Figure 4.1 DPRK Hostile Foreign Policy Activities 2000–2011

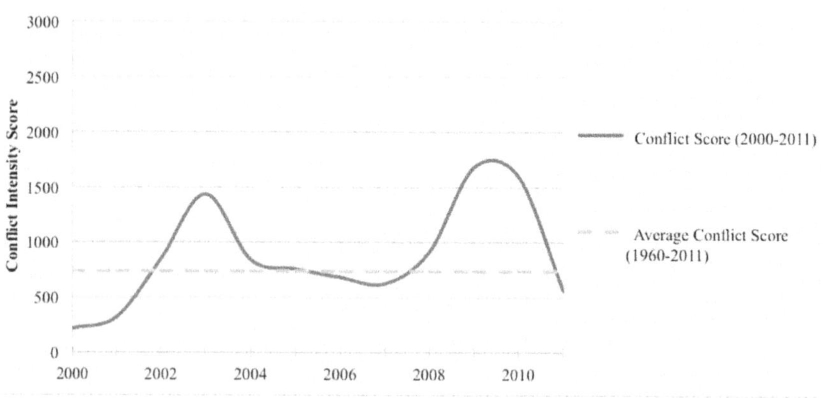

Source: Chapter 5 and the Korean Conflict Dataset (Appendix B)

North Korea's conflict levels between 2008 and 2011 are generally above the average level of conflict for the entire study period and at levels that approach the first case's scores. Compared to historical averages, conflict scores

4. Regime Succession and Case Comparisons

between 2008 and 2011 are 61 percent higher than the average for the entire case study period (1960–2011).[1] Conflict during this period also showed significant variations—both the nuclear tests and conventional military attacks against South Korea caused intensity scores to soar between 2009 and 2010.

During the case study period, North Korea achieved the status of a defacto nuclear state as the Kim regime made visible strides towards the weaponization of its nuclear technology (Nanto and Chanlett-Avery 2010, 10). These developments deeply concerned the international community, which feared not only North Korea's security threat, but also potential reactions from nearby Japan and South Korea—an Asian nuclear arms race would likely destabilize the region (Gates 2009). Beginning in March 2009, North Korea's actions demonstrated it intended to proceed with both missile development program and nuclear efforts. Additionally, the Kim regime demonstrated that it remained ready to use military and diplomatic actions to support both domestic and international policy objectives. A synopsis of the most intense conflict activities during the case study period follows.

Missile Program and Launches. North Korea's continued efforts to develop missile technology provided a number of financial and negotiation advantages for the Kim regime. These included testing of a possible weapons delivery platform for use against the U.S.–ROK alliance, continued research and development for missile exports, and a domestic source of national pride. Beginning in the spring of 2009, after refusing aid and expelling UN workers, North Korea conducted a series of ballistic missile launches. The impetus for the expulsion was unclear, although U.S. officials at the time linked it to the request for the UN's World Food Program to send Korean-speaking food aid monitor personnel, intended to ensure the proper distribution of food (Na 2009). Additionally, there was speculation that the program was shut down due to overall deterioration in relations between the DPRK and both the U.S. and ROK (Manyin 2012, 18).

North Korea's first launch included the firing of a Taepodong-2 rocket in April 2009 (KCNA 2009c), which was probably both a legitimate attempt to launch a small (albeit non-functioning) satellite and a developmental step for the DPRK's long-range missile technology efforts (Kimball 2012). Although the attempt failed (both the missile and its components fell into the sea), it demonstrated that the Kim regime had an active and potentially dangerous ICBM program (Broad 2009). This launch demonstrated that North Korea intended to continue developing both its missile technology and its nuclear weapons program: both of the components required for an active long-range nuclear capability that could threaten not only the region, but also the continental United States (Wit 2011, 3; Broad 2009).

Subsequent launches followed on July 2–4, 2009, coinciding with America's "Independence Day" holiday, and included a mix of short and intermediate range missiles (Kyodo 2009). North Korea also had previously launched a similar number of missiles on July 4–5, 2006, and Schiller (2012, 60) argued that these events were clear political signals to the United States to influence ongoing diplomatic actions. While the regime touted these as examples of North Korea's scientific progress for its domestic audiences, the timing was deliberate. These events occurred when DPRK sought direct negotiations with the United States and concessions from the international community (Asano 2009). In fact, the DPRK's ballistic missile program, often portrayed as a serious threat to the peace and stability of the region, was most likely of limited capability and primarily used as a "symbolic threat" for political purposes (Schiller 2012, 60). In fact, Schiller (2012, 20) contends that North Korea primarily uses its missile technology to "create the illusion of a sophisticated threat for domestic and foreign policy reasons." He also notes that the maximum threat posed by North Korean missiles is limited to 1,000 kilometers and DPRK systems with longer ranges "seem not to be operationally deployed or sufficiently reliable" (Schiller 2012, xvi). The international community reacted to North Korea's April 2009 missile launches with additional sanctions, rather than continued negotiations. That response was possibly one of the influential factors prompting the Kim regime to demonstrate the DPRK's other, much more dangerous, "symbolic threat": North Korea's nuclear weapons capabilities.

North Korea's Nuclear Program. Pyongyang viewed the development of nuclear technology as providing two distinct advantages: increased respect from the international community and a "credible deterrent" against external attack (Nanto and Chanlett-Avery 2010, 14). In 2009, the Kim regime gained the world's attention when it restarted its nuclear program (Landler 2009). Unconfirmed reports claimed that the DPRK had manufactured "small nuclear warheads" that were compatible with its Nodong missiles (Chosun Ilbo 2009), but North Korea's proclaimed resumption of its nuclear program and expulsion of inspectors did not arouse widespread concern about a pending nuclear test. In fact, prior to the May 2009 test, international press reporting made no apparent mention of nuclear test preparations (LexisNexis 2013). At the end of April 2009, the Kim regime stated that it was preparing to conduct "nuclear tests and test-firings of intercontinental ballistic missiles" in response to UN Security Council Sanctions (Fedchenko 2009, 1; KCNA 2009g).

In late May 2009, North Korea again caught the international community unawares by announcing that it conducted a successful underground nuclear test "as part of the measures to bolster up its nuclear deterrent for self-defence" (KCNA 2009h). The U.S. confirmed that the DPRK conducted its second nuclear test at the same location as 2006 (at the P'unggye facility) with the yield of "approximately a few kilotons" (DNI 2009). North Korea reportedly informed the U.S. and China that it would conduct a nuclear test one hour prior to the event (Fedchenko 2009, 1; AFP 2009a). At least according to one report, U.S. officials admitted that the nuclear test "caught the United States by surprise" (Rosen 2009). This test was larger than the previous one with a yield of up to seven kilotons, estimated as "about five times stronger" than the detonation in 2006 (Fedchenko 2009, 3). The DPRK also mentioned this test as part of heir-apparent Kim Jong-un's "150-day campaign" which began on April 20, 2007, and was intended to "resolve food shortages and rebuild the country's antiquated infrastructure" (Yonhap 2009; KCNA 2009h). Western analysts speculated that this campaign was an attempt to refocus public attention away from Kim Jong-il's health and questions about succession (Hoare 2012, 295–296).

The U.S. and Japan responded by drafting a proposed UN Security Resolution to tighten sanctions against the DPRK. Additionally, South Korea joined the Proliferation Security Initiative (PSI), a U.S.-led "global effort that aims to stop trafficking of weapons of mass destruction (WMD)" and associated equipment through interdicting transfers of these types of equipment between states (U.S. DoS 2013). This act by the ROK was strengthened by another UN resolution (Choe 2009c). The next day, North Korea's response was to call the South Korean PSI decision "an act of war," test launch two coastal defense missiles, and declare the 1953 Korean War Armistice null (Oh and Hassig 2010, 92; Harden 2009). Pyongyang had made the same declaration (of nullification) four times previously in 1994, 1996, 2003 and 2006 (Oh and Hassig 2010, 92; Harden 2009). These events, and the previous missile launch in April, demonstrated the advancing threat posed by North Korea to the region. These actions were taken seriously, as the test or use of a nuclear weapon by the DPRK had the potential for significant local damage on the Korean peninsula. Additionally, the actual use of nuclear weapons against the United States potentially would incite efforts to destroy the Kim regime, and the U.S. might respond with similar measures. The oft-repeated quote (attributed to U.S. Secretary of State Condoleezza Rice) was that if North Korea were to attack the U.S. or its allies with a nuclear weapon, the response would be decisive and the U.S. would turn North Korea into a "parking lot" (Natsios 2013). Nevertheless, although North Korea's test and threats associated with its nuclear program were disconcerting to the U.S. and its allies, these were actually "empty gestures" and simply a technique to force negotiations in hopes of international concessions. The Kim regime had too much to lose by actually using the nuclear weapons it was developing.

The nuclear tests served a wide range of purposes for the regime. These included a signal to the international community that North Korea required its attention; another purpose was internal propaganda. Domestically, the tests supported the idea that the DPRK's external threats were so dangerous that its only option was a "nuclear deterrent" (KCNA 2009h). As Nanto and Chanlett-Avery (2010, 14) observed

> Without the DPRK nuclear program, North Korea would be a humanitarian aid "basket case" and a reclusive society that would be hard pressed to draw more world notice than countries such as Laos or Mongolia. Instead, North Korea is high on the world's security agenda. Pyongyang has become adept at using this attention to extract economic assistance and has used actions by other countries (such as sanctions or U.S. military exercises in the region) as propaganda tools to fuel nationalism and strengthen support for its regime.

Thus, the Kim regime's efforts to maintain and further develop its nuclear capabilities should have been of little surprise to external observers. Nuclear capabilities provided a means to ensure the DPRK maintained its sovereignty, domestic stability (through both the emphasis on external threats and the acquisition of aid), and that the Kim regime remained a key issue for the international community. The test in May 2009 was a clear sign that North Korea had "no serious intention of negotiating away its nuclear capability" and that the world must accept North Korea as a nuclear state (Haggard 5, 2012). For the North Korean public, the nuclear program was a demonstration of how dangerous the world really was for the DPRK and helped the Kim regime justify "continued sacrifices by and harsh treatment of its people" (Heckler 2010, 51).

In the following months, North Korea's efforts to engage the world took another turn: the Kim regime embarked upon a "charm offensive" which sought to improve dialogue with the U.S., South Korea, and China (Japan Times 2009; Nanto and Manyin 2010). In August 2009, the North Koreans hosted former U.S. president Bill Clinton and he successfully obtained the release of two American journalists held in North Korea for almost six months (KCNA 2009i). The Kim regime also held meetings with the head of the South Korean conglomerate Hyundai, discussed a willingness to reopen Mount Kumgang for tourism, began hinting it would return to the Six-Party Talks, and concluded an agreement with Chinese Premier Wen Jiabao for substantial levels of food aid (Oh and Hassig 2010, 95). Yet these events were part of a predictable cycle in which the DPRK conducted provocative activities, sought negotiations and aid, and then returned to hostile actions when diplomatic progress stalled (Nanto and Manyin 2011, 96). In this case, the return to deadly hostile foreign policy actions occurred just a few months later.

The Kim regime's diplomatic shift lasted through the beginning of 2010, and the Kim regime's annual New Year's Message sounded "less bellicose" than in previous years (Foster-Carter 2010a, 76), stressed the importance of the historic June 2000 North-South summit, and emphasized that "National reconciliation and cooperation should be promoted actively" (KCNA 2010a). Just two weeks later, North Korea resumed hostile foreign policy statements, reportedly in reaction to press reports of discussions between the U.S. and South Korean administrations on contingency plans concerning the DPRK. The Kim regime charged that the U.S. and South Koreans had drafted a "scenario for toppling the system in the DPRK ... with an aim to bring it to a 'collapse'" (KCNA 2010b; Kim, S. 2010). As discussed below North Korea's actions during this time were among the most serious seen on the peninsula since the 1960s and the conventional attacks against naval and ground targets were the most deadly since the Korean War.

The Sinking of the *Cheonan*. The Yellow Sea and the NLL continued to be an area of both interest and tension between not only the two Koreas, but also with the Chinese whose commercial fishing ships routinely worked along the boundary areas in search of crab and a variety of fish (Van Dyke 2003, 149; Yonhap 2013a).[2] The Yellow Sea area includes South Korea's shipping routes to China and North Korea and a number of islands claimed by both the ROK and DPRK (see map in Appendix C). Additionally, the region represents a consistent security challenge for South Korea and includes a significant DPRK and ROK naval presence. Additionally, North Korea's navy has routinely used the area to insert special operations agents for operations against the South (Roehrig 2008, 25–26). Due to these considerations, South Korea maintained an active military presence along the NLL and routinely conducted maritime patrols in the area.

In November 2009, the ROK navy exchanged fire with a North Korean vessel that crossed the NLL in the Yellow Sea (Kim J. 2010). The DPRK ship sustained heavy damage and retreated back across the border line and the North Koreans sustained at least four casualties (one killed and three wounded personnel) while the South had none (CSIS 2010, 5). The South Koreans sent additional naval vessels to the area and noted that it was "a regrettable incident in which the North targeted the South" while the North Koreans called the incident a "deliberate and premeditated provocation," demanding an apology (KCNA 2009j; KCNA 2009k; Kim J. 2010). In any case, the incident did not escalate. Additionally, it was not disruptive enough to prevent a pending visit by President Obama to South Korea and ongoing nuclear negotiations between North Korea and the U.S. (AFP 2010; Choe 2010a).

For the next few months, tensions receded although North Korea demonstrated both belligerence and willingness to accept international aid. For the first time in two years, North Korea received food aid from the South, consisting of 10,000 tons of maize, while concurrently denouncing the South's discussion of contingency plans surrounding a DPRK "collapse scenario" (Foster-Carter

2010a, 77–78). Three days later, the Kim regime announced that it would not return to the Six Party Talks unless international sanctions were lifted and called for an agreement to permanently replace the 1953 Armistice (KCNA 2010c). In late January 2010, tensions also increased as the DPRK began conducting a series of naval training drills on the North Korean side of the NLL near the ROK-held islands of Baengnyeongdo and Daecheongdo in the Yellow Sea (Foster Carter 2010a, 78).

In mid–February, the South Koreans reported that the DPRK increased naval drills and reinforced the coastal areas with additional artillery (including multiple rocket launchers) (Yonhap 2010b). Additionally, at the end of February, the North Koreans began criticizing both the South Koreans and U.S. over the "KEY RESOLVE-FOAL EAGLE" exercise (slated to begin in a few weeks) stating that the event included "operations and nuclear war exercises aimed to preempt a surprise attack on the DPRK" (AFP 2010; KCNA 2010j). At the same time, analysts predicted that "absent foreign aid North Korea will be 1.2 million tons short of its food needs this year" (Foster-Carter 2010a, 88). Thus, by mid–March 2010, North Korea had not participated in the Six Party Talks since June 2008 (Liang 2012), it increased its military presence near the NLL in the west, and faced significant food shortages in the coming months. Conditions were ripe for another HFP event to force a new round of negotiations.

In mid–March 2010, the *Cheonan*, a South Korean 1,200-ton corvette-class vessel, left the ROK port of Pyeontaek on a routine patrol mission (ROK MND 2010, 36). At approximately nine p.m. on 26 March, there was an onboard explosion and the *Cheonan* sank, resulting in the deaths of 46 of the 104 crewmembers onboard (Bechtol 2010). Two months later, after an extensive investigation, the ROK's Ministry of National Defense concluded that North Korea had attacked and sunk the *Cheonan* using a submarine-launched torpedo (ROK MND 2010, 220). Additionally, U.S. Secretary of State Clinton charged "The evidence is overwhelming and condemning. The torpedo that sunk the *Cheonan* … was fired by a North Korean submarine" (Lee 2010). In April 2010, North Korea denied the charges, stating that it was a "regretful accident" and after the ROK MND report was issued, the Kim regime declared that a "state of war" existed (KCNA 2010d; KCNA 2010e).

Assuming that the DPRK conducted the attack (and all available evidence, including defector testimony, implicated the Kim regime), this was the most serious direct attack against the ROK military since the Korean War. Additionally, this incident demonstrated both North Korea's asymmetric military capabilities and willingness to conduct direct attacks against the ROK (Cha and Kim 2010, 2; Korea Times 2012). The UN Security Council discussed the *Cheonan* sinking, but China refused to approve any language that blamed North

Korea, and the final proclamation simply condemned the attack and noted South Korea's restraint in the matter (UNSC 2010; Cha 2012, 334–335). This action by China tends to support its overall position on North Korea. Beijing's first priority has historically been stability in the DPRK. As long as DPRK actions do not potentially cause circumstances that might result in U.S. military retaliation, China remains reluctant to engage in actions it considers destabilizing (such as UN resolutions condemning the North) (Song 2011, 1135). South Korea's reaction to the sinking did not include direct military retaliation. But it did include the cessation of almost all trade with North Korea (with the exception of the Kaesong Industrial Complex), implementation of additional sanctions (along with the U.S.) and ROK participation in the PSI (Hoare 2012, 85; VOA 2010b). Additionally, the U.S. and South Koreans conducted an unprecedented show of force operation, dubbed "INVINCIBLE SPIRIT," in the Yellow Sea which included a mixture of over 20 ships and submarines, 200 aircraft, and 8,000 personnel (CNN 2010a; Fackler 2010). Aside from rhetoric in the North Korean press, there was no overt military response from the DPRK to these exercises (KCNA 2010f).

The Shelling of Yeonpyeong Island. By the end of the summer of 2010, the tense atmosphere engendered by the *Cheonan* attack seemed to recede and the two Koreas experienced a slight thawing of relations. While the majority of trade between the North and South stopped, the Kaesong Industrial Complex continued to operate, with virtually no effects evident as a result of the *Cheonan* attack (Foster-Carter 2010b, 3). In fact, a South Korean government report stated that the "Kaesong Industrial Zone was almost unaffected by the *Cheonan* incident. Output at the zone in July [2010] was worth $26.4 million, only slightly down from $26.5 million in June and $28.1 million in April" (Foster-Carter 2011a, 12; Yonhap 2010c). Although the ROK and U.S. continued to conduct their annual fall military exercises (including ULCHI FREEDOM GUARDIAN), the North Korean responses were limited to public condemnations. In one of many responses, the DPRK government stated "The large-scale DPRK-targeted war maneuvers staged by the South Korean puppet forces one after another in collusion with the U.S. are very grave military provocations, little short of a declaration of war against the DPRK" (KCNA 2010g). But there was no significant increase in hostile foreign policy actions (KCNA 2010g; KINU 2011; UNC 2012). For example, the only two military events during this period included North Korea's firing of over 100 artillery rounds into the sea near the NLL in early August 2010 and a DMZ incident in October with only a few rounds fired and no injuries (KINU 2011; UNC 2012). In October 2010, South Korea provided 5,000 tons of rice aid in response to seasonal flooding two months earlier (Kim K. 2010). This is a relatively small amount of assistance compared to the previous support provided by Seoul (as much as 500,000 tons of rice per year), but it was the first aid provided by the South in over two years (Foster-Carter 2011a, 3). Additionally, the Koreas conducted North-South family reunion meetings for the first time in over a year (ROK MOU 2010).

While these events demonstrated the North Koreans' willingness to cooperate with the South (at least in some areas), the Kim regime also faced a significant amount of domestic pressure. Shortages of critical supplies continued as the World Food Program observed that the DPRK had difficulty with food and medical supplies because of both the 2009 currency reform and the August 2010 floods (Kyodo 2010a). Additionally, the North Koreans continued to call on the South to allow for renewed tourism at the Mount Kumgang Resort, which the South Koreans had disallowed for over two years (Foster-Carter 2011a, 16). While this remained a difficult time for the North Koreans, they continued to actively engage the ROK in negotiations and there were few indications that another deadly hostile foreign policy event was about to occur.

In November 2010, South Korea's military began its annual "HOGUK" amphibious training exercise with over 70,000 participants in both the Yellow Sea and along the ROK's west coast. The U.S. had planned to join the ROKs with navy and marine personnel, but a few days prior to the exercise, announced it would not participate due to "scheduling issues" (Jung 2010). On the same day, Kim Jong-il and Kim Jong-un reportedly visited the DPRK's southwest coast and may have visited a number of artillery units in the area (KCNA 2010h; *Joongang Daily* 2010). The following afternoon, the North Koreans conducted a rocket artillery attack against the South Korean-occupied island of Yeonpyeong; the North fired approximately 120 rockets and the South responded with 80 rounds of artillery (CNS 2010). The artillery exchange involved North Korean 120mm rocket launchers and South Korean K-9 self-propelled artillery (CNS 2010). This was the first artillery exchange of its kind since the 1960s. The attack left four South Koreans dead (two civilians and two ROK marines), 18 injured, 22 buildings destroyed, and resulted in the evacuation of most of the island's 1,900 residents by the South Korean navy (Yonhap 2010d; *Korea Times* 2010; CNN 2010b). It was unclear if the South Korean artillery caused any damage to North Korean personnel or facilities (JEN 2010).

North Korea commented on the incident, stating that it fired in self-defense, responding to South Korea's artillery that fell in the ocean on the DPRK side of the "maritime border" (KCNA 2010i). In fact, the North Koreans warned the South not to conduct live fire exercises in the area and the DPRK artillery attack occurred at the end of ROK maneuver exercises (Song 2010). The ROK military had previously announced these exercises (including the live firings) as it had done during similar events in the past (Hoare 2012, 407). There were also unattributed South Korean government reports that Kim Jong-il and Kim Jong-un personally ordered the attack during their visits to the area and North Korean military propaganda documents surfaced that linked the attacks to Kim Jong-un (Joongang 2010; Chosun Ilbo 2011c).

After the *Cheonan* sinking, President Lee declared that South Korea would "immediately exercise our right of self-defense if their territorial waters, airspace or territory are violated" (Armstrong 2010; CNN 2010c). In a 2013 interview, President Lee stated that he had ordered the South Korean military to attack North Korean targets, but that "a high-ranking military official blocked him, saying that the Air Force mustn't get involved per the rules of engagement, and that they needed to consult with the Americans" (Keohler 2013; Chosun Ilbo 2013a). Thus, as during previous incidents with North Korea, the South Koreans did not conduct a subsequent retaliatory military response (aside from naval exercises in the area). The ROK did immediately increase security levels, ban all travel to North Korea, cancel pending Red Cross talks, cease all programmed aid to the DPRK, and adjust the "rules of engagement" to allow for more decisive military responses in the future (Foster-Carter 2011a, 7; Fackler and McDonald 2010). China's reaction, which included blocking a UN resolution condemning the Kim regime for the attack, was seen as an "enabling response [which] appeared to write North Korea a blank check for further provocations" (Snyder and Byun 2011, 78). The U.S. also condemned the attack, and conducted two large-scale joint naval exercises with both South Korea (near the location of the attack) and Japan (off the east coast of Korea) (Foster-Carter 2011a, 8; Kyoto 2010c).

In contrast to the *Cheonan* sinking, North Korea immediately took full credit for this incident and publicly celebrated the "Victorious Yeonpyeong Island Shelling" (KCNA 2012a). As with the *Cheonan* sinking, determining the motivation behind this event is difficult. However, the attack was potentially associated with domestic efforts to solidify Kim Jong-un's place as the future ruler of North Korea (Chosun Ilbo 2011c) and concurrent efforts to restart negotiations with the South on aid and economic concerns. Kim Jong-un's lack of military experience probably made his visible involvement in Kim Jong-il's military decisions essential to establish credibility, just as his father had done under Kim Il-sung. At the same time, the DPRK sought progress between the Koreas on economic issues (such as trade and the reopening of the Mount Kumgang Resort) that had stalled (Foster-Carter 2011a, 4–5) and this action might have been considered a means to break the negotiations impasse.

The *Cheonan* sinking and Yeonpyeong shelling demonstrated the difficult situation that South Korea historically found itself in when responding to DPRK hostile military actions. While a military response by the ROK might seem like the most logical reaction, most analysts (and most likely the South Korean government) expected that retaliation against North Korea would result in additional and unpredictable DPRK aggression (Kang 2010). Yet, based on publicly available information, the South Koreans have not conducted conventional retaliatory actions since the 1960s and have instead relied on diplomatic and economic means to deal with DPRK since that time. The ROK government (and the international community) historically took the view that any military action against North Korea will lead to war on the Korean peninsula and this belief shaped South Korean responses to these types of spectacular events (McDevitt 2011). The DPRK leaders observed this behavior over the past few decades and became exceedingly adept at conducting hostile foreign policy actions short of war with little fear of military retaliation (Kaplan and Denmark 2011). North Korea's actions such as its nuclear test, continued missile firings, and naval engagements demonstrated that this was a heightened period of hostilities on the peninsula and followed previous DPRK patterns of state conduct. The increased HFP action approached the levels seen during the 1960s and again pushed the peninsula towards the possibility of war.

Was political instability associated with heightened HFP activities?

North Korea's political system was under significant stress as Kim Jong-il's health failed and the DPRK leaders sought to ensure a coherent leadership transition to Kim Jong-un. At the same time, political instability did not threaten the Kim regime's grip on power and no direct link was found between political instability and conflict. Historically, despite domestic difficulties, there were few incidents of "dissatisfaction or opposition" directed at the Kim regime (Nanto and Chanlett-Avery 2010, 14; KINU 2011b, 290–291). In fact, the unauthorized gathering of individuals in an assembly is strictly prohibited by North Korean law and can result in up to sentences of up to "5 years of correctional labor" (KINU 2011b, 291). In the 2000s, there were sporadic reports of social unrest, especially associated with Pyongyang's decision to revalue its currency in 2009. But events were localized and effects were limited to changes in the Kim regime's policies rather than wide-ranging indications of instability (Choe 2009a; KINU 2011b, 56). There were DPRK refugee reports of at least four executions of individuals accused of protesting against the 2009 currency reform (KINU 2011b, 542) and the Kim regime's successful policies of oppression eliminated many of the conditions necessary for social revolution. As Byman and Lind (2010, 70) noted, "The North Korean people may be hungry, may despise Kim Jong-il, and may envy their rich neighbors, but the people are unlikely to mobilize."

4. Regime Succession and Case Comparisons 117

During this time, the North Korean system of societal control remained intact, and substantial political difficulties faced by the regime during the succession period were not apparent to outside observers. The Kim regime most likely eliminated any high-level political dissent (associated with the arrival of Kim Jong-un) through reshuffling and promotion of key individuals during the Third Party Congress in September 2010 (Kim, J. 2011, 15). Additionally, changes were made at the provincial level with party members who were older or considered "disabled." These individuals were redesignated as "honorary members" and replaced with younger members (in their twenties and thirties) in order to support the transition to Kim Jong-un (Ah 2012, 34–35). Despite the arrival of Kim's relatively unknown son, and his rapid promotion as the future leader of the regime, there were few observable signs that North Korea's military or elite opposed Kim Jong-il's political heir (AFP 2012).

The regime's success in maintaining order and retaining power during this period resulted from North Korea's legacy of authoritarian rule and its use of "restrictive social policies; manipulation of ideas and information; use of force; co-optation; manipulation of foreign governments; and institutional coup-proofing" (Byman and Lind 2010, 45). As described later in this section, diversion became important for the regime, but only within the context of its overall system of control.

Succession rumors began almost immediately after Kim Jong-il's stroke in 2008, and in January 2009, reports surfaced stating that his youngest son was a possible choice to take KJI's place (AFP 2009c). In September 2008, the South Korean Embassy in Beijing reported that on 22 August 2008, Kim Jong-il suffered a stroke and collapsed in Pyongyang (AFP 2008). Kim was incapacitated and two months later, underwent brain surgery, reportedly by a French neurosurgeon (Kim and Yi 2008; Erlanger 2008). While Kim Jong-il's health prior to his 2008 stroke is unclear, there were reports that a pacemaker was installed in 1991 and that since the 1970s, Kim had suffered from a number of ailments attributed to his "heavy-drinking habits" (Erlanger 2008; Cha V. 2012, 94). As Kim Jong-il was recovering from his stroke, Kim Yong-nam, the Chairman of the Supreme People's Assembly (SPA), assumed visible role as "ceremonial" leader of the DPRK while actual power reportedly resided with Jang Sung-taek, Kim's brother-in-law (Jeffries 2010a; Hoare 2012, 226–227). In early October 2008, the North Korean press reported that Kim Jong-il attended a youth soccer match (KCNA 2008a), which was possibly his first public appearance in weeks. Kim suffered a setback later that month which required brain surgery and spurred rumors on the stability of the regime (Lee 2008b; Kim and Yi 2008). North Korea denied rumors that Kim Jong-il was ill or dead, stating that international press reports on the North Korean leader's condition were intended to "defame the indestructible political system in the DPRK" (KCNA 2008b).

Although the North Korean press reported that Kim had once again begun to conduct on-site guidance visits in early December 2008 (KCNA 2008c), video footage of the North Korean leader was not seen until April 2009 during the DPRK's 12th SPA meeting (which had been postponed due to his stroke the previous fall) (Pollack 2009, 156). These events most likely influenced Kim Jong-il's decision to promote his youngest son as the next leader of North Korea. Although Kim Jong-il had survived and remained firmly in control of North Korea (AP 2008), this event most likely forced the regime to take steps to solidify the process of succession to the next leader of the DPRK. The regime relied upon the same process, albeit significantly compressed, as Kim Il-sung used when he moved to install his own son as the designated successor to lead the DPRK.

Kim Jong-un's succession was "an extremely compressed version of Kim Jong-il's" and included three stages: apprenticeship, power sharing, and power transition (Ahn 2011, 27). For Kim Jong-il, the "apprenticeship" phase lasted from 1974 to 1980; from 1980 to 1991, a period of "power sharing" occurred; and from that point until Kim Il-sung's death in 1994 was the "power transition" stage (Ahn 2011, 27). The apprenticeship stage for Kim Jong-un began in early 2009, when he registered for candidacy in the upcoming March parliamentary elections; in April 2009, Kim Jong-il named his son, along with Jang Sung-taek, to the National Defense Commission (Chang 2009; CNN 2009). Just a few months later, reports surfaced that Kim Jong-il had pancreatic cancer (AFP 2009d), although during a visit in July 2009 by former President Bill Clinton (to secure the release of two American journalists), Kim was said to look "unexpectedly spry" (Landler and Mazzetti, 2009). This stage of succession culminated in the September 2010 official "unveiling" of the next ruler of Korea after he was promoted to Vice Chairman of the Central Military Committee and four-star general (Ahn 2012, 33; Kwon and Chung 2012, 186).

From this point on, Kim Jong-un shared power with the elder Kim followed by his emergence (and the beginnings of a power transition) as leader of the DPRK in December 2011 (Ahn 2012, 27). The rise of at least three key figures provided the youngest Kim legitimacy in the DPRK power structure. Elevated along with Kim Jong-un were Jang Sung-taek (Kim Jong-il's sister) and her husband and KPA Chief of Staff Ri Young-ho, who was reportedly "charged with securing the military's support for Kim Jong-un" (Kim J. 2011, 15; Choi and Shaw 2010, 189). According to some analysts, Jang was expected to assume the primary leadership role (Choi and Shaw 2010, 176) and possibly "relegate Kim Jong-un to the role of a figurehead" (Manyin 2012, 5; Economist 2011).

4. *Regime Succession and Case Comparisons*　　　119

　　Many Korean observers predicted that the succession would result in internal instability and possibly might spell the end of the Kim regimes as a "leadership transition from Kim Jong-il to Kim Jong-un ... promises even more disaffection in the party and military" (Klinger 2010; Cha and Anderson 2012, 21). Additionally, speculation persisted on how Kim Jong-un could effectively lead the reclusive state, given his age and lack of experience. The Kim family members have been relatively young when chosen to lead, as Kim Il-sung was about thirty-three years old when he was chosen by the Soviets (Cha 2012, 76) and Kim Jong-il was approximately the same age when his father introduced the younger Kim as the next DPRK ruler. Thus the choice, rushed by Kim Jong-il's ailing health, of a young successor as the next DPRK ruler somewhat followed similar events in North Korea's past. Yet questions over the future of the DPRK persisted. In fact, in March 2010, one DPRK analyst observed, "North Korea is on the verge of collapse ... not only because of Kim's illness, the food shortage, and failed currency reform, but also because of a failed government" (Ramstad 2010). Another noted that after Kim Jong-il's death, "The DPRK is now sailing into uncharted waters, formally under a greenhorn skipper whose seamanship is untested and unknown" (Foster-Carter 2012, 1). Despite these dire predictions, the succession process had been underway since 2008, three years prior to Kim's death in 2011. The Kim regime had been engineering the succession with "on-the-job training," systemic changes, and personnel changes "to ensure that the young leader would have a supportive environment" (Revere 2011).

　　During the last year of Kim Jong-il's life, there was a noticeable increase in Kim Jong-un's public appearances. This include the younger Kim's participation in on-site inspections of civilian and military units, and being present alongside Kim Jong-il during state visits of foreign dignitaries (Kim B. 2011; Foster-Carter 2012, 12). Aside from seeking domestic support for the power transition, Kim Jong-il visited both China and Russia during the succession period in order to "secure the assent of Beijing and Moscow to a second dynastic succession in North Korea" (Pollack 2011). Thus, when Kim Jong-il died at the end of 2011, efforts to place his son in a position to govern North Korea (with the help of an inner core of advisors) were well underway. Political instability did occur, yet no significant relationships between threats to the Kims' grip on power and the level of HFP activities were found in this research.

Were Economic Difficulties Associated with Increased HFP?

　　Economic difficulties continued throughout the case study period and at least one incident (the sinking of South Korea's *Cheonan* naval vessel in 2010) occurred right after the end of a "currency crisis" indicating a possible connection between these two events. During the case study period, although the DPRK's economy performed better than in the 1990s, it was still recovering from the famine period. During the 2000s, North Korea became a state with an institutionalized need for foreign humanitarian aid. Despite heavy reliance on international aid, North Korea's trade with China was at unprecedented levels and the DPRK seemed to again muddle through its economic crises. While the Kim regime faced domestic challenges on a number of fronts during this period, its own political system and the framework of a pending succession limited its reactions to these internal problems. North Korea historically blamed its economic problems on two key factors: the loss of trade with the Soviet bloc at the end of the Cold War and the restrictions imposed upon it by U.S. efforts to limit aid and enact economic sanctions (Eberstadt 2011, 3). Western scholars tend to cite North Korea's overall political structure as the primary reason for the DPRK's economic difficulties in the 2000s. North Korea's economic problems were most likely the direct result of system characteristics such as the inability to conduct long-range economic planning; the "hyper-militarization of the national economy" through the DPRK's Songun system; lack of honest feedback to decision makers on the status of the economy; poor or non-existent monetary, banking and credit policies; the inability to pay foreign debt; "allergy to licit international trade" and the development of legitimate markets for overseas customers; and a restrictive international business environment (Eberstadt 2011, 10–11). Nevertheless, the Kim regime continued to exercise continuity in its domestic policies. Even with the nomination of a young and inexperienced Kim family member as the next regime's ruler, the DPRK leadership remained, at least to external observers, stable and in control of North Korean society.

The public response to the economic chaos of the 1990s was the emergence of an alternate market system that was "outside of the state economy" consisting of private services, manufactured goods, and local markets (Lankov 2012, 15). In fact between 1998 and 2008, 78 percent of the income in North Korean households came from these types of ventures, which included agricultural products from private fields and manufactured goods in homes or at "passively tolerated private workshops" (Lankov 2012, 15; Kim and Song 2008, 373). Women generally ran these businesses, which evolved from isolated local and regional markets in the 1990s to a "unified national market" with cross-border links to China (Ishimaru 2010, 346). North Korean officials tolerated these markets and informally legitimized and regulated them beginning in 2003 (Hassig and Oh 2009, 75–76). In 2007, the North Korean government began to limit the markets and banned professionals (such as teachers and doctors) from working there. An internal KWP directive stated,

> a majority of women reaching employment age [were] working in the markets. [The report] criticizes in particular female university graduates quitting from their original jobs as teachers and doctors and becoming merchants due to poverty, saying: "Abandoning their duties to do business in the markets is an act lacking the basic conscience and morality" [Sankei Shimbun 2007].

Additionally, the KWP document quoted Kim Jong-il as criticizing the markets for "taking away our socialist system and transforming it into a place susceptible to all sorts of non-socialist phenomenon" (Ryu 2010, 111). In November 2009, the Kim regime introduced currency reform aimed at curbing black markets and other types of private enterprise to reestablish state control over the economy (Choe 2009a). North Korean citizens were forced to exchange a limited amount of old money for new currency, which set off a market panic "with the prices of staples such as rice and corn rising 6,000 percent to 8,000 percent and the black market value of the won collapsing" (Haggard and Noland 2010, 549). The limits on the currency exchange meant that any personal funds above the relatively low exchange limits were effectively worthless, thus the extra cash that many North Korean citizens had saved to tide them over during the winter was lost (Choe 2009a). In February 2010, the DPRK government took the unprecedented step of issuing a public apology for the reform effort and executed the DPRK officials associated with the new monetary policy (Choe 2010; KINU 2011b, 545).

In March 2010, North Korea sank a South Korean navy patrol craft (the *Cheonan*), as described above. The timing of this event and Pyongyang's economic chaos surrounding its currency policy suggests that a potential relationship was present. The argument that North Korea attempted to use the attack to distract the public (or elites) from internal difficulties is one of many explanations for that incident. Alternatively, North Korea's attack on the *Cheonan* could have been part of posturing by military hardliners, an effort to change the disputed sea border, an attempt to force additional aid negotiations, part of Kim Jong-un's rise as North Korea's next leader, revenge for the naval skirmish in November 2009 or retaliation for Seoul's refusal to provide additional aid in 2010 (Bechtol 2010; Pomfret and Harden 2010; Chosun Ilbo 2013a). While the motive for this action may never be known, it is clear that North Korea did not use this incident as part of its overt propaganda effort as it did with its nuclear and missile tests. Thus, this event may have been intended for a select North Korean audience, possibly to appease a specific faction in the DPRK leadership (possibly the military). The idea that the *Cheonan* sinking was instigated by the hard liners in North Korea's military is reminiscent of the alleged attackers (in Kim Il-sung's words "extreme leftists") in the Blue House attack of 1968 (SK Foreign Ministry Archive 1972). In any case, as in the Blue House attack, this incident was not something North Korea was willing to acknowledge to either the DPRK public or the international community. This event also might have been a case of attempted diversion by the Kim regime that had unintended effects (i.e., the high number of South Korean deaths), to the extent that North Korea was unwilling to publicly take credit for involvement in that event.

Between 2008 and 2011, the DPRK's economy grew slightly, averaging less than one percent per year (BOK 2012). Analysts attribute North Korea's economic stagnation to the same conditions that the DPRK faced over the years: the inability of the North's economy to interact with world markets, continued efforts at autarky, and overall industrial and technological obsolescence (Nanto and Chanlett-Avery 2010, 28). North Korea's national priorities continued to favor the military and the DPRK spent an estimated 15 to 27 percent of its GDP on national defense during the 2000s (Nanto and Chanlett-Avery 2010, 27). In fact, the DPRK government reported that it spent 15.8 percent of its GDP on defense in 2009, unchanged from 2008 (EIU 2009, 19). Outside sources contend that in the early 2000s, North Korea reportedly spent as much as $5 billion per year, or 25 percent of its GDP, on national defense (Samore 2004b). Most analysts agree that it constituted a disproportionate amount of the yearly DPRK budget and that the Kim regime had the most "militarized economy" in the world (Noland 2000, 72). Other estimates of North Korea's economy at the time were striking, such as the influence of agriculture, which constituted 20.8 percent[3] of the economy, and an underdeveloped service sector (31 percent of GDP), both of which continue to be centrally guided by the DPRK's government (EIU 2011, 18).

During this period, the DPRK remained the poorest nation in East Asia and among the most economically challenged in the world. Yet North Korea's continued economic struggles were not surprising, since the types of changes required to achieve financial success were not congruent with the Kim regime's efforts to maintain its state of authoritarian isolationism. To achieve growth and economic success, North Korea needed to make systemic changes, such as opening its economy to the international markets, taking active steps to reduce the DPRK's stance as threatening to the international community, and normalizing ROK–DPRK relations (Eberstadt 2007, 304–305). These concessions never occurred as these types of economic and political actions would have threatened the Kim regime's control over DPRK society and thus would never occur under the current political system in North Korea. Thus the North's economy had little hope of ever approaching its potential during this period.

During the last year of the succession (2011), the DPRK experienced some domestic economic gains, but also continued to struggle with food availability. After expanding trade with China, North Korea's economic output increased, but assessments from the World Food Program noted that millions of North Korean citizens still lacked adequate food (ECOS 2013; UN WFP 2011, 4). Additionally, inter-Korean aid began to show signs of resuming as Seoul approved limited amounts of food and medical aid for delivery by South Korean NGOs throughout the year (Foster-Carter 2011b, 8; 2012, 16). In 2011, the majority of North Korea's HFP policy activities became diplomatic pronouncements. It was not until after Kim Jong-il's death that the only substantial military activity occurred: the test launch of at least one short-range missile from North Korea's east coast (KINU 2011; Yonhap 2011a). In November 2011, the World Food Program (UN WFP 2011, 4) surveyed portions of the DPRK and commented that during the next year, the DPRK's estimated overall food shortage was predicted to be 414,000 tons. They also noted that North Korea had decreased PDS allowances per person from May to September 2011 to 200 grams per person per day (well below the requirement) and that

> Health officials interviewed reported a 50 to 100 percent increase in the admissions of malnourished children into pediatric wards compared to last year, a sharp rise in low-birth weight, and the mission team observed several cases of edema. Inadequate food intake has clearly compounded the health and nutrition status of vulnerable groups [UN WFP 2011, 4].

Thus there were significant economic difficulties experienced by the DPRK during this period. Additionally, as described above, there was at least one incident (the sinking of the *Cheonan*) that occurred simultaneously with these economic problems, suggesting a possible relationship between these events.

Was social instability associated with periods of increased HFP?

There were significant levels of social instability during the case study period, but no direct relationships were present between the levels of unrest and the DPRK's use of hostile foreign policy activities. North Korea's ability to feed itself improved by the mid–2000s, but problems persisted. In addition to international food aid, the North Koreans became dependent on privatized markets to support their efforts to obtain needed goods, including food. However, these markets were vulnerable to the actions of the regime and to food production levels. The Kim regime's 2005 ban on the private trade of grain resulted in criminalizing "the primary mechanism through which most Korean families obtained food" (Haggard and Noland 2009, 384). Floods in 2006 and

2007, coupled with continued efforts by the DPRK government to control the private markets, made matters worse and famine again became a real possibility for the North Korean people.

The difference between the onset of food shortages in the 2000s compared to the 1990 famine period was the level of the "marketization of the North Korean economy" (Haggard and Noland 2008, 20–21). During North Korea's Great Famine period, substantial aid did not arrive until two years after the crisis began to emerge in 1993. By the 2000s, international aid associations had monitored and accessed much of North Korea for over a decade, which allowed for more timely responses, albeit still controlled by the DPRK authorities (Haggard and Noland 2008, 20). Additionally, the increase of markets for private trading throughout North Korean society, including cross-border (DPRK-PRC) grain trade, reduced the vulnerability of the average North Korean citizen to food shortages (Haggard and Noland 2008, 20).

In July 2008, the UN reported "a progressive improvement in food security between 2000 and 2005" due to both increased domestic production and high levels of international food assistance (UN 2008a, 1). Yet flooding in 2006 and 2007 decreased harvests and left hundreds of thousands homeless resulting in significant food shortages in 2008. The military and Pyongyang's elite were not substantially affected, but more than 75 percent of the rest of North Korea reportedly had reduced their food intake and were eating "only two meals per day" (MacFarquhar 2008). The UN (2008a, 1) also noted that access to food had decreased significantly via North Korea's food distribution system (the PDS) and rations decreased from 500 grams (per person per day) in November 2007 to only 150 grams per day in June 2008. The benchmark of 450 grams per day was often used as the minimum required to satisfy human needs (Haggard and Noland 2011, 48); thus the ration of only 150 grams per day was substantially below required nutrition levels. Significant health problems for vulnerable groups, including persistent malnutrition, continued and the UN (2008b, 22) observed that

> [in North Korea] 37 percent of children under 6 were stunted, 23 percent were underweight and 7 percent were wasted. One third of all mothers with small children were malnourished, anemic, and dietary diversity (poor in protein, fats, minerals, and vitamins) was lacking.

Additionally, infant and under-five mortality rates during this period stabilized and between 2005 and 2011, were at levels fifty percent lower than during the height of the 1990s famine (World dataBank 2012). Thus while much of North Korea was suffering, the mortality rates for two of its most vulnerable groups were significantly better than during the previous decade.

4. Regime Succession and Case Comparisons 125

North Korea's relations with the international community directly influenced the levels of food available to the Kim regime during this time. The nuclear test in 2006 resulted in South Korea's suspension of fertilizer shipments, which were critical for DPRK food production. This resulted in decreased harvests and, along with "general donor fatigue" on the part of both South Korea and other states, negatively affected humanitarian aid levels (Haggard and Noland 2009, 384). The DPRK's second nuclear test (May 2009) and conventional military attacks against South Korea in 2010 also impacted aid levels. Those events negatively the international community's willingness to provide additional aid resulting, for example, in China's curtailment of its aid programs (Kim, S. 2010 and Hwang 2011). In March 2011, the UN concluded that North Korea's PDS would run out of food in two months and that over six million DPRK citizens were in "urgent need of international food assistance" (UN 2011). Yet China remained determined to support stability in the DPRK. Following Kim Jong-il's death in December 2011, China reportedly began sending "significant" amounts of food and fuel aid to "ensure a successful power transition" (Snyder and Byun, 2012).[4]

Refugee flows are another indicator of social distress for North Korea. In the 2000s, refugees arriving in South Korea were at their highest levels ever, increasing from an average of 49 per year in the 1990s to over 2,000 annually in the 2000s (ROK MOU 2012a). Significant increases began in 1999, when reported refugee numbers doubled from the previous year to 148, and numbers increased yearly thereafter. By 2002, there were over 1,000 North Koreans arriving in South Korea each year and by 2006, that number increased to over 2,000 (ROK MOU 2012a). Yet during this time, the border between China and North Korea became much "less porous" and, as a result, both states enacted measures to tighten security along the Sino-DPRK border (Lankov 2009, 64). The number of DPRK refugees living in China dropped significantly, decreasing from an estimated 100,000 individuals during the 1990s (Foster-Carter 2001, 4) to between 5,000 and 10,000 in 2009 (Haggard and Noland 2011a, 2 quoting figures from Robinson 2010). Scholars attributed this change to improved living conditions (food availability) in North Korea and increased border security (Lankov 2009, 64). This data on refugees indicate that North Koreans seeking temporary solutions to difficult circumstances in the DPRK (by relocating across the border to China) may have returned as conditions improved. Those who chose to permanently leave the DPRK are possibly reflected in the numbers of refugees who left the DPRK for other countries, including South Korea.[5]

North Korea's food availability and the DPRK's ability to feed its population also increased during this period. Improved harvests in both 2011 and 2012 narrowed the food gaps significantly and a "consistent food assistance pipeline" (probably from China)[6] helped reduce malnutrition rates (UN WFP 2012, 4). Yet North Korea's overall situation, despite its gains, remained dire. North Korea was the only industrialized society in history to accomplish "such a fateful retrogression" in its decline from a state with a relatively modern economy to one that relied heavily on the international community to feed its people (Eberstadt 2011, 5). North Korea remained subject to "exogenous shocks in the form of both weather and rising world prices" because of the Kim regime's inability and unwillingness to change its agricultural and governmental systems to function more efficiently (Haggard and Noland 2009, 385). Yet, despite these domestic challenges, the Kim regime again survived yet another significant food crisis, actually made progress (at least to external observers) towards its historic goal of juche, and reduced dependence on other states. The Kim regime remained intact and the case study analysis found no relationship between social instability and heightened HFP activities.

Were UN Security Council resolutions against the DPRK associated with increased HFP?

United Nations sanctions were related to hostile foreign policy activities, and significant increases in the level of HFP actions by the Kim Jong-il regime were often associated with UN Security Council activities. For example, North Korea's April 2009 Taepodong-2 test prompted UN Security Council condemnation and the DPRK's nuclear test resulted in its passage of Resolution 1874, intended to impose stricter sanctions on the Kim regime's missile and nuclear programs (Kimball 2012). This resolution was expected to be more comprehensive than those enacted in 2006 and provided for financial sanctions on any DPRK trade associated with its weapons programs (Nikitin 2010, 2). In 2006, the United Nations Security Council passed two resolutions (1695 and 1718) condemning North Korea's ballistic missile activities and nuclear test (UNSCR 2006a; 2006b). These sanctions were primarily focused on North Korea's trade in military and luxury goods and intended to punish both the Kim regime and its defense sector. Yet Noland (2008, 9) found that there was no evidence that these UN sanctions had any effect on the DPRK's luxury goods trade with China (its biggest trading partner) or on North Korea's overall trade. Indeed most observers contend that PRC participation and enforcement was required for any meaningful sanctions against the Kim regime (Lee and Choi 2009, 57). Thus, China's lack of enforcement of the 2006 sanctions limited their overall effectiveness (CRS 2010, 2). Additionally, rather than punishing the North Koreans, sanctions often have unintended domestic consequences and have been used by the Kim regime to fuel national sentiment as "propaganda tools" to support its grip on power (Nanto and Chanlett-Avery 2010,

14). Again, the effectiveness of these sanctions hinged on the participation of China, which continued to seek a role in negotiation and mediation, rather than active enforcement of the Security Council resolutions (Haggard and Noland 2011b, 64).

As with other high-profile hostile foreign policy actions by North Korea, this event began an oft-seen cycle of actions and reactions from the international community and North Korea. The United Nations Security Council condemned the Taepodong-2 launch as a violation of Resolution 1718 and stated that it would pursue a tightening of sanctions (UN 2009a). North Korea reacted by declaring that there "was no need for the six party talks anymore," expelling UN nuclear dismantlement inspectors, and stating that the DPRK would resume its nuclear program (Landler 2009; UN 2009b; KCNA 2009e). North Korea originally agreed in September 2005 to abandon "all nuclear weapons and existing nuclear programs," although with no agreement on the implementation date (Kahn and Sanger 2005). During the Six Party Talks in October 2007, North Korea agreed to begin physical dismantlement of its nuclear facilities (Cooper 2007). In April 2009, after disagreements over verification methods and the provision of aid, the DPRK announced it was expelling UN inspectors and restarting its nuclear program (Landler 2009). The KCNA stated that the UN Security Council's condemnation and "challenging even the satellite launch for peaceful purposes, compels the DPRK to further increase its nuclear deterrent" (KCNA 2009e). Three days after the UN Security Council Resolution passed, North Korea staged a 100,000-person rally in Pyongyang to denounce the UN action (KCNA 2009a). During the protest, North Korean officials stated that the Korean People's Army was "technically at war with the U.S." and that it would "promptly exercise the right to preemptive strike to beat back the enemies' slightest provocation" (KCNA 2009a).

United Nations Security Council Resolution 1874 provided additional means to enforce previous sanctions. This resolution included restrictions on "all arms-related trade and all training or assistance related to it" (UNSCR 2009; Haggard and Noland 2010, 562–563). North Korea responded to these sanctions by stating, "It has become an absolutely impossible option for the DPRK to even think about giving up its nuclear weapons…. Any attempted blockade of any kind will be regarded as an act of war" (KCNA 2009m). In June 2009, the Kim regime also sentenced two American journalists (apprehended two months earlier on the Sino-DPRK border while doing research for a documentary) to 12 years in prison and launched a number of short and medium-range test missiles in early July; both actions were most likely intended to pressure the United States (Oh and Hassig 2010, 92–93). Former U.S. President Bill Clinton visited Pyongyang in August 2009 to secure the journalists' release after their five month detention (Chanlett-Avery 2013, 8). North Korea's press stated that

> Clinton expressed words of sincere apology to Kim Jong Il for the hostile acts committed by the two American journalists against the DPRK after illegally intruding into it. Clinton courteously conveyed to Kim Jong Il an earnest request of the U.S. government to leniently pardon them and send them back home from a humanitarian point of view [KCNA 2009i].

After their release, the U.S. journalists stated that they entered the DPRK "for less than a minute," returned across the border, and then were arrested by DPRK guards in China and taken to North Korea (Kirk 2009).

These sanctions did little to change North Korea's military behavior, as demonstrated by high-profile military engagements against South Korea (*Cheonan* and artillery attacks) and countless other hostile foreign policy actions during this period (Hom and Thompson 2010; Klinger 2010). While the international community considered economic sanctions as a means to punish the North Koreans, these did little to inhibit their tendency to engage in high profile actions aimed at the "enemies" of the DPRK regime. Thus while the sanctions had limited effects, there were potential links between UN resolutions and increased levels of DPRK hostile actions.

Were ROK leadership changes associated with increased North Korean hostile foreign policy activities?

During the South Korean presidential election in 2007 and assumption of office in 2008, there were relatively low levels of DPRK hostilities—most were related to political rhetoric, rather than significant HFP actions. South Korea's election of conservative Lee Myung Bak as president ushered in a new, more conflict-ridden period for both North and South Korea.

As it had during previous elections, North Korea voiced its preferences for liberal rather than conservative South Korean presidential candidates during the months preceding the 2007 ROK elections (Lee 1992; Breen 1992; KCNA 2007a; KCNA 2007b). Kim Jong-il's hosting of South Korea's President Roh in the second-ever inter-Korean summit in early October 2007 demonstrated that the DPRK regime most likely preferred the liberal candidate Chung Dong-young (Sudworth 2007; Snyder 2009, 93–94). Alternatively, the North Korean regime made negative public references to Lee and commented that his conservative Grand National Party was a "pro–U.S. flunkeyist traitor party which is selling off the nation" (KCNA 2007a). Yet North Korean hostile foreign policy actions from September through December 2007 were limited to political statements and rhetoric, rather than military activities (UNC 2012). There were a number of specifically targeted statements in the North Korean press against the third candidate, ultra-conservative independent Lee Hoi-chang, who entered the race in November (one month before elections) and advocated both denuclearization and regime change for the DPRK (Onishi 2007; KCNA 2007b; KCNA 2007c).

Lee Myung-bak won the 2007 election with 48.6 percent of the vote versus liberal candidate Chung Dong-young's 26.2 percent (independent candidate Lee Hoi Chang received 15 percent). This was the largest margin of victory in recent history (Herman 2007). Lee's election spelled the end of the "Sunshine Policy" as he immediately proposed to abolish South Korea's Ministry of Unification while declaring that reinvigorating the ROK–U.S. alliance was his top policy goal (Choe 2008; Snyder 2009, 87).[7] Immediately after Lee's assumption of office, North Korea began to engage in a series of provocative actions. These began with missile launches in late March 2008 and included a series of events (generally at least one event involving the DPRK military every one to two months) through the end of 2010 (UNC 2012; KINU 2011). Thus while the election period itself was not associated with heightened levels of North Korean activity, Lee's election as president occurred at the beginning of a period of increased tensions on the peninsula.

Were U.S. leadership changes associated with increased North Korean hostile foreign policy activities?

No direct connection was found between the 2008 U.S. presidential election and DPRK hostile foreign policy actions. This election occurred at a time when the U.S. was involved in two long-term overseas conflicts (Iraq and Afghanistan). Although much of the U.S. public's attention was focused on domestic issues (especially the economy), the candidates had clear and substantially different positions on how to deal with the DPRK. The Republican Party's candidate, John McCain (a Vietnam War veteran), was reportedly dissatisfied with the Bush administration's policies towards North Korea. Aside from demanding a complete and verified dismantlement of North Korea's nuclear program, McCain also wanted to purse "human rights, illegal and illicit activities, economic and political reform, proliferation, and reduction of the conventional military threat from North Korea" (Cheon 2008; USAPC 2008; Shorts and Min 2008, 32–36).

The challenger, first-term Senator Barack Obama, advocated direct talks with North Korea along with participation in multilateral negotiations, such as the Six Party Talks, as a means to convince the DPRK to abandon its nuclear program. Obama stated that he would be willing to meet directly and unconditionally with the leaders of Iran, Syria, Venezuela, Cuba, and North Korea to improve relations with those states (USAPC 2008; Olsen 2008; Phillips 2008). Given the choice of the two candidates, it seems likely that North Korea favored Obama and his pledge to conduct open dialogue with the DPRK. This supported Kim Jong-il's previous contention that bilateral negotiations (between the DPRK and U.S.) were the only way to move forward on the nuclear issue (Shorts and Min 2008, 32; Powell 2009). McCain's hawkish policies potentially would complicate the Kim regime's negotiations by subjecting North Korea's government to international scrutiny and multilateral diplomacy (USAPC 2008). Yet, despite the characteristics of both U.S. presidential candidates, the DPRK refrained from any significant public statements of support or denouncement of either Obama or McCain (KCNAWatch 2013).

North Korea's hostile foreign policy actions during 2008 (through the November elections) were generally lower than in previous years and dominated by diplomatic pronouncements criticizing the U.S. or ROK governments (KINU 2011; UNC 2012). The most significant DPRK activities during this time included the killing of a South Korean tourist by a North Korean soldier (resulting in the closing of the Mount Kumgang tourist resort) and coastal short range missile tests in March, May and October (UNC 2012; KINU 2011; BBC 2011b). Also during this time, North Korea successfully negotiated for 500,000 tons in heavy fuel oil shipments and 500,000 tons of food aid in exchange for continued dismantling of its nuclear program (which began in 2007) and participation in the Six Party Talks (Manyin and Nikitin 2010, 5–8; Niksch 2010, 7). Along with this aid, the U.S. made two symbolic concessions to the DPRK in efforts to spur continued negotiations: the Bush administration removed North Korea from the "Trading with the Enemy Act" (allowing for the lifting of some sanctions) and delisted the DPRK from the "State Sponsors of Terrorism" designation (Niksch 2010, 8). Cheon (2008) notes that these actions seemed to be more congruent with then-candidate Obama's policy line of directly engaging "rogue regimes" than Republican candidate McCain's more hard line approach to North Korean issues. Hence, during this time the North Koreans had significant incentives to limit conduct of aggressive foreign policy actions in order to sustain the external aid provided by the Six Party Talk participants.

After Barack Obama's election win in November 2008, the DPRK issued no public statements on the results (Nagourney 2010; KCNAWatch 2013). The KCNA did acknowledge Obama's inauguration in January 2009 by noting, "Barack Obama took office as the 44th president of the United States on Jan. 20" with no accompanying rhetoric (KCNA 2009l). In March 2009, just two months after Obama was sworn in as U.S. president, negotiations with North Korea broke down. By May 2009, the DPRK launched a long range rocket (the Taepodong-2), restarted its nuclear program and conducted its second nuclear weapons test (Manyin and Nikitin 2010, 7; Choe 2009b; Kimball 2012). While the incidence of DPRK hostile foreign policy decreased significantly during the months prior to the election of Barack Obama, this hiatus did not last. The following year, hostility levels of Kim regime foreign policy actions rose to levels not seen since the late 1960s.

Did ROK/U.S. strategic-level military exercises correspond with increased hostile foreign policy activities?

During the case study period, tactical- to strategic-level military exercises continued on both sides of the DMZ and annual joint ROK–U.S. exercises seemed to cause heightened levels of DPRK denouncements. Additionally, there were linkages between other types of conflict and ROK–U.S. exercise periods. Between 2008 and 2011, ROK and U.S. military forces conducted at least five strategic-operational (and countless lower level military) exercises intended to both increase readiness and act as a visible deterrent to DPRK provocative actions (D'Orazio 2012, 276–277; author analysis). For example, the large-scale exercises listed in Table 4.1 occurred routinely during the case study period:

Table 4.1 U.S.–ROK Military Exercises (2008–2011)

Exercise	Month	Type	Purpose	Sources
Key Resolve	March (annual)	Command post	Designed to "repel assault from North Korea."	Halloran 2011, 74
Foal Eagle	March (annual)	Field training exercise	Focused on "operational plans in case of an all-out war on the Korean Peninsula"	Halloran 2011, 74; Chosun Ilbo 2010a
Invincible Spirit[8]	July 2010	Maritime and air readiness	Exercise was "in response to the sinking of the South Korean warship *Cheonan* and intended to send a strong message to Pyongyang to stop 'provocative and warlike acts'"	Halloran 2011, 75; CNN 2010a
Ulchi Freedom Guardian	August (annual)	Command post	Conducted "to ensure that our Alliance is prepared to respond to threats across the spectrum of conflict, including North Korean provocations."	USFK PAO 2010; Ham 2010
Unnamed	November 2010	Maritime readiness	Exercise was "meant as a warning to North Korea for recent provocations, including last week's deadly artillery attack on an island populated by South Koreans in the Yellow Sea."	Fackler 2010

These exercises provoked hostile statements from the North Koreans, such as a published DPRK response to the INVINCIBLE SPIRIT event (in July

2010) stating that it would respond with a "powerful nuclear deterrence" (Harlan 2010; KCNA 2010a). The U.S. and South Korea conducted INVINCIBLE SPIRIT in reaction to the North Korean sinking of a ROK naval vessel (the *Cheonan*) in March 2010 (ROK MND 2010, 220; Halloran 2011, 75; CNN 2010a). A similar exercise occurred in November 2010 after the Yeonpyeong Island shelling (Fackler 2010). Thus, while DPRK hostile foreign policy actions often occur in response to ROK–U.S. military exercises, in these two cases an ROK–U.S. "show of force" exercise was conducted as a direct result of a specific DPRK hostile action. In these instances, a DPRK military action initiated an ROK–U.S. response, but in other cases, exercises conducted by the ROK and its allies were accompanied by changes in the levels of HFP by North Korea.

Figure 4.2 DPRK Conflict Level and ROK–U.S. Military Exercises

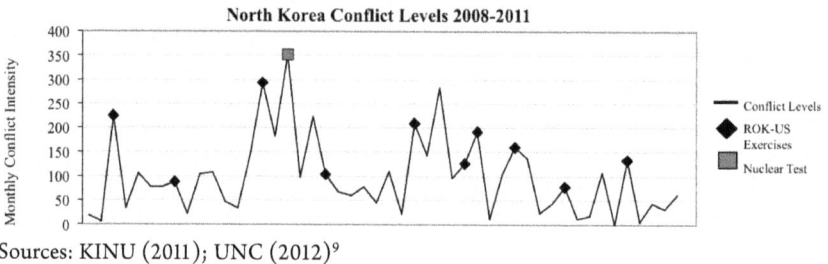

Sources: KINU (2011); UNC (2012)[9]

As shown in Figure 4.2, there is a correlation between the levels of hostility and military exercises, at least during the KEY RESOLVE—FOAL EAGLE (KR-FE) exercises (denoted by black diamonds) each March from 2008 to 2010. Additionally, significant hostile foreign policy actions occurred in August 2010, around the same time as ULCHI FREEDOM GUARDIAN (UFG), and during the Yellow Sea naval exercise in November 2010. After that point, activities decreased steadily. Concurrently, there were comparatively lower levels of activities during UFG exercises in 2008, 2009, and 2011 and during the KR-FE exercise in 2011. Yet, the evidence that at least some of the exercises coincided with heightened levels of DPRK activity does contrast with other views of DPRK military activity. For example, D'Orazio's (2012, 291) quantitative examination of military exercises from 1998–2010 found that North Korea's "response to US and South Korea joint exercises is not unique and not systematically different from regular DPRK activity." Thus, while there was a correlation between heightened levels of HFP activities and ROK–U.S. exercises, it was not consistent throughout the case study period.

4. Regime Succession and Case Comparisons 133

WAS THE PRESENCE OF A CONSERVATIVE ROK GOVERNMENT ASSOCIATED WITH INCREASED HFP?

Conservative Lee Myung-bak was the ROK president throughout the case study and his political orientation most likely contributed to increased HFP action by the DPRK. Although relations between the Koreas had historically been tenuous, the Kim Dae-jung administration (1998–2003) pursued a policy of engagement with the DPRK, culminating in the 2000 North-South Summit (ICG 2010, 8). The subsequent Roh Myoo-hung administration (2003–2008) continued to follow his predecessor's "Sunshine Policy" of cooperation and reconciliation with the DPRK (Kim, D. 1998; Kim C. 2005, 12). During his election campaign, Roh often criticized the U.S. and increased "'anti–American' sentiment (intentionally or otherwise) in an apparent effort to appeal to young Korean voters who want a more 'equal' relationship with the United States" (Levin 2004, 21). During Roh's tenure, the South Korean administration altered its relationship (at least at the national level) with the U.S. and pursued a more independent foreign policy with the DPRK. This policy was a continuation of Kim Dae-jung's efforts based on the concept of "peace and prosperity" towards North Korea and reflected rising anti–American sentiment in South Korea at the time (Zhu 2007, 75). This change in attitude was strongest among the younger Koreans, who increasingly viewed the U.S. as a major impediment to ROK–DPRK reconciliation. Incidents involving U.S. servicemembers stationed in South Korea, criticism of U.S. operations in Iraq, fewer concerns over attacks by the DPRK military, and U.S. inaction over legacy disagreements between Japan and South Korea all served to influence increasingly negative views of the United States policy towards North Korea (Zhu 2007, 75–76).

In November 2004, Roh criticized the Bush administration's pressure on the DPRK to give up its nuclear ambitions and defended "North Korea's assertion that it needed a 'nuclear deterrent' in view of its perception of a threat from the United States" (Niksch 2005, 1). Although both the U.S. and South Korea focused on the Six Party Talks as a venue to diplomatically address North Korea's nuclear program, the South seemed less concerned with North Korea's 2006 test than the U.S. In fact, South Korea seemed more worried with U.S. reactions to the nuclear test, than with the DPRK's emerging nuclear capability. The South Koreans feared that after North Korea's nuclear test, the U.S. might take military action—in fact, during a phone call with U.S. President Bush on addressing the test in the UN Security Council, Roh "rapidly read talking points about how the United States should not provoke a war in Korea" (Cha 2012, 268). The Roh administration focused on avoiding military conflict with the DPRK through an emphasis on economic relations "as a means to forestall the North's collapse and to support its economic reform" (Snyder 2007, 36–37). This emphasis on economic cooperation with North Korea despite its hostile actions contrasted with South Korean conservative Lee Myung-bak, elected to succeed Roh in 2007.

Lee's policies were exactly as the North feared: one of his first acts was to end "unconditional aid" to the DPRK and require progress on the nuclear issue as a prerequisite to economic aid cooperation with the Kim regime (Haggard and Noland 2010, 558). North Korea's reaction was to condemn Lee publicly (the first direct criticism of a South Korean leader since 2000) by stating that the "Lee regime will be held fully accountable for the irrevocable catastrophic consequences to be entailed by the freezing of the inter-Korean relations" (Foster-Carter 2008; KCNA 2008a).

In fact, many in South Korea blamed Lee's policies for antagonizing North Korea to take actions such as the sinking of the *Cheonan* (Klinger 2011). On the other hand, the Lee administration was also criticized for its seemingly tepid responses to the killing of a South Korean tourist (South Korea suspended tours to the resort and banned civilian groups from visiting the DPRK) and the *Cheonan* sinking. South Korea's responses were non-military and were described as "mild measures like reducing the South's already minuscule trade with the North" (Fackler 2010). In any case, from 2008 to 2011, the Lee administration was much less willing to negotiate with the Kim regime. This complicated DPRK efforts to gain additional humanitarian aid from the South, which (along with the United States) had provided the majority of assistance to the DPRK prior to Lee's election (Manyin 2010, 20–21). While the Lee administration sometimes interfered with North Korea's efforts to obtain international aid and continue its intra-Korean cooperative business ventures,[10] a "hostile" administration in the South did ultimately provide additional support to the Kim regime's domestic propaganda efforts. North Korea routinely referred to the Lee administration as the "puppet regime" and branded the South Korean president "Traitor Lee" and "the puppet prime minister" (KCNA 2009b; 2011b). Thus while the Lee administration made North Korea's efforts to obtain international aid more difficult, it did help sustain the Kim regime's ability to divert public attention by reminding the public that North Korea was constantly being threatened by both the Lee "puppet government" and U.S. "imperialist forces" (KCNA 2011c). Thus, the presence of Lee's conservative government was most likely related to increases in North Korea's HFP activities during the case study period.

Summary and Case Study Conclusions

On 19 December 2011, North Korean media announced that Kim Jong-il died of "great mental and physical strain … on a train during a field guidance tour" and that a medical exam confirmed it was a heart attack (KCNA 2011d; 2011e). There was speculation over the actual circumstances of Kim's death. South Korean intelligence sources note that the train Kim reportedly died on while travelling never left Pyongyang, leading to rumors that the North Korean leader had been "killed as a result of power struggles" (Straits Times 2011; Parry 2011). Whether or not this was true is difficult (if not impossible) to verify. United States and South Korean intelligence organizations apparently knew nothing about the elder Kim's death until it was acknowledged by the KCNA (Landler and Choe 2011). This was a stark reminder of the "secretive nature of North Korea, a country not only at odds with most of the world but also sealed off from it in a way that defies spies or satellites" (Landler and Choe 2011). While this event did catch the entire world by surprise, North Korea showed no signs of instability or pending collapse as a result (ITAR 2011). By all accounts, the North Koreans began a period of public mourning that was not accompanied by any detectable moves by factions to seize control of the government, mass defections, or any other sign of internal distress (JEN 2011).

North Korean media announcements not only mourned the death of their "Dear Leader," but also noted public and military allegiance to Kim Jong-un (KCNA 2011f). For example, on the same day Kim Jong-il's death was announced, the KCNA (2011g) noted, "Our army and people will struggle staunchly for an ultimate victory true to the leadership of Kim Jong-un." The younger Kim was declared "Supreme Leader" and head of both North Korea's military and the Korean Worker's Party; by the end of December 2011, Kim Jong-un formally became the leader of the DPRK (Choe 2011a; KCNA 2011h).

The Kim regimes continued to pursue hostile actions regardless of the international consequences, despite challenging domestic conditions. While there were collateral benefits to the development and testing of nuclear technology (such as regional security posturing), these types of hostile foreign policy actions seem to have also been targeting North Korea's domestic audience. The Kim Jong-il regime took a significant risk during its most provocative actions: both of the direct attacks against South Korea could have potentially escalated into a sustained conflict. Additionally, the testing of both nuclear devices and potential delivery systems (missiles) was not only alarming to South Korea, but of significant concern to the entire international community. Surprisingly (although probably not to the DPRK), the external reactions from the ROK, U.S. and other states to these events were muted and demonstrated the unique and threatening security position North Korea holds in the international order. Table 4.2 summarizes and analyzes these findings on North Korea's actions as it navigated the succession process.

Table 4.2 Structured Analysis Results: Regime Succession (2008–2011)

Category	Question	Test Result	Details
Dependent Variable (HFP)	1. What was the level of hostile foreign policy during the case study?	Higher	Conflict scores averaged 1,188 per year and were higher than historic norms.[11]
Internal Conditions (Independent Variables)	2. Was political instability associated with heightened HFP activities?	No	Instability occurred, but there were no direct links to HFP during this period.
	3. Were economic difficulties associated with increased HFP?	Yes	The DPRK conducted at least one significant event in conjunction with economic difficulties.[12]
	4. Was social instability associated with periods of increased HFP?	No	Although social instability was present in this case, no links with HFP were found.
External Conditions (Independent Variables)	5. Were UN Security Council resolutions against the DPRK associated with increased HFP?	Yes	HFP activities occurred in reaction to UN resolutions.
	6. Were ROK leadership changes associated with increased HFP actions?	No	The DPRK increased rhetoric but not significant HFP actions.
	7. Were U.S. leadership changes associated with increased HFP actions?	No	The DPRK refrained from commenting on the campaign.
	8. Were ROK/U.S. strategic-level military exercises associated with DPRK hostile actions?	Yes	There were changes, although inconsistent, in DPRK activities in conjunction with strategic exercises.
	9. Was the presence of a conservative ROK government associated with increased HFP?	Yes	Conflict levels increased with the arrival of a new ROK conservative government.

As shown above, there is a potential link support in the linkage between North Korea's economic conditions and external hostility behavior, at least in the case of its sinking of the *Cheonan*, although not without qualification. This event occurred at the same time as a significant economic crisis (currency reform), but the DPRK did not acknowledge the act. Thus, the event was only potentially linked to DPRK economic conditions. The external influence argument finds support in the relationships between UN resolutions and conflict in that heightened levels of HFP, such as missile firings and intense rhetoric, were present in the weeks following the UN Security Council declarations. Additionally, strategic-level exercises were also associated with changes in HFP levels, although on a varied basis. Finally, the explanation that DPRK conflict is simply the result of an ROK conservative administration in power is supported: the arrival of South Korea's Lee Myung-bak coincided with increases in HFP activities.

The Kim regime potentially used hostile foreign policy events (such as the nuclear and missile tests and Yellow Sea incidents) as means to coalesce domestic support around Kim Jong-il's appointed successor. While the actions also served to enable other policy objectives, such as obtaining enhanced bargaining positions with the ROK and United States, there is a clear linkage between these actions and the rise of Kim Jong-un. These actions also enabled the regime to retain its grip on power and again demonstrated that North Korea could endure pressure from the international community to change its behavior. Internal collapse had been predicted repeatedly yet it never occurred, at least to outside observers. In fact, Cumings (2011, 54) argues that North Korea had already experienced a societal "collapse" during the 1990s as a result of the loss of external communist support and famine, yet this did not result in the "collapse of state power" which often has occurred in other states. The succession between Kim Jong-il and his son, Kim Jong-un, was another perceived crisis.

Another source of domestic stress for the North Korean government was both the declining health of its leader and how to manage a second "dynastic succession." North Korea followed a compressed version of its first succession in the introduction and installation of Kim Jong-un (Ahn 2011, 27). By all external indications, aside from "administrative" shuffling (or purges) of some individuals, Kim Jong-un rose to power in North Korea with few difficulties (Kim, J. 2011, 15; ITAR 2011). The hostile foreign policy events during this period (especially the Yellow Sea incidents and nuclear test) accompanied succession efforts and helped solidify Kim Jong-un as the unquestioned successor in the minds of the DPRK public, military and elite class (Kim B. 2011; Foster-Carter 2012, 12). Thus, this case study provides some support to diversionary theory and more substantial support to the idea that North Korea is influenced by external conditions. Alternatively, it does show that diversionary behavior was a policy tool used by the Kim regime to contend with the conditions it faced.

Figure 4.3 Timeline: The Succession

North Korean Events		ROK–U.S. Events
Food security improves Kim Jong-il's health declines	2008	Lee Myung-bak elected ROK President Barack Obama elected U.S. President
Kim Jong-un chosen as KJI's successor Taepodong-2 missile test DPRK conducts second nuclear test North Korea attempts currency reform	2009	UN Security Council Resolution 1874 passed
ROK *Cheonan* naval vessel sunk Severe flooding decreases harvest levels ROK-held island shelled by DPRK	2010	Large-scale naval exercises in response to *Cheonan* sinking
Death of Kim Jong-il Kim Jong-un becomes DPRK leader	2011	Additional large-scale naval exercises in response to *Cheonan* sinking and DPRK shelling

Case Study Comparisons

These case studies provide valuable insight into the relationships between the conditions North Korea faces and its use of hostile foreign policy. These cases show that the critical periods of North Korea's development and its conflict activities had a significant impact on both regional and international systems. In the 1960s, North Korea emerged as a viable communist state that demonstrated its willingness to use military force to achieve national goals. This contrasted with the DPRK's famine in the 1990s, which left the Kim regime dependent on international aid for survival. Finally, over a decade later, the second familial leadership succession and nuclear program heralded a new phase of insecurity for both East Asia and the international community. These cases also show North Korea's progression from a lesser communist state to a nuclear-capable nation that is concurrently dependent on international aid for survival. Yet throughout its history, the DPRK never hesitated to engage in intense levels of conflict with South Korea or the U.S. to achieve its national goals. The following chart provides a comparison of the intensity levels of North Korea's hostile foreign policy throughout the study period.

The conflict levels during the late 1960s (and the first case study) are at levels higher than at any other time between 1960 and 2011 (66 percent higher than historical norms). This period includes direct attacks against South Korea and the U.S. (such as the Blue House attack, the USS *Pueblo* seizure, and the EC-121 downing) and almost daily clashes along the North-South land and maritime borders. Conflict levels varied through the end of the Cold War and were at much lower levels during the 1990s and the famine period (18 percent

4. Regime Succession and Case Comparisons 139

below the study's annual rates). During the 2000s, North Korea's hostility levels increased again, approaching the first case study's levels, and 61 percent higher than historical averages. During the third case study period, the Kim regime pursued a more aggressive foreign policy through its nuclear program, missile tests, and conventional military engagements with South Korea. Yet the historic intensity scores alone do not provide enough information about the relationships argued by the propositions or hypotheses. In Table 4.3 below, a more detailed comparison is provided of the cases in relation to the proposals, hypotheses, and structured analysis.

Figure 4.4 DPRK Hostile Foreign Policy Levels Compared

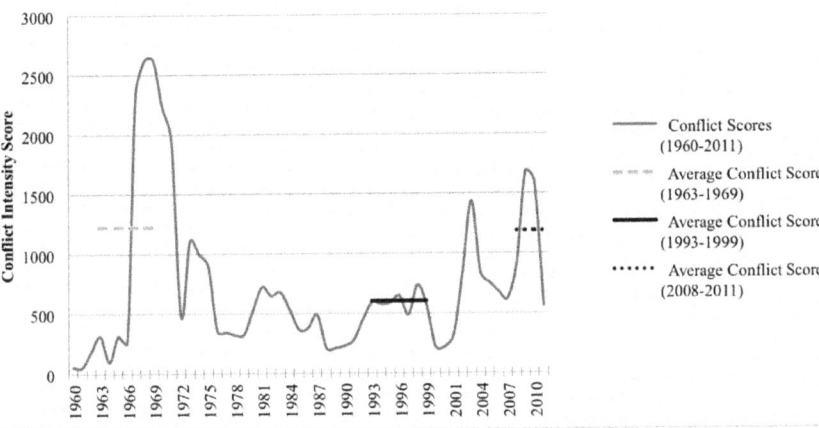

Source: Chapter 5 and the Korean Conflict Dataset (Appendix B)

Table 4.3 Case Study Comparisons

		Case 1 DPRK Emerges	Case 2 Famine	Case 3 Regime Succession
Dependent Variable	Hostile foreign policy level compared to historic norms?[13]	Higher	Lower	Higher
Diversionary Concepts Supported?	Political Instability	No	No	No
	Economic Instability	No	No	Yes
	Social Instability	No	No	No
External Conditions Argument Supported?	UN Resolutions	n/a	No	Yes
	ROK Leadership Changes	Yes	Yes	No
	U.S. Leadership Changes	Yes	No	No
	Strategic Military Exercises	Yes	Yes	Yes
	ROK Administration Type	Yes	No	Yes

The first two cases show relationships that fail to provide support for diversionary theory. In Case 1, relative domestic stability occurred within the DPRK, but there were heightened levels of external conflict that occurred during that period. During Case 2, the domestic distress caused by famine conditions should have (based on diversionary theory) caused heighted levels of conflict. In both cases, the relationship between conflict and domestic difficulties is inadequate to support the argument that diversionary theory explains North Korea's activities.

In Case 3, North Korea experienced significant levels of domestic distress (both from an economic and political perspective). Yet, direct linkages between domestic conditions and conflict were difficult to identify, except for the timing of the sinking of the *Cheonan*, which might have been related to economic conditions. But the heightened levels of HFP during the succession case study period support a potential link between domestic distress and conflict in support of diversionary concepts. In the case studies, the external conditions argument finds varying levels of support, as these were influential and often related to DPRK hostile foreign policy actions in certain instances. The characteristics of the ROK government, to include leadership changes, administration type, and military exercises, are all related to heighted levels of HFP.

At the same time, diversionary-type activities occurred in all three cases. In the 1960s, increased prosperity for North Korea occurred, but HFP behavior was at its highest levels and diversionary-type behavior, associated with Kim's efforts to reunify the Koreas, was present. Almost three decades later, the DPRK experienced significant levels of domestic distress (famine) and the Kim regime responded (albeit at lower levels than the 1960s) with HFP actions to include the development of nuclear technology, ballistic missile advances and testing, clandestine infiltration activities and naval clashes. The DPRK effectively used these events to bolster its negotiating position, obtain needed aid, and distract the public, eventually allowing the Kim regime to weather the crisis. The final case also included significant levels of economic difficulties and concurrently demonstrated that the Kim regime's primary goal is to remain in control of the DPRK. Beginning in 2008, the Kim regime began to acclimatize the DPRK public to the next hereditary succession, punctuated by additional nuclear tests, missile launches, and attacks in the Yellow Sea. These actions appeared to be related to the Kim regime's focus on maintaining sovereignty and power over North Korea's elites, military, and citizens.

Throughout all three cases, the Kim regime continued to use the threat of external actors (the U.S., ROK, and Japan) as a means to maintain an air of constant "wartime readiness." This method of maintaining political stability (control over the DPRK public) through fostering social instability has been a characteristic of all three of the Kim regimes. For example, the Kim Jong-un regime continues to emphasize that North Korea constantly faces war with both the U.S. and South Korea (KCNA 2013a). Yet, diversion was only one method used to respond to domestic conditions, and other techniques, such as suppression, imprisonment, and executions, were used as a response to the challenges experienced by the DPRK (Hassig and Oh 2009, 231; Lim 1993; Cho 1993). North Korea also continued, at least since the 1990s, to reach out to the international community for aid to sustain its economy and feed its people. This "institutionalization of support" has become required for the DPRK to survive as a sovereign state and thus actions, both of concession and hostility, often occur simultaneously. Additionally, foreign aid is potentially an "enabler" of DPRK hostile activities as North Korea might not be able to afford to "maintain such predictably destructive policies and practices" without massive amounts of international support (Eberstadt 2011, 16).

Finally, the Kim Jong-il regime pursued divergent and often conflicting policies in attempts to maintain power. One enduring characteristic was the regime's willingness to use varied foreign policy approaches (from peaceful engagement to armed conflict) to achieve its domestic goals. These foreign policy approaches were influenced by internal conditions, such as economic considerations, as well as the influence of external factors, including ROK election periods and strategic military exercises. Yet in all cases, the Kim regime continued attempts to focus its citizens on conditions outside the regime. The continued presence of a strong ROK–U.S. alliance structure (an external threat) helped to provide a justification for the DPRK to sustain efforts to distract its citizens. These case studies demonstrate that both internal and external considerations influence DPRK conflict behavior (at varying levels) and that diversion was one of many tools used by the regime to remain in power.

CHAPTER 5

Hostile Foreign Policy Event Analysis

Although the previous chapters examined North Korean conflict behavior from a qualitative (case study) perspective, more analysis is necessary to better understand the relationship between HFP actions and conditions faced by the Kim regime. This chapter examines North Korean conflict behavior using quantitative methods and linear regression to provide depth to the overall analysis. In this chapter, regression analysis, the study of relationships between variables, is used to analyze DPRK conflict data between 1960 and 2011. Scholars use regression techniques to examine "the dependence of one variable, the dependent variable, or one or more other variables, the explanatory [independent] variables, with a view to estimating and/or predicting the (population) mean or average value of the former in terms of the known or fixed (in repeated sampling) values of the latter" (Gujarati and Porter 2009, 15).

In this study, a linear regression model (commonly referred to as "AR[1]"), is used to conduct the analysis (more details are available later in the chapter).[1] The following sections provide an overview of the quantitative research design and methodology used for this project, analysis of the collected event data, and summary of the key quantitative findings on North Korean hostile foreign policy activities.

Research Design and Methods

As noted previously, this research uses a mixed-methods approach to examine North Korean conflict activities and this chapter comprises the quantitative analysis portion of this study. Although a multi-disciplined methodological approach (as is used in this study) provides significant advantages in analyzing North Korean activities, few scholars choose this method. Most of the current analytic work involving North Korean conflict is part of larger research projects focused on cross-national time-series studies. Jung's (2012) mixed-method analysis of diversionary theory and the Koreas remains an exception and this project uses some of the same methods to analyze collected data. This approach to the study of conflict provides for a more comprehensive analysis compared to single methodologies, such as social science (deductive) techniques or historical (inductive) methods, to analyze closed states (Levy 1997; Mahoney and Goertz 2006). Specifically, Levy (1989, 284) notes that using both historical and international relations methods to examine the concept of diversionary theory allows for a more complete analysis. Quantitative methods complement the qualitative (case study) analysis in this study and provide a more holistic analysis of DPRK hostile foreign policy activities. To accomplish this, the quantitative research uses time-series event data, which is the examination of specific events (or "event history data") over time (Allison 1984, 9). The output of this research is a longitudinal event data analysis of North Korean hostile foreign policy between 1960 and 2011. This event data is often referred to by other names—for example, the U.S. military often uses the term "spot reports" in reference to many of the hostile foreign policy events included in this study. The collected data includes both the military and diplomatic hostile events and includes information such as the date, intensity (based on Azar's 1993 scale, which is discussed later), and a description of the event.

The quantitative portion of this study examines events beginning in 1960. At that time, tensions were still high between North and South Korea but the South was distracted with its own domestic political chaos. In 1960, South Korea's first regime (led by U.S.-supported Syngman Rhee) came to an abrupt end after massive protests occurred in reaction to rigged national elections. The U.S. (Kennedy) administration's regional foreign policies focused on the instability in South Korea, rather than the threat posed by the DPRK. The Kennedy administration was more concerned about South Korean internal instability because it felt that with current U.S. and ROK forces, a North Korean attack could be repelled as long as China did not participate (Presidential Task Force on Korea 1961). Although U.S. interest in North Korea seemed to be waning, it still maintained over 50,000 troops stationed in South Korea (Kane 2006). In the North, this was a time of prosperity and relative stability for the Kim regime: 1960 signaled the end of post-war recovery efforts, a growing economy[2] and Kim Il-sung firmly in control of the North Korean regime (Lankov 2002, 63–65; Martin 2006, 109). The use of 1960 as a start point for analysis limits the effects of the Korean War on data from both the North and South (as both had mostly recovered at this time) and begins the research timeframe at the start of prosperity for the first Kim regime.

Beginning in the 1960s also allows for the inclusion of renewed conflict between the Koreas. Just a few years later, the DPRK embarked upon a series of high-profile attacks along the DMZ against South Korean and U.S. forces as part of Kim Il-sung's "undeclared war" against South Korea and the U.S. (Bolger 1991).

Using 2011 as the end date for the quantitative analysis allows for some of the most intense North Korean uses of force and hostile foreign policy actions to be included. This year (2011) also signified the end of the second Kim regime led by Kim Jong-il.[3] While tensions varied throughout the entire study period, using this timeframe allows for an accurate examination of conflict events over time. For example, the 2000s were characterized by a series of hostile DPRK foreign policy actions, dominated by militarized activities. These included long range missile firings (in 2006) and nuclear tests (in 2006 and 2009), the sinking of a South Korean naval vessel (the *Cheonan*) and the artillery shelling of a South Korean island (the first such attack since the Korean War) in 2010 (Hom and Thompson 2010; Klinger 2010). Thus examining conflict between the Koreas over a five decade period provides the advantage of including the actions of two North Korean regimes (Kim Il-sung and Kim Jong-il) and the beginnings of a third, led by Kim Jong-un. Additionally, using an expanded timeframe addresses methodological criticisms of short-term studies (Bronson 1997, 11; Levy 1989, 265–266).

Scholars have often used this type of event analysis in conflict research to determine potential relationships between events, trends over time, and other information that might not be apparent in other types of analysis, such as cross-sectional or case study research (Mahoney and Goertz 2006; Levy 1989). In this research, multivariate linear regression is used to test for potential relationships between political, economic and social conditions and North Korean hostile foreign policy activities. In political science terms, hostile foreign policy events (i.e., event data) constitute the dependent variable for the quantitative portion of this research, while domestic conditions and international influences are the independent variables. Kellstadt and Whitten (2009, 7) note that political theories are often conceived in terms of causal relationships between variables, which must be observable and include "any entity that can take on different values" (Trochim 2005). These variables are related to the research question and are the "building blocks" of hypotheses and theories. A theory describes the link between the individual variables and is a "reasoned and precise speculation about the answer to a research question, including a statement about why the proposed answer is correct" (King, Keohane and Verba 1994, 19). Variables are categorized according to their function: the dependent variable is the output of a particular event caused or influenced by a single or a number of independent variables. Additionally, control variables provide alternate explanations for events not associated with the independent variables that might influence the outcome of the research (such as an alternate explanation for the observations).

Control variables must be statistically addressed in this type of examination. This analysis does include one control variable (the influence of the Cold War) which helps to examine the idea that the levels of hostile foreign policy are not explained by either internal or external conditions faced by the Kim regime. In this case, the presence of the Cold War might have influenced the levels of conflict on the Korean peninsula prior to 1992 (rather than the internal or external conditions outlined in the study) and must be accounted for in the quantitative analysis. Finally, a hypothesis attempts to describe the relationship between these variables and to predict future activities. For this study, hypotheses are grouped into two major categories (ideas or "propositions"). The variables are examined in relation to the following propositions:

> **Proposition 1 (P1):** The deterioration of domestic conditions in North Korea is associated with increases in North Korean-initiated hostile foreign policy (this concept supports the diversionary theory argument).
>
> **Proposition 2 (P2):** Increased international tensions are associated with increases in North Korean-initiated hostile foreign policy (this concept focuses on external influences as an explanation for HFP actions).

Based on the two propositions above (P1 and P2), eight hypotheses were developed for testing. Three hypotheses (H1, H2, and H3) focus on internal conditions and problems with DPRK stability as the impetus for foreign policy threats or militarized actions. The first three hypotheses are based on the overarching concept of diversionary theory. For North Korea, diversionary behavior may occur when domestic conditions (identified in H1, H2, and H3) deteriorate to a level that may cause the Kim regime to increase its hostile foreign policy activities. The first three hypotheses, based on internal conditions, follow:

Proposition 1 Hypotheses (internally influenced relationships/diversionary theory):

> **H1 (Hypothesis 1):** The deterioration of **political conditions** in North Korea is potentially related to increased DPRK-initiated hostile foreign policy activities.
>
> **H2:** The deterioration of **economic conditions** in North Korea is potentially related to increased DPRK-initiated hostile foreign policy activities.
>
> **H3:** The deterioration of **social conditions** in the DPRK is potentially related to increased DPRK-initiated hostile foreign policy activities.

The other five hypotheses (H4 through H8) examine the alternative explanation for North Korea's relations with the international community. Specifically, they test the idea that external factors influence the levels of provocative events. The second set of hypotheses represents a more conventional view of DPRK conflict and are based on arguments proposed by the Kim regime itself: the level of conflict on the Korean peninsula is exclusively due to external influences (KCNA 2010a; KCNA 2010f; KCNA 2010g). North Korea's view of why conflict occurs finds theoretical support in the "traditional theorist" view of interstate relations that contends that the international system is the primary cause of international conflict (Waltz 1954; 1979). The second set of hypotheses follows:

Proposition 2 Hypotheses (external influences cause increased hostilities):

> **H4: UN resolutions** enacted involving the DPRK are correlated with increased DPRK-initiated hostile foreign policy activities.
>
> **H5: Leadership changes in the Republic of Korea** are correlated with increased DPRK-initiated hostile foreign policy activities.
>
> **H6: Leadership changes in the United States** are correlated with increased DPRK-initiated hostile foreign policy activities.
>
> **H7: Strategic-level military exercises** by the ROK and US are correlated with increased DPRK-initiated hostile foreign policy activities.
>
> **H8**: The presence of **ROK conservative governments** are correlated with increased DPRK-initiated hostile foreign policy activities.

These hypotheses are tested empirically using quantitative analysis methods that build upon previous work and concepts from other scholars such as Pickering and Kisangani (2005; 2009; 2010), Li (2008), Levy (1989; 2010), and Bueno de Mesquita (2005). To conduct these tests, linear regression analysis is used to explore potential relationships between the independent variables (internal or external DPRK conditions) and the dependent variable (hostile foreign policy activities).

Although using these techniques (propositions, hypotheses and statistical analysis) to examine North Korea might seem complicated, the practice is widely accepted among academics (and most policy analysts). For example, regression analysis is simply the study of the relationship between variables. In this research, regression analysis is used to examine the ability of the conditions faced by the regime (independent variables) to predict the value (occurrence) of the dependent variable (HFP activities). Regression analysis infuses statistics in the analytical techniques of social scientists and provides for a more comprehensive view of DPRK activities. The outputs of these techniques are results designed to make "inferences" or logical conclusions and generalized observations about North Korean conflict behavior.[4] Using regression analysis also complements the qualitative case studies in this research and the outputs support inferences and conclusions about North Korean conflict behavior. The following sections provide definitions and additional details about the variables used in this study.

The Dependent Variable: Hostile Foreign Policy Event Data

Scholars draw upon a variety of methods to measure hostile foreign policy activities and often simply use categories from event data or conflict data research. These efforts have included analysis of the onset of state-level disputes from a simple "conflict/no-conflict" (yes/no) standpoint (rather than scaling individual events) and additional analysis that measures the intensity of the disputes between states. For example, Leeds and Davis (1997) and Crescenzi, Enterline, and Long (2008) use militarized interstate dispute (MIDs) data to analyze dyadic (two-state) conflict and the onset of hostilities. Clark and Reed (2005, 615) advocate an expansion of interstate conflict research beyond the "conflict/no-conflict" typology and examine the propensity of U.S. leaders to use either economic sanctions or force (based on MIDs data) to study hostile foreign policy activities. Other techniques to analyze interstate conflict behavior focus on the examination and scaling of event data. For example, McClelland's (1999) World Event/Interaction Survey (WEIS) database includes over 98,000 interstate events from 1966 to 1978 and 63 descriptive categories ranging from cooperation to conflict. Goldstein (1992) aggregated the WEIS data and scales each category of events for comparison and analysis.

This research relies on similar methods to examine North Korea's event data and uses Edward Azar's (1993) Conflict and Peace Databank (COPDAB) as a technique to measure conflict. The COPDAB examined state-level interactions from 1945–1973 and ranked them using a 15-point cooperation vs. conflict scale (Table 5.1 below). On this scale, cooperative actions rate between one and seven, neutral actions are designated as eight, and conflict is scored from nine to fifteen (Azar et al., 1982, 36; Azar 1993). Azar (1993, 37–38) classifies conflict events into seven weighted categories and his scale provides a method to record the intensity of North Korean hostile foreign policy events. Table 5.1 shows Azar's (1993) entire scale, but only the conflict categories are used for this research on the DPRK. In discussing this research, Long (2011) noted that examining both conflict and cooperation would provide for a more complete analysis of North Korea's diversionary activities. While this observation is useful, the scope of this study is limited to only conflict events.[5]

Table 5.1 Azar's Conflict and Cooperation Scale

Scale Category	Description (See Appendix A for more details)
15	Extensive war acts causing deaths, dislocation, high strategic costs
14	Limited war acts
13	Small scale military acts
12	Political-military hostile actions
11	Diplomatic-economic hostile actions
10	Strong verbal expressions displaying hostility in interaction
9	Mild verbal expressions displaying discord in interaction

Scale Category	Weighted Value	
15	102	
14	65	
13	50	
12	44	Conflict End (used for this research)
11	29	
10	9	
9	6	
8	1	Neutral Point
7	6	
6	10	
5	14	
4	27	Cooperative End
3	31	
2	47	
1	92	

Source: Azar (1993, 37–38).

A number of international relations scholars have successfully used Azar's scaling techniques to examine and analyze event data. For example, Sprecher and DeRouen (2005, 127) examine foreign policy behavior of enduring Middle Eastern rivalries using an area-specific event database (the KEDS or Kansas Events Data System)[6] and Azar's COPDAB coding designations to analyze their dependent variable.[7] For this research on DPRK activity, Azar's COPDAB scaling (but not its database) was found to be the most efficient and the best fit for the analysis of Korea events.[8] In addition, the analysis of North Korean conflict activities required an original database of event data and unique techniques to accommodate the varied data sources. The following sections describe the database used in this portion of the research.

Database Construction

Research on a closed state can be a difficult task and North Korea is no exception. Data from the North Korean government is often either not available or highly suspect—thus any study of the DPRK must incorporate reporting from external sources. Internal surveys and research in North Korea are rare, although some important data was collected by aid organizations during the famine period on the social characteristics of North Korea (Woo-Cumings 2002). Most survey data on North Korea social and political conditions comes from refugees, especially those in China (Haggard and Noland 2011a). Fortunately, detailed information on the dependent variable data (hostile foreign policy events) was available from U.S. and South Korean sources, and from official government pronouncements from North Korea. Much of the data for the other variables was found using "mirror statistics" and relied upon information on DPRK from other states. While data limitations are a concern, one of the overarching goals of this study is to demonstrate a method (regardless of the data) to examine closed states. Despite these shortcomings, the data used in this project is among the best public information available on North Korean activities.

The dependent variable information is referred to in this book as "event data." Event data is typically taken from public sources (newspapers, journals, and broadcasts)—unfortunately, this information is often an "imperfect summary of the events ... [that] varies according to the needs of the reporters rather than the scholarly need for representativeness" (King and Lowe 2003a, 617). This demonstrates the pitfalls of using event data for analysis and the need for multiple sources of information to increase the fidelity of the research. The information used in this study includes event data taken from both government and media reports—which often overlap—in an attempt to ensure accurate recording of key events. Although the government reports and chronologies used in this research often rely on media reporting from U.S., ROK and DPRK sources, much of the information is original and from government sources (Fischer 2007; UNC 2012). The event dataset used for this research relies on the following sources: U.S. government reports (from on and off the peninsula), South Korean Unification Ministry data, and North Korea government reports from the DPRK's official news, the Korea Central News Agency (KCNA). The database is a compilation of events from these sources and approximately 45 percent (1,500 of 3,500 reviewed) of the reports had to be translated from Korean to English. The dataset is enclosed in Appendix B.

Other event data projects rely on automated collection of information, which saves a considerable amount of time and expense, as compared to individual data collection executed by hand (which was done in this project). King and Lowe (2003) have used this technique to construct a database of over 10 million dyadic interstate activities from 1990 to 2004 from press reports, coded into 200 events (using a typology based on the WEIS methodology). While automated methods are useful in other projects focused on large cross-national studies of English media sources, the information in this study of North Korea is both in English and Korean language. Thus the hand coding of events, while painstaking and time-intensive, provided the most appropriate method to systematically categorize this data. Hand coding refers to the analysis and selection of event data by an individual researcher or group of researchers without the aid of automated (computerized) scanning processes. While automated (machine) coding could have been used for some of the data (and would have been much less time-intensive), hand coding was chosen due to language, analysis and duplication concerns. For example, much of the event information was recorded and analyzed in Korean (rather than English) and other events needed additional context (relationship to other events and conditions): both of these conditions required careful attention for accurate coding. Duplicate reports of events also required that each event be carefully screened. As a result, hand coding provided the best "fit" for this analysis.

While the automated data collection technique is generally successful for states with freedom of the press (Rummel 1966; Azar 1978; McClelland 1999; King and Lowe 2003a), strictly using media reporting to analyze state behavior can result in overlooking key events that may have been unreported due to political restraints. This is particularly problematic when examining South and North Korea, due to freedom of press issues. For example, while the lack of press freedom in North Korea is well-known, the era of authoritarian regimes in South Korea (which ended with the election of Kim Young-sam in 1993) included significant limitations on media reports through measures such as the ROK's *Military Secrets Protection Act* (Youm 1994). Youm (1994) notes that critics of this law "claimed that the statute, which proscribed the unauthorized gathering and the intentional and negligent disclosure of military secrets, infringed upon their constitutional rights to free speech and free press."

Thus, the sole use of South Korean press reports to construct an event database on North Korea provides an inadequate representation of hostile foreign policy actions. This research used a mixture of official government reports, media, and other sources to obtain the best available information to construct the database for this work. For this reason, information from multiple sources was compiled and standardized to populate the database used in this study. These techniques were used to construct a database with open-source information available from North Korean, U.S. and ROK government and media sources.

The event data analyses techniques mentioned above provide the basis to analyze North Korea's hostile foreign policy events. These events were categorized and scored using Azar's COPDAB definitions and scaling.[9] Using views of state interaction that expand beyond conflict provides for a more holistic analysis of the influencers of state actions, especially for totalitarian regimes

5. Hostile Foreign Policy Event Analysis

such as North Korea. For this research, a new database was constructed using hand coding of event intensity data between 1960 and 2011.

Primary source information was used to construct the event database used in this analysis. As shown in Appendix B, sources included the USFK Command History Office, the United Nations Command (UNC), and South Korea's Korean Institute for National Unification (KINU). Additionally, this study used CRS information (Fischer 2007) and media reports from the KCNA website, New York Times Historical Archives, and Lexis-Nexis Academic Search. The dataset used for this analysis includes event information from multiple, often overlapping, sources in an attempt to ensure inclusion of all key events. While most of the reports were available in English, the KINU (2012) report from the South Korean government was only available in Korean and required translation. For those reports, the accuracy of the data is limited by the translation method used.[10] All of the events included in the database were hand coded, crosschecked for duplication, and scaled using Azar's (1993) coding system.

Figure 5.1 Event Data Sources

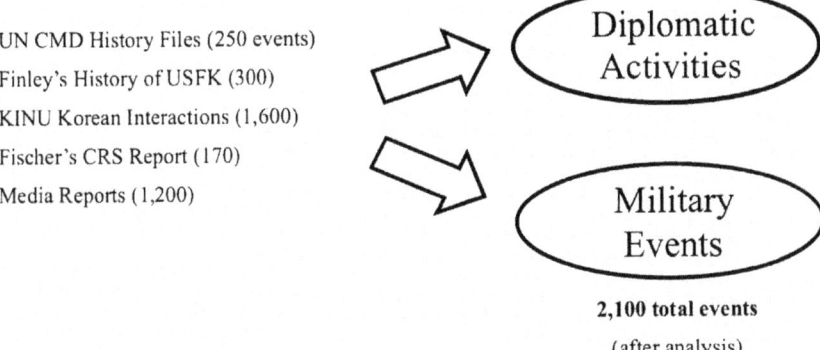

Information on military hostile foreign activity data was obtained from two primary sources: the USFK Command History Office's history of U.S. forces in Korea (which included event data from 1960–1982) (Finley 1984) and historical lists of events provided by the United Nations Command (UNC) in Korea.[11] These two sources provided over 600 diplomatic and military events, all of which were included in the database. The South Korean government's Korean Institute for National Unification (KINU) maintains a database of "Korean Civil Interactions" which includes both hostile and benign interactions between the DPRK and ROK (KINU 2011). This database, available only in Korean, lists over 1,600 events that occurred between 1960 and 2011. Bond (2003) used this information previously to analyze DPRK conflict activity (KINU 2011). Another source was the Congressional Research Service chronology of DPRK "provocations" from 1950–2007 (Fischer 2007). This report summarizes open source and media reports on DPRK activities and includes over 170 events. Finally, keyword searches were conducted for incidents and military/political pronouncements in the New York Times Historical Archive and Lexis-Nexus Academic Search media databases, and the KCNA website resulting in over 1,200 events for use.[12] In the media searches, foreign ministry and military pronouncements were used for the database (rather than all KCNA news reports which criticized the U.S. and ROK) because those announcements represent the highest level of foreign policy communication by the North Korean government. More than 3,500 events were analyzed for relevance and duplication and a database was constructed that included 2,100 incidents of DPRK hostile foreign policy.

After reviewing the data, adjustments were made to account for differences in characteristics of the dependent variable (conflict) data and the independent variables. Specifically, the DVAR was reported as events (with a specific date associated) and the IVARs and control variables were reported in yearly increments—thus the data had to be transformed to allow for statistical analysis. Initially, models were run using monthly, quarterly and yearly aggregation. The models using quarterly data provided the best representation (and best statistical fit) of the data to the research question. Monthly data, although available for the hostility (dependent variable) data, required too much manipulation of the other variables while models using only yearly data provided too few observations (52 total). Thus, using quarterly data provided a suitable "middle solution" that afforded an acceptable number of observations for analysis without causing significant problems with collapsing yearly data into reportable units. King, Keohane and Verba (1994, 221) discuss problems with research involving small numbers of observations. Using quarterly (rather than yearly) data helped address this issue.

As a result, hostile foreign policy events were aggregated by quarter in order to provide enough occurrences to allow for regression analysis and consistency with independent variables. Quarterly aggregation provided the most consistent event data calculations for analysis and provided enough fidelity to identify long-term trends without over-generalizing the data. For each quarter, the total event intensities were summed and annotated. Then quarterly hostile foreign policy events were calculated and scaled using the following equation:

5. Hostile Foreign Policy Event Analysis

$$HI_{qtr} = \sum_{i=1}^{n} S_{E_1}$$

where HI_{qtr} is the quarterly total intensity of hostile foreign policy events, S_{E_1} is the Azar score for the ith event, and n is the total number of events. A simplified example and calculation follows:

Table 5.2 Quarterly Hostile Intensity Scoring

Hostile Event (E_i) in a given quarter:

	Category	Azar Score (S_{E_1})
E1 (Event 1): DMZ firefight	13	50
E2: Kidnapping of ROK citizen	12	44
E3: Mild Diplomatic protest at UN	9	6
E4: Expulsion of Foreign Press	11	29
		HI_{qtr} = 129

Thus, the hostility intensity score for the data in Table 5.2 is 129, which is the product of all of the hostile events that occurred during that quarter (E1 through E4 denote individual events). For each quarter, the intensity level was calculated and included in the statistical analysis to account for the differences in the intensity of the events. The choice to use quarterly data required adjustments because of missing information, due to entire years in which data was not reported. To fill gaps in annual reporting, single imputation using arithmetic mean or the last known values was used. While this is not optimal (original data is always preferred) and possibly induces some bias, this is more desirable than dropping the years with incomplete data (an alternate solution) which would result in the omission of critical observations. While there are more sophisticated methods, such as multiple imputation, available (King et al., 2001), after examining imputation options, the simplest solution and best fit for this data was to simply input data based on arithmetic mean or the last known value.[13] Both the estimated and reported data were included in the analysis.

For the continuous variable data reported on a yearly basis, information was collapsed into quarterly data reports for analysis using interpolation methods. Table 5.3 provides an example of the interpolation techniques used in this analysis:

Table 5.3 Data Adjustments and Quarterly Estimate Examples[14]

Yearly Reports (original)

	2000	2001	2002
GDP Per Person (per year)	$1,500	1,600	1,700

Quarterly Reports (adjusted)

	2000 4th Qtr	2001 1st Qtr	2001 2nd Qtr	2001 3rd Qtr	2001 4th Qtr	2002 1st Qtr	2002 2nd Qtr	2002 3rd Qtr	2002 4th Qtr
GDP	$1,500	1,525	1,550	1,575	1,600	1,625	1,650	1,675	1,700

Note: GDP is interpolated each quarter and yearly data is annotated as the final quarter.

As shown in Table 5.3, yearly reports are assumed to be valid on 31 December—thus the reported data for 2000 was valid in the final quarter of that year. GDP growth for each quarter in 2001 was shown as increasing from $1,525 to $1,600 and interpolated to account for the change between 2001 and 2002. The technique shown above was used for GDP for all of the continuous independent variables except for infant mortality. For that measure, which included reporting that included averages spanning several years (especially during the Cold War period), the data was adjusted based on the reporting years and interpolated to account for increases or decreases in the observation values. Appendix B includes the results of analyzing the database (dubbed the "Korean Conflict Dataset").

Figure 5.2 DPRK Hostile Foreign Policy Activities 1960–2011

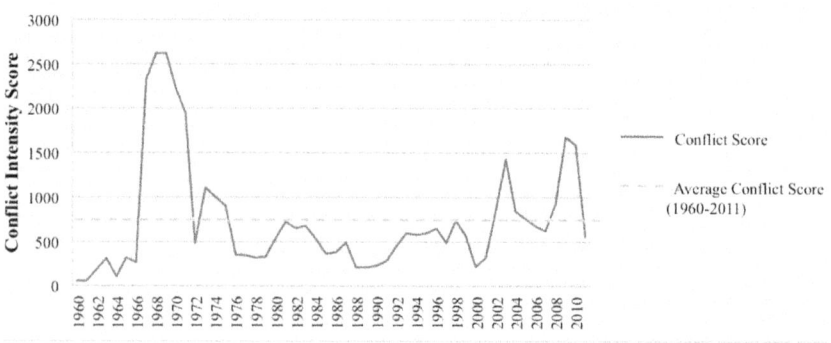

Source: The Korean Conflict Dataset (Appendix B)

The quantitative analysis in this study relies on methods used by the scholars mentioned above as the basis for examining North Korea's hostile foreign policy events. Similar to other research, variables in this study are operationalized using Azar's COPDAB definitions and scaling to account for differences in events.[15] This method was chosen because using expanded views of state interaction and conflict provides a more holistic analysis of how nations behave, especially for totalitarian regimes such as North Korea. For example, a combat engagement along the DMZ (one single event for this study) is not same as a naval clash or a diplomatic threat (also considered single events). Thus, the "intensity" of events is coded to weigh each incident appropriately for analysis following techniques established by Azar (1993).

Figure 5.2 depicts the intensity scores and variation in hostilities for over 2,100 hostile foreign policy events analyzed in this study that occurred between 1960 and 2011. These measures allow for consideration of the proportionality of events. Applying this method to all the events in the database allows for a cursory analysis of the comparative levels of DPRK hostile foreign policy activities during the research period. The following section uses quantitative analysis to identify the relationships between this data and both internal and external conditions faced by the Kim regime.

The Independent Variables: Domestic Conditions and External Influences

As noted above, the independent variables used in this analysis are domestic conditions and external influences.[16] Additionally, methods and measures used in other studies of authoritarian governments are incorporated and variables were chosen based on the characteristics of the DPRK and data availability.[17] Finally, the lack of data on North Korea makes any statistical analysis of DPRK internal activity a challenge; thus proxy (or representative and often indirect) sources are often used to analyze internal conditions.

Domestic Conditions

The first set of independent variables focus on internal conditions faced by the DPRK during the study's timeframe. These include factors that influence domestic stability (political, economic, and social conditions) and their potential relationship to HFP activities using quarterly measures. The following sections include additional details on each of the variables.

Political Stability. Political stability is the relationship between individual actors and societal norms: acts that violate those norms constitute potential evidence of instability (Ake 1975, 273). Political stability also entails "institutional consistency" and characteristics that "self-enforce" political steadiness (Gates et al., 2006, 907). For this study, political stability is measured using two indicators: government stability and national capacity.

The most relevant proxy available for government stability in North Korea is a variable measuring political stability included in Kaufmann's (2009, 2) World Governance Indicators (WGI) project. The WGI project attempts to measure the level of "good" governance using "six dimensions of governance:

Voice and Accountability, Political Stability and Absence of Violence/Terrorism, Government Effectiveness, Regulatory Quality, Rule of Law, and Control of Corruption." This index includes data from 1996 through 2008 for 212 territories and countries. Although the timeframe of the WGI data limits its explanatory capability, this index has the advantage of being one of the only structured measures of political stability applied to North Korea. Kaufmann (2009, 6) combines political stability and the level of state violence (designated as political violence or "PV" in his index) and defines PV as "perceptions of the likelihood that the government will be destabilized or overthrown by unconstitutional or violent means, including politically-motivated violence and terrorism." This variable seeks to measure the DPRK's historic levels of political violence and political instability (Hawk 2003; Kang 2002; Oh and Hassig 2009). The PV score is an aggregated indicator based on a variety of sources such as rankings and surveys from both government and non-government organizations.

The WGI PV index averages from -2.5 (higher chance of instability) to 2.5 (more stable governance) with a score of zero as the mean (Kaufmann et al 2010, 9). The scores rely on data from sources such as the Economist Intelligence Unit Democracy Index, Freedom House, Heritage Foundation Index of Economic Freedom, and a variety of other data surveys (Kaufmann et al., 2010, 29). For North Korea, the score ranges from -0.53 (lower stability) to 0.53 (higher stability) (Kaufmann 2011). The limitation of WGI data is that it is only available from 1996 to 2011, which covers only a portion of the overall time period under consideration (1960 through 2011). However, approximately 1,000 out of the 2,100 total events in the database occur during this period, and this subset is representative of a significant portion of the total event data.

The Composite Indicator of National Capabilities (CINC) index from the Correlates of War (COW) Project measures national demography, industrial capacity, and military characteristics and provides a useful proxy measure for DPRK political stability. Data from this project is available from 1960 through 2008 and includes information on civilian population levels, military personnel, defense expenditures, and usage levels of iron, steel, and energy (CINC 2011). Although this is the first time this dataset has been used as a measure of North Korean political stability, the CINC researchers note that the components of this data "reflect the breadth and depth of the resources that a nation could bring to bear in instances of militarized disputes" (NMC 2005, 3). These same "resources" (or state capacity) allow the DPRK regime to maintain stability, social order, and domestic control over its population. In other words, this research argues that increased North Korean state capacity results in enhanced control over DPRK society and more stability. While this measure is not generally used to determine political stability, it does provide, at least in North Korea's case, an indicator of the Kim regime's ability to remain stable and in power. The DPRK leaders are able to remain in power (and limit political instability) based on these capabilities. Thus CINC scores for the DPRK demonstrate the Kim regime's ability to govern and maintain control over the North Korean people.

Other options were considered for measuring political instability, such as mass and elite unrest, but after careful examination and consultation with other scholars, data for these and other measures of political stability were not found. Many scholars propose that the influencers of social unrest include the level of dissatisfaction that both the elites (privileged members) of society as well as the masses (ordinary citizens) feel towards the ruling government. Kisangani and Pickering (2009, 500) defined elite unrest in terms of "government crises and purges" and mass unrest as characterized by "general strikes, riots, and anti-government demonstrations" in their analyses of the effects of diversionary military activities. Arthur Banks' Cross-National Time-Series (CNTS) Data Archive has reporting on internal instability (including purges, strikes and riots) for many nations and has been used by a number of scholars (Kisangani and Pickering 2005; Bell 2009; Tir 2010). Unfortunately, the CNTS has limited information on DPRK instability and is an inadequate measure for this research. Thus the CINC data on North Korea remains a better option to determine political stability.

During the research period, North Korea's CINC score ranges from 0.0048 to 0.0135 (with a higher score indicating more capability to maintain political control) (CINC 2011). In comparison, the average CINC scores for South Korea between 1960 and 2007 are twice as high as North Korea and U.S. scores are an average of 18 times higher than the DPRK (CINC 2011). For North Korea, rather than simply a measure of "national capacity," CINC scores also provide a useful way to gauge the DPRK's political stability.

Economic Stability. A number of authors use economic stability and related measures to examine the inclination of leaders to pursue diversionary policies (DeRouen 1995; Chapman and Reiter 2004; Pickering and Kisangani 2005; Li, James and Drury 2009). While almost all observers agree that North Korea's economic system has struggled throughout the years, there is much debate on the magnitude and extent of Pyongyang's ability to manage its domestic economy. North Korea declined to publish official statistics for over 30 years (North Korea Country Profile 2005; Eberstadt 2007, 18) and the opaque nature of the DPRK makes economic data gathering more art than science. Statistics on North Korea's trade also remain difficult to obtain, as the DPRK is not a member of the World Trade Organization or International Monetary

Fund and is reluctant to allow access to useful economic data. This study uses proxy sources for trade data from the Correlates of War Database (COW 2012) and CIA (2009; 2010; 2011). Economic analysis organizations, such as the Economist Intelligence Unit (EIU), have attempted to report on North Korea's economy, but are subject to the same limitations of data availability as other research efforts. For example, EIU's "Country Report: North Korea" (2011) provides the following description of a Supreme People's Assembly (SPA) annual meeting:

> As usual, the main formal business at the annual meeting of the SPA was to hear economic and budget reports for 2010, and to approve the budget for 2011. This was as opaque as ever, with a complete absence of hard numbers. All that was given were a few percentages, which even if true cannot be interpreted without a baseline.

The best option for studying North Korea's economic activity is to gather and analyze information from external sources and nations who trade with the DPRK. This concept of "outside-in" (proxy) analysis has its limitations, including the reliance on reporting from other nations and lacks inclusion of illicit or unacknowledged trade. Nevertheless, this method is the most objective technique available to measure North Korea's economy and trade.

For this study, two economic indicators are used: gross domestic product (GDP) per capita and total trade. Gross domestic product refers to the overall domestic output of a nation (goods and services) and is reported on an annual basis. Economists often refer to comparisons between nations of total or per capita GDP to examine national economies and standard of living and this is used to measure the relative economic stability of North Korea. This study uses GDP per person to determine the health of North Korea's economy and whether it expands or contracts over time. A number of GDP sources considered for this research included the World Bank (World dataBank 2012), United Nations (UNdata 2012), Penn World Tables (Heston and Summers 2012), Maddison (2008) and the CIA (2009; 2010; 2011). Of these sources, only the last two adequately covered the study period and provided consistent data. This study used GDP information from Maddison's (2008) GDP database supplemented by data from the CIA (2009; 2010; 2011).

Import and export levels are also used as proxy measures for the performance of the DPRK's economy. In previous studies, Davies (2002) and Eberstadt (1996 and 1998a) used this measure as an indicator of the strength of North Korea's economy. For example, Eberstadt (1998a, 176–179) analyzes the DPRK import and export of capital goods[18] from 1970 to 1995 using "mirrored statistics" from the United Nations and North Korean trade with other nations. Eberstadt (2007, 68) begins by examining the United Nations International

Commodity Trade Database and supplements that information with data from countries that engage in the most trade with North Korea (the USSR/Russia, China, and South Korea). Additionally, Eberstadt (2007, 72–90) compares his data on North Korean trade with another survey, an unpublished dissertation by Soo-Young Choi (1992), and determines that both analyses report similar findings.[19] In the current study, a related approach is used and relies on trade information from the Correlates of War Trade database (COW Trade 2012). Total trade per person is calculated by dividing the sum of total exports and imports by the estimated DPRK population.[20] For the years 2010–2011, CIA (2010; 2011) trade data is used to supplement the COW trade information.

Social Stability. Public dissatisfaction with DPRK society also indicates domestic difficulties and instability. Measuring these indicators is challenging, but the most significant sign that DPRK citizens are discontent with the level of support they receive from the government is the willingness of individuals to flee North Korea. This assumes that a satisfied population is confident in its government's ability to provide for social needs and will have fewer incentives to leave. This measure can provide an important proxy for the social stability of the DPRK. Citizens who choose to leave the DPRK for China or the ROK commit a "drastic act" since they "know all too well that [their] family members remaining behind quite likely would be sent off to political prison camps, perhaps for the rest of their lives..."(Martin 2004, 268). Fleeing North Korea violates the DPRK's criminal code 52 (Betrayal of the Fatherland) which states "Any citizen of the Republic who flees to a foreign country or to the side of an enemy, including the seeking of asylum in a foreign embassy ... shall be subject to the death penalty'" (Demick 2010, 176).

Since the 1990s, the number of North Korean refugees who fled to the ROK has been meticulously documented by South Korea's Ministry of Unification (1996; 2001; 2010). Unfortunately, estimates of North Korean refugees in other countries (i.e., China) are only available through anecdotal information and sources that report sporadic data (Oh 2009; Haggard and Noland 2006; Margesson 2007; ICG 2006; U.S. Government 2005). Thus numbers of North Koreans who flee to the ROK (rather than other states) per year, recorded by the South Korean government, is the most reliable measure available and was chosen for this study. Refugee numbers are adjusted to account for reporting issues, as much of this data was reported in total (rather than yearly) through 1989 (ROK MOU 2012a).[21] Consequently, only refugee data during the post–Cold War period is used and the rate is calculated per 1,000 citizens (both military and civilians) based on ROK and U.S. government population data (U.S. Government 2012).

North Korea's ability to provide for the health of its citizens is another measure of social stability. Other social stability measures used in this study include infant mortality rates (IMR) and food availability per person. Fortunately, data for both of these measures is available throughout the course of this study period. Mortality rates for infants also provide an important measure for the social stability in North Korea. For example, Abouharb and Kimball (2007, 743) comment that infant mortality rates (IMR) can be useful in measuring national "development and indicate the extent to which governments provide for the economic and social welfare of their citizens, both of which are correlates of conflict." Other research studies use IMR to measure characteristics of society including the level of income equality (Kawachi et al., 1997), the effects of governance (Ross 2006), and the relationship between democracy and the availability of healthcare (Lake and Baum, 2001). From the 1960s through the late 1980s, infant mortality rates declined in North Korea. Yet between the end of the Cold War and throughout the famine, rates began to increase (World dataBank 2012; WDI 2012; UN Population 2010).[22]

For this study, IMR is used as an indication of the Kim regime's ability to provide for the welfare of its citizens. Organizations such as the UN, World Bank, and U.S. Census and individual researchers (Abouharb and Kimball 2007) provide several measures of these rates, which indicate the death rates for infants to age one, expressed in deaths per thousand births (UN World Population Estimates 2012). After analyzing several measures, this research found that the UN World Population Estimates (2012) and World Bank World Development Indicators (World databank 2012) were the best options available to reflect North Korea's infant mortality rates. The UN data was used from 1960 to 1991 and the World Bank information was used from 1992 to 2011 to provide complete reporting throughout the dates for the study.

The last proxy measure for social stability is North Korea's ability to provide food for its people. This research assumes that North Korean citizens are more satisfied with the DPRK leadership if adequate food is available (resulting in higher levels of social stability). Thus social instability potentially occurred during the 1990s famine period in which up to a million deaths occurred as a result of food shortages (Haggard and Noland 2007, 1; Hassig and Oh 2009, 116). International aid to North Korea became an important part of the DPRK economy starting in the 1990s. In fact, the U.S. provided a significant amount of the assistance to the DPRK, mostly in the form of energy and food aid. Between 1995 and 2010, the U.S. sent over $1.2 billion in aid (60 percent in food aid and 40 percent heavy fuel oil) to North Korea (Manyin, 2010). Other key donors of food aid include China, South Korea, and Japan (see Figure 3.3). From 1995 through 2008, the UN's World Food Program (and other public and private sources) provided a significant amount of food aid to North Korea.

During that time, China provided 26.9 percent of food aid, South Korea provided 26.5 percent, and the U.S., Japan, and other nations contributed 17.5 percent, 10.7 percent, and 18.4 percent respectively (Manyin 2010, 13; UN World Food Program Food Aid Information System 2011). This research assumes that the DPRK's ability to provide food increases social stability within North Korea's society and thus the availability of food in metric tons per thousand citizens was chosen as a proxy measure.[23]

External Conditions

External conditions form the next independent variable category and often involve international actions or pressure in an effort to change DPRK conflict behavior. Actions that might occur in conjunction with changes in DPRK conflict activity levels such as United Nations resolutions, ROK and U.S. election cycles, the incidence of ROK–U.S. alliance military exercises, and type of South Korean government are considered potential measures. North Korea's reactions to these external conditions range from diplomatic rhetoric to armed conflict actions.

UN Security Council Resolutions. The Kim regimes' activities have historically resulted in responses from the international community—the most notable was UN intervention after the North Korean invasion of the South in 1950. Since the Korean War, the majority of the international responses (with the exception of actions by the ROK–U.S. alliance) were overwhelmingly diplomatic. These responses are often international admonishments in an effort to change the North Korean government's behavior. Economic sanctions were also considered for inclusion as an independent variable, but most of the current sanctions against North Korea (especially those enacted by the U.S.) have been in place since the Korean War (and thus do not provide any variation).[24] Chapman and Reiter (2004, 897) use UN Security Council resolutions as an indicator for external conditions and the international community's tendency to become involved in external crises. This assumes the Kim regimes' tendency to engage in HFP activities is possibly influenced by UN Security Council Resolutions. This idea proposes that the increased international attention given to North Korea because of a new resolution might spur DPRK choices to use diversionary force. United Nations General Assembly actions and resolutions, and economic sanctions do not have similar impacts on the Kim regimes. In this study, Security Council resolutions are recorded as "one" or "zero" (political scientists refer to these as "dummy" variables): time periods (quarters) that include new resolutions are recorded as "one," and those that do not are coded as "zero."

Leadership Changes. U.S. and ROK leadership changes are used to examine possible correlations between events in the ROK and the U.S. and North Korean hostile foreign policies. Several studies exist on the relationship between government decisions to use force and national elections, although they focus primarily on the U.S. (Ostrom and Job 1986; James and Oneal 1991; Meernick 1994). In one of the only available studies of its kind, Davies (2006, 148–149) contends that U.S. elections influenced North Korea's actions during the 1990s resulting in strategic conflict avoidance (SCA),[25] while ROK election cycles had little effect on DPRK actions. Other researchers use election cycles to analyze diversion activity (Kisangani and Pickering 2005 and 2007; Li, James and Drury 2009) lending support to the inclusion of this variable. The DPRK reportedly elevates its propaganda activity during each election cycle in South Korea and has historically been accused of engaging in provocative actions in an effort to influence U.S. and ROK election outcomes (Chosun Ilbo 2010b). Additionally, scholars observe that North Korea possibly takes "into account such events as presidential elections here [ROK] and in the U.S. next year to make the North Korea issue a major variable" (*Korea Joongang Daily* 2011). Nevertheless, these observations are anecdotal and require empirical evidence to determine if statistically significant relationships exist (Enterline 2010, 411–412).

During the study period, South Korean presidential elections have historically occurred every four to seven years, while the U.S. holds elections every four years.[26] ROK and U.S. elections which include changes of leadership are coded quarterly as "one" (based on the election date) while periods without leadership changes are reflected as "zero." Exceptions to this coding are cases of assassination, coup, or other types of non-election leadership changes. For those situations, the specific quarter (as a measure of time) of the leadership change is reflected as "one."

Military Exercises. The impact of ROK–U.S. strategic-level military exercises on DPRK activities is also measured. The U.S. and the ROK conduct joint military exercises aimed at maintaining South Korea's defense capabilities every spring and fall. These include annual events, which range from units in the field to computer-simulated command-post scenarios, including exercises such as KEY RESOLVE, FOAL EAGLE, RSOI (Reception, Staging and Onward Integration), ULCHI FOCUS LENS, ULCHI FREEDOM GUARDIAN, and TEAM SPIRIT. In general, these exercises use North Korea as the adversary pitted against the ROK–U.S. alliance (D'Orazio 2012, 277–279). In fact, the U.S. agreement to cancel TEAM SPIRIT (an annual military training exercise in Korea) was part of the negotiations during the 1993 nuclear crisis (Sigal 1998, 44–51). These types of exercises often cause intense reactions from North Korea. For example, in 2011 North Korea issued the following statement in response to ROK–U.S. military exercises: "The Korean peninsula is faced with the worst crisis ever. An all-out war can be triggered by any accidents" (*Tele-

graph 2011). Unfortunately, limited research is available on the overall relationship between military exercises (conducted by the ROK and U.S.) and North Korean conflict behavior. D'Orazio (2012, 276) remains an exception and he found that joint military exercises "do not trigger a systematic escalation in conflictual rhetoric or behavior" by North Korea in his study of events between 1998 and 2010. Additionally, no published studies of diversionary theory incorporate this factor. This study uses military exercises conducted at the strategic level which employ "instruments of national power in a synchronized and integrated fashion to achieve theater, national, and/or multinational objectives" and operational exercises are those which link the "tactical [combat] employment of forces to national and military strategic objectives" (U.S. Department of Defense 2011, xi). Military war games such as the now defunct TEAM SPIRIT and the ongoing KR-FE and ULCHI FREEDOM GUARDIAN exercises fit this category of strategic events. ROK–U.S. military exercises are accounted for by designating quarters which include these types of events as "one" (and non-exercise quarters as "zero").

ROK Administration Type. The final independent variable measures the relationship between DPRK hostile foreign policy actions and the political characteristics of South Korea's ruling party. This variable is specifically focused on the internal workings of the ROK government. Davies (2006, 144) notes that DPRK actions were sometimes influenced by the domestic political conditions in the United States and this variable assumes that ROK internal political conditions potentially influence DPRK conflict behavior. The ROK Administration Type variable examines the contention that DPRK conflict was more prevalent during conservative ROK administrations, because during these times, South Korea acted with more hostility towards the Kim regime. This research assumes that a South Korean conservative ruling party typically takes a more "hardline" stance towards the DPRK (resulting in increased hostile behavior), while a liberal South Korean party is typically more inclined to engage with the North (with less conflict). North Korea's reaction to perceived threats from the ROK might have caused conflict with the DPRK during conservative administrations.

For example, although North Korea conducted dozens of military operations against ROK and U.S. forces during the mid- to late 1960s, these operations were often done in retaliation for previous activities (often military raids) by ROK forces (Michishita 2010, 20–21, quoting Vance 1968). A more recent example is the November 2010 artillery attack by North Korea against the South Korean island of Yeonpyeong. North Korea blamed this attack, which left four South Koreans dead, on previous military activities by South Korea in the Yellow Sea (Yonhap 2010a; BBC 2010). During both of these events, conservatives ruled South Korea. Thus using a variable to represent DPRK hostilities as reactions to South Korean administrations potentially provides an important way to explain these conflict events. For this study, periods that included conservative South Korean administrations are reflected as "one" and liberal administrations as "zero."[27]

The Cold War as the Control Variable

The impact of the Cold War on North Korea's HFP activity levels is a potential rival explanation for the incidence of DPRK conflict during the study period. During the Cold War, both "threats and incentives" from both the U.S. and Soviet Union potentially "kept the behavior of satellites in check" (Calaway 2001, 106–107). Some scholars argue that in the post–Cold War period, the absence of the "stabilizing" impact of the superpowers may have caused increased repression and conflict actions by these same states (Calaway 2001, 107; Milner 1998). In the North Korean case, the political, military, and economic security provided by both the PRC and Soviet Union may also have worked to dampen DPRK efforts to pursue HFP actions. The Cold War included external influences (as proposed by P2), but also had wide-ranging effects, such as ideological support to maintain the regime and Kim Il-sung's confidence that the PRC and USSR would potentially support his military "adventures" against the ROK and U.S. Alternatively, the Cold War may have provided an overarching political-military atmosphere in which the DPRK felt emboldened to pursue Kim's domestic and international policies to include hostile foreign policy activities. While the Cold War is often used as an independent variable, scholars have also used it as a control variable when analyzing conflict behavior (Doyle and Sambanis 2000, 786; Cooney 2013). The cessation of support from the Soviets and changes demanded by the Chinese also might have affected the DPRK's willingness to pursue HFP actions, not only in the 1990s, but also in the 2000s, after the worst effects of the famine period ceased. The presence (or absence) of the Cold War provides an alternative explanation for Kim regime conflict activities that have not been properly accounted for in either diversionary theory or the propositions.

The DPRK's propensity for external conflict might be influenced by the presence of the Cold War and the associated political environment regardless of North Korea's internal conditions (P1) or the associated external influences mentioned in P2. During the Cold War, the United States and Soviet Union routinely amplified regional tensions, as both states viewed the Korean peninsula as a strategic-level concern. Additionally, North Korea's reliance upon the support of both China and the Soviet Union during the Cold War was a key component of its economic health and national security. For North Korea, the end of the Cold War included the evaporation of Soviet support, significant decreases in Chinese assistance, and the beginning of a period of economic crisis and widespread famine (Eberstadt, Rubin, and Tretyakova 1995; Noland 2000; Natsios 2001; Wallace 2007). In addition, China's rapprochement with South Korea (beginning in the late 1980s) had detrimental effects on North Korea's perceived ability to maintain its regional security posture (Scobell 2004). Thus, to address this rival hypothesis, this study uses the Cold War as a control variable to account for the pre- and post- Cold War activities of North Korea. Years prior to 1992 are coded "one" to measure the Cold War period, with years 1992–2011 coded as "zero."[28]

Time Series Linear Regression Models

Using social science research and analysis techniques, four statistical models were constructed to represent HFP relationships of events between 1960 and 2011. Model 1 (the "Base Model") includes all of the variables noted above that included reliable reporting and variance during and after the Cold War between 1960 and 2011. In this model, WGI was omitted due to limited reporting (1996–2011), UN resolutions were omitted because they did not vary during the Cold War (none were passed), and defector (refugee) rates prior to 1992 were not reliably reported by the ROK government. Models 2, 3, and 4 are variations of the first model and include the addition of WGI, UN Resolutions, and defector (refugee) rates respectively.

The models test P1 and P2 by examining the relationship between the independent variables (described above) and the level of hostile foreign policy. Changes in these independent variables (noted as "IVAR") or conditions are related to changes in the dependent variable (Hostile Foreign Policy). Conceptually, this relationship is as follows:

$$\text{Hostile Foreign Policy}_t = \beta_0 + \beta_1 DPRK\ CINC_{t-1} + \beta_2 WGI_{t-1} + \beta_3 GDP_{t-1} + \beta_4 Trade_{t-1} + \beta_5 Refugees_{t-1} + \beta_6 Infant\ Mort_{t-1} + \beta_7 Food_{t-1} + \beta_8 UN\ Resolutions_{t-1} + \beta_9 Mil\ Exercises_{t-1} + \beta_{10} US\ Leadership_{t-1} + \beta_{11} ROK\ Leadership_{t-1} + \beta_{12} ROK\ Admin_{t-1} + \beta_{13} Cold\ War_{t-1} + \mu_t$$

Hostile Foreign Policy$_t$ represents the dependent variable (also called the "DVAR") during a given quarter (t), β signifies the coefficients, and μ_t is the error term. To ensure that data is analyzed in the correct temporal order (IVAR followed by DVAR), the independent variables are lagged by one quarter (denoted by "t-1") and only the lagged data is included in the regressions. Additionally, four individual models are identified to test these relationships based on differences in data, such as the span of observations. As noted above, in the first model (the Base Model), the variables WGI, Refugees, and UN Resolutions are omitted to allow for consistent reporting throughout the study period. This allows for an analysis of the DVAR over the entire study period (1960–2011) with most of the independent variables. The other three models introduce the omitted variables and only include observations during the post–Cold War period. The Cold War variable is omitted from the other three models because it does not vary during the periods examined by those models. Additionally, UN resolutions were not included in Models 1, 2, and 3 because of lack of variance prior to 1992. The second model includes the addition of WGI to Model 1 as an independent, external condition variable and examines the relationship between conditions faced by North Korea and its HFP activities from 1996 to 2011. Model 3 adds UN Resolutions to the Base Model and examines the relationship between these conditions and DPRK conflict levels during the post–Cold War period (1992–2011). The final model (Model 4) examines Model 1 with the addition of defector (refugee) data. Additionally, Model 4 only includes data from the post–Cold War period (due to lack of reliable reporting on defectors prior to 1992).

Data Transformations and Tests

After the initial examination of independent variable data, the models were adjusted to ensure the use of valid social science and regression analysis techniques. Data was also adjusted account for differences in characteristics of the dependent variable (conflict) data and the independent variables. Specifically, the DVAR is reported as events (with a specific date associated) while the IVARs and control variables are only available in yearly increments. Thus, data was collapsed into a uniform time period and each model was initially tested using monthly, quarterly and yearly aggregation to see which provided the best statistical fit. The dependent variable (HFP events) was available in monthly data, but there were difficulties (related to over-manipulation) with adjusting the other variables to fit monthly reporting. Alternatively, using yearly data for all models resulted in 52 observations (considered too few for valid statistical analysis).[29] Based on these results, using quarterly data (rather than monthly or yearly) provided feasible solution resulting in an adequate number of observations (208) without causing significant analytical problems. This provides enough occurrences to allow for regression analysis and consistency for analysis with other data (such as military exercises and leadership changes). Monthly and yearly aggregation of events were both considered and tested. After a number of sample test runs, quarterly aggregation provided the most consistent event data calculations for analysis and provided enough fidelity to identify long-term trends without over-generalizing the data.

Additionally, models were evaluated using statistical (regression) analysis techniques to determine their predictive value.[30] Diagnostic tests were conducted on each model to ensure conformity with multivariate assumptions, which is required for valid statistical analysis. Multivariate regression assumes that the dependent variable (conflict) is continuous, that relationships between the IVARs and DVAR are linear, that the error term is not correlated with each IVAR, and that each independent variable exhibits an additive effect on the dependent variable (Berry and Sanders 2000, 38). Linear regression analysis also assumes that the model is "correctly specified," meaning that it includes variables that are necessary and excludes those that are not. Specification bias tests indicated that this condition was possibly present in the models, but it was difficult to implement typical solutions (to include selecting new variables) due to the lack of information on the Kim regime. As a result, specification bias is acknowledged as a potential risk in this analysis. Robust standard errors were used to account for potential heteroscedasticity, a condition where the error terms are constant and not related to the DVAR.

Additionally, the data demonstrates autocorrelation (relationships between successive time variables), which is a common problem with time-series data. To correct for this, Cochrane-Orcutt AR(1) regressions are used. Ordinary least squares (OLS) regression was initially tested, but autocorrelation was detected. To correct for this, "autoregressive process of order 1" or AR(1) regression (Cochrane-Orcutt) was used for the analysis and found to be a better fit for the data. The advantage of using the Cochrane-Orcutt AR(1) regression technique is that it initially provides an estimate of the autocorrelation error, then includes that error while estimating new regression coefficients, and finally provides a regression output that confirms that the "fitted residuals are independent" (Maggin et al., 2011, 308).[31]

Finally, the data was tested for multicollinearity (a measure of relationships between variables) and high levels of correlation did exist between some of the variables. Mean variable inflation factor (VIF) scores for each of the models (1 to 4) are at 10 or below, but individual variable scores were often higher. After conducting diagnostic tests of joint significance or the "joint f test" (Blackwell 2008), Model 1 was found to contain variables that are influential in relation to the dependent variable, regardless of their correlation. Similar tests run on Models 2, 3 and 4 show that their removal caused little effect on the DVAR, indicating significant correlation between variables in those models. A number of standard remedies were attempted with little effect. These included tests and transformations performed on the data (i.e., log, square or cube), but this resulted in either insignificant changes to the overall model outputs or significant skewing of the data. Thus, the research simply uses the original quarterly data without additional statistical transformations. As a result, multicollinearity is also considered an assumed risk for this study.[32]

Quantitative Analysis

The following section discusses the results of the quantitative analysis of North Korea's HFP activities between 1960 and 2011. This analysis used longitudinal research, which involves the consistent and methodological collection and analysis of data across time (Menard 1991, 4). The research data was obtained through repeated observation of DPRK-related activities (designated as the dependent and independent variables) during a given historical context (52 years, divided into 208 quarters). This method of focusing solely on the long-term activity of North Korea allows for a more structured and detailed examination of the DPRK and its conflict activities. Statistical analysis, with the help of the computer program Stata, is used to examine the data and help support conclusions on relationships between the variables. Stata is a commercially available statistical software package often used by social scientists to analyze the relationships between measurable characteristics (variables) of a specific phenomenon (Stata 2012).

In this analysis, support for Proposition 1 (diversionary theory) was found and a correlation between heightened levels of conflict and both political and social instability was present. There was also some support for Proposition 2 (external conditions), although the external conditions associated with increased HFP were primarily based on the South Korean government and its activities. Additionally, relationships between the levels of conflict and the presence of the Cold War suggest that North Korean HFP activities were more prevalent during the post–Cold War period. Table 5.4 characterizes and summarizes the data by showing the number of data points, mean, standard deviation, and minimum and maximum (range) of observations.

Table 5.4 Descriptive Statistics for All Variables (1960–2011)

Variable	Variable Description	N	Mean	Std. Dev.	Min	Max
Hostile Foreign Policy Activities	Dependent	208	183.8269	184.0945	0	982

5. Hostile Foreign Policy Event Analysis

DPRK CINC	Independent (Political)	208	0.008994	0.002955	0.004855	0.013581
WGI	Independent (Political)	64	-0.0803125	0.3116647	-0.53	0.53
GDP	Independent (Economic)	208	1987.762	746.0711	1104.994	2841.079
Trade	Independent (Economic)	208	.1148044	.0738334	.030464	.368898
Refugees	Independent (Social)	80	0.0449841	.0446442	.0007884	.1209954
Infant Mort	Independent (Social)	208	38.65601	13.13068	24	67
Food	Independent (Social)	208	0.154359	0.009751	0.13531	0.175528
UN Resolutions	Independent (External)	80	0.1	0.3018928	0	1
Mil Exercises	Independent (External)	208	0.091346	0.288796	0	1
ROK Leadership	Independent (External)	208	0.913462	0.2887958	0	1
U.S. Leadership	Independent (External)	208	0.072115	0.259303	0	1
ROK Admin	Independent (External)	208	0.7788462	0.2887958	0	1
Cold War	Control	208	0.6153846	0.4160251	0	1

As shown in Table 5.4, the dependent variable (Hostile Foreign Policy Activities) includes 208 quarterly observations with an intensity level ranging from 0 to 982, a mean (average) of 183.82 and standard deviation of 184.09. The political stability variables follow, with the DPRK national capabilities (CINC) measurements ranging from 0.0048 to 0.0135, a mean of 0.0089, and standard deviation score of 0.0029. The other political variable, WGI score, has a range of -0.53 to 0.53, with a mean of -0.080 and standard deviation of 0.311. The economic stability variables include GDP per person (in U.S. dollars) per quarter, ranging from 1104.99 to 2841.07 with a mean of 1987.76 and standard deviation of 746.07. The economic variable, total trade per person, was measured in millions of U.S. dollars and ranged from .0304639 to .3688978 with a mean of .1148 and a standard deviation of .0738. The first social stability variable (defectors) ranges from .0007884 to .1209954 per person, with an average of .0449 and standard deviation of .0446. Infant mortality rate per 1000 had quarterly averages ranging from 24 to 67 with a mean score of 38.65 and standard deviation of 13.13. The final social variable, food availability per person (in metric tons) ranges from 0.135 to 0.175 with an average of 0.154 and standard deviation of 0.097. The other independent (external condition) variables and the control variable were recorded as dummy variables (designated as either one or zero) denoting the presence or absence of the condition. The external condition independent variables include UN Resolutions, Military Exercises, ROK Leadership Change, U.S. Leadership Change, and ROK Admin. The control variable was Cold War. For example, periods that included the binary variables, such as UN Resolutions or the Cold War, were recorded as "one" and all other times as "zero." Table 5.5 shows the results of regression analysis on each of the four models. As stated above, Cochrane-Orcutt AR(1) regression is used for each model.

Table 5.5 Statistical Analysis Results: All Models

Variable	Model 1 (1960–2011) (Base Model)[33]	Model 2 (1996–2011) (Base + WGI)	Model 3 (1992–2011) (Base + UN Resolutions)	Model 4 (1992–2011) (Base + Refugees)
DPRK CINC$_{(t-1)}$	-55154.67 (17969.03)***	77237.74 (80520.1)	3736.401 (41331.83)	-3189.311 (37417.85)
WGI$_{(t-1)}$	—	161.1741 (277.9712)	—	—
GDP$_{(t-1)}$	-0.0917953 (0.0705419)	0.1348404 (0.3197684)	-0.0527 (0.0612981)	0.0102596 (0.0714668)
Trade$_{(t-1)}$	-43.57502 (494.4618)	-502.8026 (1056.531)	116.7253 (703.9506)	-828.2668 (847.7516)
Refugees$_{(t-1)}$	—	—	—	2868.563 (1633.79)*
Infant Mortality$_{(t-1)}$	-7.236242 (5.246148)	7.708937 (11.94308)	-2.374974 (5.832422)	2.756085 (6.745713)
Food$_{(t-1)}$	-3634.759 (2140.799)*	-11065.66 (12884.88)	-3537.73 (5751.358)	-2949.348 (5301.901)
UN Resolutions$_{(t-1)}$	—	—	-16.00958 (29.87347)	—
Military Exercises$_{(t-1)}$	-18.91945 (16.17652)	23.24864 (21.95039)	10.60475 (20.5928)	11.43339 (20.29014)
ROK Leadership Change$_{(t-1)}$	93.37184 (48.12031)*	98.92562 (70.27786)	107.4748 (61.30165)*	100.9797 (65.67377)
U.S. Leadership Change$_{(t-1)}$	-29.74627 (23.42722)	-5.589573 (58.80727)	3.086805 (50.64341)	16.76734 (53.91637)
ROK Admin$_{(t-1)}$	110.6997 (49.11612)**	-14.34915 (118.7285)	46.22309 (81.23314)	52.4943 (77.06109)
Cold War$_{(t-1)}$	-179.9121 (58.40437)***	—	—	—
R2	0.1221	.2025	.1789	0.2235
Number	208	62	78	78

*p< 0.10, **p < 0.05, ***p < 0.01

Note: Coefficients are listed and then followed by standard errors (in parentheses). Robust standard errors are used for all models.

Model 1 tests the overall relationships between the DVAR (hostility score) and the independent variables that were observed throughout the study period (1960–2011). In this model (as noted previously), WGI is omitted due to limited reporting (only available from 1996 to 2011). This model also does not include UN Resolution and Refugee data due to lack of variance or unreliable reporting during the Cold War period. The Base Model includes a number of statistically significant and negative relationships between hostility levels and the independent variables such as DPRK CINC and food availability. Thus, between 1960 and 2011, decreases in North Korea's national capacity and food supplies are potentially related to increases in hostile foreign policy behaviors. Additionally, ROK leadership changes and ROK administration type are associated with increased North Korean conflict.

Finally, the control variable (Cold War) is also statistically significant, and demonstrates a negative relationship to the level of HFP. In other words, the presence of the Cold War is related to decreased levels of HFP, while the absence of the Cold War has the opposite effect. Many scholars support the idea that the DPRK felt less secure after the loss of USSR and PRC support (Mceachern 2010, 68–70; Park 2012, 324; Cha and Kang 2003, 19; Oh 2000, 185) and the quantitative analysis seems to support that viewpoint. As stated previously, one of the reasons for using the Cold War as a control is to address that alternate hypothesis. Yet, as the qualitative portion of this research demonstrated, the end of the Cold War was less related to DPRK conflict than it might seem. In many respects, support to North Korea from its communist benefactor (China) never really stopped at the end of the Cold War. While the support from the Soviets evaporated (Radchenko 2011, 309), the Chinese continued to provide aid (either direct or in the form of subsidized goods) throughout the 1990s (Noland 2000, 187) and the PRC continues to do this today (Jayshree and Xu 2013). In fact, when Kim Jong-il died, there were reports of substantial PRC aid to North Korea to ensure stability (Yonhap 2012). China's policy towards northeast Asia remains stability and the status quo and an intact North Korea is a key part of that strategy (Choi 2012, 54–55). Despite the end of the Cold War, North Korea still received a significant amount of aid from China which helped to ensure the DPRK remained solvent and sovereign.

Model 2 adds the World Governance Indicators (WGI) to Model 1, but limits the temporal scope of the analysis to 1996–2011. While this model uses the WGI political stability measures to test for correlations between conflict and the independent variables, no relationships are found and the model itself is not statistically significant. Model 3 includes the variables in the first model and adds UN resolutions, but limits the scope of the analysis to the post–Cold

War period. Aside from the resolutions in the 1950s, the UN did not enact any resolutions until 1993, during the first DPRK nuclear crisis. In this model, the only significant variable is an ROK leadership change (which provides additional support to P2) although the model is also not statistically significant. Finally, Model 4 examines the relationship between refugee (defector) levels and hostile foreign policy activities during the post–Cold War period. This statistically significant model finds a relationship between increased levels of refugees and heightened DPRK conflict during this period (in support of P1). This lends support to the contention that increased levels of North Korean hostile foreign policy occur in conjunction with higher refugee numbers.

The R^2 values for all of the models are relatively low, although Gujaradi and Porter (2009, 206–207) note that a low score is not "necessarily bad." R^2 is a measure of proportional reduction in error and helps determine the ability of the independent variables to explain or predict the dependent variable (DPRK hostilities) (Pollock 2005, 163–164). Alternatively, Gujaradi and Porter (2009, 206–207) warn that overemphasizing R^2 is a common problem and that scholars "should be more concerned about the logical or theoretical relevance of the explanatory variables to the dependent variable and their statistical relevance." Based on the R^2 value, Model 1 explains 12 percent of the variance in the level of conflict (DVAR) while Model 4 accounts for 22 percent of the change in the dependent variable. These two statistically significant models (Model 1 and Model 4) do provide support for Proposition 1 (internal conditions) and limited support for external or international community-based conditions (Proposition 2). Model 1 also shows that other factors are influential, such as ROK election periods, conservative administrations, and the control variable (presence of the Cold War). Additionally, Model 4 is the most robust (with the highest explanatory power) and does provide limited support for the contention that after the Cold War, domestic distress (based on the numbers of defectors/refugees) experienced by the DPRK is related to the propensity for increased hostile foreign policy behavior. Models 2 and 3 add little to these arguments and show (with the exception of ROK leadership changes in Model 3) no significant relationships between the variables.

Comparing the most significant variables is a useful method to analyze the changes in HFP activities over time. This provides more accurate insight into the complicated relationships found in this research. Figure 5.3 shows the relationship between HFP, CINC, food availability, and refugee (defector) levels. CINC and food availability were scaled to allow for comparison.

Examining CINC scores reveals near constant increases throughout much of the study period. Yet at the end of the Cold War (and just prior to the famine period), there was an increase in CINC scores (42 percent between 1988 and

1992) that accompanied a relatively low level of HFP activity. This increase in capabilities, along with the continued support of both the USSR and China, might have allowed North Korea to rely less upon HFP activities to achieve its national goals. The end of the Cold War and loss of support saw a gradual increase in HFP activities and the accompanying economic and social disasters that occurred during the famine period in the 1990s.

Figure 5.3 Significant Variable Comparisons[34]

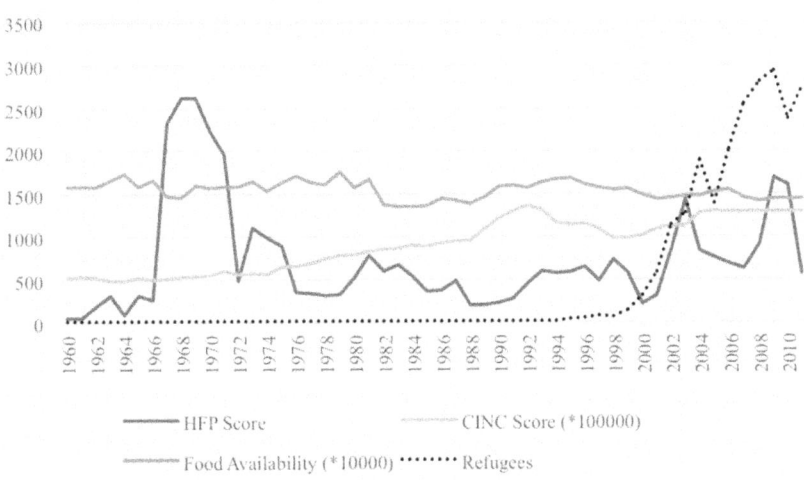

Additionally, food availability statistics indicate that between 1966 and 1967, HFP scores increased dramatically (almost 800 percent) and during the same period, there was a 12 percent decrease in food availability per person. Additionally, the increase on hostilities in 2009 (84 percent higher than in 2008) was preceded by a nine percent decrease in food availability per person between 2006 and 2008. These observations provide support to the idea that as the Kim regime encounters difficulties in feeding its people, it turns to HFP activities and diversion in efforts to gain concessions and distract the public's attention from food shortages.

Finally, examining the refugee (defector) levels and both increases in refugee levels during two periods (2000–2003 and 2007–2009) and decreases in refugees between 2004 and 2005, one sees that between 2000 and 2003, refugee levels increased over 300 percent and during the same time, conflict levels increased over 500 percent; between 2007 and 2009, increases in HFP activities (170 percent) accompanied increases in refugee (defector) levels (15 percent) during the same period. Decreases in refugee (defector) levels occurred either just after or in the same year as decreases in HFP levels in both 2005 and 2010. This lends support to the idea that decreases in hostilities are potentially related to refugee levels, especially after the famine period. In other words, as diversionary incentives (such as domestic distress, indicated by refugee levels) disappear, the levels of North Korea's HFP activities also decrease.

Summary and Conclusions

This quantitative analysis of North Korean activity demonstrates the complex nature of dealing with unruly sources of data on a reclusive state. It also shows statistically significant relationships between conflict and the conditions the Kim regime has faced over the past 52 years. The data provides support to P1 and two of its hypotheses (H1 and H3): increases in conflict activities (DVAR) are associated with decreases in political stability (measured by DPRK CINC) and social stability (Food and Refugees). In other words, evidence for the predicted relationship between internal conditions and external conflict is present and there is a statistical correlation between the levels of internal instability and increased levels of HFP. This analysis also provides some support to P2, but only with the variables focused on the characteristics of the ROK government. Two of the hypotheses (H5 and H8) associated with external influences positively correlate with conflict levels and indicate that the actions of South Korea are associated with increases in conflict activity.

The control variable (Cold War) is significant, but associated with decreased hostile foreign policy activities. This indicates that prior to 1992, North Korea demonstrated a lower propensity to conduct external conflict activities compared to the post–Cold War period. The lower overall incidence of conflict during the entire Cold War (despite the spike in activity in the late 1960s) may have been due to a combination of the overall economic difficulties experienced beginning in the 1970s and the overarching security and economic "umbrella" provided by the USSR and PRC. After the Cold War ended (and subsequent loss of support), the Kim regime might have been more inclined to engage in conflict to increase its security posture within the region and in an attempt to ensure domestic stability.

Some of the most important results of this examination come from the relationships not present between the DVAR and variables such as UN Resolutions, ROK–U.S. military exercises and internal DPRK economic conditions. For example, throughout all of the models, economic conditions and infant mortality levels have no relationship with hostility levels. Similarly, military exercises and U.S. leadership changes are not associated with variances in North Korean conflict levels. Perhaps most striking is the lack of relationship between UN resolutions and DPRK actions, which are found to be uncorrelated in Model 2. Thus, these observations lead to questions about which external conditions (or actions by the international community) actually affect North Korea's conflict behaviors.

Although this research reveals the challenges associated with analyzing North Korea, it also yields important and empirically-supported findings. Coupled with the case studies, evidence is found in support of the idea that domestic conditions (i.e., political and social instability) did influence North Korea's external conflict behavior, which is consistent with the diversionary argument. Additionally, there is also some limited support found the idea that some external factors (such as ROK election periods) were related to Kim regime's actions. Also significant were the relationships not found between other internal and external conditions (such as the DPRK's domestic economy, UN resolutions and ROK–U.S. military exercises) and DPRK hostile foreign policy activities.

Based on the empirical evidence presented, this chapter shows there is a correlation between North Korea's internal conditions and its external activities. Yet these findings are not without limitations. Determining if particular events were actual cases of diversion, or related to other motivations, remains problematic and a much more thorough analysis of individual events is required. Unfortunately, the quantitative analysis presented above only provides evidence of statistical linkages between hostile events and conditions and is insufficient to explain the relationships between conditions faced by the regime and external conflict. These findings potentially support the contention that diversionary behavior might be present (i.e., rising conflict because of internal instability). Additionally, while the analysis above uses some of the best proxy data available on North Korean activities, the concept of "intent" of the regime to divert the public's attention is difficult to quantify. But combination of this quantitative analysis and case studies supports the argument that diversionary concepts were influential in the levels of North Korean conflict during the research period. In other words, by combining these two analytical methods (qualitative and quantitative), this research finds that there were relationships between the conditions faced by the Kim regime and the associated levels of conflict activities.

CHAPTER 6

Comparisons and Conclusions

When comparing case study analysis with statistical outputs (quantitative analysis), scholars cannot simply extend the methods used in quantitative analysis to qualitative analysis (George and Bennett 2005, 106). For example, each of the case studies encompasses a specific number of years, ranging from four to seven, while the quantitative analysis examines fifty-two years of conflict. Thus, the quantitative analysis demonstrates overall trends, but provides limited evidence on why particular trends actually occurred. Nevertheless, this study does demonstrate that both research methods (quantitative and qualitative analysis) have revealed important characteristics related to North Korean conflict. For example, the case studies provide detailed information on why particular hostile foreign policy events occurred in relation to overall conditions faced by the Kim regime, but are limited in scope and have difficulty in accounting for conflict over the entire study period. However, the mixing of these methods provides evidence of relationships between conditions faced by the regime and hostile foreign policy conflict levels throughout North Korea's history. Table 6.1 compares the case studies and quantitative analysis as follows:

Table 6.1 Case Study and Statistical Analysis Comparison

		Qualitative (Case Study) Analysis	Quantitative (Statistical) Analysis
Diversionary Concepts Supported?	Political Instability	No	Yes
	Economic Instability	No	No
	Social Instability	No	Yes

176

6. Comparisons and Conclusions

		Qualitative (Case Study) Analysis	Quantitative (Statistical) Analysis
External Conditions Argument Supported?	UN Resolutions	Yes	No
	ROK Leadership Changes	Yes	Yes
	U.S. Leadership Changes	Yes	No
	Strategic Military Exercises	Yes	No
	ROK Administration Type	Yes	Yes

As shown above, both internal conditions and external conditions find mixed support across both the case studies and statistical analysis. The argument that internal conditions are related to external conflict finds support in the quantitative analysis but not the case studies. Additionally, the decreases in political and social stability (and increased HFP) were evident in the longer-term analysis rather than in the cases, which might indicate that the case periods were inadequate to analyze specific relationships between those conditions and conflict. Within the case studies, a limited number of historic events support the diversionary argument, but only the quantitative analysis provides substantial evidence of a relationship between deteriorating internal conditions and heighted HFP activities.

The idea that external factors are influential in North Korea's foreign policy choices finds support in both the case studies and statistical analysis. Two of the hypotheses (ROK leadership changes and leadership type) demonstrate continuity in the case studies and quantitative analysis. This demonstrates that within the cases and throughout the DPRK's history, the characteristics of the ROK government have impacted the level of hostile foreign policy activities. Additionally, throughout most of the case studies, external events did have an impact on the Kim regime's tendency to use diplomatic or military force against the ROK or U.S. However, as with the evidence found in examining diversionary events, the comparisons between the case studies and regression analysis require further explanation. For example, while the case studies indicate relationships between UN resolutions, U.S. leadership changes, and military exercises, the statistical analysis of these events show that between 1960 and 2011 there was no correlation between these events. The case studies demonstrate anecdotal evidence of relationships that exist to a limited extent during the research periods, but that are not consistently present over time. For example, the presence of ROK–U.S. military exercises might seem to increase hostilities on the Korean peninsula based on case study evidence, but when considered over the span of the study, these events demonstrate a limited relationship with HFP activities. This mixed-method approach sheds light on the conditions that influence North Korean conflict actions, but also demonstrates the complexity of these relationships.

Goals, Methods and Limitations

This research examined the relationship between conflict behavior and conditions faced by the DPRK regime to determine the value of diversionary theory as explanation for these actions. In this research, hypotheses focused on the internal and external factors that are potentially related to the Kim regimes' use of hostile actions are examined and tested. Under some circumstances, domestic conditions do influence the Kim regimes' tendency to engage in hostile foreign policy activities. However, there is also substantial support for the idea that external conditions were influential in HFP levels. To North Korean observers, these conclusions will come as no surprise. Yet this study provides both statistically-sound (quantitative) and case study (qualitative) evidence to support the argument that North Korean conflict activities are related to specific conditions faced by the Kim regimes, rather than purely anecdotal evidence (which is often relied upon by policymakers). The following paragraphs summarize this information and include a synopsis of the study, a brief review of the findings, policy implications, and suggestions for future research.

The initial premise for this examination of DPRK activity was to examine if there was a positive relationship between domestic difficulties and the Kim regime's external conflict activities. To test these ideas, three case studies and North Korean event data were examined, analyzed and compared. Another purpose of this study was to demonstrate a viable method to examine closed states using mixed-method approaches. Academics have rarely used both history and political science methodology to examine North Korean activities,[1] often because of the lack of empirical data, but also because these two disciplines have separate research philosophies. In this study, the strengths of both disciplines are demonstrated—these include the inductive approach preferred by historians and the deductive analysis favored by political scientists. International relations scholars have used these methods to examine other states, but this research is one of only a few publicly available longitudinal studies of its type on North Korea.[2]

Additionally, this research demonstrates that despite being considered a closed state, North Korea's characteristics and actions do allow for empirical study. The U.S. and other states have declassified large amounts of information on the DPRK and the use of "mirror statistics" from nations that interact with North Korea provides an extensive amount of detailed data for analysis. This study also supports the contention that the DPRK is a unique country, perhaps unprecedented not only among communist nations, but among all states. North Korea's national character is similar to former Stalinist states such as Romania and Albania, but it has managed to remain intact without substantial change (Buzo 1999, 245). Although North Korea was similar to these states, "it has not shared their fate" (Buzo 1999, 245) and has survived despite difficult circumstances, mostly related to its own shortcomings. The fact that North Korea has eluded collapse over the past few decades (especially during periods of severe distress, such as the famine in the 1990s) has continued to puzzle scholars and policymakers. Analysts, such as Eberstadt (1993, 1999), have consistently predicted the end of North Korea is near, yet the Kim regime continues to muddle through. In addition, unlike China and Vietnam, North Korea has not attempted significant reform or engagement of the international community, retaining the moniker "the Hermit Kingdom" despite the vast progress experienced by those states and its other half, South Korea. This analysis is an important effort to analyze a state that is both distinctive and rarely studied in a mixed-methods manner.

As with all studies, this one has its limitations. The presence of my own "Western bias" and personal experiences while working for the U.S. government and in South Korea might have affected this examination of North Korea.[3] Yet North Korea's actions are generally recognized as threatening to the region and the international community shares concerns about the effects of DPRK foreign policy activities. The use of accepted research methods and analysis has assisted efforts to be objective in explaining Kim regime actions. Specifically, careful attention was paid to why North Korea engages in peaceful interaction at some times and in hostile behavior during others, regardless of the consequences of those activities (e.g., significant levels of ROK and U.S. casualties). Another limitation for this study was the availability of dependent variable data (conflict events).

Although the sources used for this analysis are among the best currently available, not all diplomatic and conflict incidents are reported in the open press. Additionally, there is only limited reporting on ROK and U.S. military actions taken against the DPRK. For example, over the last few decades, the ROK conducted infiltration operations against the DPRK that were rarely acknowledged in the open press (Rennie and Mars 2000). A full account of actions on both sides of the DMZ (rather than just North Korean activities) would provide for a better understanding of the nature of conflict on the peninsula. Finally, this study only considered diversionary theory as an explanation for the Kim regimes' actions. Diversionary concepts are important, but might be sufficient to completely explain North Korea's conflict activities. Expanding the scope of this study to examine other conflict theories that can provide explanations for North Korean conflict, a technique used by Jung (2012), might have resulted in more comprehensive theoretical explanations. While this is an important limitation of this study, both of the propositions (P1 and P2) are theoretically-grounded. The first is based on diversionary theory and the second (external influences) is based on traditional views of conflict (Waltz 1954 and 1979; Wendt 1992). Nevertheless, for the intended scope of this study, the sole focus on diversionary theory is sufficient to support the examination of DPRK conflict.

Despite the limitations mentioned above, one of the most important outputs of this research is to provide an example of how to analyze North Korea's conflict behaviors. While the data sources and the statistical analysis methods might change, the overall concept of how to approach this security dilemma in a systematic manner is an important contribution of this book.

Findings

This study provides insight to conflict activities of a closed state that is rarely studied in a systematic manner. The findings provide support to the argument that diversion is an influential factor and related to the Kim regimes' external conflict actions. This contrasts with Michishita's (2009 and 2011) findings that diversion was not the primary impetus for DPRK conflict activities. Additionally, external conditions, especially those associated with the ROK government and strategic exercises, were found to be significant across both the quantitative and qualitative studies. This study also shows that diversionary theory provides only a partial explanation for North Korean HFP activities. Diversion might be a necessary component of the Kim regimes' policies to achieve national goals, but it remains insufficient to explain the scope of conflict actions pursued by the DPRK. Finally, this research also confirms the idea that the Kim family's primary objective is to maintain power and survive, which is consistent with other scholars' conclusions (Suh 2002, 170; Haggard and Noland 2011b).

The case study and quantitative analyses demonstrate that some of the domestic conditions experienced by the Kim regimes occurred in conjunction with changes in the levels of conflict. The qualitative study added that specific economic events (e.g., the economic downturns in the late 1960s and 1990s, and the currency crisis in the 2000s) were related to specific hostile foreign policy events. The quantitative study demonstrates that as North Korea's political and social stability decreases, there are increases in conflict. Additionally, both the quantitative and qualitative studies find that conflict actions were influenced by a number of external conditions in South Korea, such as election cycles and type of ROK government, throughout the entire span of the study.

The research also revealed that North Korea did engage in heightened levels of conflict after the Cold War (as supported by the quantitative analysis), but also during the height of the Cold War (as supported by both the event data and first case study). Finally, the proposal that diversionary behavior occurred was difficult to discern from the three case studies alone and required additional analysis (quantitative) to provide more depth to the results. Yet when the overall hostilities levels were compared to the conditions present in the case studies, support for diversionary concepts were insufficient as the only means to explain North Korea's activities. Diversion was one of many methods used by the Kim regimes to control the people and other more oppressive methods were routinely used in response to domestic challenges.

Policy Implications

An important output of this research is identification of how North Korea uses force as a means to achieve policy objectives, whether oriented towards domestic goals or in reaction to external threats. The conclusions in this study, including observations on the use of diversionary means and the Kim regimes' emphasis on retaining power, help provide insight into the cyclic nature of how the DPRK interacts with other states. The DPRK continues to use a cycle of threats or provocative actions in attempts to start dialogue or force concessions, participation in negotiations, and a resurgence of HFP actions when those efforts fail. The strength of this research is that it provides empirical evidence on the historic characteristics and patterns of the Kim regimes. The findings support the view that international community actions have only a limited effect on North Korea's behaviors and one of the strongest influencers tend to be the activities of the ROK government.

International diplomatic efforts and economic sanctions that have sought to change North Korea's behavior have generally failed, as evidenced in the second and third case studies. All three of the case studies show that internal dynamics are important influencers of DPRK behaviors. This research provides support to the idea that international community policies aimed at changing those internal conditions are more likely to be successful. Additionally, China's efforts to sustain North Korea in times of extreme domestic challenges have most likely kept the Kim regimes solvent. Based on its historic interactions with the DPRK, Beijing seems to prefer a divided Korean peninsula with a sovereign North Korean state. Thus, this study provides support to the contention that China's primary policy objective is to keep North Korea solvent through aid and economic support (CRS 2010, 1; Lee and Choi 2009, 57). Any policy action that leaves the support channel between China and North Korea intact is likely to have little impact.

Yet, North Korea poses a significant threat to the international community and the Kim Jong-un regime seems more willing than his father's to directly threaten both the U.S. and South Korea with nuclear warfare (KCNA 2013b). Additionally, the DPRK's actions since the death of Kim Jong-il, which have included additional nuclear testing and missile launches, have demonstrated that the North possesses the capability to make good on its threats of attack against the U.S. or ROK. Consequently, the international community has little choice but to take North Korea's actions seriously. Deterrence efforts, such as strong regional security alliances and anti-proliferation activities, are useful international responses to these types of activities.

Despite international community efforts to change North Korea's behavior, the Kim regimes' enduring trait has been their ability to chart an independent course regardless of internal or external circumstances. Thus, while deterrence efforts remain necessary to keep North Korea's actions from destabilizing the region, they often have little effect on North Korea's proclivity to engage in conflict actions. Other methods of engagement with North Korea that focus on its lack of information about the outside world are viable alternative policy options. Exposing the DPRK population to external press reports, entertainment, and technology might help the North Korean people understand the nature of both their government and its leader. Hassig and Oh (2009, 251–252) discuss the merits of "information warfare" and note that an effective campaign could "successfully introduce the North Korean people to a new way of thinking about their government and their society."

Additionally, continued exposure of North Korea to the outside world through academic, cultural, or even technological exchanges might also serve to lessen the strict control that the Kim Jong-un regime has on its people. These types of exchanges had a profound impact on the Soviet Union (Richmond 2003) and, while the DPRK is culturally different from the former USSR, visits by sports teams, scholars, or musicians are often welcomed by the regime (Wakin 2008; Zinser 2013). These types of exchanges do occur in North Korea, but they are relatively rare. "Soft power" actions of these types are relatively inexpensive, entail little risk to participants, and might spur small changes to North Korean society that would otherwise be impossible.

Future Research

This analysis of North Korea only begins to explore what is possible given publicly available DPRK conflict data. Additionally, this study provides a foundation for further research and debate on North Korea's armed and political actions. Methods described here, especially the longitudinal analysis of a single state, can be used as a template for gathering and analyzing data on other states with limited outside access. In addition, analyzing other sources of event data information on North Korea, such as King and Lowe's (2003b) "10 Million International Dyadic Events," might provide additional insight to DPRK activities. The use of automated methods to extract data from media sources to compare against these findings might also be an important way to verify (or refute) the conclusions in this study. In addition, as mentioned in the limitations discussion above, expanding the view of DPRK actions beyond the theoretical concept of diversionary war might provide for a better understanding of North Korea's willingness to engage in conflict and peace. For example, Jung (2012, 20) uses not only diversionary war theory, but also offensive realism, opportunistic war, and his own "diversionary target theory" to analyze DPRK activities. Finally, as more accurate or updated DPRK data becomes available, using these same methods to examine new information would be an important way to determine if the trends identified in this study continue to occur in the "newest" Kim regime.

Final Thoughts

Policymakers, political scientists, and historians continue efforts to study and attempt to understand the characteristics and solitary nature of North Korea. These individuals generally continue to pursue the same question: "What should be done about North Korea?" As noted in this study, despite the vast amount of literature available on the DPRK, only a handful of scholars have attempted to blend social science and historical methods to analyze this isolated state. This research begins to help fill this gap in current knowledge about this reclusive, yet potentially very dangerous nation. This study's conclusion that conditions faced by the regime are an influential force behind North Korea's actions is a significant observation. More importantly, the extensive use of historical data to empirically support this contention is a valuable step in understanding the recurrence of conflict on the Korean peninsula. Although deterrence and efforts to mitigate North Korea's military threat to the international community are important, other actions (such as the sociocultural options mentioned above) also might help to nudge the Kim regime towards becoming a more active (and peaceful) participant in world affairs. In any case, this research provides not only important observations on the characteristics of the Kim regimes, but also gives scholars a means to analyze a security problem that confounds the international community. The systematic method demonstrated in this study to examine North Korea's conflict activities provides a useful example of how to study the actions of closed states. Most importantly, this research potentially can inform more effective policymaking in hopes of solving an enduring security dilemma in East Asia.

Appendix A

Azar's Event Categories

Azar (1993, 27–29) provided the following descriptions for each of his numbered categories for coding events:

9. *Mild verbal expressions displaying discord in interaction*: Low key objection to policies or behavior; communicating dissatisfaction through third party; failing to reach an agreement; refusing protest note; denying accusations; objecting to explanation of goals, position, etc.; requesting change in policy.

10. *Strong verbal expressions displaying hostility in interaction*: Warning retaliation for acts; making threatening demands and accusations; condemning strongly specific actions or policies; denouncing leaders, system, or ideology; postponing heads of state visits; refusing participation in meetings or summits; leveling strong propaganda attacks; denying support; blocking or vetoing policy or proposals in the UN or other international bodies.

11. *Diplomatic-economic hostile actions*: Increasing troop mobilization; boycotts; imposing economic sanctions; hindering movement on land, waterways, or in the air; embargoing goods; refusing mutual trade rights; closing borders and blocking free communication; manipulating trade or currency to cause economic problems; halting aid; granting sanctuary to opposition leaders; mobilizing hostile demonstrations against target country; refusing to support foreign military allies; recalling ambassador for emergency consultations regarding target country; refusing visas to other nationals or restricting movement in country; expelling or arresting nationals or press; spying on foreign government officials; terminating major agreements.

12. *Political-military hostile actions*: Inciting riots or rebellions (training or financial aid for rebellions); encouraging guerrilla activities against target country; limited and sporadic terrorist actions; kidnapping or torturing foreign citizens or prisoners of war; giving sanctuary to terrorists; breaking diplomatic relations; attacking diplomats or embassies; expelling military advisors; nationalizing companies without compensation.

13. *Small scale military acts*: Limited air, sea, or border skirmishes; border police acts; annexing territory already occupied; seizing material of target country; imposing blockades; assassinating leaders of target country; material support of subversive activities against target country.

14. *Limited war acts*: Intermittent shelling or clashes; sporadic bombing of military or industrial areas; small scale interception or sinking of ships; mining of territorial waters.

15. *Extensive war acts causing deaths, dislocation or high strategic costs*: Use of nuclear weapons; full scale air, naval, or land battles; invasion of territory; occupation of territory; massive bombing of civilian areas; capturing of soldiers in battle; large scale bombing of military installations; chemical or biological warfare.

Appendix B

Korean Conflict Dataset

This appendix displays the conflict data used to support HFP research and findings. The headings indicate measured items and show dates, indicated by Year and Quarter ("Qtr"), and conflict intensity rating (Score). Internal conditions measured for this study follow and include the DPRK Composite Indicator of National Capabilities (CINC), World Governance Indicators (WGI), Gross Domestic Product (GDP), Trade, Refugees, Infant Mortality and Food Availability. External influences follow and include UN Resolutions, Military Exercises, US Leaders, ROK Leaders, ROK Administration type and the presence of the Cold War.

Korea Conflict Dataset (by quarter)

Year	Qtr	Score	DPRK CINC	WGI	GDP pp	Trade pp	Refugees	Infant Mort	Food pp	UN Resolutions	Mil Exercise	U.S. Leader	ROK Leader	ROK Admin	Cold War
1960	1	6	0.005502		1116.2	0.033491		67	0.159218	0	0	0	0	1	1
1960	2	0	0.005401		1112.46	0.032537		67	0.159097	0	0	0	1	1	1
1960	3	6	0.005299		1108.73	0.031582		67	0.158975	0	0	0	1	0	1
1960	4	42	0.005198		1104.99	0.030628		67	0.158853	0	0	1	0	0	1
1961	1	6	0.00523		1109.74	0.030587		67	0.158731	0	0	0	0	0	1
1961	2	18	0.005261		1114.49	0.030546		67	0.15861	0	0	0	0	0	1
1961	3	6	0.005293		1119.24	0.030505		67	0.158488	0	0	0	0	0	1
1961	4	24	0.005325		1123.99	0.030464		67	0.158366	0	1	0	0	0	1
1962	1	6	0.005306		1123.48	0.030868		67	0.158321	0	1	0	0	0	1
1962	2	18	0.005286		1122.98	0.031272		67	0.158276	0	0	0	0	0	1
1962	3	50	0.005267		1122.47	0.031676		67	0.158232	0	0	0	1	1	1
1962	4	112	0.005248		1121.96	0.032080		67	0.158187	0	1	0	1	1	1
1963	1	0	0.00515		1137.98	0.033380		67	0.160255	0	0	0	0	1	1
1963	2	50	0.005052		1154	0.034679		67	0.162324	0	0	0	1	1	1
1963	3	230	0.004953		1170.03	0.035978		67	0.164392	0	1	0	1	1	1
1963	4	30	0.004855		1186.05	0.037278		67	0.166461	0	0	1	0	1	1
1964	1	56	0.004861		1202.8	0.036903		67	0.168218	0	0	1	0	1	1
1964	2	18	0.004866		1219.55	0.036529		64.25	0.169974	0	0	0	0	1	1
1964	3	12	0.004872		1236.3	0.036154		61.5	0.17173	0	1	1	0	1	1
1964	4	12	0.004877		1253.05	0.035780		58.75	0.173487	0	1	0	0	1	1
1965	1	24	0.004974		1263.54	0.036052		56	0.169855	0	0	0	0	1	1
1965	2	124	0.005071		1274.02	0.036324		56	0.166222	0	0	1	0	1	1
1965	3	50	0.005168		1284.51	0.036597		56	0.16259	0	1	0	0	1	1
1965	4	118	0.005265		1295	0.036869		56	0.158958	0	1	0	0	1	1
1966	1	24	0.005204		1325	0.037042		56	0.160591	0	0	0	0	1	1
1966	2	62	0.005144		1355	0.037215		56	0.162225	0	0	0	0	1	1
1966	3	86	0.005084		1384.99	0.037387		56	0.163858	0	1	0	0	1	1
1966	4	92	0.005023		1414.99	0.037560		56	0.165492	0	0	0	0	1	1
1967	1	474	0.005037		1431.99	0.037988		56	0.161031	0	0	0	1	1	1
1967	2	212	0.005051		1449	0.038416		56	0.15657	0	0	0	1	1	1
1967	3	982	0.005065		1466	0.038843		56	0.15211	0	1	0	0	1	1
1967	4	660	0.005079		1483	0.039271		56	0.147649	0	1	0	0	1	1
1968	1	430	0.005151		1520.49	0.042687		56	0.147272	0	0	0	0	1	1

Appendix B

Year	Qtr	Score	DPRK CINC	WGI	GDP pp	Trade pp	Refugees	Infant Mort	Food pp	UN Resolutions	Mil Exercise	U.S. Leader	ROK Leader	ROK Admin	Cold War
1968	2	730	0.005223		1557.98	0.046103		56	0.146895	0	0	0	0	1	1
1968	3	824	0.005296		1595.47	0.049519		56	0.146518	0	1	0	0	1	1
1968	4	636	0.005368		1632.97	0.052935		56	0.146141	0	1	1	0	1	1
1969	1	430	0.005363		1684.47	0.051748		56	0.149443	0	0	0	0	1	1
1969	2	730	0.005359		1735.97	0.050562		53	0.152746	0	0	0	0	1	1
1969	3	824	0.005354		1787.47	0.049376		50	0.156048	0	1	0	0	1	1
1969	4	636	0.00535		1838.98	0.048190		47	0.15935	0	0	0	0	1	1
1970	1	156	0.005401		1867.73	0.048765		44	0.158987	0	0	0	1	1	1
1970	2	718	0.005453		1896.49	0.049340		44	0.158624	0	1	0	1	1	1
1970	3	554	0.005505		1925.25	0.049916		44	0.158261	0	1	0	0	1	1
1970	4	798	0.005556		1954.01	0.050491		44	0.157898	0	1	0	0	1	1
1971	1	236	0.005661		2096.03	0.053529		44	0.158015	0	0	0	1	1	1
1971	2	604	0.005765		2238.06	0.056566		44	0.158131	0	0	0	1	1	1
1971	3	692	0.00587		2380.08	0.059604		44	0.158248	0	1	0	0	1	1
1971	4	418	0.005975		2522.11	0.062642		44	0.158365	0	1	0	0	1	1
1972	1	192	0.005892		2531.82	0.064366		44	0.158411	0	0	0	0	1	1
1972	2	148	0.005809		2541.53	0.066090		44	0.158457	0	0	0	0	1	1
1972	3	54	0.005726		2551.24	0.067813		44	0.158503	0	1	1	1	1	1
1972	4	89	0.005643		2560.95	0.069537		44	0.15855	0	1	1	0	1	1
1973	1	254	0.005658		2626.79	0.073897		44	0.159945	0	0	0	0	1	1
1973	2	506	0.005673		2692.63	0.078257		44	0.16134	0	0	0	0	1	1
1973	3	142	0.005687		2758.47	0.082617		44	0.162735	0	1	0	0	1	1
1973	4	204	0.005702		2824.31	0.086976		44	0.16413	0	1	0	0	1	1
1974	1	268	0.005689		2828.46	0.097394		44	0.161583	0	0	0	0	1	1
1974	2	318	0.005676		2832.6	0.107811		41.75	0.159035	0	0	1	0	1	1
1974	3	174	0.005663		2836.75	0.118229		39.5	0.156488	0	1	0	0	1	1
1974	4	236	0.00565		2840.89	0.128646		37.25	0.15394	0	0	0	0	1	1
1975	1	292	0.005849		2840.91	0.125756		35	0.15623	0	1	0	0	1	1
1975	2	262	0.006049		2840.93	0.122866		35	0.15852	0	0	0	0	1	1
1975	3	222	0.006248		2840.95	0.119975		35	0.16081	0	1	0	0	1	1
1975	4	124	0.006447		2840.97	0.117085		35	0.163101	0	1	0	0	1	1
1976	1	24	0.006502		2840.96	0.110138		35	0.165034	0	0	0	0	1	1
1976	2	144	0.006557		2840.94	0.103191		35	0.166968	0	1	1	0	1	1
1976	3	134	0.006611		2840.93	0.096244		35	0.168902	0	1	0	0	1	1
1976	4	50	0.006666		2840.92	0.089297		35	0.170836	0	1	1	0	1	1

190　APPENDIX B

Year	Qtr	Score	DPRK CINC	WGI	GDP pp	Trade pp	Refugees	Infant Mort	Food pp	UN Resolutions	Mil Exercise	U.S. Leader	ROK Leader	ROK Admin	Cold War
1977	1	56	0.006715		2840.92	0.092059		35	0.169082	0	1	0	0	1	1
1977	2	174	0.006764		2840.92	0.094820		35	0.167327	0	1	0	0	1	1
1977	3	56	0.006813		2840.92	0.097582		35	0.165573	0	1	0	0	1	1
1977	4	56	0.006862		2840.92	0.100344		35	0.163819	0	1	0	0	1	1
1978	1	34	0.007014		2840.95	0.103021		35	0.163128	0	1	0	0	1	1
1978	2	168	0.007167		2840.98	0.105698		35	0.162437	0	1	0	1	1	1
1978	3	0	0.007319		2841	0.108375		35	0.161747	0	1	0	1	1	1
1978	4	118	0.007472		2841.03	0.111052		35	0.161056	0	1	0	0	1	1
1979	1	50	0.007555		2841	0.121584		35	0.164674	0	1	0	0	1	1
1979	2	50	0.007639		2840.98	0.132116		33.75	0.168292	0	0	0	0	1	1
1979	3	174	0.007723		2840.95	0.142648		32.5	0.17191	0	1	0	0	1	1
1979	4	50	0.007807		2840.93	0.153181		31.25	0.175528	0	1	0	1	1	1
1980	1	162	0.007843		2840.96	0.145784		30	0.171102	0	1	0	0	1	1
1980	2	144	0.007879		2841	0.138387		30	0.166676	0	1	0	0	1	1
1980	3	18	0.007915		2841.03	0.130991		30	0.16225	0	1	0	1	1	1
1980	4	206	0.007952		2841.07	0.123594		30	0.157824	0	1	0	0	1	1
1981	1	62	0.008035		2841.05	0.116438		30	0.160321	0	1	0	1	1	1
1981	2	194	0.008118		2841.04	0.109283		30	0.162817	0	1	0	0	1	1
1981	3	329	0.008201		2841.02	0.102127		30	0.165313	0	1	1	0	1	1
1981	4	194	0.008285		2841	0.094971		30	0.167809	0	1	0	0	1	1
1982	1	84	0.008364		2841.02	0.095307		30	0.160131	0	1	0	0	1	1
1982	2	268	0.008444		2841.04	0.095644		30	0.152452	0	1	0	0	1	1
1982	3	185	0.008524		2841.06	0.095981		30	0.144774	0	1	0	0	1	1
1982	4	56	0.008604		2841.08	0.096317		30	0.137095	0	1	0	0	1	1
1983	1	100	0.008635		2841.06	0.094307		30	0.136649	0	1	0	0	1	1
1983	2	210	0.008667		2841.04	0.092296		30	0.136203	0	1	0	0	1	1
1983	3	156	0.008699		2841.02	0.090286		30	0.135756	0	1	0	0	1	1
1983	4	212	0.008731		2841	0.088275		30	0.13531	0	1	0	0	1	1
1984	1	138	0.008822		2841	0.086236		30	0.13534	0	0	0	0	1	1
1984	2	210	0.008914		2841	0.084197		29	0.13537	0	1	0	0	1	1
1984	3	116	0.009005		2841.01	0.082157		28	0.1354	0	1	0	0	1	1
1984	4	72	0.009096		2841.01	0.080118		27	0.13543	0	1	1	0	1	1
1985	1	66	0.009061		2841	0.080122		26	0.135592	0	1	0	0	1	1
1985	2	44	0.009026		2840.99	0.080126		26	0.135754	0	0	0	0	1	1
1985	3	56	0.008991		2840.97	0.080131		26	0.135916	0	1	0	0	1	1

Appendix B

Year	Qtr	Score	DPRK CINC	WGI	GDP pp	Trade pp	Refugees	Infant Mort	Food pp	UN Resolutions	Mil Exercise	U.S. Leader	ROK Leader	ROK Admin	Cold War
1985	4	200	0.008955		2840.96	0.080135		26	0.136079	0	1	0	0	1	1
1986	1	90	0.009043		2840.95	0.079897		26	0.138274	0	1	0	0	1	1
1986	2	54	0.00913		2840.94	0.079659		26	0.14047	0	0	0	0	1	1
1986	3	210	0.009218		2840.93	0.079422		26	0.142665	0	1	0	0	1	1
1986	4	22	0.009306		2840.92	0.079184		26	0.14486	0	1	0	0	1	1
1987	1	252	0.00937		2840.95	0.084605		26	0.14435	0	1	0	0	1	1
1987	2	56	0.009435		2840.99	0.090027		26	0.143839	0	0	0	0	1	1
1987	3	24	0.0095		2841.02	0.095448		26	0.143329	0	1	0	1	1	1
1987	4	156	0.009565		2841.06	0.100869		26	0.142818	0	1	0	0	1	1
1988	1	46	0.009562		2841.04	0.105468		26	0.141969	0	1	0	0	1	1
1988	2	58	0.00956		2841.02	0.110066		26	0.14112	0	0	0	0	1	1
1988	3	24	0.009557		2841	0.114665		26	0.14027	0	1	0	0	1	1
1988	4	80	0.009555		2840.98	0.119263		26	0.139421	0	1	1	0	1	1
1989	1	124	0.009902		2840.99	0.115766		26	0.141026	0	1	0	0	1	1
1989	2	18	0.010249		2841.01	0.112268		25.5	0.142632	0	0	0	0	1	1
1989	3	24	0.010596		2841.02	0.108771		25	0.144237	0	0	0	0	1	1
1989	4	42	0.010943		2841.03	0.105273		24.5	0.145843	0	1	0	0	1	1
1990	1	90	0.01124		2841.04	0.106452		24	0.14913	0	1	0	0	1	1
1990	2	66	0.011537		2841.05	0.107632		24.175	0.152418	0	0	0	0	1	1
1990	3	42	0.011834		2841.06	0.108811		24.35	0.155705	0	1	0	0	1	1
1990	4	30	0.012131		2841.07	0.109990		24.525	0.158993	0	1	0	0	1	1
1991	1	78	0.012367		2841.05	0.108820		24.7	0.159065	0	1	0	0	1	1
1991	2	34	0.012604		2841.04	0.107650		25.55	0.159137	0	0	0	0	1	1
1991	3	74	0.01284		2841.02	0.106480		26.4	0.15921	0	1	0	0	1	1
1991	4	92	0.013077		2841.01	0.105311		27.25	0.159282	0	1	0	0	1	1
1992	1	86	0.013203		2775.22	0.105431	0.00081324	25.55	0.158697	0	0	0	0	1	0
1992	2	236	0.013329		2709.43	0.105551	0.00080968	26.4	0.158113	0	0	0	0	1	0
1992	3	30	0.013455		2643.65	0.105671	0.00080613	27.25	0.157528	0	1	0	0	1	0
1992	4	98	0.013581		2577.86	0.105791	0.0008026	28.1	0.156943	0	1	1	1	1	0
1993	1	289	0.013462		2568.72	0.107337	0.00079902	29.325	0.158532	1	1	0	1	1	0
1993	2	114	0.013344		2559.58	0.108882	0.00079548	30.55	0.16012	1	0	0	0	1	0
1993	3	72	0.013225		2550.44	0.110428	0.00079193	31.775	0.161708	0	1	0	1	1	0
1993	4	120	0.013106		2541.3	0.111974	0.0007884	33	0.163296	0	1	0	0	1	0
1994	1	102	0.012756		2368.59	0.108201	0.00079722	34.425	0.164326	0	0	0	0	1	0
1994	2	254	0.012405		2195.87	0.104427	0.00080606	35.85	0.165356	0	0	0	0	1	0

192   APPENDIX B

Year	Qtr	Score	DPRK CINC	WGI	GDP pp	Trade pp	Refugees	Infant Mort	Food pp	UN Resolutions	Mil Exercise	U.S. Leader	ROK Leader	ROK Admin	Cold War
1994	3	130	0.012055		2023.16	0.100653	0.00081489	37.275	0.166386	0	1	0	0	1	0
1994	4	92	0.011704		1850.44	0.096879	0.0008237	38.7	0.167416	0	0	0	0	1	0
1995	1	126	0.01163		1768.14	0.099549	0.00108145	40.05	0.167592	0	0	0	0	1	0
1995	2	189	0.011555		1685.83	0.102219	0.00133917	41.4	0.167768	0	1	0	0	1	0
1995	3	96	0.011481		1603.53	0.104889	0.00159689	42.75	0.167944	0	1	0	0	1	0
1995	4	180	0.011406		1521.22	0.107559	0.0018546	44.1	0.16812	0	0	0	0	1	0
1996	1	66	0.011453		1454.38	0.114312	0.00201809	45.1	0.166358	0	0	0	0	1	0
1996	2	338	0.0115	-0.53	1387.55	0.121064	0.00218156	46.1	0.164596	0	0	0	0	1	0
1996	3	114	0.011547	-0.53	1320.71	0.127817	0.00234504	47.1	0.162834	0	0	0	0	1	0
1996	4	130	0.011595	-0.53	1253.87	0.134570	0.0025085	48.1	0.161071	0	0	0	0	1	0
1997	1	72	0.011432	-0.5175	1234.4	0.127040	0.00283937	48.55	0.160269	0	0	1	0	1	0
1997	2	136	0.011269	-0.505	1214.93	0.119510	0.00317022	49	0.159466	0	0	0	0	1	0
1997	3	154	0.011106	-0.4925	1195.46	0.111980	0.00350108	49.45	0.158664	0	1	0	0	1	0
1997	4	128	0.010943	-0.48	1175.99	0.104450	0.0038319	49.9	0.157861	0	1	0	1	1	0
1998	1	149	0.010671	-0.4675	1178.27	0.101147	0.00366343	49.725	0.156979	0	0	0	0	0	0
1998	2	172	0.010398	-0.455	1180.55	0.097844	0.00349494	49.55	0.156097	0	0	0	0	0	0
1998	3	250	0.010125	-0.4425	1182.83	0.094541	0.00332644	49.375	0.155214	0	1	0	0	0	0
1998	4	164	0.009853	-0.43	1185.11	0.091238	0.0031579	49.2	0.154332	0	1	0	0	0	0
1999	1	136	0.009843	-0.41375	1188.68	0.090646	0.00400606	48.475	0.154646	0	1	0	0	0	0
1999	2	174	0.009834	-0.3575	1192.26	0.090054	0.00485418	47.75	0.154961	0	0	0	0	0	0
1999	3	174	0.009824	-0.30125	1195.83	0.089463	0.00570229	47.025	0.155275	0	1	0	0	0	0
1999	4	86	0.009815	-0.245	1199.41	0.088871	0.0065504	46.3	0.15559	0	1	0	0	0	0
2000	1	110	0.009909	-0.18875	1197.13	0.099872	0.00833611	45.175	0.154008	0	1	0	0	0	0
2000	2	58	0.010003	-0.1325	1194.86	0.110874	0.01012182	44.05	0.152426	0	0	0	0	0	0
2000	3	30	0.010097	-0.07625	1192.58	0.121875	0.01190752	42.925	0.150844	0	1	0	0	0	0
2000	4	18	0.010191	0.02	1190.31	0.132876	0.0136932	41.8	0.149262	0	0	0	0	0	0
2001	1	48	0.010359	0.0375	1187.1	0.145749	0.01661321	40.5	0.147781	0	0	1	0	0	0
2001	2	58	0.010526	0.055	1183.9	0.158622	0.01953321	39.2	0.146301	0	0	0	0	0	0
2001	3	70	0.010694	0.0725	1180.7	0.171495	0.02245320	37.9	0.14482	0	1	0	0	0	0
2001	4	142	0.010862	0.09	1177.5	0.184368	0.0253732	36.6	0.14334	0	0	0	0	0	0
2002	1	86	0.010981	0.1075	1174.55	0.172596	0.03131136	35.475	0.143831	0	1	0	0	0	0
2002	2	184	0.011101	0.125	1171.6	0.160823	0.03724952	34.35	0.144322	0	0	0	0	0	0
2002	3	114	0.01122	0.1425	1168.66	0.149051	0.04318768	33.225	0.144813	0	1	0	0	0	0
2002	4	462	0.01134	0.16	1165.71	0.137279	0.0491258	32.1	0.145305	0	0	0	1	0	0
2003	1	577	0.011321	0.1475	1163.23	0.136805	0.05057134	31.25	0.145924	0	1	0	0	0	0

Appendix B

Year	Qtr	Score	DPRK CINC	WGI	GDP pp	Trade pp	Refugees	Infant Mort	Food pp	UN Resolutions	Mil Exercise	U.S. Leader	ROK Leader	ROK Admin	Cold War
2003	2	386	0.011301	0.135	1160.75	0.136332	0.05201684	30.4	0.146543	0	0	0	0	0	0
2003	3	272	0.011282	0.1225	1158.28	0.135859	0.05346234	29.55	0.147162	0	1	0	0	0	0
2003	4	198	0.011263	0.11	1155.8	0.135386	0.0549078	28.7	0.147781	1	0	0	0	0	0
2004	1	218	0.011635	0.11	1153.71	0.144138	0.06134956	28.175	0.147761	0	0	0	0	1	0
2004	2	122	0.012006	0.11	1151.71	0.152891	0.06779127	27.65	0.147741	1	1	0	0	1	0
2004	3	195	0.012378	0.11	1149.66	0.161643	0.07423299	27.125	0.147722	0	0	0	0	1	0
2004	4	302	0.01275	0.11	1147.61	0.170395	0.0806747	26.6	0.147702	1	0	0	0	1	0
2005	1	216	0.012809	0.065	1145.75	0.173408	0.07514343	26.4	0.148728	0	0	0	0	1	0
2005	2	176	0.012869	0.02	1143.89	0.176420	0.06961215	26.2	0.149755	1	0	0	0	1	0
2005	3	122	0.012928	-0.025	1142.03	0.179433	0.06408087	26	0.150781	0	0	0	0	1	0
2005	4	242	0.012988	-0.07	1140.16	0.182446	0.0585496	25.8	0.151808	0	0	0	0	1	0
2006	1	140	0.012958	-0.0775	1138.47	0.187499	0.06514179	25.85	0.15243	1	0	0	0	1	0
2006	2	126	0.012928	-0.085	1136.77	0.192551	0.07173398	25.9	0.153051	0	0	0	0	1	0
2006	3	209	0.012898	-0.0925	1135.07	0.197604	0.07832617	25.95	0.153673	1	0	0	0	1	0
2006	4	205	0.012868	-0.1	1133.37	0.202657	0.0849184	26	0.154294	0	0	0	0	1	0
2007	1	64	0.012882	0.055	1131.83	0.216320	0.09029075	26.05	0.151856	1	0	0	0	1	0
2007	2	380	0.012896	0.21	1130.28	0.229982	0.09566313	26.1	0.149417	0	0	0	0	1	0
2007	3	146	0.012911	0.365	1128.73	0.243645	0.10103551	26.15	0.146979	1	0	0	0	1	0
2007	4	34	0.012925	0.52	1127.18	0.257308	0.1064079	26.2	0.144541	0	0	0	0	1	0
2008	1	249	0.012925	0.5225	1125.79	0.285205	0.10900429	26.25	0.143748	1	1	0	0	1	0
2008	2	218	0.012925	0.525	1124.41	0.313103	0.11160069	26.3	0.142956	0	0	1	0	0	0
2008	3	188	0.012925	0.5275	1123.02	0.341000	0.11419708	26.35	0.142164	1	0	0	1	0	0
2008	4	259	0.012925	0.53	1121.63	0.368898	0.1167935	26.4	0.141371	0	0	0	1	1	0
2009	1	474	0.012925	0.3825	1316.22	0.345119	0.11784396	26.4	0.141836	1	0	0	1	1	0
2009	2	631	0.012925	0.235	1510.82	0.321341	0.11889445	26.4	0.1423	0	0	0	1	1	0
2009	3	395	0.012925	0.0875	1705.41	0.297563	0.11994493	26.4	0.142765	1	0	0	1	1	0
2009	4	183	0.012925	-0.06	1900	0.273784	0.1209954	26.4	0.143229	1	0	0	1	1	0
2010	1	341	0.012925	-0.145	1875	0.283855	0.11516488	26.375	0.143229	0	0	0	1	1	0
2010	2	522	0.012925	-0.23	1850	0.293926	0.10933434	26.35	0.143229	1	0	0	1	1	0
2010	3	330	0.012925	-0.315	1825	0.303997	0.10350381	26.325	0.143229	0	0	0	1	1	0
2010	4	401	0.012925	-0.4	1800	0.314067	0.0976733	26.3	0.143229	1	0	0	1	1	0
2011	1	146	0.012925	-0.4125	1800	0.324554	0.10123263	26.3	0.143229	1	0	0	1	1	0
2011	2	138	0.012925	-0.425	1800	0.335040	0.10479199	26.3	0.143229	0	0	0	1	1	0
2011	3	139	0.012925	-0.4375	1800	0.345526	0.10835134	26.3	0.143229	1	0	0	1	1	0
2011	4	138	0.012925	-0.45	1800	0.356013	0.1119107	26.3	0.143229	0	0	0	1	1	0

Appendix C

Map of the Korean Peninsula

Source: CIA 2011. Map of the Korean Peninsula. Library of Congress. *http://www.loc.gov/resource/g7900.ct003454/*. Accessed 31 October 2015.

Chapter Notes

Preface

1. This book and the supporting research used both methods to examine North Korea's conflict behavior.
2. These include Clark, Fordham and Nordstrom (2011); Kim (2010); Kisangani and Pickering (2007); Davies (2005, 2006, 2007); Fordham (2005); Bueno de Mesquita et al. (2004); Peceny and Butler (2004); and Peceny, Beer, and Sanchez-Terry (2002).
3. See Toft (2010) and Li (2008) for mixed-method study examples.
4. The statements of fact, opinion, or analysis expressed in the book are those of the author and do not reflect the official policy or position of the U.S. Government, the Department of Defense, or any of its components.

Introduction

1. This is not an inclusive list as many other conflicts have been associated with diversionary war such as the Franco-Prussian Wars, World War I, the United States' war with Vietnam, and the 1996 conflict in Rwanda (Mayer 1969, 299; Lenin 1930, 76; Fordham 1998, 568; Kisangani and Pickering 2005, 23).

Chapter 1

1. Relevant literature on the modern history of the Koreas includes Eckert (1990), Cumings (2005), Robinson (2007) and Salvada (1994) and Worden (2008). These scholars provide an important perspective on Korea's initial relations with other nations and opening to the West in the 1800s, the domination and occupation by the Japanese and the arrival of the Cold War and influence of the Soviet Union and United States. Additionally, there are number of important works that discuss the rise of the Korean communist party (Suh 1967; Nam 1974; Kim I. 1975; Van Ree 1989), Kim Il-sung's background and ascension (Suh 1988, Lankov 2002; Szalontai 2005), and the early formation of the North Korean state (Cumings 1981; Cumings 1990; Armstrong 2003; Millett 2005).
2. Salvada (1994, 9–11) provides a concise review of this period in Korea's history.
3. The early history of Kim and his guerrilla activities against the Japanese are available in Martin (2006, 29–46) and Suh (1988, 30–54).
4. The USSR did not achieve its pre-war production levels until 1948 and its subsequent support to North Korea weighed heavily on the Soviet economy (Carter 1972, 9).
5. The People's Republic of China was formally established on October 1, 1949, and Mao's first visit to the Soviet Union and Stalin occurred in December 1949 (Spence 1990 512, 524).
6. Cumings (1990, 568–621) devotes an entire chapter to the question of who started the Korean War and concludes, "Who caused the Korean war? No one and everyone, [it was caused by] all who where party to the tapestry of events since 1945." More recent scholarship that focuses on the prelude period (1945–1950) to the war includes Cumings (1981; 1990), Armstrong (2003), Millett (2005), the Wilson Center's Cold War International History Project (2012), North Korea International Documentation Project (2012), and the CIA's FOIA portal (2012).
7. For a detailed account of the activities during that period, see Ridgeway (1967, 185–

225), MacDonald (1986, 116–198), and Stueck (2002, 143–181).

8. The majority of the heavy industry in Korea was located in the northern half of the peninsula (CIA 1947a, 4; Salvada 1993, 31).

9. Cumings (2005, 297–298) was quoting a Thames Television transcript for "Korea: The Unknown War" (Thames 1986).

10. Kim (1968a, 715) obtained these figures from both Kim Il Sung and Nodong Shinmun (North Korea's leading newspaper).

11. This is also spelled "Yan'an" or "Yenan."

12. During the late 1950s, North Korea began to place an "emphasis on all things Korean over all things foreign" (Lankov 2002b, 67).

13. See Barnhart (1987) for details on Japanese efforts to achieve autarky.

14. Unfortunately, Shimotomai (2011, 131) provides no details or evidence of the relationship between diversion and these juche campaigns. These types of assertions about diversion are often made by both scholars and policymakers, but require evidence to substantiate.

15. The text of Eisenhower's policy is detailed in NSC 162/2 (FRUS 1953).

16. In this treaty, the U.S. pledged to assist South Korea in case of an "armed attack" and currently remains in effect (USFK 2012b).

17. Hostilities initiated by the DPRK increased after the deployments of new weapons to the South (1958–1959) and decreased during the time in which the ROK transitioned power from Rhee to Park (1960–1961).

18. As Sobek (2007, 31) notes, diversion provides these types of capabilities to leaders.

Chapter 2

1. Collier and Mahoney (1996, 59) define selection bias as "occurring when some form of selection process in either the design of the study or the real-world phenomena under investigation results in inferences that suffer from systematic error."

2. Not all of these cases are "perfectly" congruent and comparable (although no case selection can achieve perfect symmetry), but this selection allows for a representative sample of events that have occurred between 1960 and 2011.

3. This includes conflicts involving North and South Korea.

4. Six data sources were used to construct the event database in this analysis: the USFK Command History Office, the United Nations Command (UNC), the South Korean government's Korean Institute for National Unification (KINU), Fischer's CRS Report, the New York Times Historical Archive, and Lexis-Nexis Academic Search.

5. In this research, ongoing resolutions are discussed, but only newly enacted resolutions are counted for this measure.

6. The turmoil during this period has been analyzed by a few scholars including Bolger (1991), Michishita (2009, 1–51), and Park (2009). Additionally, recently opened archival and declassified information has provided important perspectives to this period such as the Wilson Center's North Korea International Documentation Project (2012), which includes primary source information on diplomatic relations with North Korea by the Soviet Union, China, and a number of other former communist states as Hungary, Bulgaria, and the German Democratic Republic. The CIA's Freedom of Information Act Site (CIA FOIA 2012), Foreign Relations of the United States (FRUS 2012), and Finley's (1984) history of U.S. Forces in Korea also provide in-depth analysis of DPRK and regional interactions from a U.S. perspective during this period.

7. Bolger (1991, 62–65) provides a useful synopsis of the attack and an analysis of the effectiveness of ROK anti-infiltration efforts. He noted that the incident had resulted in too many casualties, but the attack had been successfully stopped due to "DMZ enhancements" (which provided evidence of the infiltration) and ROK quick reaction force operations (Bolger 1991, 62–65).

8. The USS *Pueblo* remained in North Korea as a tourist attraction and, as of this writing, possibly being refurbished for installation in a museum in Pyongyang (NK News 2013).

9. Lerner (2002), Mobley (2003), and Armbister (2004) provide useful and in-depth narratives of the entire *Pueblo* incident. Additionally, the U.S. House Armed Services Committee meeting reports (HASC 1969) include a detailed investigation of the incident and the lessons learned from the U.S. government's perspective.

10. More narrative details on the EC-121 incident are available in Zagoria and Zagoria (1979, 39–58), Mobley (2003, 98–167) and CINCPAC (1970, 133–145).

11. Other scholars have measured political instability based on mass and elite unrest in a given society. For example, Banks' Cross-National Time-Series (CNTS) Data Archive

has reporting on internal instability (including purges, strikes and riots) and has been cited by a number of scholars as a measure of political unrest (Kisangani and Pickering 2005; Bell 2009; Tir 2010). Unfortunately, the CNTS contains only limited information on North Korean instability.

12. The World Governance Indicators (WGI) are not discussed in this case as that index is only available beginning in the 1990s.

13. Shimotomai (2011) and Koh (1969) provide useful historical discussions on Kim Il-sung's ability to maintain North Korea's independence and generally cordial relations with both communist hegemons.

14. Maddison's (2008) data is reported in 1990 international dollars.

15. For more details on the Seven-Year Plan, see Chung (1972).

16. See Appendix B.

17. South Korean government statistics on defectors are only published in aggregated form prior to 1989. This database shows that "prior to 1989," 607 refugees from the DPRK entered South Korea (ROK MOU 2012a). Most likely, this means that between 1953 and 1989, the ROK documented 607 refugees fled the DPRK.

18. Ironically, a few young American soldiers defected to North Korea during the 1960s. Between 1961 and 1965, four U.S. Army enlisted soldiers (all between 19 and 21 years old) defected to North Korea including Charles Robert Jenkins, an American NCO who was released by North Korea in 2004 to reside in Japan (UNC 2012; Brooke 2012). Jenkins reportedly crossed the DMZ and defected to the DPRK in order to "avoid military service in Vietnam" (Brooke 2012).

19. This classification system remains in place today.

20. This exercise still occurs, now designated "ULCHI FREEDOM GUARDIAN," and remains focused on "strengthening the readiness of Republic of Korea and U.S. forces" (USFK 2012).

21. Beginning in 1968, FOCUS LENS (or a similar exercise) occurred annually in the fall.

22. Very little information is available on other ROK military actions, but these activities by the South Korean defense forces happened often enough to warrant the attention of both USFK and the U.S. Congress (FRUS 1967a).

23. The average hostile foreign policy yearly conflict score between 1960 and 2011 was 735 (Appendix B).

24. The DPRK always issued provocative statements during these exercise periods, but the intensity of military conflict during exercises did not vary consistently during the 1960s (KINU 2011; Finley 1984).

25. Lerner's (2010) archival analysis provides some of the best information on the motivations of the Kim regime's activities from the perspective of diplomats stationed in the DPRK. The examination of similar communications during the other two case study periods (diplomatic communications in Pyongyang throughout the 1990s and in the late 2000s) might hold similarly revealing insights into Kim regime actions, although that information is not currently available.

Chapter 3

1. Farmers and their families were given their rations for a year at the end of harvest and were not included in the standard PDS system food allocations (Natsios 2000, 94).

2. Eberstadt (1997, 233) was quoting an article in a South Korean newspaper, the *Tong-a Ilbo* (13 May 1994).

3. This term harks back to the "Arduous March" period of Kim Il Sung. According to the DPRK Government (2001, 86–87), Kim Il Sung and the unit under his command (the 2nd Directional Army) marched for 100 days while being pursued by Japanese Army forces in southern Manchuria. The DPRK Government (2001, 86) notes, "The KPRA [Korean People's Revolutionary Army] had to continue its forced march and fight bloody battles against the enemy all the while, without properly eating, sleeping or resting in the face of the tenacious and persistent attacks of the enemy, biting cold and raging snow storms unprecedented for 100 years."

4. The HFP scores for the famine period averaged 601 per year and the first case study scores were 1222 per year (Appendix B).

5. Conflict intensity scores during the famine period were 601 compared to 735 during the entire study period (1960–2011) (Appendix B).

6. President Bush directed the removal in November 1991 (CINCPAC 1991, 91).

7. This crisis has been well documented by scholars such as Wit (2004) and Oberdorfer (2001, 249–336), who both provide a detailed and detailed account of the entire nuclear crisis period.

8. For more information on North Korea's ballistic missile program and its relationship to

the Kim regime's foreign policy and security goals, see Bermudez (1999; 2001, 236–291) and Michishita (2009, 117–137).

9. Michishita (2009, 132) notes that "in terms of missile range and capabilities, the Nodong was designed for use against Japan and the Taepo Dong, or more specifically, the Taepodong-2 was designed for use against the United States."

10. The average conflict intensity from 1960 to 1970 was twice as high as during the 1990s (Appendix B).

11. In the 1990s, these units were considered well-trained and capable of conducting a variety of clandestine missions deep into South Korea (MCIA 1997, 102–104; Martin 2004, 538–542).

12. In the Imjin river incident, one agent escaped, the other was killed by ROK security forces; the two North Koreans who entered South Korea via Cheju island conducted operations for about two months before being detected in Puyo (about 100 miles south of Seoul) with both agents being killed by ROK soldiers (Bermudez 1997, 160; Fischer 2007, 12).

13. Bermudez (1997, 161–168) provides a detailed account of the incident focusing on the equipment and methods used by the DPRK special operations forces.

14. Seoul National University is generally considered South Korea's most prestigious university.

15. Appendix C includes a map of the Yellow Sea area.

16. On both the north and south side of the MDL there is a two-kilometer buffer zone (or DMZ) that is the land-based separation zone between the DPRK and ROK.

17. Kim Il-sung was the founding father of the North Korean state, appointed and sponsored by the Soviets during their post–World War II occupation of the DPRK. After spending the 1930s as a communist guerrilla fighter against the Japanese in Manchuria and much of the 1940s training in Soviet camps, Kim returned to Korea in September 1945 to a hero's welcome (Eckert and Lee 1990, 341). Kim was instrumental in the early formation of the DPRK and by early 1948, after a purge of older communists, he established firm control of the North Korean Workers Party (Buzo 2002, 56). In September 1948, the Democratic People's Republic of Korea announced itself as an independent nation, with Kim Il-sung as its leader. Kim led North Korea for over 45 years: through war with the South and rebuilding (supported by both the Soviets and the PRC); challenges to his authority in the late 1950s; industrial and social achievements and an "undeclared war" with South Korea and the U.S. in the 1960s; limited reconciliation with the ROK in the 1970s; and the beginnings of economic stagnation in the 1980s.

18. The term "Great Leader" is an honorific phrase referring to Kim Il-sung. Kim Jong-il was often referred to as the "Dear Leader" by the North Korean public.

19. Defector testimony is the primary source of information on North Korea's police and penal system. See Haggard and Noland (2007, 81–99), Hassig and Oh (2009, 195–215), Martin (2006, 290–304) and Kang and Rigoulet (2001).

20. While these events might be considered instances of petty crime in most states, this type of activity rarely occurs in North Korea and indicated growing public dissatisfaction with the Kim regime. Pictures and statues of both Kim Il-sung and Kim Jong-il are considered "the very embodiment of those leaders, beyond mere art, and are treated accordingly" and disrespect or defamation usually incurs severe penalties or imprisonment (Korea Times 1999).

21. Author's experience while living in South Korea.

22. The threat, issued in 1994 by a DPRK diplomat, was intended to remind the ROK of the DPRK's development and potential use of nuclear weapons if needed (Financial Times 1994).

23. For a more detailed discussion on North Korea's political "caste" system, see Hassig and Oh (2009, 198–204).

24. Kaufman's (2010) World Governance Indicators assessment of North Korea between 1996 and 2000 actually showed an increasing level of political stability during the famine period.

25. Many authors (Noland 1997; Cha 2004; Eberstadt 1993) have used this phrase to describe North Korea's ability, despite all odds, to survive both economic and social crises intact.

26. There were no other UN Security Council Resolutions enacted on North Korea until the mid-2000s.

27. Wit (2004) provides a detailed account of the crisis and negotiations from a U.S. diplomat's vantage point.

28. See Eckert (1990, 379–387) and Cumings (2005, 342–403) for more detailed information.

29. Kim Dae-jung had a long history of con-

flict with the South Korean political establishment and was a presidential challenger to longtime authoritarian ruler Park Chung Hee in 1971. Park had intelligence operatives in Tokyo kidnap Kim in 1973 and Kim remained either in prison or under house arrest until 1978 (Oberdorfer 1997, 126 and Eckert 1990, 364–372).

30. Kim Young-sam had resigned from the ruling party and declared that he was "neutral" in the election (Sullivan 1997). South Korean law limits each president to a single five-year term limit.

31. For a review of the crisis and its effects on Korea and the region, see Nanto (1998), Yoo (1999), and Noland (2000, 195–250).

32. North Korea publically threatened a number of South Korean media organizations for publishing first-hand accounts of incidents ranging from the relationship between Kim Il-sung and Kim Jong-il to the daily lives of North Korean citizens (Fischer 2007, 14–15 and DPRK 1997).

33. The DPRK had previously supported Kim Dae-jung in the 1992 elections (Lee 1992; Breen 1992).

34. The official DPRK explanation was that the submarine had engine trouble in North Korean waters and drifted to the South Korean coast (Browne 1996).

35. The average yearly conflict score between 1960 and 2011 was 735 (see Appendix B).

36. In 1993, the "nuclear club" only included the five signatories to the NPT (the U.S., China, Russia, Great Britain, and France) and two non–NPT states (Israel and India) (Norris and Kristensen 2010, 82; Sagan 1996, 59).

37. Author observations while working in Seoul in 1998.

Chapter 4

1. Conflict scores for this period (2008–2011) average 1188 per year while the historical (yearly) average is 735 (1960–2011) (Appendix B).

2. A description of the history of the NLL is included in the Famine case study above in the section entitled the "The Battle of Yeonpyeong." Additionally, a map of this area is included in Appendix C.

3. In comparison, South Korea's agricultural section makes up only 2.6 percent of its GDP, yet the ROK produces more food each year than the North (EIU 2011, 18).

4. Details on the amount and type of Chinese humanitarian and energy aid were not made public.

5. This description omits the complicated situations and extreme hardships faced by DPRK defectors (refugees). For more details on both the circumstances and motives of DPRK refugees, see KINU (2011b), Hassig and Oh (2009) and Haggard and Noland (2011a).

6. This may have been referring to the Chinese food and energy support cited by Snyder and Byun (2012).

7. In November 2010, South Korea's Ministry of Unification formally declared the end of the "Sunshine Policy" and that "a decade of cooperation, cross-border exchanges and billions of dollars in aid did not change Pyongyang's behavior or improve the lives of North Korean citizens" (ROK MOU 2010).

8. This was the first time this exercise was held and it was considered a direct response to the sinking of the ROK naval vessel *Cheonan* in March 2010.

9. Although this chart is formatted differently than previous ones, it provides an important example of the relationship between military exercises and hostile foreign policy actions by month. This shows that there is a potential correlation, at least during some events, of conflict to strategic exercises.

10. North and South Korea operated two joint economic ventures during this time: the Kaesong Industrial Complex and the Mount Kumgang tourist resort. Both of these special economic zones were accessible to South Koreans, the result of Kim Dae-jung's Sunshine Policy, and intended to "nudge the North toward embracing economic reforms and opening up to the world" (Onishi 2006). While the Mount Kumgang tourist resort was closed in 2008 (BBC 2011b), the Kaesong Industrial complex included around 100 South Korean companies employing 40,000 North Koreans to produce "light industrial goods to be sold in South Korea" (Oh and Hassig 2010, 93) and was still in operation as of 2016.

11. The average yearly conflict score between 1960 and 2011 was 735 (see Appendix B).

12. North Korea never admitted responsibility for this incident (the *Cheonan* sinking), which occurred in conjunction with the end of the DPRK's 2009–2010 currency crisis (Chosun Ilbo 2013a).

13. Cases 1 and 3 were 66 percent and 61 percent higher than yearly historical averages respectively. Case 2 was 18 percent lower than annual averages (Appendix B).

Chapter 5

1. More details on this model are available later in this chapter and in Gujarati (2009, 634–639).

2. According to some reports, North Korea's economy outpaced South Korea's well into the 1970s (Oh and Hassig 2000, 8).

3. Kim Jong-il, the son of North Korea's first leader (Kim Il-sung) died of a heart attack on December 17, 2011 after ruling the DPRK for 17 years. North Korea's government quickly affirmed that Kim Jong-il's son, Kim Jong-un, was its next leader.

4. This is the goal of all social science research—to make conclusions that "go beyond the particular observations collected" (King, Keohane, and Verba 1999, 8).

5. In the future, examining DPRK cooperative events would be an important contribution to the overall analysis of the political behaviors of North Korea and the Kim regimes.

6. The KEDS database (Kansas Events Data System 2012) is now in the Penn State Events Data Project (2012). That project is focused primarily on areas such as the Balkans, West Africa, and the Middle East (but not East Asia).

7. Sprecher and DeRouen (2005, 127) note that "Hostile actions in COPDAB are those events coded nine and above. In KEDS, events coded 110 and above are considered hostile actions." The KEDS coding is more specific than the COPDAB method and uses over 60 categories (Sprecher and DeRouen 2005, 137–138). For this research on DPRK activity, Azar's (1993) COPDAB scaling was more efficient and a better fit for the analysis of Korea events.

8. Vincent (1983) notes systemic problems with both COPDAB and WEIS event data and comments that these included both significant levels of "regional bias" and an inability to predict changes in conflict that occurred.

9. This method is based on Nincic (1975, 624), Azar (1982, 36), McClelland (1999, 1), and Goldstein (1992, 376–377).

10. These reports were translated initially using automated methods (Google Translate) and then reviewed by a native-speaking Korean research assistant for accuracy.

11. An official with the United Nations Command in Seoul provided event data on DPRK–U.S.–ROK interactions from 1960–2011 (UNC 2012). The same information is publicly available in media reports.

12. These sources were searched and often reported duplicate information (which allowed for cross-checking and verification). Again, the only provocative statements used in the analysis were from Lexis-Nexus, *New York Times*, and KCNA databases for foreign ministry and military pronouncements (rather than all negative reports on the U.S.) since they represent the highest level of communication from the DPRK government.

13. Baraldi and Enders (2010) and Howell (2012) discuss the merits and risks of this approach.

14. These numbers are simulated for clarity.

15. This method is based on Nincic (1975, 624), Azar (1982, 36), McClelland (1999, 1); and Goldstein (1992, 376–377). See previous text for an explanation of the scaling in the COPDAB and WEIS data.

16. Park (2011) notes that both of these factors are influential in North Korean aggressive foreign policy choices.

17. This includes research by Weeks (2011), Pickering and Kisangani (2010), Lai and Slater (2006) and Peceny and Butler (2004).

18. Capital goods are finished items that governments use for the production of other items. For North Korea, these include items such as metal, machinery, and other manufactured items (Eberstadt 1998, 180).

19. U.S. government researchers also used this approach to analyze North Korea's economy (Nanto and Chanlett-Avery, 2010).

20. North Korea population figures are from the U.S. Census (2012) international population data.

21. Detailed data on pre-1994 refugees held by the ROK government is not publicly releasable (ROK MOU 2012b).

22. More information on the causes of the increase in infant mortality during the 1990s is available in case studies on North Korea's famine by Natsios (2000) and Haggard and Noland (2007).

23. This data is available from the Food and Agriculture Organization of the United Nations (FAOSTAT 2012).

24. Rennack (2011) provides a useful discussion of the background and the status of sanctions on North Korea while Noland (2008) contends that they are overwhelmingly ineffective.

25. This concept involves state-level efforts to avoid conflict with other states through "conciliatory" actions or attitudes (Fordham 2005).

26. ROK elections or regime changes have occurred in 1948, 1952, 1956, 1960, 1963, 1967,

1971, 1978, 1981, 1987 and every five years thereafter (for this study, 2007 was the most recent). U.S. elections generally occur every 4 years (2008 was the most recent).

27. South Korean administrations that are coded as "liberal" include Yun Bo-seon (1960–1962), Kim Dae-jung (1998–2003) and Roh Myoo-hung (2003–2008). Yun Bo-seon, along with his Prime Minister Chang Myon, took power after Syngman Rhee's resignation in 1960 and was the leader of "South Korea's first democratic regime" (Cumings 2005, 350–351; Eckert 1990, 355–357). The more recent administrations of Kim and Roh were more centrist and liberal compared to other ROK presidencies.

28. This project uses December 31, 1991, as the date of the official dissolution of the Soviet Union and end of the Cold War.

29. King, Keohane and Verba (1994, 221) discuss problems with research involving small numbers of observations.

30. For more detailed explanations on the types of adjustments required for this type of analysis, see Gujarati and Porter (2009, 34–54), Ostrom (1990, 7–16) and Downing and Clark (1996, 107–128).

31. See Cochrane and Orcutt (1949), Gujarati and Porter (2009, 55–85), Gujarati (2011), and DSS (2012) for a detailed discussion of this method of regression analysis and AR(1), OLS, and associated tests for validity.

32. Gujarati and Porter (2009, 342) note that one method to deal with multicollinearity is to "do nothing" and given the characteristics of this data, this is the best option for this research.

33. In this first model, WGI, UN Resolutions, and Refugees are omitted although these are tested in each of the other models. See next section for a detailed explanation for the characteristics and outputs of each model.

34. Only the statistically significant variables that are continuous (CINC, Food Availability, and Refugees) are included in this figure.

Chapter 6

1. As previously discussed, Michishita (2011) and Jung (2012) are the only other scholars that have used these types of methods to examine DPRK conflict activities.

2. Jung's (2012) study remains an exception and his study of diversion using quantitative cross-national analysis. His case studies on Korea are useful additions to scholarship on the DPRK.

3. The author has spent over a decade in Korea working for the Department of Defense and U.S. Army as an intelligence officer. The first (1995 to 1997) was with 2ID and the 501st Military Intelligence Brigade, and during the second and third (2002–2004 and 2005–2008), he was assigned to the USFK J2. As of this writing, the author is again working in Korea for USFK.

Bibliography

Abouharb, M., and Anessa Kimball. 2007. "A New Dataset on Infant Mortality Rates, 1816–2002." *Journal of Peace Research* 44(6): 743–754.

AFP (*Agence France Presse*). 1992. "North Korea Slams Election of Kim Young-Sam." *Agence France Presse*. 21 December 1992. Accessed via LexisNexis, 21 August 2012.

AFP (*Agence France Presse*). 1993. "Pyongyang Denounces U.N. Security Council Resolution." *Agence France Presse*. 13 May 1993. Accessed via LexisNexis, 21 August 2012.

AFP (*Agence France Presse*). 1998. "Medecins Sans Frontieres Forced to Withdraw from North Korea." *Agence France Presse*. 30 September 1998. Accessed via LexisNexis, 19 August 2012.

AFP (*Agence France Presse*). 2006a. "U.S. Diplomacy in High Gear After 'Provocative' North Korea Launches." 5 July 2006. *Agence France Presse*. Accessed via LexisNexis, 26 January 2013.

AFP (*Agence France Presse*). 2006b. "Nkorea Says Sanctions 'Act of War.'" 7 July 2006. *Agence France Presse*. Accessed via LexisNexis, 26 January 2013.

AFP (*Agence France Presse*). 2008. "Nkorea's Kim May Have Suffered Stroke: U.S. Intelligence." 9 September 2008. *Agence France Presse*. Accessed via LexisNexis, 30 January 2013.

AFP (*Agence France Presse*). 2009a. "Nkorea's Kim Attends Lunar New Year Concert: State Media." 26 January 2009. *Agence France Presse*. Accessed via LexisNexis, 10 February 2013.

AFP (*Agence France Presse*). 2009b. "Nkorea Informed U.S. of Nuclear Test: Official." 25 May 2009. *Agence France Presse*. Accessed via LexisNexis, 10 February 2013.

AFP (*Agence France Presse*). 2009c. "Nkorea's Kim Has Cancer: Report." 13 July 2009. *Agence France Presse*. Accessed via LexisNexis, 10 February 2013.

AFP (*Agence France Presse*). 2009d. "Two Koreas in Naval Clash Off West Coast: Official." *Agence France Presse*. 10 November 2009. Accessed via LexisNexis, 11 February 2013.

AFP (*Agence France Presse*). 2010. "S.Korea, U.S. Launch War Games Despite N.Korean Threats." *Agence France Presse*. 8 March 2010. Accessed via LexisNexis, 11 February 2013.

AFP (*Agence France Presse*). 2012a. "N. Korea Deal Raises Hopes Over Young Leader." 29 February 2012. *Agence France Presse*. Accessed via LexisNexis, 3 February 2013.

AFP (*Agence France Presse*). 2012b. "Chronology of North Korean Missile Development." 12 December 2012. *Agence France Presse*. Accessed via LexisNexis, 26 January 2013.

The Age. 1993. "Food Riots in N Korea—Defector." *The Age*. Melbourne. 26 August 1993. Accessed via LexisNexis, 17 August 2012.

Agreed Framework Between the United States of America and the Democratic People's Republic of Korea. 21 October 1994. Korea Peninsula Energy Development Organization Website. http://www.kedo.org/pdfs/AgreedFramework.pdf. Accessed 7 Aug 2012.

Ahn, Byung-Joon. 1985. "The Soviet Union and the Korean Peninsula." *Asian Affairs* 11(4): 1–20

Ahn, Mun Suk. 2012. "Kim Jong-Il's Death and His Son's Strategy for Seizing Power in North Korea." *Problems of Post-Communism* 59(4): 27–37.

Ake, Claude. 1975. "A Definition of Political Stability." *Comparative Politics* 7(2): 271–283.

Allison, Paul David. 1984. *Event History Analysis: Regression for Longitudinal Event Data*. Beverly Hills, CA: Sage Publications.

AP (*Associated Press*). 1999a. "North Korea's Famine May Be Easing." *Associated Press Online*. 11 May 1999. Accessed via LexisNexis, 16 August 2012.

AP (*Associated Press*). 1999b. "North Korea Still Has Food Shortage." *Associated Press Online*. 27 October 1999. Accessed via LexisNexis, 16 August 2012.

AP (*Associated Press*). 2001. "U.S., S. Korea Announce Joint Exercise." 6 November 2001. *Air Force Times*. http://www.airforcetimes.com/legacy/new/1-292925-583717.php. Accessed 18 January 2013.

AP (*Associated Press*). 2006. "South Korea Delays Food Aid to the North." 7 July 2006. *The Associated Press*. Accessed via LexisNexis, 28 January 2013.

AP (*The Associated Press*). 2008. "Skorea Says Nkorea Running Normally Under Kim." 22 October 2008. *The Associated Press*. Accessed via LexisNexis, 30 January 2013.

Appleman, Roy Edgar. 1961. *South to the Naktong, North to the Yalu: June-November 1950*. Washington, D.C.: Office of the Chief of Military History, Department of the Army.

Armbrister, Trevor. 2004. *A Matter of Accountability: The True Story of the Pueblo Affair*. Guilford, CT: Lyon's Press.

Armstrong, Charles. 2010. "The Korean War Never Ended." *CNN Online*. 26 May 2010. http://www.cnn.com/2010/OPINION/05/24/armstrong.north.korea/ index.html. Accessed 13 February 2013.

Armstrong, Charles K. 2003. *The North Korean Revolution, 1945–1950*. Ithaca: Cornell University Press.

Asano, Yoshiharu. 2009. "DPRK Missile Launch a Calculated Move; Pyongyang Sought Powerful Message for Domestic, International Consumption." *The Daily Yomiuri* (Tokyo). 7 April 2009. Accessed via LexisNexis, 9 February 2013.

Azar, Edward E. 1978. *Conflict and Peace Data Bank (COPDAB), 1948–1978* [Computer file]. ICPSR07767-v4. Ann Arbor, MI: Interuniversity Consortium for Political and Social Research.

Azar, Edward E. 1980. "The Conflict and Peace Data Bank (COPDAB) Project." *Journal of Conflict Resolution* 24(1): 143–152.

Azar, Edward E. 1982. "The Codebook of the Conflict and Peace Data Bank (COPDAB): A Computer-Assisted Approach to Monitoring and Analyzing International and Domestic Events." The Center for International Development and Conflict Management, University of Maryland, College Park, MD.

Azar, Edward E. 1993. *Conflict and Peace Data Bank (COPDAB), 1948–1978 Codebook*. Ann Arbor, MI: Inter-university Consortium for Political and Social Research.

Azar, Edward E., Stanley H. Cohen, Thomas O. Jukam, and James M. McCormick. 1972. "The Problem of Source Coverage in the Use of International Events Data." *International Studies Quarterly* 16(3): 373–388.

Bajoria, Jayshree, and Beina Xu. 2013. "The China-North Korea Relationship." 21 February 2013. *Council on Foreign Relations*. http://www.cfr.org/china/china-north-korea-relationship/p11097. Accessed 1 November 2013.

Bak, Daehee, and Glenn Palmer, 2011. "Domestic Unrest and International Conflict in Authoritarian Regimes: Diversion Vs. Constraints." Paper presented at the annual meeting of the International Studies Association Annual Conference, Montreal, Canada, 16 March 2011.

Bank of Korea (BOK). 2005. "GDP of North Korea." *Bank of Korea Online*, www.bok.or.kr/index.jsp, keyword search: North Korea. Accessed 6 February 2005.

Bank of Korea (BOK). 2012. "News Release: Gross Domestic Product Estimates for North Korea for 2011." http://www.bok.or.kr/down.search?file_path=/attach/eng/626/2012/07/1341575591392.pdf&file_name=GDP+of+North+Korea+in+2011.pdf. Accessed 2 February 2012.

Bank of Korea (BOK). 2013. *Bank of Korea Economic Statistics System*. http://ecos.bok.or.kr/flex/EasySearch_e.jsp. Accessed 3 May 2013.

Banks, Arthur S. 2004. *Cross-National Time-Series Data Archive*. Binghamton: Center for Social Analysis.

Banks, Arthur S., and Robert B. Textor, 1972. *A Cross-Polity Survey*. Cambridge, MA: MIT.

Baraldi, Amanda N., and Craig K. Enders. 2010. "An Introduction to Modern Missing Data Analyses." *Journal of School Psychology* 48(1): 5–37.

Barnhart, Michael A. 1987. *Japan Prepares for Total War: The Search for Economic Security, 1919–1941*. Ithaca: Cornell University Press.

Barrett, Jasmine. 2011. "The North Korean Healthcare System: On the Fine Line Between Resilience and Vulnerability." *Resilience:*

Interdisciplinary Perspectives on Science and Humanitarianism 2: 52–65.

BBC. 2001. "Japan Expels N Korean Leader's 'Son.'" *BBC News Online*. 4 May 2001. http://news.bbc.co.uk/2/hi/asia-pacific/1310374.stm. Accessed 29 January 2013.

BBC. 2011a. "North Korea Fury at South Korea-U.S. Military Exercise." 16 August 2011. *BBC News Online*. http://www.bbc.co.uk/news/world-asia-pacific-14541988. Accessed 7 February 2013.

BBC. 2011b. "North Korea Seizes South's Mount Kumgang Resort Assets." 22 August 2011. *BBC News Online*. http://www.bbc.co.uk/news/world-asia-pacific-14611873. Accessed 8 February 2013.

BBC News. 2010. "N Korea Warns War Drills Take Region to 'Brink of War.'" *BBC News Online*. 26 November 2010. http://www.bbc.co.uk/news/world-asia-pacific-11844387. Accessed 7 November 2012.

Bechtol, Bruce E. 2010. "The *Cheonan* Incident and North Korea's Northern Limit Line Strategy." *American Enterprise Institute Center for Defense Studies*. http://www.defensestudies.org/cds/the-cheonan-incident-and-north-koreas-northern-limit-line-strategy/. Accessed 29 August 2012.

Bechtol, Bruce E. 2011. *Confronting Security Challenges on the Korean Peninsula*. Quantico, VA: Marine Corps University Press.

Becker, Jasper. 2004. *Rogue Regime: Kim Jong Il and the Looming Threat of North Korea*. Oxford: Oxford University Press.

Beecher, William. 1969a. "U.S. Scout Plane with 31 Is Lost, Reported Downed by 2 North Korean Mig's." *New York Times*. 19 April 1969: 1.

Beecher, William. 1969b. "Aides Say Nixon Weighed Reprisal." *New York Times*. 6 May 1969: 1.

Beecher, William. 1970. "U.S. to Shift 54 Phantom Jets to Bases in South Korea." *New York Times*. 17 August 1970: 2.

Bell, B.B. 2006. "Statement of General B.B. Bell Commander in Chief United Nations Command/Combined Forces Command & Commander, United States Forces Korea Before the Senate Armed Services Committee." *U.S. Senate Armed Services Committee*. 7 March 2006. http://www.armed-services.senate.gov/statemnt/2006/March/Bell%2003-07-06.pdf. Accessed 25 January 2013.

Bell, B.B. 2008. "Statement of General B.B. Bell Commander in Chief United Nations Command/Combined Forces Command & Commander, United States Forces Korea Before the Senate Armed Services Committee." *U.S. Senate Armed Services Committee*. 11 March 2008. http://www.dod.mil/dodgc/olc/docs/testBell080311.pdf. Accessed 25 January 2013.

Bell, Sam R. 2009. *What You Don't Know Can Hurt You: Information, Transparency, Domestic Challenges, and Interstate Conflict*. Dissertation. State University of New York.

Bennett, A., and C. Elman. 2006a. "Complex Causal Relations and Case Study Methods: The Example of Path Dependence." *Political Analysis* 14: 250–267.

Bennett, Andrew, and Colin Elman. 2006b. "Qualitative Research: Recent Developments in Case Study Methods." *Annual Review of Political Science* 9:455–76.

Bennett, Bruce. 2010. "Uncertainties in the North Korean Nuclear Threat." *RAND Documented Briefing*. http://www.rand.org/pubs/documented_briefings/2010/RAND_DB589.pdf. Accessed 15 September 2011.

Bennett, Bruce W. 2012. "The Korean Defense Reform 307 Plan." *The Asan Institute for Policy Studies, Policy Brief* 8. http://www.asaninst.org/. Accessed 5 February 2013.

Bennett, Bruce W., and Jennifer Lind. 2011. "The Collapse of North Korea: Military Missions and Requirements." *International Security* 36(2): 84–119.

Bennett, Jon. 1999. *North Korea: The Politics of Food Aid*. London: Overseas Development Institute.

Bermudez, Joseph S. 1998. *North Korean Special Forces*. Annapolis, MD: Naval Institute Press.

Bermudez, Joseph S. 1999. *A History of Ballistic Missile Development in the DPRK*. Monterey, CA: Monterey Institute of International Studies, Center for Nonproliferation Studies.

Bermudez, Joseph S. 2001. *The Armed Forces of North Korea*. London: I.B. Tauris.

Bernstein, Lewis. 2008. Interview and Personal Communication, 9 July 2008.

Bernstein, Lewis. 2010. Personal communication with the author, 11 August 2010 (email from Lewis Bernstein to Robert Wallace).

Bernstein, Lewis. 2012. "North Korea Nuclear and Missile Development Chronology, 1955–2012." *Eighth United States Army Historian's Office*. Unpublished report provided to the author.

Bernstein, Thomas P. 1984. "Stalinism, Famine,

and Chinese Peasants: Grain Procurements During the Great Leap Forward." *Theory and Society* 13(3): 339–377.

Berry, William D., and Mitchell S. Sanders. 2000. *Understanding Multivariate Research: A Primer for Beginning Social Scientists*. Boulder, CO: Westview Press.

Blackwell, Matthew. 2008. "Multiple Hypothesis Testing: The F-Test." http://www.mattblackwell.org/files/teaching/ftests.pdf. Accessed 13 May 2013.

Blainey, Geoffrey. 1988. *The Causes of War*. New York: The Free Press.

Blair, Clay. 1987. *The Forgotten War*. New York: Times Books.

Bluth, Christoph. 2011. *Crisis on the Korean Peninsula*. Washington, D.C.: Potomac Books.

Bodin, Jean. 1955[1606] *Six Books of the Commonwealth*, translated by M J. Tooley. Oxford: Basil Blackwell.

Bolger, Daniel P. 1991. *Scenes from an Unfinished War: Low-Intensity Conflict in Korea, 1966–1969*. Fort Leavenworth, KS: Combat Studies Institute, U.S. Army Command and General Staff College. http://purl.access.gpo.gov/GPO/LPS30608. Accessed 24 August 2012.

Bolger, Daniel P. 1999. "Unconventional Warrior: General Charles H. Bonesteel III and the Second Korean Conflict 1966–69." *Small Wars & Insurgencies* 10(1): 65–77.

Bond, Doug, Joe Bond, Churl Oh, J. C. Jenkins, and Charles Lewis Taylor. 2003. "Integrated Data for Events Analysis (IDEA): An Event Typology for Automated Events Data Development." *Journal of Peace Research* 40(6): 733–745.

Bond, Joe, Doug Bond and Churl Oh. 2000. "Charting the Korean Peninsula: A 1990–2000 Assessment of North Korea Event Interactions." Paper prepared for 5th International Command and Control Research and Technology Symposium, Australia War Memorial, Canberra ACT, Australia.

Borunkov, A. 1966. "Memorandum on Sino-Korean Relations in 1966." 2 December 1966. Cold War International History Project. http://www.wilsoncenter.org/document-collections. Accessed 20 December 2012.

Borunkov, A., and Gorovoi, V. 1965. "Excerpts from the Report of the Soviet Embassy in Pyongyang, "Some New Aspects of Korean-Chinese Relations in the First Half of 1965." 4 June 1965. *Cold War International History Project*. http://www.wilsoncenter.org/document-collections. Accessed 14 December 2012.

Breen, Michael. 1992. "Seoul Misses Top N. Korean Agent; but Smashes One of Largest Rings." *The Washington Times*. 8 October 1992: A11.

Breen, Michael. 2004. *Kim Jong-Il: North Korea's Dear Leader*. New York: Wiley.

Brigham, Robert K. 1998. *Guerrilla Diplomacy: The NLF's Foreign Relations and the Viet Nam War*. Ithaca: Cornell University Press.

Broad, William J. 2009. "Korean Missile Was a Failure, Trackers Say." *New York Times*. 6 April 2009: A1.

Bronson, Rachel. 1997. *Searching for Legitimacy: Diversionary Theory Reconsidered*. Dissertation, Columbia University.

Brooke, James. 2004. "G.I. Deserter Tells of Cold, Hungry Times in North Korea." *New York Times*. 4 November 2004: A3.

Brooke, James. 2005. "North Korea Is Said to Plan for Dynasty's Next Generation." *New York Times*. February 1, 2005: A4.

Brooke, James. 2006. "By Order of North Korea, U.N. Halts Food Assistance There." *New York Times*. 7 January 2006: A5.

Brown, Winthrop G. 1964. "Memorandum of Conversation : ROK Assistance to Viet Nam." 19 December 1964. *Foreign Relations of the United States, 1964–1968, Volume XXIX, Part 1, Korea*, Document 28. http://history.state.gov/historicaldocuments/frus1964-68v29p1/d28. Accessed 18 December 2012.

Browne, Andrew. 1996. "Seoul Hits Back Over Pyongyang Sub Claim." *The Herald*. Glasgow. 24 September 1996: 10. Accessed via LexisNexis, 22 August 2012.

Bueno de Mesquita, Bruce. 1985. "Toward a Scientific Understanding of International Conflict: A Personal View." *International Studies Quarterly* 29(2): 121–136.

Bueno de Mesquita, Bruce, and David Lalman. 1992. *War and Reason*. New Haven: Yale University Press.

Bueno de Mesquita, Bruce, et al. 2005. *The Logic of Political Survival*. Cambridge, MA: MIT Press.

Bumiller, Elisabeth, and Edward Wong. 2010. "China Warily Eyes U.S.–Korea Drills." 20 July 2010. *New York Times Online*. http://www.Nytimes.com/2010/07/21/world/asia/21military.html?ref=northkorea&_r=0. Accessed 7 February 2013.

Burr, William (ed). 2002. "National Security Archive Electronic Briefing Book No. 66: September 1970-July 1971." 27 February 2002. *George Washington University National*

Security Archive. http://www.gwu.edu/~ns archiv/NSAEBB/NSAEBB66/#docs. Accessed 16 January 2013.

Burrowes, Robert, and Bertram Spector. 1973. *The Strength and Direction of Relationships Between Domestic and External Conflict and Cooperation: Syria, 1961–1967*. New York: David McKay.

Buzo, Adrian. 1999. *The Guerilla Dynasty: Politics and Leadership in North Korea*. Boulder, CO: Westview Press.

Buzo, Adrian. 2002. *The Making of Modern Korea: A History (Asia's Transformations)*. New York: Routledge.

Byman Daniel, and Jennifer Lind. 2010. "Pyongyang's Survival Strategy: Tools of Authoritarian Control in North Korea." *International Security* 35(1): 44–74.

Cairo Communiqué. 1943. "Text of Cairo Communiqué." http://www.ndl.go.jp/con stitution/e/shiryo/01/002_46/002_46tx. html. Accessed 14 November 2012.

Callaway, Rhonda Lynn. 2001. *Is the Road to Hell Paved with Good Intentions? The Effect of United States Foreign Assistance and Economic Policy on Human Rights*. Ph.D. dissertation, University of North Texas.

Callow, Thomas W. 1995. *Nation Building in Korea*. Fort Belvoir, VA: Defense Technical Information Center. Http://handle.dtic.mil /100.2/ADA328381. Accessed 7 August 2012.

Carter, James Richard. 1972. *The Net Cost of Soviet Foreign Aid*. New York: Praeger Publishers.

Cattell, Raymond B. 1949. "The Dimensions of Culture Patterns by Factorization of National Characteristics." *The Journal of Abnormal and Social Psychology* 44(4): 443–469.

Cha, John H., and K. J. Sohn. 2012. *Exit Emperor Kim Jong-Il: Notes from His Former Mentor*. Bloomington, IN: Abbott Press.

Cha, Victor D. 1996. "Bridging the Gap: The Strategic Context of the 1965 Korea-Japan Normalization Treaty." *Korean Studies* 20(1): 123–160.

Cha, Victor D. 2001. "Strategic Culture and the Military Modernization of South Korea." *Armed Forces and Society* 28(1): 99–127.

Cha, Victor D. 2004a. "The North Korean Nuclear Calculus: Beyond the Six-Power Talks." Congressional Testimony. Hearing before the Committee on Foreign Relations, 108th Congress, 2nd Session, 2 March 2004. Washington, D.C.: Government Printing Office.

Cha, Victor D. 2004b. "Can North Korea Be Engaged?" *Survival* 46(2): 89–107.

Cha, Victor D. 2012. *The Impossible State: North Korea, Past and Future*. New York: Ecco.

Cha, Victor D., and Balbina Y. Hwang. 2008. "Government and Politics." In *North Korea : A Country Study*, ed. Robert L. Worden and Library of Congress. Federal Research Division. Washington, D.C.: U.S. Government Printing Office: 181–234.

Cha, Victor D., and David C. Kang. 2003. *Nuclear North Korea: A Debate on Engagement Strategies*. New York: Columbia University Press.

Cha, Victor, and Ellen Kim. 2010. "U.S.–Korea Relations: The Sinking of the *Cheonan*." *Comparative Connections* 12(2). http://csis. org/files/publication/1002qus_korea.pdf. Accessed 11 February 2013.

Cha, Victor D., and Nicholas D. Anderson. 2012. "A North Korean Spring?" *The Washington Quarterly* 35(1): 7–24.

Chang, Jae-Soon. 2009a. "N. Korea Steps Up Rhetoric Ahead of Clinton Trip." *Associated Press Online*. 19 February 2009. Accessed via LexisNexis, 10 February 2013.

Chang, Jae-soon. 2009b. "North Korea Bans Ships from Coastal Waters." *Huffington Post Online*. 8 June 2009. http://www. huffingtonpost.com/2009/06/08/north-korea-bans-ships-fr_n_212584.html. Accessed 25 January 2013.

Chapman, Terrence L., and Dan Reiter. 2004. "The United Nations Security Council and the Rally 'Round the Flag Effect." *The Journal of Conflict Resolution* 48(6): 886–909.

Chen, Jian. 2001. *Mao's China and the Cold War*. Chapel Hill: University of North Carolina Press.

Chen, Jian. 2011. "Reorienting the Cold War: The Implications of China's Early Cold War Experience, Taking Korea as a Central Test Case." In *The Cold War in East Asia, 1945–1991*. Tsuyoshi Hasegawa (ed), 81–97. Washington, D.C.: Woodrow Wilson Center Press.

Cheon, Seongwhun. 2008. "The Question President Bush Needs to Answer." *The Korea Herald*. 16 October 2008. Accessed via LexisNexis, 8 February 2013.

Chi, Hae-pom. 1999. "Rumors of Riot in DPRK Viewed." 1 November 1999. *Chosun Ilbo*. Seoul.

Chiozza, Giacomo, and Henk E. Goemans. 2003. "Peace Through Insecurity: Tenure and International Conflict." *Journal of Conflict Resolution* 47(4): 443–467.

Chiozza, Giacomo, and Henk E. Goemans. 2004. "Avoiding Diversionary Targets." *Journal of Peace Research* 41(4): 423–443.

Cho, Il Hyun. 2009. *Global Rogues and Regional Orders: The North Korean Challenge in Post–Cold War East Asia*. Dissertation. Cornell.

Cho, Se-hyon. 1993. "South Korean Cabinet Meeting Hears of Riots and Troop Movements in North Korea." 3 May 1993. *South Korean News Agency*. Seoul. Accessed via LexisNexis, 17 August 2012.

Cho, Soon Sung. 1968. "Korea: Election Year." *Asian Survey* 8(1): 29–42.

Cho, Yun-Jo. 2005. "The Sources of Regime Stability in North Korea: Insights from Democratization Theory." *Stanford Journal of East Asian Affairs* 5(1): 90–99.

Choe Sang-Hun. 2007. "U.N. Inspectors Confirm Shutdown of North Korean Reactor." *New York Times*. 17 July 2007: A3.

Choe, Sang-Hun. 2008. "South Korea's Sunshine Policy." 17 January 2008. *New York Times Online*. http://www.Nytimes.com/2008/01/17/world/asia/17korea.html?_r=0. Accessed 7 February 2013.

Choe, Sang-Hun. 2009a. "North Korea Claims to Conduct 2nd Nuclear Test ." 24 May 2009. *The New York Times Online*. http://www.Nytimes.com/2009/05/25/world/asia/25nuke.html?ref=northkorea. Accessed 8 February 2013.

Choe, Sang-Hun. 2009b. "North Korea Threatens Military Strikes." 27 May 2009. *New York Times Online*. http://www.Nytimes.com/2009/05/28/world/asia/28korea.html?_r=0. Accessed 10 February 2013.

Choe, Sang-Hun. 2009c. "Pyongyang Calls Naval Clash a 'Brazen Violation'; Seoul Sends More Ships to Border Area, but Direct Talks with U.S. Unaffected." *The International Herald Tribune*. 13 November 2009: 3. Accessed via LexisNexis, 11 February 2013.

Choe, Sang-Hun. 2009d. "North Korea Revalues Its Currency: Limits on Exchanges Seem Aimed at Curbing Private Markets." 2 December 2009. *The New York Times*: A6.

Choe, Sang-Hun. 2010. "Economic Measures by North Korea Prompt New Hardships and Unrest." 4 February 2010. *The New York Times*: 4.

Choe, Sang-Hun. 2011. "North Korea Heralds Kim Jong-Un." 29 December 2011. *The New York Times*. http://www.Nytimes.com/2011/12/30/world/asia/north-korea-declares-kim-jong-un-as-supreme-leader.html?_r=0. Accessed 16 September 2013.

Choe, Won-ki. 1995. "DPRK to Suffer 'Worst Food Crisis' in May to August." [in Korean] *Chungang Ilbo*. 24 April 1995. Accessed via LexisNexis, 14 August 2012.

Choe, Yong-ho, Peter H. Lee, and William DeBary. 1997. *Sources of Korean Tradition. Vol. 2, from the Sixteenth to the Twentieth Centuries*. New York: Columbia University Press.

Choi, Jinwook. 1999. *Changing Relations Between Party, Military, and Government in North Korea and Their Impact on Policy Direction*. Stanford, CA: Shorenstein Asia-Pacific Research Center.

Choi, Jinwook, and Meredith Shaw. 2010. "The Rise of Kim Jong Eun and the Return of the Party." *International Journal of Korean Unification Studies* 19(2): 175–202.

Choi, Myeong-hae. 2013. "Prospects for China's North Korea Strategy." *International Journal of Korean Unification Studies*. 30 June 2012: 45–74.

Choi, Soo-Young. 1992. *Foreign Trade of North Korea, 1946–1988: Structure and Performance*, Dissertation, Northwestern University.

Choi, Tae Y., and Su G. Lee. 1989. *Effect Analysis of U.S. Military Aid to the Republic of Korea*. Master's Thesis. Monterey, CA: Naval Postgraduate School.

Chon, Yo-ok. 1993. "Details on Last Month's Riots Given by Tokyo-Based Organization." *KBS Radio*. Seoul. 14 May 1993. *BBC Summary of World Broadcasts*. Accessed via LexisNexis, 17 August 2012.

Chong, Chang-yol. 1996. "10 Million People Face Starvation in February 1997." *Chugan Chosun* [in Korean]. Seoul. 19 December 1996.

Chosun Ilbo. 1994. "Pyongyang Reportedly Trains Spies in Subterranean Model of Seoul." *Chosun Ilbo* [in Korean]. 4 October 1994: 31. *BBC Summary of World Broadcasts*. Accessed via LexisNexis, 22 August 2012.

Chosun Ilbo. 1995. "Serious Food Shortage." *Chosun Ilbo*. 27 April 1995. Accessed via LexisNexis, 14 August 2012.

Chosun Ilbo. 2009. ""N.Korea 'Has Nuclear Warheads.'" *Chosun Ilbo* (Seoul). *BBC Monitoring Asia Pacific—Political*. 1 April 2009. Accessed via LexisNexis, 10 February 2013.

Chosun Ilbo. 2010a. "Annual South Korea-U.S. Military Exercise to Start in March." 18 February 2010. *Chosun Ilbo* [Seoul]. *BBC Monitoring Asia Pacific—Political*. Accessed via LexisNexis, 3 February 2013.

Chosun Ilbo. 2010b. "N. Korea Steps Up Propaganda to Influence Elections in South."

Bibliography

Chosun Ilbo. 28 May 2010. http://english.chosun.com/site/data/html_dir/2010/05/28/2010052800859.html. Accessed 21 June 2011.

Chosun Ilbo. 2011a. "N.Korea Refuses to Budge Over Mt. Kumgang." Chosun Ilbo. 27 July 2011. http://english.chosun.com/site/data/html_dir/2011/07/27/2011072700683.html. Accessed 12 February 2012.

Chosun Ilbo. 2011b. "Kim Jong-Un 'Masterminded Attacks on S.Korea.'" *Chosun Ilbo Online*. 3 August 2011. http://english.chosun.com/site/data/html_dir/2011/08/03/2011080300499.html. Accessed 12 February 2013.

Chosun Ilbo. 2011c. "Kaesong Firms Worry as N.Korea Seizes Mt. Kumgang Assets." Chosun Ilbo. 24 August 2011. http://english.chosun.com/site/data/html_dir/2011/08/24/2011082401039.html. Accessed 12 February 2012.

Chosun Ilbo. 2013a. "*Cheonan* Sinking 'Was Revenge for Refusing Aid.'" *Chosun Ilbo Online*. 3 January 2013. *BBC Monitoring Asia Pacific—Political*. Accessed via LexisNexis, 11 February 2013

Chosun Ilbo. 2013b. "Interview with President Lee." *Chosun Ilbo Online* (in Korean). 5 February 2013. http://news.chosun.com/site/data/html_dir/2013/02/05/2013020500132.html?news_top. Accessed 12 February 2013.

Chung, Joseph Sang-Hoon. 1972. "North Korea's "Seven Year Plan." (1961–70): Economic Performance and Reforms." *Asian Survey* 12(6): 527–545.

Chungang Ilbo. 1996a. "Workers Reportedly Use Labour Boycott to Protest Suspended Rations." Chungang Ilbo. Seoul (in Korean). 14 March 1996: 2. *BBC Summary of World Broadcasts*. Accessed via LexisNexis, 17 August 2012.

Chungang Ilbo. 1996b. "Seoul Newspaper Says North's Soldiers Executed for 'Massive' Riots." Chungang Ilbo. Seoul. 2 October 1996: 1. Accessed via LexisNexis, 17 August 2012.

CIA (U.S. Central Intelligence Agency). 1946. "Soviet Foreign and Military Policy: ORE 1." *CIA Freedom of Information Website*. http://www.foia.cia.gov/docs/DOC_00002566 01/DOC_0000256601.pdf. Accessed 14 Nov 2012.

CIA. 1947a. "The Situation in Korea: ORE 5/1." *CIA Freedom of Information Website*. http://www.foia.cia.gov/sites/default/files/document_conversions/89801/DOC_0000256989.pdf. Accessed 19 Nov 2012.

CIA. 1947b. "Implementation of Soviet Objectives in Korea (CIA ORE 62)." *CIA Freedom of Information Website*. http://www.foia.cia.gov/sites/default/files/document_conversions/89801/DOC_0000256631.pdf. Accessed 19 Nov 2012.

CIA. 1949. "Consequences of U.S. Troop Withdrawal from Korea in Spring, 1949: ORE 3–49." *CIA Freedom of Information Website*. http://www.foia.cia.gov/sites/default/files/document_conversions/89801/DOC_0000258388.pdf. Accessed 17 Nov 2012.

CIA. 1950. "Current Capabilities of the North Korean Regime: ORE 18–50." *CIA Freedom of Information Website*. http://www.foia.cia.gov/docs/DOC_0000256601/DOC_0000256601.pdf. Accessed 14 Nov 2012.

CIA. 1954. "Reconstruction in North Korea (RR IM-390)." *Intelligence Assessments*. 27 July 1954. *CIA Freedom of Information Website*. http://www.foia.cia.gov/sites/default/files/document_conversions/89801/DOC_0000494212.pdf. Accessed 19 Nov 2012.

CIA. 1957a. "Economic Relations Between the Soviet Bloc and the Communist Far East 1950 Through mid-1956." 15 April 1957. *CIA Freedom of Information Website*. http://www.foia.cia.gov/sites/default/files/document_conversions/DOC_0000968997.pdf. Accessed 19 Nov 2012.

CIA. 1961a. "NIE 10–61: Authority and Control in the Communist Movement." 8 August 1961. *CIA Freedom of Information Website*. http://www.foia.cia.gov/sites/default/files/document_conversions/89801/DOC_0001086089.pdf. Accessed 14 November 2012.

CIA. 1961b. "Current Intelligence Staff Study: Sino-Soviet Competition in North Korea (Reference Title: ESAU XV-61)." 5 April 1961. *CIA Freedom of Information Website*. http://www.foia.cia.gov/sites/default/files/document_conversions/14/esau-14.pdf. Accessed 14 November 2012.

CIA. 1961c. "Current Intelligence Weekly Review: South Korea." 25 May 1961. *CIA Freedom of Information Website*. http://www.foia.cia.gov/sites/default/files/document_conversions/89801/DOC_0000617175.pdf. Accessed 19 Nov 2012.

CIA. 1969a. "Intelligence Memorandum: North Korean Political Strategy." 8 August 1969. *CIA Freedom of Information Website*.

http://www.foia.cia.gov/sites/default/files/document_conversions/89801/DOC_0000253386.pdf. Accessed 13 January 2013.

CIA. 1969b. "National Intelligence Estimate 14.2–69: The Confrontation in Korea." *Foreign Relations of the United States, 1969–1976, Volume XIX, Part 1, Korea, 1969–1972.* Document 1. http://history.state.gov/historicaldocuments/frus1969-76v19p1/d1. Accessed 14 October 2011.

CIA. 1970. "Recent Soviet and Communist Chinese Aid to North Korea." 19 November 1970. *CIA Freedom of Information Website.* http://www.foia.cia.gov/sites/default/files/document_conversions/89801/DOC_0000307670.pdf. Accessed 15 January 2013.

CIA. 1972. "Central Intelligence Bulletin—Korea: A Review of the Negotiations and Their Prospects." 14 September 1972. *CIA Freedom of Information Website.* http://www.foia.cia.gov/sites/default/files/document_conversions/5829/CIA-RDP79T00975A022700120001-6.pdf. Accessed 18 January 2013.

CIA. 1982. "North Korea: Nuclear Reactor." *CIA Freedom of Information Website.* http://www.foia.cia.gov/sites/default/files/document_conversions/89801/DOC_0000835115.pdf. Accessed 28 January 2013.

CIA. 1993. "North Korea: The World Through P'yongyang's Eyes." *National Intelligence Daily.* 18 March 1993. http://www.gwu.edu/~nsarchiv/NSAEBB/NSAEBB164/. Accessed 18 August 2012.

CIA. 2005. *Political Map of North Korea.* Perry-Castañeda Library Map Collection at the University of Texas (Austin). http://www.lib.utexas.edu/maps/middle_east_and_asia/korea_north_pol_2005.jpg Accessed 29 August 2012.

CIA. 2008. *CIA World Factbook.* Washington, D.C.: Central Intelligence Agency. http://www.umsl.edu/services/govdocs/wofact2008/index.html. Accessed 23 January 2013.

CIA. 2012. *CIA World Factbook.* Washington, D.C.: Central Intelligence Agency. http://www.credoreference.com/book/cia. Accessed 20 May 2012.

CIA FOIA. 2012. *Baptism by Fire: CIA Analysis of the Korean War.* http://www.foia.cia.gov/KoreanWar.asp. Accessed 17 November 2012.

CIA IM (Intelligence Memorandum). 1969. "Intelligence Memorandum: Major Directions in Soviet Military Assistance." May 1969. *CIA Freedom of Information Website.* http://www.foia.cia.gov/sites/default/files/document_conversions/89801/DOC_0000496069.pdf. Accessed 14 December 2012.

CIA NIE (National Intelligence Estimate). 1966. *NIE Number 40/50–66: Security Conditions in Five Countries of the Western Pacific Area.* 13 October 1966. *CIA Freedom of Information Website.* http://www.foia.cia.gov/sites/default/files/document_conversions/89801/DOC_0000014087.pdf. Accessed 19 Dec 2012.

CIA NIE (National Intelligence Estimate). 1967. *NIE Number 14.2–67: North Korean Intentions and Capabilities with Respect to South Korea.* 21 September 1967. *CIA Freedom of Information Website.* http://www.foia.cia.gov/sites/default/files/document_conversions/89801/DOC_0000661633.pdf. Accessed 18 Dec 2012.

CIA NIE (National Intelligence Estimate). 1970. *NIE Number 42–70: The Changing Scene in South Korea.* 2 December 1970. *CIA Freedom of Information Website.* http://www.foia.cia.gov/sites/default/files/document_conversions/89801/DOC_0001218152.pdf. Accessed 20 Dec 2012.

CIA NIE (National Intelligence Estimate). 1972. CIA NIE 42/14.2-72: The Two Koreas. 11 May 1972. *CIA Freedom of Information Website.* http://www.foia.cia.gov/sites/default/files/document_conversions/89801/DOC_0001218022.pdf. Accessed 6 January 2013.

CINC (Composite Indicator of National Capabilities Index). 2005. "Correlates of War Project National Material Capabilities Data Documentation Version 3.0." *Correlates of War Project.* http://www.correlatesofwar.org/COW%20Data/Capabilities/NMC_Documentation.pdf. Accessed 23 August 2012.

CINC (Composite Indicator of National Capabilities Index). 2012. "Composite Indicator of National Capabilities Database." *Correlates of War Project.* http://www.correlatesofwar.org/COW%20Data/Capabilities/nmc3-02.htm#cinc. Accessed 23 August 2012.

CINCPAC (Commander in Chief Pacific). 1962. *CINCPAC Command History 1961.* Honolulu, HI: Commander in Chief Pacific. http://nautilus.org/projects/by-name/foia/command-histories/. Accessed 10 January 2013.

CINCPAC. 1963. *CINCPAC Command History 1962*. Honolulu, HI: Commander in Chief Pacific. http://nautilus.org/projects/by-name/foia/command-histories/. Accessed 10 January 2013.

CINCPAC. 1964. *CINCPAC Command History 1963*. Honolulu, HI: Commander in Chief Pacific. http://nautilus.org/projects/by-name/foia/command-histories/. Accessed 10 January 2013.

CINCPAC. 1965. *CINCPAC Command History 1964*. Honolulu, HI: Commander in Chief Pacific. http://nautilus.org/projects/by-name/foia/command-histories/. Accessed 10 January 2013

CINCPAC. 1968. *CINCPAC Command History 1967*. Honolulu, HI: Commander in Chief Pacific. http://nautilus.org/projects/by-name/foia/command-histories/. Accessed 16 January 2013.

CINCPAC. 1969. *CINCPAC Command History 1968*. Honolulu, HI: Commander in Chief Pacific. http://nautilus.org/projects/by-name/foia/command-histories/. Accessed 17 January 2013.

CINCPAC. 1970. *CINCPAC Command History 1969*. Honolulu, HI: Commander in Chief Pacific. http://nautilus.org/projects/by-name/foia/command-histories/. Accessed 10 January 2013

CINCPAC. 1971. *CINCPAC Command History 1970*. Honolulu, HI: Commander in Chief Pacific. http://nautilus.org/projects/by-name/foia/command-histories/. Accessed 10 January 2013.

CINCPAC. 1972. *CINCPAC Command History 1971*. Honolulu, HI: Commander in Chief Pacific. http://nautilus.org/projects/by-name/foia/command-histories/. Accessed 10 January 2013.

CINCPAC. 1973. *CINCPAC Command History 1972*. Honolulu, HI: Commander in Chief Pacific. http://nautilus.org/projects/by-name/foia/command-histories/. Accessed 10 January 2013.

CINCPAC. 1991. *CINCPAC Command History 1991*. CIA FOIA Document. Honolulu, HI: Commander in Chief Pacific. http://nautilus.wpengine.netdna-cdn.com/wp-content/uploads/2012/01/1992.pdf. Accessed 14 August 2012.

Clark, David H. 2003. "Can Strategic Interaction Divert Diversionary Behavior? A Model of U.S. Conflict Propensity." *The Journal of Politics* 65(4): 1013–1039.

Clark, David H., and William Reed. 2005. "The Strategic Sources of Foreign Policy Substitution." *American Journal of Political Science* 49(3): 609–624.

Clark, David H., Benjamin O. Fordham and Timothy Nordstrom. 2011. "Preying on the Misfortune of Others: When Do States Exploit Their Opponents' Domestic Troubles?" *The Journal of Politics* 73(1): 248–264.

CNN. 2009. "Report: Kim Jong Il Has Pancreatic Cancer." 13 July 2009. *CNN Online*. http://articles.cnn.com/2009-07-13/world/kim.jong.il.ill_1_chang-sung-taek-korea-institute-reclusive-leader?_s=PM:WORLD. Accessed 13 February 2013.

CNN. 2010a. "U.S., South Korea Begin Military Exercises." 24 July 2010. *CNN World News*. http://articles.cnn.com/2010-07-24/world/south.korea.drills_1_cheonan-incident-military-exercises-cheonan-attack?_s=PM:WORLD. Accessed 5 February 2013.

CNN. 2010b. "South Korea: Artillery Firing from North Korea Stays on North's Side." 8 December 2010. *CNN Online*. www.cnn.com. Accessed via LexisNexis, 12 February 2013.

CNN. 2010c. "N. Korea Offers No Retaliation for Drill, Agrees to Measures." 20 December 2010. *CNN Online*. Accessed via LexisNexis, 12 February 2013.

CNS (Center for Non-Proliferation Studies). 2010. "CNS Experts Available for Comment on North Korea's Artillery Bombardment of Yeonpyeong Island and Revelation of LWR and Uranium Enrichment at Yongbyon." *Center for Non-Proliferation Studies*. 29 November 2010. http://cns.miis.edu/activities/101124_dprk_artillery_heu.htm. Accessed 12 February 2013.

Cohen, Eliot A. 1988. "The Chinese Intervention in Korea, 1950." *CIA Historical Files, CIA Freedom of Information Website*. http://www.foia.cia.gov/sites/default/files/document_conversions/44/1988-11-01.pdf. Accessed 18 Nov 2012.

Collier, David, and James Mahoney. 1996. "Insights and Pitfalls: Selection Bias in Qualitative Research." *World Politics* 49(1): 56–91.

Collins, Robert M. 2011. "North Korea's Strategy of Compellence, Provocations, and the Northern Limit Line." In Bruce E. Bechtol (ed.). *Confronting Security Challenges on the Korean Peninsula*: 13–36. Quantico, VA: Marine Corps University Press.

Cooney, Kevin. 2013. *Japan's Foreign Policy Maturation a Quest for Normalcy*. Hoboken: Taylor and Francis.

Cooper, Helene. 2007. "North Koreans in Nuclear Pact: Are to Disable Facilities by the End of the Year." *New York Times*. 4 October 2007: A1.

Cooper, Helene, and Jim Yardley. 2007. "Pact with North Korea Draws Fire from a Wide Range of Critics in U.S." *New York Times*. 14 February 2007: A10.

Coppedge, Michael. 1999. "Thickening Thin Concepts and Theories: Combining Large N and Small in Comparative Politics." *Comparative Politics* 31(4): 465–476

Coser, Lewis A. 1956. *Functions of Social Conflict*. Glencoe, IL: The Free Press.

Country Profile: North Korea. Washington, D.C.: Library of Congress—Federal Research Division. http://lcweb2.loc.gov/frd/cs/profiles/North_Korea.pdf. Accessed 2 January 2013.

COW (Correlates of War). 2012. *Correlates of War Website*. http://www.correlatesofwar.org. Accessed 23 August 2012.

COW MID (Correlates of War Militarized Interstate Dispute) Data. 2012. *Correlates of War Website*. http://www.correlatesofwar.org. Accessed 15 October 2012.

COW Trade Data. 2012. *COW International Trade 1870–2009*. http://www.correlatesofwar.org/COW%20Data/Trade/Trade.html. Accessed 22 October 2012.

Creamer, Dewayne J. 2003. *The Rise and Fall of Chosen Soren: Its Effect on Japan's Relations on the Korean Peninsula*. Master's Thesis (Naval Postgraduate School). Ft. Belvoir: Defense Technical Information Center. http://handle.dtic.mil/100.2/ADA420217. Accessed 4 January 2013.

Crescenzi, Mark, Andrew Enterline, and Stephen Long. 2008. "Bringing Cooperation Back In: A Dynamic Model of Interstate Interaction." *Conflict Management and Peace Science* 25(3): 264–280.

CRS (Congressional Research Service). 2010. "Implementation of U.N. Security Council Resolution 1874." Memorandum for Hon. Richard G. Lugar. 8 October 2010. http://fpc.state.gov/documents/organization/152630.pdf. Accessed 4 February 2013.

CSIS (Center for Strategic and International Studies). 2010. *Record of North Korea's Major Conventional Provocations Since 1960s*. Washington, D.C.: CSIS Office of the Korea Chair. http://csis.org/files/publication/100525_North_Koreas_Provocations.pdf. Accessed 22 August 2012.

Cumings, Bruce. 1981. *The Origins of the Korean War: Liberation and the Emergence of Separate Regimes 1945–1947*. Princeton: Princeton University Press.

Cumings, Bruce. 1990. *The Origins of the Korean War 2, the Roaring of the Cataract, 1947–1950*. Princeton: Princeton University Press.

Cumings, Bruce. 1997. *Korea's Place in the Sun: A Modern History*. New York: W.W. Norton.

Cumings, Bruce. 1998. "The Legacy of Japanese Colonialism in Korea." In *Showa Japan: Political, Economic and Social History, Vol. 2, 1941–1952*, 215–232. Large, Stephen S. (ed). London: Routledge.

Cumings, Bruce. 2005. *Korea's Place in the Sun: A Modern History*. New York: W.W. Norton.

Cumings, Bruce. 2008. "Chapter 1. Historical Setting." In *North Korea: A Country Study*. Robert L. Worden and Library of Congress Federal Research Division, eds., 1–58. Washington, D.C.: U.S. Government Printing Office.

Cumings, Bruce. 2011. "Why Did So Many Influential Americans Think North Korea Would Collapse?" In *The Survival of North Korea: Essays on Strategy, Economics and International Relations*, 44–63. Suk H. Kim, Terence Roehrig, and Bernhard Seliger. Jefferson, N.C.: McFarland & Co.

CWIHP (Cold War International History Project). 1949. "Telegram from Tunkin to Soviet Foreign Ministry, in Reply to 11 September Telegram." Dated 09/14/1949. The Wilson Center. http://digitalarchive.wilsoncenter.org/document/112132. Accessed 17 November 2012.

Dahrendorf, Ralf. 1964. "The New Germanies." *Encounter* 22(April): 50–58.

Daily NK. 2008. "Expert Forecasts Next Five Years in North Korea." 11 January 2008. *The Daily NK*. BBC Monitoring Asia Pacific—Political. Accessed via LexisNexis, 29 January 2013.

Daily Telegraph. 1999. "Japanese Shoot at Spy Ships." *The Daily Telegraph*. Sydney, Australia. 25 March 1999: 31.

Dassel, Kurt, and Eric Reinhardt. 1999. "Domestic Strife and the Initiation of Violence at Home and Abroad." *American Journal of Political Science* 43(1): 56–85.

Davies, Graeme A. M. 2007a. "Coercion or Engagement? A Quantitative Test of the Effect of Regional Actors on North Korean Behaviour 1990–2000." *British Journal of Politics and International Relations* 9(3): 477–493.

Davies, Graeme A.M. 2007b. "U.S. Presidential

Popularity and Opportunities to Coerce North Korea: A Quantitative Test 1990–2000." *International Relations of the Asia-Pacific* 7(2): 129–153.

Davies, Graeme A. M. 2008a. "Inside Out or Outside In: Domestic and International Factors Affecting Iranian Foreign Policy Towards the United States 1990–2004." *Foreign Policy Analysis* 4: 209–225.

Davies, Graeme. 2008b. "Strategic Cooperation, the Invasion of Iraq and the Behaviour of the 'Axis of Evil,' 1990–2004." *Journal of Peace Research* 45(3): 385–399.

Debs, Alexandre, and H.E. Goemans. 2010. "Regime Type, the Fate of Leaders, and War." *American Political Science Review* 104(3): 430–445.

Demick, Barbara. 2010. *Nothing to Envy: Ordinary Lives in North Korea*, New York: Spiegel and Grau.

DeRouen, Karl. 1995. "The Indirect Link: Politics, the Economy and the Use of Force." *Journal of Conflict Resolution* 39: 671–696.

DeRouen, Karl. 2000. "Presidents and the Diversionary Use of Force: A Research Note." *International Studies Quarterly* 44(2): 317–328.

DeVos, George A., and William O. Wetherall. 1974. *Japan's Minorities: Burakumin, Koreans and Ainu*. London: Minority Rights Group.

DNI (U.S. Office of the Director of National Intelligence). 2009. "Statement by the Office of the Director of National Intelligence on North Korea's Declared Nuclear Test on 25 May 2009." ODNI News Release No. 23–09, *DNI Public Affairs Office*. 15 June 2009. http://www.dni.gov/files/documents/Newsroom/Press%20Releases/2009%20Press%20Releases/20090615_release.pdf. Accessed 10 February 2013.

Dockrill, Saki. 1996. *Eisenhower's New-Look National Security Policy, 1953–61*. Houndmills, Basingstoke, Hampshire: Macmillan Press.

D'Orazio, Vito. 2011. "War Games in Korea: United States and South Korea Joint Military Exercises and the North Korean Response." Conference paper for the International Studies Association Meeting, Montreal, Canada, March 16–19, 2011.

D'Orazio, Vito. 2012. "War Games: North Korea's Reaction to U.S. and South Korean Military Exercises." *Journal of East Asian Studies* 12(2): 275–294.

Downing, Douglas, and Jeff Clark. 1996. *Forgotten Statistics: A Self-Teaching Refresher Course*. Hauppauge, N.Y.: Barron's Educational Series.

Downs, Erica Strecker, and Phillip C. Saunders. 1998. "Legitimacy and the Limits of Nationalism: China and the Diaoyu Islands." *International Security* 23: 114–146.

Doyle, Michael W., and Nicholas Sambanis. 2000. "International Peacebuilding: A Theoretical and Quantitative Analysis." *The American Political Science Review* 94(4): 779–801.

DPRK. 1961. "Contents of the [May] 18th [North] Korean Party Central Standing Committee Meeting." 21 May 1961. Chinese Foreign Ministry Archive, File Number: 106-00581-02. *Cold War International History Project*. http://legacy.wilsoncenter.org/va2/index.cfm?topic_id=1409&fuseaction=HOME.document&identifier=B5C478D6-D991-9FE2-CE78BA68EF49F2E7&sort=Coverage&item=Korea (North). Acessed 26 November 2012.

DPRK. 1999. *Kim Jong Il: Brief History*. Pyongyang: Foreign Languages Publishing House.

DPRK. 2001. *Kim Il Sung: Condensed Biography*. Pyongyang: Foreign Languages Publication House.

DPRK Radio Central Broadcasting Station. 1996a. "Pyongyang Radio Calls South Report of Soldiers' Riot 'Groundless.'" *Central Broadcasting Station*. Pyongyang. 5 October 1996. BBC Summary of World Broadcasts. Accessed via LexisNexis, 17 August 2012.

DPRK Radio Central Broadcasting Station. 1996b. "Radio Reports on Re-Election of U.S. President Bill Clinton." 9 November 1996. BBC Summary of World Broadcasts. Accessed via LexisNexis, 22 August 2012.

DPRK Radio Central Broadcasting Station. 1997. "North Korea Vows Revenge for South Newspaper's Editorial." DPRK Central Broadcasting Station. Pyongyang. 30 June 1997. BBC Summary of World Broadcasts. Accessed via LexisNexis, 22 August 2012.

DPRK Radio Central Broadcasting Station. 2011. "North Korean Army Command Slams South's Military Drills." DPRK Central Broadcasting Station. Pyongyang. 24 November 2011. BBC Summary of World Broadcasts. Accessed via LexisNexis, 7 November 2011.

Drury, A. Cooper. 1998. "Revisiting Economic Sanctions Reconsidered." *Journal of Peace Research* 35(4): 497–509.

DSS (Data and Statistical Services). *Introduction to Regression.* Princeton University. http://dss.princeton.edu/online_help/analysis/regression_intro.htm. Accessed 23 October 2012.

Durdin, Tillman. 1972. "Opposition in Seoul Says It Is Stifled, Calls Park's Tactics Self-Perpetuating." *New York Times.* 7 July 1972: 3.

Durkheim, E. (1951 [1897]) *Suicide: A Study in Sociology.* New York: Free Press.

DVO [Soviet Far East Department]. 1967. "Memorandum About Sino-Korean Relations." 7 March 1967. *Cold War International History Project.* http://www.wilsoncenter.org/program/cold-war-international-history-project. Accessed 3 January 2013.

Eberstadt, Nicholas. 1993. *North Korea: Reform, Muddling Through, or Collapse?* Seattle, WA: National Bureau of Asian Research.

Eberstadt, Nicholas. 1997. "North Korea as an Economy Under Multiple Severe Stresses: Analogies and Lessons from Past and Recent Historical Experience." *Communist Economies and Economic Transformation* 9(2): 233–255.

Eberstadt, Nicholas. 1998a. "International Trade in Capital Goods, 1970–1995." *Journal of East Asian Affairs* 12(1): 165–223.

Eberstadt, Nicholas. 1998b. "North Korea's Interlocked Economic Crises: Some Indications from 'Mirror Statistics.'" *Asian Survey* 38(3): 203–230.

Eberstadt, Nicholas. 1999. *The End of North Korea.* Washington, D.C.: American Enterprise Institute.

Eberstadt, Nicholas. 2000. "Disparities in Socioeconomic Development in Divided Korea: Indications and Implications." *Asian Survey* 40(6): 867–893.

Eberstadt, Nicholas. 2004. "The Persistence of North Korea." *Policy Review* (127): 23–48.

Eberstadt, Nicholas. 2007. *The North Korean Economy: Between Crisis and Catastrophe,* New Brunswick, NJ: Transaction Publishers.

Eberstadt, Nicholas. 2011. "Western Aid: The Missing Link for North Korea's Economic Revival?" *The American Enterprise Institute.* Working Paper Series on Development Policy Number 6, April 2011. http://www.aei.org/files/2011/04/26/files/2011/04/26/Updated-Eberstadt-DPWorkingPaper-April2011.pdf. Accessed 31 January 2013.

Eberstadt, Nicholas, Marc Rubin, and Albina Tretyakova. 1995. "The Collapse of Soviet/Russian Trade with the DPRK: Impact and Implications." *Korean Journal of National Unification* 4: 87–104.

Eckert, Carter Joel, and Ki-baik Lee. 1990. *Korea Old and New: A History.* Seoul: Published for the Korea Institute Harvard University by Ilchokak.

The Economist [U.S.]. 1994. "Son King or Sinking?" *The Economist.* 16 July 1994: 13.

The Economist. 2011. "Succession in North Korea: Grief and Fear." *The Economist Online.* 31 December 2011. http://www.economist.com/node/21542227?zid=309&ah=80dcf288b8561b012f603b9fd9577f0e. Accessed 13 February 2013.

ECOS (Economic Statistics System). 2013. "DPRK GDP Growth." *Bank of Korea* (Seoul). http://ecos.bok.or.kr/. Accessed 13 February 2013.

Eisenhower Presidential Library. 2103. "The Korean War." Dwight D. Eisenhower Presidential Library and Museum. http://www.eisenhower.archives.gov/research/online_documents/korean_war.html. Accessed 1 January 2013.

EIU (Economist Intelligence Unit). *Country Report North Korea, May 2009.* 1 May 2009. London: The Economist Intelligence Unit.

EIU (Economist Intelligence Unit). *Country Report North Korea, November 2011.* 16 November 2011. London: The Economist Intelligence Unit.

Enterline, Andrew J. 2010. "Introduction to CMPS Special Issue: Diversionary Theory." *Conflict Management and Peace Science* 27(5): 411–416.

Enterline, A. J., and K. S. Gleditsch. 2000. "Threats, Opportunity, and Force: Repression and Diversion of Domestic Pressure, 1948–1982." *International Interactions* 26: 21–53.

Erlanger, Steven. 2008. "Doctor Confirms Kim Jong Il Stroke." 11 November 2008. *New York Times Online.* http://www.Nytimes.com/2008/12/11/world/asia/11iht-12kim.1860 2447.html?_r=0. Accessed 30 January 2013.

EUSA (Eighth United States Army). 1968a. "Operational Report of Headquarters, Eighth United States Army, for Period Ending 30 April 1968, RCS CSFOR-65." 6 July 1968. Seoul: Eighth United States Army Historian's Office.

EUSA (Eighth United States Army). 1968b. "Critical Analysis Paper: Operations Summary—Blue House Raid Team Sequence of Events." Eighth United States Army. Seoul: Eighth United States Army History Office.

Fackler, Martin. 2010. "U.S. and South Korea Begin Joint Naval Exercises." 27 November 2010. *New York Times Online*. http://www.Nytimes.com/2010/11/28/world/asia/28korea.html?_r=0. Accessed 5 February 2013.

Fackler, Martin, and Mark McDonald. 2010. "South Korea Reassesses Its Defenses After Attack." 25 November 2010. *New York Times Online*. http://www.Nytimes.com/2010/11/26/world/asia/26korea.html?ref=northkorea. Accessed 7 February 2013.

FAOSTAT (Food and Agriculture Organization of the United Nations). 2012. Online database. http://faostat.fao.org/site/616/DesktopDefault.aspx?PageID=616#ancor. Accessed 20 May 2012.

FBIS (Foreign Broadcast Information Service). 1953. "Korean Truce: Moscow Claims Major Role in Success of Korean Armistice." *USSR Survey*. 6 August 1953. *CIA Freedom of Information Website*. http://www.foia.cia.gov/. Accessed 19 Nov 2012.

Fearon, James D. 1994. "Domestic Political Audiences and the Escalation of International Disputes." *The American Political Science Review* 88(3): 577–92

Fedchenko, Vitaly. 2009. "North Korea's Nuclear Test Explosion, 2009." *SIPRI Fact Sheet*. December 2009. http://books.sipri.org/files/FS/SIPRIFS0912.pdf. Accessed 10 February 2013.

Fehrenbach, T.R. 1963. *This Kind of War: A Study in Unpreparedness*. New York: The Macmillan Company.

Filippov, Mikhail. 2009 "Diversionary Role of the Georgia–Russia Conflict: International Constraints and Domestic Appeal." *Europe-Asia Studies* 61(10): 1825–1847

Financial Times. 1994. "North Korea's 'Sea of Fire' Threat Shakes Seoul." *Financial Times* [London], 22 March 1994, 6.

Finley, James P. 1983. *The U.S. Military Experience in Korea, 1871–1982: In the Vanguard of ROK–U.S. Relations*. San Francisco, CA: Command Historian's Office USFK/EUSA.

Fischer, Hannah. 2007. "North Korean Provocative Actions, 1950–2007." *Congressional Research Service Report*. Washington, D.C.: Congressional Research Service.

Fordham, Benjamin O. 2005. "Strategic Conflict Avoidance and the Diversionary Use of Force." *The Journal of Politics* 67(1): 132–153.

Fordham, Benjamin O. 2011. "U.S. Uses of Force, 1870–1995." Available at http://bingweb.binghamton.edu/~bfordham/data.html. Accessed 15 October 2011.

Fordham, Benjamin O., and Christopher C. Sarver. 2001. "Militarized Interstate Disputes and United States Uses of Force." *International Studies Quarterly* 45(3): 455–466.

Foster, Dennis M., and Glenn Palmer. 2006. "Presidents, Public Opinion, and Diversionary Behavior: The Role of Partisan Support Reconsidered." *Foreign Policy Analysis* 2: 269–287.

Foster, Dennis, and Jonathan Keller. 2010. "Rallies and the 'First Image' Leadership Psychology, Scapegoating Proclivity, and the Diversionary Use of Force." *Conflict Management and Peace Science* 27(5): 417–441.

Foster-Carter, Aidan. 1978. "Development and Self-Reliance: A Critical Appraisal." In Gavan McCormack and Mark Selden, *Korea, North and South: The Deepening Crisis*, 115–149. New York: Monthly Review Press.

Foster-Carter, Aidan. 2001. "DPR Korea: North Korean Refugees—An Escalating Crisis?" *UNHCR Centre for Documentation and Research*. http://www.unhcr.org/refworld/pdfid/3c4bf63e7.pdf. Accessed 4 February 2013.

Foster-Carter, Aidan. 2008. "North Korea–South Korea Relations: Lee Outflanked." July 2008. *Comparative Connections*. http://csis.org/files/media/csis/pubs/0802qnk_sk.pdf. Accessed 7 February 2013.

Foster-Carter, Aidan. 2010a. "South Korea–North Korea Relations: Torpedoed?" *Comparative Connections*. April 2010: 75–90. http://csis.org/files/publication/1001q.pdf. Accessed 11 February 2013.

Foster-Carter, Aidan. 2010b. "South Korea–North Korea Relations: Picking Up the Pieces." *Comparative Connections*. October 2010. http://csis.org/publication/comparative-connections-v12-n3-north-korea-south-korea. Accessed 11 February 2013.

Foster-Carter, Aidan. 2011a. "South Korea–North Korea Relations: Playing with Fire." *Comparative Connections*. January 2011. http://csis.org/publication/comparative-connections-v12-n4-north-korea-south-koera. Accessed 11 February 2013.

Foster-Carter, Aidan. 2011b. "South Korea–North Korea Relations: Picking Up the Pieces." *Comparative Connections*. September 2010. http://csis.org/files/publication/1102qnk_sk.pdf. Accessed 11 February 2013.

Foster-Carter, Aidan. 2012. "A New Era?" *Comparative Connections*. January 2012. http://

csis.org/files/publication/1103qnk_sk.pdf. Accessed 11 February 2013.

Fravel, M. Taylor. 2010. "The Limits of Diversion: Rethinking Internal and External Conflict." *Security Studies* 19(2): 307–341.

French, Howard W. 2002. "North Korea Adding a Pinch of Capitalism to Its Economy." *New York Times*. 9 August 2002: A1.

French, Paul. 2007. *North Korea: The Paranoid Peninsula: A Modern History*. New York: Zed Books.

FRUS (Foreign Relations of the United States). 1943. *The Conferences at Cairo and Tehran, 1943*. Section V. Post-conference papers: 833–891. http://digital.library.wisc.edu/1711.dl/FRUS.FRUS1943CairoTehran. Accessed 14 November 2012.

FRUS. 1953. "NSC 162/2: Basic National Security Policy General Considerations." Document 100 in *Foreign Relations of the United States, 1952–1954, Volume II, Part 1, National Security Affairs*, U.S. Department of State, Office of the Historian. http://history.state.gov/historicaldocuments/frus1952-54v02p1/d100. Accessed 25 November 2012.

FRUS. 1954. "The Geneva Conference on Korea: April 26-June 15, 1954." *Foreign Relations of the United States, 1952–1954. the Geneva Conference. Volume XVI*. Washington, D.C.: U.S. Government Printing Office. http://digital.library.wisc.edu/1711.dl/FRUS. Accessed 7 January 2012.

FRUS. 1957. "NSC 5702/2." 9 August 1957. *Foreign Relations of the United States, 1955–1957, Volume XXIII, Part 2, Korea*, Document 240. http://history.state.gov/historicaldocuments/frus1955-57v23p2/d240. Accessed 26 November 2012.

FRUS. 1961a. "Telegram from the Commander in Chief, U.S. Forces Korea (Magruder) to the Joint Chiefs of Staff: Document 213." 16 May 1961. *Foreign Relations of the United States, 1961–1963*. http://history.state.gov/historicaldocuments/frus1961-63v22/d213. Accessed 4 December 2012.

FRUS. 1961b. "Telegram from the Department of State to the Embassy in Korea." *Foreign Relations of the United States 1961–1963, Volume XXII, China; Korea; Japan*. Document 239. 5 August 1961. http://www.state.gov/www/about_state/history/frusXXII/201to240.html. Accessed 9 January 2013.

FRUS. 1966a. "Telegram from the Embassy in Korea to the Department of State." *Foreign Relations of the United States 1964–1968*, Volume XXIX, Korea. Document 93. 19 October 1966. http://www.state.gov/www/about_state/history/vol_xxix/j.html. Accessed 9 January 2013.

FRUS. 1966b. "Memorandum of Conversation Between President Johnson and President Pak." 1 November 1966. *Foreign Relations of the United States, 1964–1968, Volume XXIX, Part 1, Korea*, Document 97. http://www.state.gov/www/about_state/history/vol_xxix/j.html. Accessed 13 January 2013.

FRUS. 1966c. "Intelligence Memorandum No. 1620/66." 8 November 1966. *Foreign Relations of the United States, 1964–1968, Volume XXIX, Part 1, Korea*, Document 98. http://history.state.gov/historicaldocuments/frus1964-68v29p1/d98. Accessed 11 January 2013.

FRUS. 1967a. "Telegram from the Embassy in Korea to the Department of State." *Foreign Relations of the United States 1964–1968, Volume XXIX*. Document 129. 19 September 1967. http://www.state.gov/www/about_state/history/vol_xxix/m.html. Accessed 9 January 2012.

FRUS. 1967b. "Telegram from the Embassy in Korea to the Department of State." *Foreign Relations of the United States 1964–1968, Volume XXIX, Korea*. Document 134. 25 November 1967. http://www.state.gov/www/about_state/history/vol_xxix/n.html. Accessed 15 January 2013.

FRUS. 1968a. "Editorial Note." *Foreign Relations of the United States 1964–1968, Volume XXIX, Korea*. Document 144. http://www.state.gov/www/about_state/history/vol_xxix/o.html. Accessed 13 January 2013.

FRUS. 1968b. "Telegram from the Department of State to the Embassy in the Soviet Union." 23 January 1968. Document 212. *Foreign Relations of the United States 1964–1968, Volume XXIX, Korea*. http://www.state.gov/www/about_state/history/vol_xxix/v.html. Accessed 13 January 2013.

FRUS. 1968c. "Summary Minutes of Meeting—USS *Pueblo* Group." 24 January 1968. Document 217. *Foreign Relations of the United States 1964–1968, Volume XXIX, Korea*. http://www.state.gov/www/about_state/history/vol_xxix/v.html. Accessed 15 January 2013.

FRUS. 1968d. "Memorandum from the President's Special Assistant (Rostow) to President Johnson." 28 January 1968. Document 235. *Foreign Relations of the United States 1964–1968, Volume XXIX, Korea*. http://

www.state.gov/www/about_state/history/vol_xxix/y.html. Accessed 15 January 2013.

FRUS. 1968e. "Telegram from the Department of State to the Embassy in Korea." 28 January 1968. Document 237. *Foreign Relations of the United States 1964–1968, Volume XXIX, Korea.* http://www.state.gov/www/about_state/history/vol_xxix/y.html. Accessed 15 January 2013.

FRUS. 1968f. "Information Memorandum from the Director of the Korean Task Force (Berger) to Secretary of State Rusk." 16 February 1968. Document 278. *Foreign Relations of the United States 1964–1968, Volume XXIX, Korea.* http://www.state.gov/www/about_state/history/vol_xxix/zc.html. Accessed 15 January 2013.

FRUS. 1968g. "Summary of Conversations Between President Johnson and President Pak." 17 April 1968. Document 194. *Foreign Relations of the United States 1964–1968, Volume XXIX, Korea.* http://www.state.gov/www/about_state/history/vol_xxix/t.html. Accessed 15 January 2013.

FRUS. 1969. "Memorandum from the President's Assistant for National Security Affairs (Kissinger) to President Nixon [Footnote 3]." December, 1969. Document 46. *Foreign Relations of the United States, 1969–1976, Volume XIX, Part 1, Korea, 1969–1972.* http://history.state.gov/historicaldocuments/frus1969-76v19p1/d46. Accessed 16 January 2013.

FRUS. 1970. "Telegram from the Department of State to the Embassy in Korea." 23 April 1970. Document 57. *Foreign Relations of the United States, 1969–1976, Volume XIX, Part 1, Korea, 1969–1972.* http://history.state.gov/historicaldocuments/frus1969-76v19p1/d57. Accessed 16 January 2013.

Gaddis, John Lewis. 1997. "History, Theory, and Common Ground." *International Security* 22(1): 75–85.

Gallery, Daniel V. 1970. *The Pueblo Incident.* Garden City, N.Y.: Doubleday.

Gates, Robert. "Roundup: U.S. Defence Chief Warns Against New Arms Race in Asia." 30 May 2009. *Deutsche Presse-Agentur.* Accessed via LexisNexis, 8 February 2013.

Gates, Scott, Håvard Hegre, Mark P. Jones and Håvard Strand. 2006. "Institutional Inconsistency and Political Instability: Polity Duration, 1800–2000." *American Journal of Political Science* 50(4): 893–908.

Gause, Ken E. 2012. *Coercion, Control, Surveillance and Punishment: Examination of the North Korean Police State.* Washington, D.C.: The Committee for Human Rights in North Korea.

Geddes, Barbara. 2006. "Stages of Development in Authoritarian Regimes." In *World Order After Leninism*, ed. Vladimir Tismaneanu, Marc M. Howard, and Rudra Sil. Seattle, WA: University of Washington Press, 149–70.

Gelpi, Christopher, 1997. "Democratic Diversions: Governmental Structure and the Externalization of Domestic Conflict." *Journal of Conflict Resolution* 41(2): 255–82.

George, Alexander. 1979. "Case Studies and Theory Development: The Method of Structured, Focused Comparison." In *Diplomacy: New Approaches in History, Theory, and Policy*, ed. Paul Lauren, New York: Free Press.

George, Alexander. 1982. "Case Studies and Theory Development." Paper presented to the Second Annual Symposium on Information Processing in Organizations, Carnegie-Mellon University, Pittsburgh, October, 1982.

George, Alexander L., and Andrew Bennett. 2005. "The Congruence Method." In George and Bennett, *Case Studies and Theory Development in the Social Sciences.* Cambridge, MA: MIT Press.

George, Alexander L., and Andrew Bennett. 2005. *Case Studies and Theory Development in the Social Sciences.* Cambridge, MA: MIT Press.

George, Alexander L., and Timothy J. McKeown. 1985. "Case Studies and Theories of Organizational Decisionmaking." *Advances in Information Processing in Organizations* 2, 21–58.

Gerring, John. 2001. *Social Science Methodology: A Criterial Framework.* Cambridge: University Press

Gerring, John. 2005. "Causation: A Unified Framework for the Social Sciences." *Journal of Theoretical Politics* 17(2): 163–198.

Goertz, Gary, and Paul F. Diehl. 1995. "The Initiation and Termination of Enduring Rivalries: The Impact of Political Shocks." *American Journal of Political Science* 39(1): 30–52.

Goldstein, Joshua S. 1992. "A Conflict-Cooperation Scale for WEIS Events Data." *Journal of Conflict Resolution* 36(2): 369–385.

Goodkind, Daniel, and Loraine West. 2001. "The North Korean Famine and Its Demographic Impact." *Population and Development Review* 27(2): 219–238.

Gowa, J. 1998. "Politics at the Water's Edge: Parties, Voters, and the Use of Force Abroad." *International Organization* 52: 307–325.

Gujarati, Damodar N. 2011. *Econometrics by Example*. New York: Palgrave Macmillan.

Gujarati, Damodar N., and Dawn C. Porter. 2009. *Basic Econometrics*. Boston: McGraw-Hill.

Gurr, Ted. 1968. "A Causal Model of Civil Strife: A Comparative Analysis Using New Indices." *The American Political Science Review* 62(4): 1104–1124.

Gurr, Ted. 1969. "A Comparative Study of Civil Strife." In *The History of Violence in America*. Eds. H. D. Graham and T. R. Gurr. New York: Bantam Books, 572–632.

Ha, Yong-Chool. 1986. "Soviet Perceptions of Soviet–North Korean Relations." *Asian Survey* 26(5): 573–590.

Hagan, Joe D. 1986. "Domestic Political Conflict, Issue Areas, and Some Dimensions of Foreign Policy Behavior Other than Conflict." *International Interactions* 12(4): 291–313.

Haggard, Stephan. 2012. "Changing Military Dynamics in East Asia, Policy Brief 3, January 2012: Grand Strategies on the Korean Peninsula." *University of California Institute on Global Conflict and Cooperation*. http://igcc.ucsd.edu/assets/001/503585.pdf. Accessed 31 January 2013.

Haggard, Stephan, and Marcus Noland. 2006. *The North Korean Refugee Crisis: Human Rights and International Response*. Washington, D.C.: U.S. Committee for Human Rights in North Korea.

Haggard, Stephan, and Marcus Noland. 2007. *Famine in North Korea: Markets, Aid, and Reform*. New York: Columbia University Press.

Haggard, Stephan, and Marcus Noland. 2008a. "North Korea in 2007: Shuffling in from the Cold." *Asian Survey* 48(1): 107–115.

Haggard, Stephen, and Marcus Noland. 2008b. *Famine in North Korea Redux?* Washington, D.C.: Peterson Institute for International Economics.

Haggard, Stephen, and Marcus Noland. 2009. "Famine in North Korea Redux?" *Journal of Asian Economics* 20(4): 384–395.

Haggard, Stephen, and Marcus Noland. 2010a. "Sanctioning North Korea: The Political Economy of Denuclearization and Proliferation." *Asian Survey* 50(3): 539–568.

Haggard, Stephan, and Marcus Noland. 2010b. *Winter of Their Discontent: Pyongyang Attacks the Market*. Washington, D.C.: Peterson Institute for International Economics.

Haggard, Stephan, and Marcus Noland. 2011a. *Witness to Transformation: Refugee Insights into North Korea*. Washington, D.C.: Peterson Institute for International Economics.

Haggard, Stephan, and Marcus Noland. 2011b. *Engaging North Korea: The Role of Economic Statecraft*. Honolulu: East-West Center.

Haggard, Stephan, Marcus Noland, and Erik Weeks. 2008. *North Korea on the Precipice of Famine*. Washington, D.C.: Peterson Institute for International Economics.

Hailey, Foster. 1956. "Big Armies in Korea Observe Uneasy Truce: Buildup on Communist Side." *New York Times*. 17 June 1956: 174.

Halloran, Richard. 1968. "Nixon, Greeting Park, Stresses South Korean Responsibility for Defense." *New York Times*. 22 August 1969: 8.

Halloran, Richard. 1972. "Koreans Report Deal on Vietnam: Delay on Troop Pullout Tied to U.S. Pledge to Seoul." *New York Times*. 15 September 1972: 9.

Halloran, Richard. 2011. "Sharpening the Spear." *Air Force Magazine*. February 2011: 73–76. http://www.airforce-magazine.com/MagazineArchive/Pages/2011/February%202011/0211spear.aspx. Accessed 5 February 2013.

Ham, Walter T. 2010. "Eighth Army Participates in ULCHI FREEDOM GUARDIAN." 16 August 2010. 8th U.S. Army Public Affairs Online. http://www.army.mil/article/43770/Eighth_Army_participates_in_Ulchi_Freedom_Guardian/ Accessed 5 February 2013.

Han, Duk-soo. 2010. "Briefing on the *Cheonan* Situation—Presented by H.E. Ambassador Han, Duk-Soo." 25 May 2010. http://csis.org/files/attachments/100525_Presentation_Cheonan.pdf. Accessed 11 February 2013.

Han, Sungjoo. 1978. "South Korea's Participation in the Vietnam Conflict." *Orbis* 21(4): 893–912.

Hanguk Ilbo. 1996. "Support of North Korea Should Observe Principle." *Hanguk Ilbo* [in Korean]. Seoul. 16 July 1996.

Harden, Blaine. 2009a. "North Korea Disavows 1953 Armistice, Warns South Korea—North Korea Fires Missiles After Nuclear Test." *Washington Post*. 27 May 2009. http://www.washingtonpost.com/wp-dyn/content/

article/2009/05/26/AR2009052600555. html. Accessed 10 February 2013.

Harden, Blaine. 2009b. "Value of U.N. Sanctions on North Korea Disputed." 12 June 2009. http://www.washingtonpost.com/wp-dyn/content/article/2009/06/11/AR2009061102323.html. Accessed 4 February 2013.

Harlan, Chico. 2010. "South Korea and U.S. Send Message to North Korea with Drills in Sea of Japan." 26 July 2010. *Washington Post Online*. http://www.washingtonpost.com/wp-dyn/content/article/2010/07/25/AR2010072500754.html. Accessed 5 February 2013.

HASC (United States House Armed Services Committee, Special Subcommittee on the USS *Pueblo*). 1969. *Inquiry into the USS Pueblo and EC-121 Plane Incidents*. HASC 91-12. Washington, D.C.: U.S. Government Printing Office.

Hassig, Ralph C., and Kong Dan Oh. 2009. *The Hidden People of North Korea: Everyday Life in the Hermit Kingdom*. Lanham, MD: Rowman & Littlefield Publishers.

Hawk, David. 2003. *The Hidden Gulag: Exposing North Korea's Prison Camps*. Washington, D.C.: U.S. Committee for Human Rights in North Korea.

Hayashi, Nasuko. 2004. *The Linkage Between Domestic and International Conflict: The Case of Japanese Foreign Policy, 1891-1941*. Dissertation, University of Michigan.

Hazlewood, Leo A. 1975. "Diversion Mechanisms and Encapsulation Processes: The Domestic Conflict Foreign Conflict Hypothesis Reconsidered." In *Sage International Yearbook of International Studies*, ed. Patrick J. McGowan. Beverly Hills, CA: Sage, 213-243.

Herman, Burt. 2007. "Lee Claims Win in South Korea Election." 19 December 2007. *Associated Press Online*. Accessed via Lexis-Nexis, 7 February 2013.

Heston, Alan, Robert Summers and Bettina Aten. 2009. *Penn World Table Version 6.3*. University of Pennsylvania: Center for International Comparisons of Production, Income and Prices.

Hoare, James. 2012. *Historical Dictionary of the Democratic People's Republic of Korea*. Lanham, MD: Scarecrow Press.

Hodge, H. T. 2003. " North Korea's Military Strategy." *Parameters: Journal of the U.S. Army War College* 33: 68-81.

Hom, Daniel, and Jennifer Thompson. 2010. "Timeline: North Korean Provocations." *Financial Times*, http://www.ft.com/cms/s/0/0c4d68e2-f6e7-11df-8feb-00144feab49a.html#axzz1Y1qyOnI3. Accessed 15 Sept 2011.

Howell, David C. 2012. "Treatment of Missing Data—Part 1." *Dave Howell's Statistical Home Page*. http://www.uvm.edu/~dhowell/Stat Pages/More_Stuff/Missing_Data/ Missing .html#Little. Accessed 21 February 2013.

Howell, Llewellyn D. 1983. "A Comparative Study of the WEIS and COPDAB Data Sets." *International Studies Quarterly* 27(2): 149-159.

Hungarian Embassy. 1962. "Report, Embassy of Hungary in North Korea to the Hungarian Foreign Ministry." August 1962. *Cold War International History Project*. http://www.wilsoncenter.org/document-collections. Accessed 29 January 2013.

Hungarian Embassy. 1963. "Report, Embassy of Hungary in North Korea to the Hungarian Foreign Ministry." 15 February 1963. *Cold War International History Project*. http://www.wilsoncenter.org/document-collections. Accessed 20 December 2012.

Hungarian Embassy. 1964. "Report, Embassy of Hungary in North Korea to the Hungarian Foreign Ministry." 10 March 1964. *Cold War International History Project*. http://www.wilsoncenter.org/document-collections. Accessed 20 December 2012.

Hungarian Embassy. 1967. "Report, Embassy of Hungary in North Korea to the Hungarian Foreign Ministry." 25 November 1967. *Cold War International History Project*. http://www.wilsoncenter.org/document-collections. Accessed 13 January 2013.

Hwang, Doo-hyong, 2011. "U.S. Repeats Calls for N. Korea to Mend Ties with S. Korea Ahead of 6-Way Talks' Reopening." 30 April 2011. *Yonhap News* (Seoul). BBC Monitoring Asia Pacific—Political. Accessed via LexisNexis, 3 February 2013.

Hwang, Jang Yop. 1998. *North Korea: Truth or Lies* (in Korean). Seoul: Institute for Reunification Policy Studies.

Hyun, Joo Chon. 2004. *A Study of the Social Control System in North Korea: Focusing on the Ministry of People's Security*. Seoul: Korea Institute of National Unification.

IAEA (International Atomic Energy Agency). 2011. "IAEA Safeguards Overview: Comprehensive Safeguards Agreements and Additional Protocols." http://www.iaea.org/Publications/Factsheets/ English/sg_over view.html. Accessed 30 October 2011.

ICG (International Crisis Group). 2010. *North Korea the Risks of War in the Yellow Sea.* Seoul, ROK: International Crisis Group. http://www.crisisgroup.org/en/regions/asia/north-east-asia/north-korea/198-north-korea-the-risks-of-war-in-the-yellow-sea.aspx. Accessed 29 August 2012.

Ignatius, Adi. 1993. "Russia Turns Away from North Korea." *The Wall Street Journal.* 12 February 1993: A10. Accessed via ProQuest on 3 September 2012.

IISS (International Institute for Strategic Studies). 2010. *The Military Balance 2010.* Oxfordshire: Routledge.

IISS (International Institute for Strategic Studies). 2011. *The Military Balance 2011.* Oxfordshire: Routledge.

IISS (International Institute for Strategic Studies). 2013. "The Conventional Military Balance on the Korean Peninsula." *International Institute for Strategic Studies.* http://www.iiss.org/publications/strategic-dossiers/north-korean-dossier/north-koreas-weapons-programmes-a-net-asses/preface/. Accessed 5 February 2013.

IMF (International Monetary Fund). 2005. *Direction of Trade Statistics Yearbook 2005.* Washington, D.C.: International Monetary Fund.

IMF (International Monetary Fund). 2010. *Direction of Trade Statistics Yearbook 2010.* Washington, D.C.: International Monetary Fund.

IMF (International Monetary Fund). 2011. *International Monetary Fund's Country Profile.* http://www.imf.org/external/country/index.htm. Accessed 19 September 2011.

IMH (South Korean Institute for Military History). 2012. "Ask! Vietnam War and the ROK." [In Korean]. *Institute for Military History Compilation, South Korean Department of Defense.* http://www.imhc.mil.kr/imhcroot/upload/resource/V27.pdf. Accessed 22 December 2012.

Institute for Far Eastern Studies. 1979. *North Korea's Foreign Trade.* Seoul: Kyungnam University Press.

Institute for Japan-China Economy. 1977. *The Chinese Economic Statistical Data Collection: The Focus on the Status of the Third and Fourth Five-Year Plan.* Tokyo: Institute for Japan-China Economy.

International Crisis Group. 2003. "North Korea: A Phased Negotiation Strategy." *ICG Asia Report N°61*, Washington/Brussels 1 August 2003, http://merln.ndu.edu/archive/icg/northkoreaphasednegotiation.pdf. Accessed 19 September 2011.

International Crisis Group. 2006. "Perilous Journeys: The Plight of North Koreans in China and Beyond." *ICG Asia Report N°122*, Washington/Brussels, 26 October 2006, http://www.nautilus.org/publications/essays/napsnet/reports/0694IGC.pdf/view. Accessed 19 September 2011.

Ishimaru, Jiro. 2010. "The Twilight of the Kim Jong-Il Regime." In *Rimjin-Gang: News from Inside North Korea,* 322–382. Osaka, Japan: Asia Press International.

ISS (Institute for Strategic Studies). 1968. "Appendix: Military Activity Between July 1967 and July 1968." *The Military Balance* 68(1): 60–61.

ITAR-TASS. 2011. "Mourning Events in N Korea Continue, Situation in All Areas Calm." *ITAR-TASS News.* 23 December 2011. Accessed via LexisNexis, 14 February 2013.

Jackson, Michael Gordon. 2005. "Beyond Brinkmanship: Eisenhower, Nuclear War Fighting, and Korea, 1953–1968." *Presidential Studies Quarterly* 35(1): 52–75.

James, Patrick. 1987. "Conflict and Cohesion: A Review of the Literature and Recommendations for Future Research." *Cooperation and Conflict* 22:21–33.

James, Patrick, and Jean Sébastien Rioux. 1998. "International Crises and Linkage Politics: The Experiences of the United States, 1953–1994" *Political Research Quarterly* 51(3): 781–812.

James, Patrick, and John R. Oneal, 1991. "The Influence of Domestic and International Politics on the President's Use of Force." *The Journal of Conflict Resolution* 35(2): 307–332.

Japan Economic Newswire. 1997. "North Voices Hopes for Better Ties Under Kim Dae Jung." *Japan Economic Newswire, Kyodo News Service.* Tokyo. 22 December 1997. Accessed via LexisNexis, 22 August 2012

Japan Economic Newswire. 1999. "Missing Adults Sign of N. Korean Starvation." *Japan Economic Newswire, Kyodo News Service.* Tokyo. 30 January 1999. Accessed via LexisNexis, 16 August 2012.

Japan External Trade Organization (JETRO). 1982. *China Newsletter* 36, January-February.

Japan Times. 2009. "North Korea's Charm Offensive." *The Japan Times.* 1 September 2009. http://www.japantimes.co.jp/opinion/2009/09/01/editorials/north-koreas-charm-offensive/. Accessed 11 February 2013.

Jasinski, Michael P. 2011. *Social Trust, Anarchy and Conflict*, New York: Palgrave MacMillan.

Jeffries, Ian. 2010. *Contemporary North Korea: A Guide to Economic and Political Developments*. London: Routledge.

JEN (*Japanese Economic Newswire*). 2010. "Satellite Image Suggests S. Korea Shelling of North Was Ineffective." *Japan Economic Newswire*. 2 December 2010. Accessed via LexisNexis, 12 February 2013.

JEN (*Japanese Economic Newswire*). 2011. "China Told Regional Powers After the Death of North Korean Leader Kim Jong Il." *Japan Economic Newswire*. 24 December 2011. Accessed via LexisNexis, 12 February 2013.

Johnston, Alastair Iain. 1998. "China's Militarized Interstate Dispute Behaviour 1949–1992: A First Cut at the Data." *The China Quarterly* 153: 1–30.

JoongAng (Daily). 2010. "ROK Daily: Kim and Jong-Un Ordered Bombardment: Source." *JoongAng Daily Online*. 25 November 2010. http://joongangdaily.joins.com. Accessed 12 February 2013.

Jung, Sung-chul. 2012. *Fear and Greed: Domestic Unrest, Foreign Target, and Interstate Conflict*. Ph.D. Dissertation. New Brunswick, NJ: Rutgers University.

Jung, Sung-ki. 2010a. "Marines to Join Drills in Thailand." 8 January 2010. *Korea Times*. Accessed via LexisNexis, 3 February 2013.

Jung, Sung-ki. 2010b. "U.S. Marines Won't Participate in Exercise in West Sea." *Korea Times*. 18 November 2010. Accessed via LexisNexis, 12 February 2013.

Jung, Won-Il. 2004. "The Future of the United Nations Command in the Republic of Korea." U.S. Army War College Strategy Research Project. Carlisle Barracks, PA: U.S. Army War College.

Kaarbo, Juliet, Jeffrey S. Lantis, and Ryan K. Beasley. 2002. "The Analysis of Foreign Policy in Comparative Perspective." In Beasley, Ryan K. ed. 2002. *Foreign Policy in Comparative Perspective: Domestic and International Influences on State Behavior*. Washington, D.C.: CQ Press.

Kagan, Richard Clark, Matthew Oh, and David S. Weissbrodt. 1988. *Human Rights in the Democratic People's Republic of Korea*. Washington, D.C.: Asia Watch.

Kahn, Joseph, and David Sanger. 2005. "U.S.-Korean Deal on Arms Leaves Key Points Open." *New York Times*. 20 September 2005: A1.

Kane, Tim. 2006. "Global U.S. Troop Deployments 1950–2005." *The Heritage Foundation*, http://www.heritage.org/research/reports/2006/05/global-us-troop-deployment-1950-2005. Accessed 15 Sept 2011.

Kang, Chol-Hwan. 2002. *The Aquariums of Pyongyang: Ten Years in the North Korean Gulag*, New York: Basic Books.

Kang, David C. 2005. "Japan: U.S. Partner or Focused on Abductees?" *The Washington Quarterly* (Autumn): 107–117.

Kang, David C. 2011. Email correspondence with author. 30 August 2011.

Kang, Erica. 2000. "Relief Without Protection." *Refugee Survey Quarterly* 19(2): 110–112.

Kang, Won-taek. 2010. Quoted in Bumiller, Elisabeth and Edward Wong. 2010. "South Korea Reassesses Its Defenses After Attack." 25 November 2010. *New York Times Online*. http://www.Nytimes.com/2010/11/26/world/asia/26korea.html?ref=northkorea. Accessed 7 February 2013.

Kansas Events Data System (KEDS). *Kansas Events Data System Website*. http://web.ku.edu/~keds/. Accessed 6 February 2012.

Kaplan, Robert D., and Abraham M. Denmark. 2011. "The Long Goodbye: The Future North Korea." *World Affairs*. May/June 2011. http://www.worldaffairsjournal.org/article/long-goodbye-future-north-korea. Accessed 13 February 2013.

Katona-Apte, J., and Ali Mokdad. 1998. "Malnutrition of Children in the Democratic People's Republic of North Korea." *The Journal of Nutrition* 128(8): 1315–9.

Kaufmann, Daniel, Aart Kraay and Massimo Mastruzzi. 2009. "Governance Matters VIII: Aggregate and Individual Governance Indicators, 1996–2008 (June 29, 2009)." *World Bank Policy Research Working Paper No. 4978*. Available at SSRN: http://ssrn.com/abstract=1424591. Accessed 2 September 2011.

Kaufmann, Daniel, Aart Kraay and Massimo Mastruzzi. 2010a. *The Worldwide Governance Indicators: Methodology and Analytical Issues*. Brookings Institution. http://info.worldbank.org/governance/wgi/sc_country.asp. Accessed 3 September 2012.

Kaufmann, Daniel, Aart Kraay and Massimo Mastruzzi. 2010b. "The Worldwide Governance Indicators: Methodology and Analytical Issues." *World Bank Policy Research Working Paper No. 5430* (http://papers.ssrn.com/sol3/papers.cfm?abstract_id=1682130). Accessed 5 October 2013.

Kawachi, I., B.P. Kennedy, K. Lochner and D.

Prothrow-Stith. 1997. "Social Capital, Income Inequality, and Mortality." *American Journal of Public Health* 87(9): 1491–8.

KBS (Korea Broadcasting Service) Radio. 1993. "Troops Reportedly Used Against 30,000 Rioters in North Korea." *KBS Radio*. Seoul. 4 May 1993. BBC Summary of World Broadcasts. Accessed via LexisNexis, 17 August 2012.

KBS (Korea Broadcasting Service) TV. 1998. "ROK Joint Chiefs of Staff on Details of Sub Incident." *Korea Broadcasting Service*. Seoul. 26 June 1998. Accessed via LexisNexis, 24 July 2012.

KBSM (Korea Buddhist Sharing Movement). 1998. "'The Food Crisis of North Korea: Witnessed by 770 Food Refugees." *Relief Web*. http://reliefweb.int/report/democratic-peoples-republic-korea/food-crisis-north-korea-witnessed-770-food-fefugees-4th. Accessed 13 August 2012.

KCBN (Korean Central Broadcasting Network) Radio. 1995. "Questions Aid from Capitalists." *Pyongyang Korean Central Broadcasting Network* [in Korean]. Pyongyang. 28 December 1995. Accessed via LexisNexis, 24 August 2012.

KCBN (Korean Central Broadcasting Network) Radio. 1998. "Radio Announces Successful 'Satellite' Launch." *P'yongyang Korean Central Broadcasting Network* [in Korean]. 4 September 1998. Accessed via LexisNexis, 24 August 2012.

KCBN (Korean Central Broadcasting Network) Radio. 1999. "DPRK Radio Denounces Firing Incident as ROK Provocation." *P'yongyang Korean Central Broadcasting Network* [in Korean]. 15 June 1999.

KCNA (Korea Central News Agency). 1995. "Foreign Relations; U.S. 'Attempt to Stifle' North Korea 'Unchanged.'" *Korea Central News Agency*. Pyongyang. 26 November 1995. Accessed via LexisNexis, 24 August 2012.

KCNA (Korea Central News Agency). 1996a. "Spirit of 'Arduous March.'" *Korea Central News Agency*. Pyongyang. 2 January 1996. Accessed Via Lexisnexis, 24 August 2012.

KCNA (Korea Central News Agency). 1996b. "ROK Remarks on 'Exaggerated' Damages Viewed." *Korea Central News Agency*. Pyongyang. 12 January 1996. Accessed via LexisNexis, 24 August 2012.

KCNA (Korea Central News Agency). 1996c. "ROK Condemned for Obstructing Aid to North." *Korea Central News Agency*. Pyongyang. 25 January 1996. Accessed via LexisNexis, 24 August 2012.

KCNA (Korea Central News Agency). 1996d. "DPRK Warns It Will Not Accept Further Aid with Conditions." *Korea Central News Agency*. Pyongyang. 29 January 1996. Accessed via LexisNexis, 24 August 2012.

KCNA (Korea Central News Agency). 1996e. "Vice Marshal: DPRK Took 'Self-Defense Measure' to Deter War." *Korea Central News Agency*. Pyongyang. 24 April 1996. Accessed via LexisNexis, 24 August 2012.

KCNA (Korea Central News Agency). 1996f. "Further on Vice Premier Discussing Food Aid at FAO Meeting." *Korea Central News Agency*. Pyongyang. 21 November 1996. Accessed via LexisNexis, 24 August 2012.

KCNA (Korea Central News Agency). 1997. "SKNDF Urges 'Overthrow' of U.S.-Backed Kim Yong-Sam." *Korea Central News Agency*. Pyongyang. 5 June 1997. Accessed via LexisNexis, 24 August 2012.

KCNA (Korea Central News Agency). 1998a. "Daily on 'Successful' Launch of 'Kwangmyongsong No.1.'" *Korea Central News Agency*. Pyongyang. 7 September 1998. Accessed Via Lexisnexis, 24 August 2012.

KCNA (Korea Central News Agency). 1998b. "Satellite Launch 'Fruit' of Kim Chong-Il's Guidance." *Korea Central News Agency*. Pyongyang. 19 September 1998. Accessed via LexisNexis, 24 August 2012.

KCNA (Korea Central News Agency). 1998c. "Dailies Blast Japan's UN Statement on 'Satellite.'" *Korea Central News Agency*. Pyongyang. 26 September 1998. Accessed Via Lexisnexis, 24 August 2012.

KCNA (Korea Central News Agency). 1998d. "Foreign Leaders Laud DPRK's Satellite Launch." *Korea Central News Agency*. Pyongyang. 29 September 1998. Accessed via LexisNexis, 24 August 2012.

KCNA (Korea Central News Agency). 1999a. "North Korea Denounces Us, South's Joint Military Manoeuvres." *Korea Central News Agency*. Pyongyang. 2 February 1999. www.kcna.co.jp/index-e.htm. Accessed 24 May 2012.

KCNA (Korea Central News Agency). 1999b. "Agency Says South's War Ships Intruded into North's Waters." *Korea Central News Agency*. Pyongyang. 7 June 1999. *BBC Worldwide Monitoring*. Accessed via LexisNexis, 29 August 2012.

KCNA (Korea Central News Agency). 1999c. "*KCNA* Reports on 15 Jun General Officers'

Talks.'" *Korea Central News Agency*. Www. Kcna.Co.Jp/Index-E.Htm. Pyongyang. 15 June 1999.

KCNA (*Korea Central News Agency*). 2002. "DPRK Committee for Peaceful Reunification of Fatherland Secretariat Issues White Paper Rejecting NLL." *Korea Central News Agency*. www.kcna.co.jp/index-e.htm. Pyongyang. 1 August 2002.

KCNA (*Korea Central News Agency*). 2003. "Rodong Sinmun on Army-Based Policy." *Korea Central News Agency*. Pyongyang. 21 March 2003. www.kcna.co.jp/index-e.htm. Accessed 24 January 2013.

KCNA (*Korea Central News Agency*). 2006a. "DPRK Foreign Ministry Clarifies Stand on New Measure to Bolster War Deterrent." 3 October 2006. *Korea Central News Agency Online*. http://www.kcna.co.jp/index-e.htm. Accessed 28 January 2013.

KCNA (*Korea Central News Agency*). 2006b. "DPRK Successfully Conducts Underground Nuclear Test." 9 October 2006. *Korea Central News Agency Online*. http://www.kcna.co.jp/index-e.htm. Accessed 28 January 2013

KCNA (*Korea Central News Agency*). 2007a. "Gnp's Servile Attitude Toward Outside Forces Denounced in S. Korea." 11 Oct 2007. *Korea Central News Agency Online*. www.kcna.co.jp/index-e.htm. Accessed 7 February 2013.

KCNA (*Korea Central News Agency*). 2007b. "Ri Hoe Chang's Foolish Remarks Blasted in S. Korea." 3 December 2007. *Korea Central News Agency Online*. www.kcna.co.jp/index-e.htm. Accessed 7 February 2013.

KCNA (*Korea Central News Agency*). 2007c. "Actions for Foiling U.S. Plot and Eliminating Ri Hoe Chang Called for in S. Korea." 15 December 2007. *Korea Central News Agency Online*. www.kcna.co.jp/index-e.htm. Accessed 8 February 2013.

KCNA (*Korea Central News Agency*). 2008a. "Kim Jong Il Enjoys Student Football Match." 6 October 2008. *Korea Central News Agency Online*. www.kcna.co.jp/index-e.htm. Accessed 30 January 2013.

KCNA (*Korea Central News Agency*). 2008b. "*KCNA* Dismisses False Reports Released by Japanese Newspapers." 24 October 2008. *Korea Central News Agency Online*. www.kcna.co.jp/index-e.htm. Accessed 30 January 2013.

KCNA (*Korea Central News Agency*). 2008c. "Kim Jong Il Visits Sariwon Chicken Farm and Migok Cooperative Farm." 12 December 2008. *Korea Central News Agency Online*. www.kcna.co.jp/index-e.htm. Accessed 30 January 2013.

KCNA (*Korea Central News Agency*). 2009a. "Barack Obama Takes Office as U.S. President." 21 January 2009. *Korea Central News Agency Online*. www.kcna.co.jp/index-e.htm. Accessed 8 February 2013.

KCNA (*Korea Central News Agency*). 2009b. "Anti-DPRK Outbursts of Commander of U.S. Forces in S. Korea Blasted." 7 April 2009. *Korea Central News Agency Online*. www.kcna.co.jp/index-e.htm. Accessed 7 February 2013.

KCNA (*Korea Central News Agency*). 2009c. "*KCNA* on Dprk's Successful Launch of Satellite Kwangmyongsong-2." 5 April 2009. *Korea Central News Agency Online*. www.kcna.co.jp/index-e.htm. Accessed 7 February 2013.

KCNA (*Korea Central News Agency*). 2009d. "KCNA Report on One More Successful Underground Nuclear Test." 19 April 2009. *Korea Central News Agency Online*. www.kcna.co.jp/index-e.htm. Accessed 7 February 2013

KCNA (*Korea Central News Agency*). 2009e. "Rodong Sinmun Refutes Unsc's 'Presidential Statement.'" 19 April 2009. *Korea Central News Agency Online*. www.kcna.co.jp/index-e.htm. Accessed 7 February 2013.

KCNA (*Korea Central News Agency*). 2009f. "UNSC Urged to Retract Anti-DPRK Steps." 29 April 2009. *Korea Central News Agency Online*. www.kcna.co.jp/index-e.htm. Accessed 10 February 2013.

KCNA (*Korea Central News Agency*). 2009g. "Dprk's Power Increased by Dint of Songun." 26 May 2009. *Korea Central News Agency Online*. www.kcna.co.jp/index-e.htm. Accessed 7 February 2013.

KCNA (*Korea Central News Agency*). 2009h. "Lee Myung Bak Group's Sycophancy and Servility to Japan Flayed." 29 May 2009. *Korea Central News Agency Online*. www.kcna.co.jp/index-e.htm. Accessed 7 February 2013.

KCNA (*Korea Central News Agency*). 2009i. "DPRK Foreign Ministry Declares Strong Counter- Measures Against Unsc's 'Resolution 1874.'" 13 June 2009. *Korea Central News Agency Online*. www.kcna.co.jp/index-e.htm. Accessed 10 February 2013.

KCNA (*Korea Central News Agency*). 2009j. "Mammoth Pyongyang Rally Denounces UNSC 'Resolution.'" 15 June 2009. *Korea

Central News Agency. http://www.kcna.co.jp. Accessed 4 February 2013.
KCNA (*Korea Central News Agency*). 2009k. "Report on Bill Clinton's Visit to DPRK Made Public." 5 August 2009. *Korea Central News Agency Online*. www.kcna.co.jp/index-e.htm. Accessed 10 February 2013.
KCNA (*Korea Central News Agency*). 2009l. "DPRK Demands S. Korea Apologize for Armed Provocation." 10 November 2009. *Korea Central News Agency Online*. www.kcna.co.jp/index-e.htm. Accessed 10 February 2013.
KCNA (*Korea Central News Agency*). 2009m. "S. Korea Will Be Forced to Pay Dearly for Armed Provocation." 12 November 2009. *Korea Central News Agency Online*. www.kcna.co.jp/index-e.htm. Accessed 10 February 2013.
KCNA (*Korea Central News Agency*). 2010a. "DPRK Warns S. Korean Authorities of Anti-DPRK Operation." 15 January 2010. *Korea Central News Agency Online*. www.kcna.co.jp/index-e.htm. Accessed 10 February 2013.
KCNA (*Korea Central News Agency*). 2010b. "DPRK on Reasonable Way for Sept. 19 Joint Statement." 18 January 2010. *Korea Central News Agency Online*. www.kcna.co.jp/index-e.htm. Accessed 10 February 2013.
KCNA (*Korea Central News Agency*). 2010c. "KPA General Staff Blasts US-S. Korea Military Exercises." 25 February 2010. *Korea Central News Agency Online*. www.kcna.co.jp/index-e.htm. Accessed 10 February 2013.
KCNA (*Korea Central News Agency*). 2010d. "Military Commentator Denies Involvement in Ship Sinking ." 17 April 2010. *Korea Central News Agency Online*. www.kcna.co.jp/index-e.htm. Accessed 10 February 2013.
KCNA (*Korea Central News Agency*). 2010e. "CPRK Accuses S.Korea of Linking Ship Sinking with North." 21 May 2010. *Korea Central News Agency Online*. www.kcna.co.jp/index-e.htm. Accessed 10 February 2013.
KCNA (*Korea Central News Agency*). 2010f. "NDC States to Counter US-S. Korea War Exercises with Nuclear Deterrence." 24 July 2010. *Korea Central News Agency Online*. www.kcna.co.jp/index-e.htm. Accessed 12 February 2013.
KCNA (*Korea Central News Agency*). 2010g. "Will to Take Retaliatory Measures Against Warmongers Declared." 25 July 2010. Korea Central News Agency. http://www.kcna.co.jp. Accessed 5 February 2013.
KCNA (*Korea Central News Agency*). 2010h. "Dangerous Saber-Rattling of Warmongers Blasted." *Korea Central News Agency Online*. 17 August 2010. www.kcna.co.jp/index-e.htm. Accessed 12 February 2013.
KCNA (*Korea Central News Agency*). 2010i. "U.S. Invariable Scenario for Invading DPRK Assailed." *Korea Central News Agency Online*. 16 November 2010. www.kcna.co.jp/index-e.htm. Accessed 12 February 2013.
KCNA (*Korea Central News Agency*). 2010j. "Kim Jong Il Inspects Fish Farm and Fish Breeding Ground." *Korea Central News Agency Online*. 22 November 2010. www.kcna.co.jp/index-e.htm. Accessed 12 February 2013.
KCNA (*Korea Central News Agency*). 2010i. "Panmunjom Mission of KPA Sends Notice to U.S. Forces Side." *Korea Central News Agency Online*. 25 November 2010. www.kcna.co.jp/index-e.htm. Accessed 12 February 2013.
KCNA (*Korea Central News Agency*). 2011a. "Traitor Lee Myung Bak Branded Chieftain of Anti-DPRK Confrontation Racket." 30 June 2011. *Korea Central News Agency Online*. www.kcna.co.jp/index-e.htm. Accessed 7 February 2013.
KCNA (*Korea Central News Agency*). 2011b. "Puppet Group of Traitors Indicted for Enforcing 'NSL.'" 23 July 2011. *Korea Central News Agency Online*. www.kcna.co.jp/index-e.htm. Accessed 7 February 2013.
KCNA (*Korea Central News Agency*). 2011c. "U.S.-S. Korea Joint Military Exercises Under Fire." 16 August 2011. *Korea Central News Agency Online*. www.kcna.co.jp/index-e.htm. Accessed 7 February 2013.
KCNA (*Korea Central News Agency*). 2011d. "Kim Jong Il Passes Away (Urgent)." *Korea Central News Agency Online*. 19 December 2011. www.kcna.co.jp/index-e.htm. Accessed 14 February 2013.
KCNA (*Korea Central News Agency*). 2011e. "Korean People Fully Determined to Win Final Victory Under Leadership of Kim Jong Un ." *Korea Central News Agency Online*. 19 December 2011. www.kcna.co.jp/index-e.htm. Accessed 14 February 2013.
KCNA (*Korea Central News Agency*). 2011f. "Medical Analysis of Kim Jong Il's Demise." *Korea Central News Agency Online*. 19 December 2011. www.kcna.co.jp/index-e.htm. Accessed 14 February 2013.
KCNA (*Korea Central News Agency*). 2011g. "Notice to All Party Members, Serviceper-

sons and People." *Korea Central News Agency Online.* 19 December 2011. www.kcna.co.jp/index-e.htm. Accessed 14 February 2013.

KCNA (*Korea Central News Agency*). 2011h. "Kim Jong Un Assumes Supreme Commander." *Korea Central News Agency Online.* 31 December 2011. www.kcna.co.jp/index-e.htm. Accessed 14 February 2013.

KCNA (*Korea Central News Agency*). 2012a. "North Korean Paper Says U.S. 'Imperialists' Launched Korean War." *Korea Central News Agency.* Pyongyang. 27 June 2012. BBC Worldwide Monitoring. Accessed via Lexis-Nexis, 17 November 2012.

KCNA (*Korea Central News Agency*). 2012b. "Army-People Meeting Marks Anniversary of Victorious Yonphyong Island Shelling." *Korea Central News Agency Online.* 23 November 2012. www.kcna.co.jp/index-e.htm. Accessed 12 February 2013.

KCNA (*Korea Central News Agency*). 2013c. "S. Korean Authorities Accused of Fabricating UN 'Resolution' with Foreign Forces." *Korea Central News Agency Online.* 25 January 2013. www.kcna.co.jp/index-e.htm. Accessed 26 February 2013.

KCNA (*Korea Central News Agency*). 2013d. "U.S. and S. Korean War Manoeuvres Against DPRK Under Fire." *Korea Central News Agency Online.* 23 February 2013. www.kcna.co.jp/index-e.htm. Accessed 26 February 2013.

Kcnawatch. 2013. Keyword searches: "John McCain" and "Barack Obama." *KCNA Watch.* http://kcnawatch.org/. Accessed 8 February 2013.

KEDO (Korea Peninsula Energy Development Organization). 1994. *Agreed Framework Between the United States of America and the Democratic People's Republic of Korea.* Geneva, 21 October 1994. http://www.kedo.org/pdfs/AgreedFramework.pdf. Accessed 7 August 2012.

KEDO (Korea Peninsula Energy Development Organization). 2001. *KEDO 2001 Annual Report.* http://www.kedo.org/annual_reports.asp. Accessed 24 August 2012.

KEDO (Korea Peninsula Energy Development Organization). 2005. *KEDO 2005 Annual Report.* http://www.kedo.org/annual_reports.asp. Accessed 7 August 2012.

KEDO (Korea Peninsula Energy Development Organization). 2012. *About Us: Our History.* http://www.kedo.org/au_history.asp. Accessed 7 Aug 2012.

Kellstedt, Paul M., and Guy D. Whitten. 2009. *The Fundamentals of Political Science Research*, Cambridge, MA: Cambridge University Press.

Kennan, George. 1946 "The Charge in the Soviet Union (Kennan) to the Secretary of State [The Long Telegram]." 22 February 1946. http://www.gwu.edu/~nsarchiv/coldwar/documents/episode-1/kennan.htm. Accessed 15 January 2013.

Kennedy-Pipe, Caroline. 2000. "International History and International Relations Theory: A Dialogue Beyond the Cold War." *International Affairs* 76(4): 741–754.

Khrushchev, Nikita S. 1959. "On Peaceful Coexistence." *Foreign Affairs* 38(1): 1–18.

Kim, Bong Seob. 2011. "A Year in the Life." *The Daily NK.* 27 September 2011. http://www.dailynk.com/english/. Accessed 13 February 2013

Kim, Byung-Yeon, and Dongho Song. 2008. "The Participation of North Korean Households in the Informal Economy: Size, Determinants, and Effect." *Journal of Economics* (Seoul) 21(2): 361–385.

Kim, Byung-Yeon, Suk Jin Kim, and Keun Lee. 2007. "Assessing the Economic Performance of North Korea, 1954–1989: Estimates and Growth Accounting Analysis." *Journal of Comparative Economics* 35: 564–582.

Kim, Cayman. 1992. "Sudden Freeze Hits Korean Relations." *Japan Economic Newswire.* Kyodo. 12 November 1992. Accessed via LexisNexis, 21 August 2012.

Kim, Choong Nam. 2005. *The Roh Moo Hyun Government's Policy Toward North Korea.* Honolulu, HI: East-West Center.

Kim, Dae-jung. 1998. "Let Us Open a New Era: Overcoming National Crisis and Taking a New Leap Forward [Inaugural Address]." Seoul, South Korea. 25 February 1998. http://shlel.tripod.com/krinaug.htm. Accessed 29 August 2012.

Kim, Dongsoo, and Yongseok Choy. 2012. "The Impact of Domestic Politicson North Korea's Foreign Policy." *International Journal of Korean Unification Studies* 21(2): 61–84.

Kim, Hak-Joon. 1977. *The Unification Policy of South and North Korea: A Comparative Study.* Seoul: Seoul National University Press.

Kim, Hong-Cheol. 2010. *The Paradox of Power in Conflict Between the Strong and the Weak When and Why Do Weaker States Challenge the Hegemon's International Status Quo?* Dissertation. Tallahassee, FL: Florida State University.

Kim, Hyon-hui. 1993. *The Tears of My Soul.* New York: William Morrow and Co.

Kim, Hyung-A. 2004. *Korea's Development Under Park Chung-Hee: Rapid Industrialization, 1961–79*. London: RoutledgeCurzon.

Kim, Ilpyong J. 1962. "North Korea's Fourth Party Congress." *Pacific Affairs* 35(1): 37–50.

Kim, Ilpyong J. 1975. *Communist Politics in North Korea*. New York: Praeger.

Kim, Ji-hyun. 2009. "Navies of 2 Koreas Clash Off West Coast." *The Korea Herald*. 11 November 2009. Accessed via LexisNexis, 11 February 2013.

Kim, Jin-Ha. 2011. "On the Threshold of Power, 2011/12: Pyongyang's Politics of Transition." *International Journal of Korean Unification Studies* 20(2): 1–25.

Kim, Joungwon A. 1970. "Soviet Policy in North Korea." *World Politics: A Quarterly Journal of International Relations* 22(2): 237–254.

Kim, Joungwon A. 1975. *Divided Korea: The Politics of Development, 1945–1972*. Cambridge, MA: East Asian Research Center, Harvard University.

Kim, Kwang-tae. 2010. "Koreas Meet to Discuss Family Reunions." *The Associated Press*. Accessed via LexisNexis, 12 February 2013.

Kim, Kyong-ho. 1996. "Article Says DPRK Toning Down Rhetoric Against ROK, U.S." *The Korean Herald*. Seoul. 6 November 1996.

Kim, Roy U. T. 1968. "Sino-North Korean Relations." *Asian Survey* 8(8): 708–722.

Kim, Se-jeong. 2010. "NK Threatens to Wage Holy War on South." *Korea Times*. 15 January 2010. Accessed via LexisNexis, 11 February 2013.

Kim, Se Jin. 1970. "South Korea's Involvement in Vietnam and Its Economic and Political Impact." *Asian Survey* 10(6): 519–532.

Kim, So-hyun. 2010. "Kim, Hu Hold Talks in Beijing." 6 May 2010. *The Korea Herald* (Seoul). Accessed via LexisNexis, 3 February 2013.

Kim, Tong-ho, and Yi Yong-chong. 2008. "'Who Is That Doctor Seeing Kim Jong Il?'—Intelligence War Heats Up." 30 October 2008. JoongAng Ilbo Online [Seoul, in Korean]. http://joongangdaily.joins.com/. Accessed 30 January 2013.

Kim, Woon Keun, Hyunok Lee, and Daniel A. Sumner. 1998. "Assessing the Food Situation in North Korea." *Economic Development and Cultural Change* 46(3): 519–535.

Kim, Yong-ho. 2011. *North Korean Foreign Policy: Security Dilemma and Succession*. Lanham, MD: Lexington Books.

Kim, Young Jak. 2011. "Park Chung Hee's Governing Ideas: Impact on National Consciousness and Identity." In *Reassessing the Park Chung Hee Era, 1961–1979: Development, Political Thought, Democracy & Cultural Influence*, 66–84. Hyung-A Kim and Clark W. Sorensen (eds). Seattle: University of Washington Press.

Kim Il Sung: Condensed Biography. 2001. Pyongyang: Foreign Languages Publication House.

Kimball, Daryl. 2012. "Chronology of U.S.-North Korean Nuclear and Missile Diplomacy." *Arms Control Association*. http://www.armscontrol.org/factsheets/dprkchron. Accessed 22 January 2013.

King, Gary, and Will Lowe. 2003a. "An Automated Information Extraction Tool for International Conflict Data with Performance as Good as Human Coders: A Rare Events Evaluation Design." *International Organization* 57(3): 617–642.

King, Gary, and Will Lowe. 2003b. "10 Million International Dyadic Events." http://hdl.handle.net/1902.1/FYXLAWZRIA UNF:3:dSE0bsQK2o6xXlxeaDEhcg== IQSS Dataverse Network [Distributor] V3 [Version]

King, Gary, Robert O. Keohane, and Sidney Verba. 1994. *Designing Social Inquiry: Scientific Inference in Qualitative Research*. Princeton, NJ: Princeton University Press.

King, Gary, et.al. 2001. "Analyzing Incomplete Political Science Data: An Alternative Algorithm for Multiple Imputation." *American Political Science Association* 95(1): 49–69.

KINU (Korea Institute for National Unification). 2011a. "Inter-Korean Relations Chronology, 1948–2011." http://www.unied u.go.kr/uniedu/PdsDataroomHome.do?cmd=readArticle&dataroomArticleDTO .atclSn=1382. Accessed 22 October 2011.

KINU (Korea Institute for National Unification). 2011b. "White Paper on Human Rights in North Korea." Seoul: Center for North Korean Human Rights Studies.

Kirk, Donald. 2009. "Journalists Held in North Korea Recount Their Capture." *Christian Science Monitor Online*. 2 September 2009. http://www.csmonitor.com/World/GlobalNews/2009/0902/journalists-held-in-north-korea-recount-their-capture. Accessed 10 February 2013.

Kirk, Mark. 1998. "Mission to North Korea and China, August 11–23, 1998." Report prepared for the International Relations Committee of the U.S. House of Representatives. Available at http://nkorelief.tripod.com/kirkrep.htm. Accessed 20 May 2012.

KIS (Kim Il-sung). 1955. "On Eliminating Dogmatism and Formalism and Establishing Juche [Chuche] in Ideological Work." In *Sources of Korean Tradition. Vol. 2, from the Sixteenth to the Twentieth Centuries*. 2008, 582–606. Yong-ho Choe, Peter H. Lee, and William DeBary (eds.). New York: Columbia University Press.

KIS (Kim Il-sung). 1961. "Report on the Work of the Central Committee to the Fourth Congress of the Workers' Party of Korea." In *Kim Il Sung: Selected Works, Volume 3*. 1976, 57–204. Pyongyang: Foreign Languages Publication House.

KIS (Kim Il-sung). 1962. "On the Immediate Tasks of the Government of the Democratic People's Republic of Korea." October 23, 1962. *Kim Il Sung: Selected Works, Volume 3*. 1976, 372–422. Pyongyang: Foreign Languages Publication House.

KIS (Kim Il-sung). 1964. "Let Us Strengthen the Revolutionary Forces in Every Way to Achieve the Cause of Reunification of the Country." In *Kim Il Sung: Selected Works, Volume 4*. 1971: 84–103. Pyongyang: Foreign Languages Publication House.

KIS (Kim Il-sung). 1965. "To Give Full Play to the Great Vitality of the Unified and Detailed Planning of the National Economy." In *Kim Il Sung: Selected Works, Volume 4*. 1971: 252–290. Pyongyang: Foreign Languages Publication House.

KIS (Kim Il-sung). 1967. "Let Us Intensify the Anti-Imperialist, Anti-U.S. Struggle." In *Kim Il Sung: Selected Works, Volume 4*. 1971: 538–545. Pyongyang: Foreign Languages Publication House.

KIS (Kim Il-sung). 1976. *Selected Works. [Volume] III*. Pyongyang, Korea: Foreign Languages Publishing House.

Kisangani, Emizet F., and Jeffrey Pickering. 2007. "Diverting with Benevolent Military Force: Reducing Risks and Rising Above Strategic Behavior." *International Studies Quarterly* 51, 277–299.

Kisangani, Emizet F., and Jeffrey Pickering. 2009. "The Dividends of Diversion: Mature Democracies' Proclivity to Use Diversionary Force and the Rewards They Reap from It." *British Journal of Political Science* 39(3): 483–515.

KJI (Kim Jong-il). 1997. *On Preserving the Juche Character and National Character of the Revolution and Construction*. Pyongyang, Korea: Foreign Languages Pub. House.

KJI (Kim, Jong-il). 2004 [1982]. *On the Juche Idea*. Whitefish, MT: Kessinger Publishing.

Klinger, Bruce. 2010a. "New Leaders, Old Dangers: What North Korean Succession Means for the U.S." *Heritage Foundation Backgrounder*, No. 2397. 7 April 2010. http://s3.amazonaws.com/thf_media/2010/pdf/bg_2397.pdf. Accessed 13 February 2013.

Klinger, Bruce. 2010b. "North Korea Pressures U.S. Through Provocations." *The Heritage Foundation*, 24 Nov 2010. http://www.heritage.org/research/reports/2010/11/north-korea-pressures-us-through-provocations. Accessed 15 September 2011.

Klinger, Bruce. 2011. "The *Cheonan*: A Retrospective Assessment." 25 March 2011. *The Heritage Foundation*. http://www.heritage.org/research/commentary/2011/03/the-cheonan-a-retrospective-assessment. Accessed 7 February 2013.

Koh, B. C. 1965. "North Korea and Its Quest for Autonomy." *Pacific Affairs* 38(3/4): 294–306.

Koh, B.C. 1969. "North Korea and the Sino-Soviet Schism." *The Western Political Quarterly* 22(4): 940–962.

Koh, B. C. 1977. "North Korea 1976: Under Stress." *Asian Survey* 17(1): 61–70.

Koh, B. C.. 1984. *The Foreign Policy Systems of North and South Korea*. Berkeley: University of California Press.

Koh, B. C. 1997. "South Korea in 1996: Internal Strains and External Challenges." *Asian Survey* 37(1): 1–9.

Korea Herald. 1999a "NIS Reports North Korean Famine Easing." *The Korea Herald*. Seoul. 4 February 1999.

Korea Joongang Daily. 2011. "North Korea Playing with Fire." 7 June 2011, *Korea Joongang Daily* http://joongangdaily.joins.com/article/view.asp?aid=2937211. Accessed 21 June 2011.

Korea Newsreview. 1995. "World Vision International to Donate Grain to P'yang." *Korea Newsreview*. 11 February 1995: 8–13.

Korea Times. 1998a. "Financial Crisis Strips ROK of Ability to Give DPRK Aid." *Korea Times* [internet version] Seoul. 7 January 1998.

Korea Times. 1998b. "Around 3 Million Reportedly Die of Famine in DPRK." *Korea Times* [internet version] Seoul. 11 May 1998.

Korea Times. 1998c. "NK Maintains Numerical Military Superiority Over ROK." *Korea*

Times. Seoul. 28 September 1998. Accessed via LexisNexis, 23 August 2012.

Korea Times. 1999a. "Kim IS Statues in NK Vandalized: Reports." *Korea Times.* Seoul. 30 March 1999. Accessed via LexisNexis, 16 August 2012.

Korea Times. 1999b. "Possible Reasons for DPRK Intrusion." *The Korea Times* (internet version). Seoul. 16 June 1999.

Korea Times. 2004. "Kim Jong-Il May Soon Appoint Heir: Analyst." 7 January 2004. *The Korea Times.* Accessed via LexisNexis, 29 January 2013.

Korea Times. 2010. "U.S. Denounces N. Korea's Artillery Attack." *Korea Times.* 24 November 2010. Accessed via LexisNexis, 12 February 2013.

Korea Times. 2012. "*Cheonan* Sinking Ordered by Kim Jong-Un: NK Defector Testifies." *The Korea Times Online.* 27 March 2012. http://www.koreatimes.co.kr/www/news/nation/2012/03/113_107857.html. Accessed 12 February 2013.

Kristof, Nicholas D. 1997a. "A Hungry North Korea Swallows a Bit of Pride." *New York Times.* 29 May 1997: A6.

Kristof, Nicholas D. 1997b. "Seoul Said to Foil Spy Ring for North That Included a Top Scholar." *New York Times.* 21 November 1997: A7.

Kristof, Nicholas D. 1997c. "Seoul's Heroic Failure: Departing Chief, Kim Young Sam." *The New York Times.* 22 December 1997: A12. Accessed via LexisNexis, 22 August 2012.

Kristof, Nicholas D. 1998a. "North Korea Says Its Food Is Nearly Gone." *New York Times.* New York. 3 March 1998: A9.

Kristof, Nicholas D. 1998b. "Congressman Fears Famine Is Decimating North Koreans." *The New York Times.* 15 November 1998: 9.

Kuark, Yoon T. 1963. "North Korea's Industrial Development During the Post-War Period." *China Quarterly* (14): 51–64.

Kun, Joseph C. 1967. "North Korea: Between Moscow and Peking." *The China Quarterly* (31): 48–58.

Kuznetsov, Vasily. 1965. "Record of Conversation Between Soviet Deputy Foreign Minister Vasily Kuznetsov and the North Korean Ambassador to the Soviet Union Kim Pyeongchaek." 21 May 1965. *Cold War International History Project.* http://www.wilsoncenter.org/document-collections. Accessed 14 December 2012.

Kwon, Heonik, and Byung-Ho Chung. 2012. *North Korea: Beyond Charismatic Politics.* Lanham, MD Rowman & Littlefield Publishers.

Kyodo News. 1992. "Widespread Rioting as Monetary Controls Cause Severe Cash Shortage." *Kyodo News.* Tokyo. 4 September 1992. BBC Summary of World Broadcasts. Accessed via LexisNexis, 17 August 2012.

Kyodo News. 1995. "North Reportedly Deploying Nodong-1 Missiles." *Kyodo News.* Tokyo. 12 September 1995.

Kyodo News. 2009. "Japan Says North Korea's Missile Launches Act of 'Provocation.'" *Kyodo News* (Japan). 6 July 2009. BBC Monitoring Asia Pacific—Political. Accessed via LexisNexis, 9 February 2013.

Kyodo News. 2010a. "U.N. Humanitarian Chief Considering N. Korea Visit." *Kyodo News* (Japan). 30 September 2010. Japan Economic Newswire. Accessed via LexisNexis, 12 February 2013.

Kyodo News. 2010b. "Japan, U.S. Begin Biggest Ever Joint Military Exercises." *Kyodo News* (Japan). 3 December 2010. BBC Summary World Broadcast. Accessed via LexisNexis, 12 February 2013.

Lai, Brian, and Dan Slater. 2006. "Institutions on the Offensive: Domestic Sources of Dispute Initiation in Authoritarian Regimes, 1950–1992." *American Journal of Political Science* 50: 113–26.

Lake, David A., and Matthew A. Baum. 2001. "The Invisible Hand of Democracy: Political Control and the Provision of Public Services." *Comparative Political Studies* 34(6): 587–621.

Landler, Mark. 2009. "North Korea Says It Will Halt Talks and Restart Its Nuclear Program." *New York Times.* 15 April 2009: A5.

Landler, Mark, and Choe Sang-Hun. 2011. "In Kim's Undetected Death, Sign of Nation's Opacity." *The New York Times.* 19 December 2011. http://www.Nytimes.com/2011/12/20/world/asia/in-detecting-kim-jong-il-death-a-gobal-intelligence-failure.html?pagewanted=all. Accessed 14 February 2013.

Landler, Mark, and Mark Mazzetti. 2009. "In North Korea, Clinton Helped Unveil a Mystery." *New York Times Online.* 18 August 2009. http://www.Nytimes.com/2009/08/19/world/asia/19korea.html. Accessed 13 February 2013.

Lankov, A. N. 2002a. "Kim Takes Control: The "Great Purge." In North Korea, 1956–1960." *Korean Studies* 26(1): 87–119.

Lankov, A. N. 2002b. *From Stalin to Kim Il Sung: The Formation of North Korea, 1945–1960.* New Brunswick, N.J.: Rutgers University Press.

Lankov, Andrei N. 2009. "Pyongyang Strikes Back: North Korean Policies of 2002–08 and Attempts to Reverse 'De-Stalinization from Below.'" *Asia Policy* 8(July 2009): 7–71.

Lankov, Andrei N. 2011. "North Korea-China Special Economic Zones." *East Asia Forum,* 14 July 2011, http://www.eastasiaforum.org/2011/07/14/north-korea-china-special-economic-zones/. Accessed 5 February 2012.

Lankov, Andrei. 2012. "Kim Jong-Un's North Korea: What Should We Expect?" *International Journal of Korean Unification Studies* (21) 1: 1–20.

Lee, Doowon. 2008. "Assessing North Korean Economic Reform: Historical Trajectory, Opportunities, and Constraints." *Pacific Focus* 8(2): 5–29.

Lee, J. S. 1931. "The Periodic Recurrence of Internecine Wars in China." *The China Journal* (1931: March–April):111–163.

Lee, Julia Joo-A. 2009. "To Fuel or Not to Fuel: China's Energy Assistance to North Korea." *Asian Security* 5(1): 45–72.

Lee, Karin, and Julia Choi. 2009. *North Korea: Unilateral and Multilateral Economic Sanctions and U.S. Department of Treasury Actions 1955-April 2009.* The National Committee on North Korea. Washington, D.C.: National Committee on North Korea.

Lee, Matthew. 2010. "Clinton: Nkorea Must Face Consequences for Attack." *The Associated Press.* 21 May 2010. Accessed via Lexis-Nexis, 11 February 2013.

Lee, Suk. 2003. Food Shortages and Economic Institutions in the Democratic People's Republic of Korea. Thesis (doctoral). http://webcat.warwick.ac.uk/record=b1735804~S9, University of Warwick, 2003.

Lee, Suk. 2005. *The DPRK Famine of 1994–2000: Existence and Impact.* Seoul, Korea: Korea Institute for National Unification.

Lee, Suk. 2006. "Reliability and Usability of the DPRK Statistics: Case of Grain Statistics in 1946-2000." *International Journal of Korean Unification Studies* 15(1): 132–172.

Lee, Sung-Yul. 1998. "Agents Suspected of Committing Suicide Before Vessel Sank." *The Korean Herald.* Seoul. 21 December 1998: 3.

Lee, Young-Sun, and Deok Ryong Yoon. 2004. *The Structure of North Korea's Political Economy: Changes and Effects.* Seoul, Korea: Korea Institute for International Economic Policy.

Leeds, Brett Ashley, and David R. Davis. 1997. "Domestic Political Vulnerability and International Disputes." *Journal of Conflict Resolution* 41(6): 814–834.

Lenin, V.I. 1930. *The Imperialist War: The Struggle Against Social Chauvinism and Social Pacifism.* New York: International Publishers.

Lerner, Mitchell B. 2002. *The Pueblo Incident: A Spy Ship and the Failure of American Foreign Policy.* Lawrence, Kan: University Press of Kansas.

Levy, Jack S. 1986. "Organizational Routines and the Causes of War." *International Studies Quarterly* 30(2): 193–222.

Levy, Jack S. 1997. "Too Important to Leave to the Other: History and Political Science in the Study of International Relations." *International Security* 22(1): 22–33.

Levy, Jack S. 1998. "The Causes of War and Conditions of Peace." *Annual Review of Political Science* 1: 139–165.

Levy, Jack S. 2001a. "Explaining Events and Developing Theories: History, Political Science, and the Analysis of International Relations." Colin Elman and Miriam Elman, eds. *Bridges and Boundaries: Historians, Political Scientists, and the Study of International Relations,* Cambridge, MA: MIT Press.

Levy, Jack S. 2001b. "Theories of Interstate and Intrastate War: A Levels-Of-Analysis Approach." In *Turbulent Peace: The Challenges of Managing International Conflict,* eds. Chester A. Crocker, Fen Osler Hampson, Pamela Aall. Washington, D.C.: United States Institute of Peace, 3–27.

Levy, Jack S. 2007. "Qualitative Methods and Cross-Method Dialogue in Political Science." *Comparative Political Studies* 40(2): 196–214.

Levy, Jack S. 2008. "Case Studies: Types, Designs, and Logics of Inference." *Conflict Management and Peace Science* 25(1): 1–18.

Levy, Jack S., and William R. Thompson. 2010. *Causes of War.* Malden, MA: Wiley-Blackwell.

LexisNexis, 2013. Keyword search— "North Korea Nuclear." from 1 April 2009 to 23 May 2009. www.LexisNexis.com. Accessed 10 February 2013.

Li, Yitan. 2008. *A Two-Level Analysis of Foreign Policy Decision Making: An Empirical Investigation of the Case of China Taiwan,* Dissertation, University of Southern California.

Li, Yitan, Patrick James and A. Cooper Drury. 2009. "Diversionary Dragons, or 'Talking Tough in Taipei': Cross-Strait Relations in the New Millennium." *Journal of East Asian Studies* 9(3): 369–398.

Liang, Xiaodon. 2012. "The Six-Party Talks at a Glance." Arms Control Association. May 2012. http://www.armscontrol.org/factsheets/6partytalks. Accessed 11 February 2013.

Lijphart, Arend 1971. "Comparative Politics and the Comparative Method." *The American Political Science Review* 65(3): 682–693

Lim, C.W. 1993. "Report: 18 North Korean Officers Executed in 1992 Coup." *The Associated Press*. 25 August 1993. Accessed via LexisNexis, 17 August 2012.

Lim, Phillip Wonhyuk. 1997. "North Korea's Food Crisis." *Korea and World Affairs* 21(4) Winter: 568–585.

Lintner, Bertil. 2005. *Great Leader, Dear Leader: Demystifying North Korea Under the Kim Clan.* Chiang Mai: Silkworm Books.

Long, Andrew G. 2008. "Bilateral Trade in the Shadow of Armed Conflict." *International Studies Quarterly* 52, 81–101.

Long, Andrew G. 2011. Personal communication with the author, 28 January 2011.

Low, Alfred D. 1976. *The Sino-Soviet Dispute: An Analysis of the Polemics.* Rutherford, NJ: Fairleigh Dickinson University Press.

Lydons, Christopher. 1968. "U.S. Is Reducing Fleet Off Korea." *New York Times.* 28 April 1969: 1.

MacDonald, C. A. 1987. *Korea, the War Before Vietnam.* New York: Free Press.

MacFarquhar, Neil. 2008. "North Korea Faces Worst Food Crisis in Decade, U.N. Says." 24 October 2008. *The New York Times*: A10.

MacFarquhar, Neil. 2009. "U.N. Council May Rebuke North Korea." *New York Times.* 12 April 2009: 8.

Machiavelli, Niccolò. 1882 [1513]. *The Historical, Political, and Diplomatic Writings of Niccolo Machiavelli,* Volume II, translated by Christian E. Detmold. Boston: James R. Osgood and Company.

Mack, A. 1975. "Numbers Are Not Enough: A Critique of Internal/External Conflict Behavior Research." *Comparative Politics* 7: 597–618

Mack, R. W. 1965. "The Components of Social Conflict." *Social Problems* 22(4): 388–397.

Maddison, Angus. 2008. *Statistics on World Population, GDP and Per Capita GDP, 1–2008 AD.* University of Groningen. http://www.ggdc.net/MADDISON/oriindex.htm. Accessed 21 October 2012.

Mahoney, J., and G. Goertz. 2004. "The Possibility Principle: Choosing Negative Cases in Comparative Research." *American Political Science Review* 98(4): 653–669.

Mahoney, J., and G. Goertz. 2006. "A Tale of Two Cultures: Contrasting Quantitative and Qualitative Research." *Political Analysis* 14: 227–249.

Maliniak, D., A. Oakes, S. Peterson and M. J. Tierney. 2011. "International Relations in the U.S. Academy." *International Studies Quarterly* 55: 437–464.

Manyin, Mark E. 2012. *Kim Jong-Il's Death Implications for North Korea's Stability and U.S. Policy.* Washington, D.C.: Congressional Research Service, Library of Congress.

Manyin, Mark E., and Mary B. Nikitin. 2012. *Foreign Assistance to North Korea.* Washington, D.C.: Congressional Research Service.

Manyin, Mark E., and Ryun Jun. 2003. *U.S. Assistance to North Korea.* Washington, D.C.: Congressional Research Service.

Margesson, Rhoda. 2007. "North Korean Refugees in China and Human Rights Issues: International Response and U.S. Policy Options." *Congressional Research Service,* 26 September 2007, RL34189, http://www.fas.org/sgp/crs/row/RL34189.pdf. Accessed 15 September 2011.

Marolda, Edward J. 1994. *By Sea, Air, and Land: An Illustrated History of the U.S. Navy and the War in Southeast Asia.* Washington, D.C.: Naval Historical Center, Department of the Navy.

Martin, Bradley K. 2006. *Under the Loving Care of the Fatherly Leader: North Korea and the Kim Dynasty.* New York: Griffin.

Martin, Curtis H. 2002. "Rewarding North Korea: Theoretical Perspectives on the 1994 Agreed Framework." *Journal of Peace Research* 39(1): 51–68.

Matern, Hermann, and Hermann Axen. 1967. "Memorandum on a Meeting with a Delegation from the Supreme People's Assembly of the DPRK on 3 July 1967." 3 July 1967. *Cold War International History Project.* http://www.wilsoncenter.org/program/cold-war-international-history-project. Accessed 6 January 2013.

Mayer, Arno J. 1967. "Domestic Causes of the First World War." In *The Responsibility of Power,* ed. Leonard Krieger and Fritz Storn. Garden City, New York, 286–293.

Mayer, Arno J. 1969. "Internal Causes and Pur-

pose of War in Europe, 1870–1956." *Journal of Modern History* 41(3): 291–303.
Mazarr, Michael J. 1995. "Going Just a Little Nuclear: Nonproliferation Lessons from North Korea." *International Security* 20(2): 92–122.
Mazzetti, Mark. 2006. "Preliminary Samples Hint at North Korean Nuclear Test." *New York Times*. 14 October 2006: A7.
McClelland, Charles. 1999. "World Event/Interaction Survey (WEIS) Project Codebook, 1966–1978." ICPSR05211-v3. Ann Arbor, MI: Inter-university Consortium for Political and Social Research [distributor].
McDevitt, Michael. 2011. "Deterring North Korean Provocations." *Brookings Northeast Asia Commentary* 46 (February). http://www.brookings.edu/research/papers/2011/02/north-korea-mcdevitt. Accessed 12 February 2013.
McEachern, Patrick, 2010. *Inside the Red Box: North Korea's Post-Totalitarian Politics*. New York: Columbia University Press.
MCIA (U.S. Marine Corps Intelligence Activity). 1997. *North Korea Country Handbook*. Quantico, VA: Dept. of Defense Intelligence Production Program. http://purl.access.gpo.gov/GPO/LPS42016. Accessed 24 August 2012.
Meernik, James. 2001. "Domestic Politics and the Political Use of Military Force by the United States." *Political Research Quarterly* 54(4): 889–904.
Meernik, James, and Peter Waterman, 1996. "The Myth of the Diversionary Use of Force by American Presidents." *Political Research Quarterly* 49(3): 573–590.
Meernik, John J. 1994. "Presidential Decision-Making and the Political Use of Force." *International Studies Quarterly* 38:121–138.
Michishita, Narushige. 2003. *Calculated Adventurism: North Korea's Military-Diplomatic Campaigns, 1966–2000*. Dissertation, Johns Hopkins University.
Michishita, Narushige. 2010. *North Korea's Military-Diplomatic Campaigns, 1966–2008*. New York, NY: Routledge.
Michishita, Narushige. 2011. Email correspondence with the author. 5 June 2011.
Milbank, Dan. 2002. "Democrats Question Iraq Timing; Talk of War Distracts from Election Issues." *Washington Post*, 16 September 2002, A1.
Militarized Interstate Disputes (MID). 2010. "Militarized Interstate Disputes Database." *Correlates of War (COW) Website*. http://www.correlatesofwar.org/COW2%20Data/MIDs/MIDA_3.10.csv/. Accessed 27 August 2010.
Miller, Ross. 1995. 'Domestic Structures and the Use of Force,' *American Journal of Political Science* 39(3): 760–785.
Miller, Ross, 1999. "Regime Type, Strategic Interaction, and the Diversionary Use of Force." *Journal of Conflict Resolution* 43(3): 388–402
Millett, Allan Reed. 2005. *The War for Korea, 1945–1950: A House Burning*. Lawrence, KS: University Press of Kansas.
Milner, Wesley. 1998. *Progress or Decline? International Political Economy and Human Rights*. Ph.D. Dissertation, University of North Texas.
Mitchell, Richard H. 1967. *The Korean Minority in Japan*. Berkeley: University of California Press.
Mitchell, Sara McLaughlin, and Brandon C. Prins. 1999. "Beyond Territorial Contiguity: Issues at Stake in Democratic Militarized Interstate Disputes." *International Studies Quarterly* 43(1): 169–183.
Mitchell, Sara McLaughlin, and Brandon C. Prins. 2004. "Rivalry and Diversionary Uses of Force." *The Journal of Conflict Resolution* 48(6): 937–961.
Mitchell, Sara McLaughlin, and Clayton L. Thyne. 2010. "Contentious Issues as Opportunities for Diversionary Behavior." *Conflict Management and Peace Science* 27(5): 461–485.
Mobley, Richard A. 2003. *Flash Point North Korea: The Pueblo and EC-121 Crises*. Annapolis, MD: Naval Institute Press.
Morgan, T. Clifton. 1990. "The Concept of War: Its Impact on Research and Policy." *Peace and Change* 15(4): 413–41.
Morgan, T. Clifton, and Christopher J. Anderson. 1999. "Domestic Support and Diversionary External Conflict in Great Britain, 1950- 1992." *The Journal of Politics* 61(3): 799–814.
Morgan, T. Clifton, and Kenneth N. Bickers. 1992. "Domestic Discontent and the External Use of Force." *The Journal of Conflict Resolution* 36(1): 25–52.
Morris-Suzuki, Tessa. 2005. "A Dream Betrayed: Cold War Politics and the Repatriation of Koreans from Japan to North Korea." *Asian Studies Review* 29(4): 357–381.
Morris-Suzuki, Tessa. 2006. "Defining the Boundaries of the Cold War Nation: 1950s

Japan and the Other Within." *Japanese Studies* 26(3): 303–316.

Moskovsky, Vasily. 1962. "Memorandum of Conversation Between Soviet Ambassador to North Korea Vasily Moskovsky and Kim Il Sung." 1 November 1962. *Cold War International History Project*. http://www.wilsoncenter.org/document-collections. Accessed 14 December 2012.

Moskovsky, Vasily. 1963. "Entry from the Diary of Soviet Ambassador Moskovsky." 4 September 1963. *Cold War International History Project*. http://www.wilsoncenter.org/document-collections. Accessed 14 December 2012.

Most, Benjamin, and Harvey Starr. 1989. *Inquiry, Logic, and International Politics*. Columbia: University of South Carolina Press.

Mulready-Stone, Kristin. 2013. Email communication with author.

Myers, B. R. 2010. *The Cleanest Race: How North Koreans See Themselves and Why It Matters*. Brooklyn, N.Y.: Melville House.

Myers, Steven Lee. 1996. "U.S. Reports Foes in Korea Willing to Discuss Peace." *The New York Times*. 31 December 1996: A1.

Myers, Steven Lee. 1997. "U.S. Giving North Korea More Food: Reply Due Today on Holding Talks." *New York Times*. 15 April 1997: A9.

Na, Jeong-ju. 2009. "North Korea Rejects U.S. Food Aid." *Korea Times*. 18 March 2009. Accessed via LexisNexis, 9 February 2013.

Nagourney, Adam. 2008. "Mccain Is Undone by Economy, Bush and Star Power." 6 November 2008. *The International Herald Tribune*. Accessed via LexisNexis, 8 February 2013.

NAM (Non-Aligned Movement). 2012. "The Non-Aligned Movement: Description and History." NAM Website. http://www.nam.gov.za/background/history.htm. Accessed 3 January 2012.

Nam, Koon Woo. 1974. *The North Korean Communist Leadership, 1945–1965; a Study of Factionalism and Political Consolidation*. University, AL: University of Alabama Press.

Nam, L. J. 2006. "The Revival of Chinese Nationalism: Perspectives of Chinese Intellectuals.." *Asian Perspective* 30: 141–166.

Nanto, Dick K. 1998. *The 1997–98 Asian Financial Crisis*. Washington, D.C.: Congressional Research Service.

Nanto, Dick K., and Emma Chanlett-Avery. 2008. *The North Korean Economy Background and Policy Analysis*. Washington, D.C.: Congressional Research Service, Library of Congress.

Nanto, Dick K., and Emma Chanlett-Avery. 2010. *North Korea: Economic Leverage and Policy Analysis*. Washington, D.C.: Congressional Research Service, Library of Congress.

Nanto, Dick K., and Mark E. Manyin. 2011. "China–North Korea Relations." *North Korean Review* 7(2): 94–101.

Nanto, Dick K., Mark E. Manyin, and Kerry Dumbaugh. 2010. *China-North Korea Relations*. Washington, D.C: Congressional Research Service, Library of Congress.

National Security Archive. 2005. "National Security Archive Electronic Briefing Book No. 164." *National Security Archive*. http://www.gwu.edu/~nsarchiv/NSAEBB/NSAEBB164/. Accessed 24 August 2012.

Natsios, Andrew S. 1999. "The Politics of Famine in North Korea." *United States Institute of Peace*, Special Report 51, 2 August 1999. http://www.usip.org/files/resources/sr990802.pdf. Accessed 15 August 2012.

Natsios, Andrew S. 2001. *The Great North Korean Famine: Famine, Politics, and Foreign Policy*. Washington, D.C.: United Stated Institute of Peace, 2001.

Natsios, Andrew. 2013. "Why North Korea Is Testing Nuclear Weapons Now?" *U.S. News and World Report*. 8 February 2013. http://www.usnews.com/opinion/blogs/world-report/2013/02/08/why-north-korea-is-testing-nuclear-weapons-now. Accessed 10 February 2013.

Nihon Keizai Shimbun. 1998. "Missile Tests Tokyo's Crisis Management." *Nihon Keizai Shimbun* [in Japanese]. Tokyo. 2 September 1998: 2.

Nikitin, Mary B. 2010. *North Korea's Second Nuclear Test: Implications of U.N. Security Council Resolution 1874*. Washington, D.C.: Congressional Research Service.

Niksch, Larry A. 2005. *North Korea's Nuclear Weapons Program*. CRS Report, Washington, D.C.: Congressional Research Service, Library of Congress.

Niksch, Larry A. 2006. *North Korea's Nuclear Weapons Program*. CRS Report, Washington, D.C.: Congressional Research Service, Library of Congress.

Niksch, Larry A. 2010a. *North Korea's Nuclear Weapons Development and Diplomacy*. Ft. Belvoir, VA: Defense Technical Information Center.

Niksch, Larry A. 2010b. *North Korea's Nuclear*

Weapons Program. CRS Report, Washington, D.C.: Congressional Research Service, Library of Congress.

Nincic, Miroslav. 1975. "Determinants of Third World Hostility Toward the United States: An Exploratory Analysis." *Journal of Conflict Resolution* 19(4): 620–642.

NK News (NK News.org). 2012. "USS *Pueblo* Disappears from Pyongyang: Koryo Tours Reports Mysterious Disappearance of North Korea's Most Famous American War Trophy." *NK News*, http://www.nknews.org/2012/11/uss-pueblo-dissapears-from-pyongyang/. Accessed 11 Jan 2013.

NMC (National Material Capabilities) (CINC) Documentation. 2005. *Correlates of War Website*. http://www.correlatesofwar.org. Accessed 15 October 2012.

No, Chae-hyon, and Choe Won-ki. 1996. "Ministry Official Notes Student 'Disturbance' in DPRK." *Chungang Ilbo*. Seoul. 9 March 1996.

Nodong Sinmun. 1999. "Kim Chong-Il's Military–1st Policy Lauded." *Nodong Sinmun* [in Korean]. Pyongyang. 28 February 1999: 2.

Noland, Marcus. 1997. "Why North Korea Will Muddle Through." *Foreign Affairs* 76(4): 105–118.

Noland, Marcus. 2000. *Avoiding the Apocalypse: The Future of the Two Koreas*. Washington, D.C.: Institute for International Economics.

Noland, Marcus. 2002. "North Korea's External Economic Relations: Globalization in 'Our Own Style'" in *North Korea and Northeast Asia*. Samuel S. Kim and Tai Hwan Lee. Lanham, MD: Rowman and Littlefield.

Noland, Marcus. 2003a. Testimony to the U.S. Congress, Senate, Subcommittee on East Asian and Pacific Affairs of the Committee on Foreign Relations, *Life Inside North Korea*, 108th Cong., 1st sess., 5 June 2003, S. Hrg. 108–131. Washington, D.C.: U.S. Government Printing Office.

Noland, Marcus. 2003b. "Famine and Reform in North Korea: Working Paper 03–5." *Institute for International Economics Website*, July 2003. www.iie.com/publications/wp/2003/03–5.pdf. Accessed 24 January 2013.

Noland, Marcus. 2005. "Famine and Reform in North Korea: Working Paper 03–5." *Institute for International Economics Website*, July 2003. www.iie.com/publications/wp/2003/03–5.pdf. Accessed 30 April 2005.

Noland, Marcus. 2008. "The (Non) Impact of UN Sanctions on North Korea." *Working Paper*. Washington, D.C.: Institute for International Economics.

Noland, Marcus, Sherman Robinson, and Tao Wang. 2001. "Famine in North Korea: Causes and Cures." *Economic Development and Cultural Change* 49(4): 741–767.

Norris R.S., and Kristensen H.M. 2010. "Global Nuclear Weapons Inventories, 1945–2010." *Bulletin of the Atomic Scientists* 66(4): 77–83.

Nozoe, Shinichi. 1997. "The Collapsing Planned Economic System." In *Kim Jong Il's North Korea: An Arduous March*. Edited by Kazunobu Hayashi and Teruo Komaki. Tokyo, Japan: Institute of Developing Economies.

Nye, J.S. Jr. 1992. "New Approaches to Nuclear Proliferation Policy." *Science (New York, N.Y.)*. 256 (5061): 1293–7.

NYT (*New York Times*). 1950. "Truman Orders U.S. Air, Navy Units to Fight in Aid of Korea; U.N." *New York Times*. 28 June 1950: 1.

NYT (*New York Times*). 1955. "Atomic Artillery Sent to Far East." *New York Times*. 29 July 1955: 3.

NYT (*New York Times*). 1957. "Reds' Reply to the U.N. at Panmunjon." *New York Times*. 22 June 1957: 3.

NYT (*New York Times*). 1961. "TASS Hints U.S. Had Role in Korea Coup." 17 May 1961, p. 3.

NYT (*New York Times*). 1962. "Troops Sent to Thailand Drawn from Far-Flung Pacific Force." *New York Times*. 16 May 1962: 12.

NYT (*New York Times*). 1966a. "Cuba and North Korea Ask World Red Force in Vietnam." *New York Times*. 2 November 1966: 2.

NYT (*New York Times*). 1966b. "6 G.I.'S Killed as North Koreans Attack in South." *New York Times*. 2 November 1966: 1.

NYT (*New York Times*). 1967a. "North Korean Shore Guns Sink Southern Gunboat: 11 Dead, 28 Missing." *New York Times*. 20 January 1967: 3.

NYT (*New York Times*). 1967b. "Park Will Run Again." *New York Times*. 3 February 1966: 6.

NYT (*New York Times*). 1967c. "North Korea Tells Its People War Is Imminent." *New York Times*. 15 May 1967: 8.

NYT (*New York Times*). 1968a. "North Korean Says Aim Was to Assassinate Park." *New York Times*. 23 January 1968: 6.

NYT (*New York Times*). 1968b. "Korea Resents the U.S. Emphasis on the *Pueblo*." *New York Times*. 11 February 1968: E2.

NYT (*New York Times*). 1968c. "Pyongyang Assails Nixon." *New York Times*. 9 November 1968: 12.

NYT (*New York Times*). 1969. "North Korea Accuses U.S." *New York Times*. 20 April 1969: 3.

NYT (*New York Times*). 1997. "Tidal Wave Destroys Crops in North Korea." *New York Times*. 2 September 1997: A6.

NYT (*New York Times*). 1998. "U.S. Provides Fuel Oil for North Korea." *New York Times*. 1 October 1998: A8.

NYT (*New York Times*). 1999. "U.S. Outlines Aid for North Korea." *The New York Times*. 23 March 1999: A11.

NYT (*New York Times*). 2003. "North Korea Fires Antiship Missile in Test Launch." *New York Times*. 10 March 2003: A14.

O, Yong-chin. 1997. "Task of NK Agents to Recruit Social Leaders.*" Korea Times*. Seoul. 20 November 1997.

Oakes, Amy. 2006. "Diversionary War and Argentina's Invasion of the Falkland Islands." *Security Studies* 15(3): 431–463.

Oberdorfer, Donald. 1997. *The Two Koreas: A Contemporary History*, Indianapolis: Basic Books.

Oberdorfer, Donald. 2001. "North Korea's Historic Shift: From Self-Reliance to Engagement." In *North Korea's Engagement: Perspectives, Outlooks and Implications*. National Intelligence Council. Washington, D.C.: National Intelligence Council.

Oh, Chul Ho (ed.). 1999. *Korea Annual 1999*. Seoul: *Yonhap News* Agency.

Oh, Gyung Chan. 1997. *North Korea's Food Problem Could Be Solved*. Seoul: Daewangsa.

Oh, Kong Dan. 1988. *Leadership Change in North Korean Politics: The Succession to Kim Il Sung*. Santa Monica, CA: Rand.

Oh, Kong Dan, and Ralph C. Hassig. 2000. *North Korea Through the Looking Glass*. Washington, D.C.: Brookings Institution Press.

Oh, Kong Dan, and Ralph C. Hassig. 2009. *The Hidden People of North Korea: Everyday Life in the Hermit Kingdom*. Lanham, MD: Rowman and Littlefield Publishers.

Oh, Kong Dan, and Ralph C. Hassig. 2010. "North Korea in 2009: The Song Remains the Same." *Asian Survey* 50(1): 89–96.

Olsen, Edward A. 2008. "Obama Sunshine on N. Korea." *The Korea Herald*. 21 November 2008. Accessed via LexisNexis, 8 February 2013.

Onishi, Norimitsu. 2006. "South Brings Capitalism, Well Isolated, to North Korea: Benefits of Training and High Wages." 18 July 2006. The *New York Times*: A3.

Onishi, Norimitsu. 2007. "Election in South Korea Is Missing Its Suspense." 17 December 2007. *The New York Times Online*. http://www.Nytimes.com/2007/12/17/world/asia/17korea.html?pagewanted=all&_r=0. Accessed 8 February 2013.

Oreskes, Michael. 1990. "Bush Trying a New Topic; Is Talk of War Driven by Policy or Politics?" *New York Times*, 31 October 1990: A21.

Ostrom, Charles W. 1990. *Time Series Analysis: Regression Techniques*. Newbury Park, Calif: Sage Publications.

Ostrom, Charles W., Jr., and Brian L. Job. 1986. "The President and the Political Use of Force." *The American Political Science Review* 80(2): 541–566.

Paige, Glenn D., and Dong Jun Lee. 1963. "The Post-War Politics of Communist Korea." *China Quarterly* (14): 17–29.

Pak, Chi-yong. 2000. *Korea and the United Nations*. The Hague: Kluwer Law International.

Park, Chung Hee. 1971. *To Build a Nation*. Washington, D.C.: Acropolis Books.

Park, Jae Kyu. 1984. "North Korea's Political and Economic Relations with China and the Soviet Union: From 1954 to 1980." *Comparative Strategy* 4(3): 273–305.

Park, Tae-Gyun. 2009. "Beyond the Myth: Reassessing the Security Crisis on the Korean Peninsula During the mid-1960s." *Pacific Affairs* 82 (1): 93–110.

Park, Young-June, 2011. Korea National Defense University, personal communication with the author [email]. 8 June 2011.

Park, Young-taek. 2012. "The Structural Elements of North Korea's Insecurity: Applying the 'Regional Security Complex Theory.'" *The Korean Journal of Defense Analysis* 24 (3): 321–333.

Peceny, Mark, and Caroline C. Beer, with Shannon Sanchez-Terry. 2002. "Dictatorial Peace?" *American Political Science Review* 96: 15–26.

Peceny, Mark, and Caroline C. Beer. 2003. "Peaceful Parties and Puzzling Personalists." *American Political Science Review* 97: 339–42.

Peceny, Mark, and Christopher K. Butler. 2004. "The Conflict Behavior of Authoritarian Regimes." *International Politics* 41: 565–81.

Penn State Event Data Project, 2012. *The Penn State Event Data Project Website*. http://eventdata.psu.edu/. Accessed 5 February 2012.

Person, James F. 2006. "'We Need Help from Outside': The North Korean Opposition Movement of 1956." Washington, D.C.: Woodrow Wilson International Center for Scholars.

Phillips, Kate. 2008. "Obama and the Preconditions Meme." 23 May 2008. *The New York Times Online*. http://thecaucus.blogs.Nytimes.com/2008/05/23/obama-and-the-preconditions-meme/. Accessed 8 February 2013.

Pickering, Jeffrey. 2011. Email communication with the author (14 October 2011).

Pickering, Jeffrey, and Emizet F. Kisangani. 2005. "Democracy and Diversionary Military Intervention: Reassessing Regime Type and the Diversionary Hypothesis." *International Studies Quarterly* 49(1): 23–43.

Pickering Jeffrey, and Emizet F. Kisangani. 2009. "The International Military Intervention Dataset: An Updated Resource for Conflict Scholars." *Journal of Peace Research* 46(4): 589–599.

Pickering, Jeffrey, and Emizet F. Kisangani. 2010. "Diversionary Despots? Comparing Autocracies' Propensities to Use and to Benefit from Military Force." *American Journal of Political Science* 54(2): 477–493.

Pinkston, Daniel A. 2008. *The North Korean Ballistic Missile Program*. Carlisle Barracks, PA: Strategic Studies Institute, U.S. Army War College. http://purl.access.gpo.gov/GPO/LPS91582. Accessed 15 August 2012.

Podgorny, N.V. 1967. "Record of Conversation Between Podgorny, N.V. and Extraordinary and Plenipotentiary Ambassador of the DPRK in the USSR Kim Chunbong." 20 January 1967. *Cold War International History Project*. http://www.wilsoncenter.org/document-collections. Accessed 11 January 2013.

Pollack, Jonathan D. 2009. "Kim Jong-Il's Clenched Fist." *The Washington Quarterly* 32(4): 153–173.

Pollack, Jonathan D. 2011. "Kim Jong-Il to Kim Jong-Un: North Korea in Transition." The Brookings Institute. 19 December 2011. http://www.brookings.edu/research/opinions/2011/12/19-north-korea-pollack. Accessed 13 February 2013.

Pollock, Philip H. 2005. *The Essentials of Political Analysis*. Washington, D.C.: CQ Press.

Porter, William J. 1968. "Telegram from the Embassy in Korea to the Department of State/1/ Seoul, January 24, 1968, 2105Z." 24 January 1968. *Cold War International History Project*. http://www.wilsoncenter.org/document-collections. Accessed 20 December 2012.

Powell, Bill. 2009. "U.S. Tries Direct Talks with North Korea." 8 December 2009. *Time Online*. http://www.time.com/time/world/article/0,8599,1946145,00.html#ixzz2KJmT9GF0. Accessed 8 February 2013.

Presidential Task Force on Korea (U.S.). 1961. "Report to the National Security Council." 5 June 1965. *Papers of John F. Kennedy*, Presidential Papers, President's Office Files. http://www.jfklibrary.org/Asset-Viewer/Archives/JFKPOF-121-004.aspx#. Accessed 22 Sep 2011.

Prybyla, Jan S. 1964. "Soviet and Chinese Economic Competition Within the Communist World." *Soviet Studies* 15(4): 464–473.

Purdum, Todd S. 1998. "U.S. Fury on 2 Continents: Congress; Critics of Clinton Support Attacks." *New York Times*, 21 August 1998: A1.

Putnam, Robert D. 1988. "Diplomacy and Domestic Politics: The Logic of Two-Level Games." *International Organization* 42(3): 427–460.

Quinones, Kenneth C. 2003. "Beyond Collapse-Continuity and Change in North Korea." http://ckquinones.com/wp-content/uploads/2008/08/2003-1-dprk-economy-beyond-collapse.pdf. Accessed 19 February 2013.

Radchenko, Sergy. 2011. "Inertia and Change: Soviet Policy Toward Korea 1985–1991." In *The Cold War in East Asia, 1945–1991*. Hasegawa Tsuyoshi (ed), 289–320. Washington, D.C.: Woodrow Wilson Center Press.

Ramstad, Evan. 2010. "North Korea Strains Under New Pressures." *The Wall Street Journal Online*. 30 March 2010. http://online.wsj.com/article/SB10001424052702304434404575149520133311894.html. Accessed 13 February 2013.

Ramstad, Evan. 2011. "North Korea Warns South in Annual Message." *Wall Street Journal Online*. 1 January 2011. http://online.wsj.com/article/ SB10001424052748704543604576054890727297846.html. Accessed 15 October 2011.

Raymond, Jack. 1957. "U.N. Korea Force to Get New Arms to Offset Reds' Communist Build-Up." *New York Times*. 21 June 1957: 1.

Raymond, Jack. 1958. "Rhee Will Reduce Forces in Korea: Yields to Pressure from U.S." *New York Times*. 21 February 1958: 6.

Ree, Erik van. 1989. *Socialism in One Zone:*

Stalin's Policy in Korea, 1945–1947. Oxford [England]: Berg.
Reilly, David 2004. "The Growing Importance of the Failing State: Sovereignty, Security, and the Return to Power Politics." *Journal of Conflict Studies* 24(June). http://journals.hil.unb.ca/index.php/JCS/article/view/289/459. Accessed 27 Sep. 2011.
Rennack, Dianne E. 2010. "North Korea Legislative Basis for U.S. Economic Sanctions." CRS Report RL31696. Washington, D.C.: Congressional Research Service, Library of Congress.
Rennack, Dianne E. 2011. *North Korea: Legislative Basis for U.S. Economic Sanctions*. Washington, D.C.: Congressional Research Service.
Rennie, David, and Roger du Mars. 2000. "Seoul Spy Protest Over Colleagues Left Out in the Cold." *The Telegraph*. http://www.telegraph.co.uk/news/worldnews/asia/southkorea/1373156/Seoul-spy-protest-over-colleagues-left-out-in-the-cold.html. Accessed 23 February 2013.
Revere, Evans J.R. 2011. "Dealing with North Korea's New Leader: Getting It Right." *The Brookings Institute Online*. 21 December 2011. http://www.brookings.edu/research/opinions/2011/12/21-north-korea-revere. Accessed 13 February 2013.
RFE (Radio Free Europe) Research Report. 1966. "Strengthening North Korean-Soviet Economic Relations." 22 June 1966. Retrieved from Open Society Archives at Central European University. www.osaarchivum.org. Keyword search: Strengthening North Korean-Soviet Economic Relations. Accessed 18 December 2012.
Rhee, Syngman. 1957. "Letter from President Rhee to President Eisenhower." Seoul, 24 June 1957. *Foreign Relations of the United States, 1955–1957, Volume XXIII, Part 2, Korea*, Document 227. http://history.state.gov/historicaldocuments/frus1955-57v23p2/d227. Accessed 26 November 2012.
Richmond, Yale. 2003. *Cultural Exchange & the Cold War: Raising the Iron Curtain*. University Park: Pennsylvania State University Press.
Robinson, Michael Edson. 2007. *Korea's Twentieth-Century Odyssey*. Honolulu: University of Hawaii Press.
Robinson, W. Courtland. 2010. "Population Estimation of North Korean Refugees and Migrants and Children Born to North Korean Women in Northeast China." Unpublished paper, 9 April 2010.
Robinson, W. Courtland, Myung Ken Lee, Kenneth A. Hill, Edbert B. Hsu, and Gilbert M. Burnham. 2001. "Demographic Methods to Assess Food Insecurity: A North Korean Case Study." *Prehospital and Disaster Medicine* 16(4): 286–292.
Rochester, J. Martin. 2008. *U.S. Foreign Policy in the Twenty-First Century: Gulliver's Travails*. Boulder, CO: Westview Press.
Roehrig, Terence. 2007. "Restructuring the U.S. Military Presence: Implications for Korean Security and the U.S.-ROK Alliance." *Korea Economic Institute Issue Papers* 2 (1). http://keia.org/publication/restructuring-us-military-presence-korea-implications-korean-security-and-us-rok-allianc. Accessed 25 January 2013.
Roehrig, Terence. 2008. "Korean Dispute Over the Northern Limit Line: Security, Economics, or International Law?" *Maryland Series in Contemporary Asian Studies* 2008(3): 1–59.
ROK Government. 2012a. "History: Founding of Korea." http://www.korea.net/AboutKorea/Korea-at-a-Glance/History. Accessed 17 November 2012.
ROK Government. 2012b. "Korean War Casualties." Institute for Military History Compilation. http://www.imhc.mil.kr/imhcroot/data/korea_view.jsp?seq=4&page=1 [in Korean]. Accessed 18 November 2012.
ROK MND (Republic of Korea Ministry of National Defense). 1986. *The Brief History of ROK Armed Forces*. 1986. Seoul: Ministry of National Defense, Republic of Korea.
ROK MND (Republic of Korea Ministry of National Defense). 2002. *The Republic of Korea Position Regarding the Northern Limit Line*. August 2002. http://www.military.co.kr/english/NLL/NLL.htm. Accessed 29 August 2012.
ROK MND (Republic of Korea Ministry of National Defense). 2010. *Joint Investigation Report on the Attack Against the ROK Ship Cheonan*. Seoul: ROK Ministry of National Defense.
ROK MOU (Ministry of Unification). 2010. "North and South Koreas Agreed to Hold the Next Family Reunion at the Reunion Center Near Mt. Geumgang from October 30 to November 5." *States News Service*. 4 October 2010. Accessed via LexisNexis, 12 February 2013.
ROK MOU (Republic of Korea Ministry of Unification). 2012a. *Major Statistics in Inter-Korean Relations*. http://eng.unikorea.go.kr/

CmsWeb/viewPage.req?idx =PG00000005 41. Accessed 23 October 2012.
ROK MOU (Republic of Korea Ministry of Unification). 2012b. "Data on Number of North Korean Refugees Prior to 1990 Cannot Be Released to the Public." Email communication with author. 1 November 2012.
Romanian Embassy. 1968a. "Telegram from Pyongyang to Bucharest, Top Secret, No: 75.015, Flash." 24 January 1968. *Cold War International History Project*. http://www.wilsoncenter.org/document-collections. Accessed 11 January 2013.
Romanian Embassy. 1968b. "Telegram from Pyongyang to Bucharest, Top Secret, No. 76.017, Flash." 25 January 1968. *Cold War International History Project*. http://www.wilsoncenter.org/document-collections. Accessed 11 January 2013.
Romanian Government. 1971. "Minutes of Conversation on the Occasion of the Party and Government Delegation on Behalf of the Romanian Socialist Republic to the Democratic People's Republic of Korea." 10 June 1971. *Cold War International History Project*. http://www.wilsoncenter.org/program/cold-war-international-history-project. Accessed 9 January 2013.
Rosen, James. 2009. "North Korean Nuclear Test Catches U.S. by Surprise." *Fox News Online*. 25 May 2009. http://www.foxnews.com/politics/2009/05/25/north-korean-nuclear-test-catches-surprise/. Accessed 10 February 2013.
Rosenau, James N. 1969. *Linkage Politics: Essays on the Convergence of National and International Systems*. New York: Free Press.
Rosenau, James N. 1971. *The Scientific Study of Foreign Policy*. New York: Free Press.
Rosenau, James N., and George H. Ramsey. 1975. "External and Internal Typologies of Foreign Policy Behavior." In Patrick J. Macgowan (ed.) *Sage International Yearbook of Foreign Policy Studies*. Vol. 3. Beverly Hills, Sage: 245–262.
Ross, Michael. 2006. "Is Democracy Good for the Poor?" *American Journal of Political Science* 50(4): 860–874.
Rummel, R.J. 1963. "Dimensions of Conflict Behavior Within and Between Nations." *General Systems Yearbook* 8.
Rummel, R.J. 1966. "Dimensions of Conflict Behavior Within Nations, 1946–59" *The Journal of Conflict Resolution* 10(1): 65–73.
Rummel, R.J. 1973. "Dimensions of Conflict Behavior Within and Between Nations." In *Conflict Behavior and Linkage Politics*, ed. Jonathan Wilkenfeld. New York: McKay, 59–106.
Ryu, Kyung-won. 2010. "Endless Attempts at Market Reform." In *Rimjin-Gang: News from Inside North Korea*, 90–121. Osaka, Japan: Asia Press International.
Ryu, Kyung-won, and Jiro Ishimaru. 2010. "The Secret History of the North Korean Economy: An Interview with a North Korean Economic Official." In *Rimjin-Gang: News from Inside North Korea*, 23–83. Osaka, Japan: Asia Press International.
Sagan, Scott D. 1997. "Why Do States Build Nuclear Weapons?: Three Models in Search of a Bomb." *International Security* 21(3): 54–86.
Samore, Gary Samuel. 2004a. *North Korea's Weapons Programmes: A Net Assessment*. Basingstoke: Palgrave Macmillan.
Samore, Gary Samuel. 2004b. *North Korea's Weapons Programmes: A Net Assessment*. London: International Institute for Strategic Studies. http://www.iiss.org/publications/strategic-dossiers/north-korean-dossier/north-koreas-weapons-programmes-a-net-asses/. Accessed 25 January 2013.
Sanger, David E. 2002. "Bush, Focusing on Terrorism, Says Secure U.S. Is Top Priority." *New York Times*. 30 January 2002: A1.
Sanger, David E. 2005. "U.S. Widens Campaign on North Korea: An Effort to Curb Weapons Program." *New York Times*. 24 October 2005: A7.
Sanger, David E. 2007. "News Analysis: Outside Pressures Snapped Korean Deadlock." *New York Times*. 14 February 2007: A1.
Sankei Shimbun. 2007. "North Korea Orders Tighter Control Out of Alarm at Expansion of Black Markets." 13 November 2007. *Sankei Shimbun* Tokyo [in Japanese]. http://sankei.jp.msn.com/. Accessed 1 February 2013.
Sarkesian, Sam C., John Allen Williams, and Stephen J. Cimbala. 2008. U.S. *National Security: Policymakers, Processes, and Politics*. Boulder, CO: Lynne Rienner.
Savada, Andrea Matles. 1994. *North Korea: A Country Study*. Washington, D.C.: Federal Research Division, Library of Congress.
Savada, Andrea M., and William Shaw. 1990. *South Korea: A Country Study*. Washington, D.C.: Federal Research Division, Library of Congress.
Scalapino, Robert A. 1963. "The Foreign Policy of North Korea." *The China Quarterly* 14: 30–50.

Scalapino, Robert A., and Chong-Sik Lee. 1972. *Communism in Korea*. Berkeley: University of California Press.

Schiller, Markus. 2012. *Characterizing the North Korean Nuclear Missile Threat*. Santa Monica, CA: RAND.

Schneider, William. 2000. *Foreign Missile Developments and the Ballistic Missile Threat to the United States Through 2015*. Testimony before the Subcommittee on International Security, Proliferation, and Federal Services Committee on Government Affairs, U.S. Senate. Washington, D.C.: National Intelligence Council.

Scobell, Andrew. 2004. *China and North Korea from Comrades-In-Arms to Allies at Arm's Length*. Carlisle, PA: Strategic Studies Institute, U.S. Army War College.

Scobell, Andrew. 2005. *North Korea's Strategic Intentions*, Carlisle, PA: U.S. Army War College Strategic Studies Institute.

Scobell, Andrew. 2006. *Kim Jong Il and North Korea the Leader and the System*. Carlisle, PA: Strategic Studies Institute, U.S. Army War College.

Scobell, Andrew, and John M. Sanford. 2007. *North Korea's Military Threat Pyongyang's Conventional Forces, Weapons of Mass Destruction, and Ballistic Missiles*. Carlisle, PA: Strategic Studies Institute, U.S. Army War College.

Seawright, Jason, and John Gerring. 2008. "Case Selection Techniques in Case Study Research." *Political Research Quarterly* 61: 294–308.

Shabecoff, Philip. 1969. "Long-Distance Deployment of U.S. Troops for Airdrop in South Korea Stirs Seoul's Fear of Pullout." *New York Times*. 20 March 1969: 13.

Shakespeare, William. 1823. "King Henry IV, Act 4." In *The Dramatic Works of William Shakespeare*, London: Chiswick.

Shimotomai, Nobuo. 2011. "Kim Il Sung's Balancing Act Between Moscow and Beijing." In *The Cold War in East Asia, 1945–1991*. Tsuyoshi Hasegawa (ed). Washington, D.C.: Woodrow Wilson Center Press.

Shin, Paul. 1994. "U.S. Patriot Missiles Arrive in S. Korea—Tense Standoff with N. Korea Prompted Shipment." *Seattle Times*. 19 April 1994. http://community.seattletimes.nwsource.com/archive/?date=19940418&slug=1906116. Accessed 23 August 2012.

Shirk, Susan L. 2008. *China: Fragile Superpower*. New York: Oxford University Press.

Shorts, Dennis, and Vincent Min. 2008. "Obama's Asia Policy: A Look Back at the Presidential Race to Understand America's Next Steps in Asia." *International Journal of Korean Unification Studies* 17(2): 27–47.

Shtykov, Terenti. 1950. "Telegram from Shtykov to Vyshinski Regarding Meeting with Kim Il Sung." 12 May 1950. *Cold War International History Project*. http://legacy.wilsoncenter.org/va2/index.cfm?topic_id=1409&fuseaction=HOME.document&identifier=5034BF56-96B6-175C-9ED40B8C84C0F12B&sort=Coverage&item=Korea (North). Accessed 27 November 1950.

Sigal, Leon V. 1998. *Disarming Strangers: Nuclear Diplomacy with North Korea*. Princeton, N.J.: Princeton University Press.

Simmel, Georg. 1898. "The Persistence of Social Groups." *American Journal of Sociology* 3(5): 662–698.

Simmel, Georg. 1904. "The Sociology of Conflict. II." *American Journal of Sociology* 9(5): 672–689.

Simmel, Georg. 1955 [1898]. *Conflict*. K. Wolf, trans. Glencoe, IL: Free Press.

SK Foreign Ministry Archive (South Korean Foreign Ministry Archive). 1972. "Conversation with Kim Il Sung." 4 May 1972. *Cold War International History Project*. http://www.wilsoncenter.org/document-collections. Accessed 11 January 2013.

Slater D., and Simmons E. 2010. "Informative Regress: Critical Antecedents in Comparative Politics." *Comparative Political Studies* 43(7): 886–917.

Small, Melvin. 2004. "The Election of 1968." *Diplomatic History* 28(4): 513–528.

Smith, Alastair, 1996. "Diversionary Foreign Policy in Democratic Systems." *International Studies Quarterly* 40(1): 133–153.

Smith, Hazel. 1999. "'Opening Up' by Default: North Korea, the Humanitarian Community and the Crisis." *Pacific Review* 12(3): 453–478.

Smith, Hazel. 2000. "Bad, Mad, Sad or Rational Actor? Why the 'Securitization' Paradigm Makes for Poor Policy Analysis of North Korea." *International Affairs* 76(3): 593–617.

Smith, Hedrick. 1969. "U. S. Perplexed by Okinawa Issue: Weighs Demands by Tokyo and Military Value of Island." *New York Times*. 31 March 1969: 2.

Smith, Walter B. 1950. "Memorandum for the President: Five Critical Situations in the Far East." 12 October 1950. *CIA Freedom of Information Website*. http://www.foia.cia.gov/sites/default/files/document_conversions/

89801/DOC_0000121494.pdf. Accessed 18 Nov 2012.

Snyder, Jack. 2002. "Anarchy and Culture: Insights from the Anthropology of War." *International Organization* 56(1): 7–45.

Snyder, Scott. 1999. *Negotiating on the Edge: North Korean Negotiating Behavior*. Washington, D.C.: United States Institute of Peace Press,

Snyder, Scott. 2001. "North Korea's Challenge of Regime Survival: Internal Problems and Implications for the Future." *Pacific Affairs* 73(4): 517–533.

Snyder, Scott. 2007. "Responses to North Korea's Nuclear Test: Capitulation or Collective Action?" *The Washington Quarterly* 30(4): 33–43.

Snyder, Scott. 2009. "Lee Myung-Bak's Foreign Policy: A 250-Day Assessment." *Korean Journal of Defense Analysis* 21(1): 85–102.

Snyder, Scott, and See-Won Byun. 2011. "Cheonan and Yeonpyeong." *The RUSI Journal* 156(2): 74–81.

Snyder, Scott, and See-won Byun. 2012. "China-Korea Relations: China's Post-Kim Jong Il Debate." May 2012. *Comparative Connections*. http://csis.org/files/publication/1201q china_korea.pdf. Accessed 3 February 2013.

Sobek, David. 2007. "Rally Around the Podesta: Testing Diversionary Theory Across Time." *Journal of Peace Research* 44(1): 29–45.

Song, Jooyoung. 2011. "Understanding China's Response to North Korea's Provocations." *Asian Survey* 51(6): 1134–1155.

Song, Sang-ho. 2010. "North Korea Fires Artillery into Sea Near Western Border." *The Korea Herald*. 23 November 2010. http://nwww.koreaherald.com/view.php?ud=20101123000840. Accessed 13 February 2013.

Sorokin, Pitirim. 1957 [1937]. *Social and Cultural Dynamics*. New York: American Book Company.

Soviet Embassy. 1966. "Memorandum of the Soviet Embassy in the DPRK About Embassy Measures Against Chinese Anti-Soviet Propaganda in the DPRK." 30 December 1966. *Cold War International History Project*. http://www.wilsoncenter.org/program/cold-war-international-history-project. Accessed 3 January 2013.

Soviet Embassy. 1968. "A Conversation with the 1st Secretary of the Embassy of the USSR in the DPRK, Comrade Zvetkov, and Comrade Jarck." 29 July 1968. *Cold War International History Project*. http://www.wilsoncenter.org/program/cold-war-international-history-project. Accessed 3 January 2013.

Spector, Leonard S. "Repentant Nuclear Proliferants." *Foreign Policy* 88: 21–37.

Spence, Jonathan D. 1990. *The Search for Modern China*. New York: Norton.

Sprecher, Christopher, and Karl DeRouen. 2005. "The Domestic Determinants of Foreign Policy Behavior in Middle Eastern Enduring Rivals, 1948–1998." *Foreign Policy Analysis* 1(1): 121–141.

Starr, Barbara. 1994. "Nodongs May Be Nuclear, Warns USN." *Jane's Defence Weekly* 21(24). 18 June 1994.

Starr, Barbara. 2003. "N. Korean Jets Intercept U.S. Plane." *CNN*. 4 March 2003. http://www.cnn.com/2003/WORLD/asiapcf/east/03/03/nkorea.intercept/. Accessed 25 January 2013.

Starr, Barbara. 2011. "North Korea Willing to Resume U.S. Missions to Recover Remains of Mias." *CNN*. http://www.cnn.com/2011/WORLD/asiapcf/01/18/us.north.korea.mias/index.html. Accessed 11 December 2012.

Stata (Stata Data Analysis and Statistical Software). 2012. http://stata.com/. Accessed 11 September 2012.

Stein, Arthur A. 1976. "Conflict and Cohesion: A Review of the Literature." *the Journal of Conflict Resolution* 20(1): 143–172.

Stohl, Michael, 1980. "The Nexus of Civil and International Conflict." In *Handbook of Political Conflict*, ed. Ted Robert Gurr. New York: Free Press, 297–330.

Straits Times. 2011. "Suspicions Linger Over Kim's Death." *The Straits Times* (Singapore). 23 December 2011. Accessed via LexisNexis, 14 February 2013.

Stueck, William. 2002. *Rethinking the Korean War: A New Diplomatic and Strategic History*. Princeton, NJ: Princeton University Press.

Stueck, William. 2009. "Reassessing U.S. Strategy in the Aftermath of the Korean War." *Orbis* 53(4): 571–590.

Sudworth, John. 2007. "Mixed Feelings Over Koreas Summit." 2 October 2007. BBC Online. http://news.bbc.co.uk/2/hi/asia-pacific/7022080.stm. Accessed 7 February 2013.

Suh, Choo-suk. 2002. "North Korea's 'Military-First' Policy and Inter-Korean Relations." *Korean Journal of Defense Analysis* 14(2): 167–185.

Suh, Dae-Sook. 1967. *The Korean Communist*

Movement, 1918–1948. Princeton, N.J.: Princeton University Press.

Suh, Dae-Sook. 1988. *Kim Il Sung: The North Korean Leader*. New York: Columbia University Press.

Suh, Dae-Sook. 1993. "North Korea: The Present and the Future." *Korean Journal of Defense Analysis* 5(1): 246–247.

Suh, Dae-Sook. 1998. "Kim Jong Il and New Leadership in North Korea." In Dae-Sook Suh and Chae-Jin Lee (eds) *North Korea After Kim Il Sung*. Boulder: Lynne Rienner Publishers: 13–31.

Suh, Dae-Sook, and Chae-Jin Lee. 1998. *North Korea After Kim Il Sung*. Boulder: Lynne Rienner Publishers.

Suh, Jae-Jung. 2004. "Assessing the Military Balance in Korea." *Asian Perspective* 28(4): 63–88.

Suh, Sang-Chul. 1983. "North Korean Industrial Policy and Trade." In Robert A. Scalapino and Chun-yop Kim (eds), *North Korea Today: Strategic and Domestic Issues*. Berkeley: University of California, Institute of East Asian Studies: 197–213.

Suk, Hi Kim. 2003. *North Korea at a Crossroads*. Jefferson. NC: McFarland.

Sullivan, Kevin. 1997. "South Korean Voters Ignore Economic Ills; Despite Currency Chaos, Establishment Candidate Holds Own in Polls." Washington Post. 26 November 1997: A27. Accessed via LexisNexis, 22 August 2012.

Sumner, W. G. 1906. *Folkways: A Study of the Sociological Importance of Usages, Manners, Customs, Mores and Morals*. Boston: Ginn.

Szalontai, Balazs. 2006. *Krushchev Versus Kim Il-Sung: Soviet-DPRK Relations and the Roots of North Korean Despotism, 1953–1964*. Stanford, CA: Stanford University Press.

Szarvas, Pál. 1955. "Report, Embassy of Hungary in North Korea to the Hungarian Foreign Ministry, 26 February 1955." *Cold War International History Project*, Washington, D.C.: Woodrow Wilson International Center for Scholars.

Tanter, Raymond. 1966. "Dimensions of Conflict Behavior Within and Between Nations, 1958–1960." *Journal of Conflict Resolution* 10: 41–64;

Tanter, Raymond. 1969. "International War and Domestic Turmoil: Some Contemporary Evidence." In *Violence in America: Historical and Comparative Perspectives*, eds. Hugh Davis Graham and Ted Robert Gurr. New York: Praeger.

The Telegraph (UK). 2011. "North Korea Says Korean Peninsula Faces 'Worst Crisis.'" 16 August 2011, http://www.telegraph.co.uk/news/worldnews/asia/northkorea/8703786/North-Korea-says-Korean-peninsula-faces-worst-crisis.html. Accessed on 19 Sep 2011.

Tir, Jaroslav. 2010. "Territorial Diversion: Diversionary Theory of War and Territorial Conflict." *The Journal of Politics* 72(2): 413–425.

Toft, Monica Duffy. 2010. *Securing the Peace: The Durable Settlement of Civil Wars*. Princeton: Princeton University Press.

Tong-a Ilbo. 1997. "Kim Chong-Il in 'Symbiotic' Relationship with Military." *Tong-A Ilbo*. Seoul. 6 January 1997.

Triandis, Harry C. 2001. "Individualism-Collectivism and Personality." *Journal of Personality* 69(6): 907–924.

Trochim, William M. 2005. *Research Methods: The Concise Knowledge Base*. Atomic Dog Publishers, Cincinnati, OH.

Truman, Harry S. 1947. "Recommendation for Assistance to Greece and Turkey." Address to Congress on 12 March 1947. http://trumanlibrary.org/publicpapers/viewpapers.php?pid=2189. Accessed 18 November 2012.

Truman, Harry S. 1950. "Notes Regarding Meeting with Congressional Leaders, June 27, 1950." *The Korean War and Its Origins 1945–1953*. Truman Library Online. http://www.trumanlibrary.org/whistlestop/study_collections/korea/large/documents/pdfs/ki-2-40.pdf#zoom=100. Accessed 27 November 2012.

Trumbull, Robert. 1958. "Korea Status Unchanged by Chinese Withdrawal." *New York Times*. 23 February 1958: E5.

Trumbull, Robert. 1967. "Economic Strains Beset Korea Reds: Morale in North Said to Sag as Goals Remain Unrealized." *New York Times*. 9 May 1967: 14.

Trumbull, Robert. 1968. "Vance and Park Reach an Accord." *New York Times*. 15 February 1968: 1.

Tures, John A. 2004. "Will New Blood in the Leadership Produce New Blood on the Battlefield? The Impact of Regime Changes on Middle East Military Rivalries." *Middle East Journal* 58(4): 612–635.

UN (United Nations) 1968. "Complaint by the United States (*Pueblo* Incident)." 26 January 1968. In *Repertoire of the Practice of the Security Council: Supplement 1966–1968*. 1971: 168. New York: United Nations. http://www.un.org/en/sc/repertoire/66-68/66-68___c.pdf, Accessed 15 January 2013.

UN (United Nations). 1969. *Resolution 2516: The Question of Korea.* UN General Assembly, 24th Session. 25 November 1969. http://documents.un.org/advance.asp. Accessed 7 January 2013.

UN (United Nations). 1970. *Resolution 2668: The Question of Korea.* UN General Assembly, 25th Session. 7 December 1970. http://documents.un.org/advance.asp. Accessed 7 January 2013.

UN (United Nations). 1993. *United Nations Security Council Resolution 825.* United Nations. New York: United Nations. http://daccess-dds-ny.un.org/doc/UNDOC/GEN/N93/280/49/IMG/N9328049.pdf?OpenElement. Accessed 20 August 2012.

UN (United Nations). 1994. *United Nations Convention on the Law of the Sea.* New York: United Nations Dept. of Public Information.

UN (United Nations). 1995a. "DPR Korea—Floods Situation Report No.1." United Nations. http://reliefweb.int/report/democratic-peoples-republic-korea/dpr-korea-floods-situation-report-no1. Accessed 13 August 2012.

UN (United Nations). 1995b. "DPR Korea—Floods Situation Report No. 2." United Nations. http://reliefweb.int/report/democratic-peoples-republic-korea/dpr-korea-floods-situation-report-no2. Accessed 7 September 2012.

UN (United Nations). 1995c. "DPR Korea—Floods Situation Report No.11." United Nations. http://reliefweb.int/report/democratic-peoples-republic-korea/dpr-korea-floods-situation-report-no11. Accessed 13 August 2012.

UN (United Nations). 1995d. "DPR Korea—Floods Situation Report No.12." United Nations. http://reliefweb.int/report/democratic-peoples-republic-korea/dpr-korea-floods-situation-report-no12. Accessed 14 August 2012.

UN (United Nations). 1996a. "Special Alert No.267—Democratic People's Republic of Korea." United Nations FAO/WFP. http://www.fao.org/docrep/004/W1302e/W1302e00.htm#I3. Accessed 15August 2012.

UN (United Nations). 1996b. "Special Alert No. 270—Democratic People's Republic of Korea." United Nations FAO/WFP. http://www.fao.org/docrep/004/w2706e/w2706e00.htm. Accessed 15August 2012.

UN (United Nations). 1997a. "Special Alert No. 275—Democratic People's Republic of Korea." United Nations FAO/WFP. http://www.fao.org/docrep/004/W5502E/W5502E00.HTM. Accessed 15August 2012.

UN (United Nations). 1997b. "Special Alert No. 277—Democratic People's Republic of Korea." United Nations FAO/WFP. http://www.fao.org/docrep/004/w6300e/w6300e00.htm. Accessed 15August 2012.

UN (United Nations). 1997c. "Special Report FAO/WFP Crop and Food Supply Assessment Mission to the Democratic People's Republic of Korea." United Nations FAO/WFP. http://www.fao.org/docrep/004/W7289E/W7289E00.HTM. 25 November 1997. Accessed 15 August 2012.

UN (United Nations). 1998a. "DPR of Korea Humanitarian Situation Report : 15 May–15 Jun. 1998." United Nations Office for the Coordination of Humanitarian Affairs. http://reliefweb.int/report/democratic-peoples-republic-korea/dpr-korea-humanitarian-situation-report-15-may-15-jun-1998. Accessed 16 August 2012.

UN (United Nations). 1998b. "Special Report FAO/WFP Crop and Food Supply Assessment Mission to the Democratic People's Republic of Korea." United Nations FAO/WFP. 25 June 1998. http://www.fao.org/docrep/004/w9066e/w9066e00.htm#E11E3. Accessed 16 August 2012.

UN (United Nations). 1998c. "Special Report FAO/WFP Crop and Food Supply Assessment Mission to the Democratic People's Republic of Korea." United Nations FAO/WFP. 12 November 1998. http://www.fao.org/docrep/004/x0449e/x0449e00.htm#E61E4. Accessed 16 August 2012.

UN (United Nations). 1999. "Special Report FAO/WFP Crop and Food Supply Assessment Mission to the Democratic People's Republic of Korea." United Nations FAO/WFP. 29 June 1999. http://www.fao.org/docrep/004/x2437e/x2437e00.htm#P308_17791. Accessed 16 August 2012.

UN (United Nations). 2000. "Special Report: Chronic Food Supply Problems Persist in DPR Korea Suggesting Continued Dependence on Large Scale Food Assistance." United Nations FAO/WFP. 7 June 2000. http://www.fao.org/docrep/004/X7426E/X7426E00.HTM. Accessed 15 August 2012.

UN (United Nations). 2008a. "Executive Summary: Rapid Food Security Assessment Democratic People's Republic of Korea." *United Nations FAO/WFP.* June/July 2008. http://documents.wfp.org/stellent/gro

ups/public/documents/ena/wfp193549.pdf. Accessed 3 February 2013.
UN (United Nations). 2008b. "WFP/FAO/UNICEF Food Security Assessment Mission to the Democratic People's Republic of Korea." *United Nations FAO/WFP*. 8 December 2008. http://documents.wfp.org/stellent/groups/public/documents/ena/wfp193548.pdf. Accessed 2 February 2013.
UN (United Nations). 2009a. "Security Council Condemns DPR Korea's Recent Launch." *United Nations Online*. 13 April 2009. http://www.un.org/apps/news/story.asp?NewsID=30461&Cr=dprk. Accessed 9 February 2013.
UN (United Nations). 2009b. "UN Nuclear Inspectors Leave DPR Korea." *United Nations Online*. 16 April 2009. http://www.un.org/apps/news/story.asp?NewsID=30488&Cr=dprk&Cr1=&Kw1=Korea&Kw2=Missile&Kw3=. Accessed 9 February 2013.
UN (United Nations). 2011. "WFP/FAO/UNICEF Rapid Food Security Assessment Mission to the Democratic People's Republic of Korea." *United Nations FAO/WFP*. 24 March 2011. http://documents.wfp.org/stellent/groups/public/documents/ena/wfp233442.pdf. Accessed 2 February 2013.
UN (United Nations). 2011. "FAO/WFP Crop and Food Security Assessment Mission to the Democratic People's Republic of Korea." 25 November 2011. http://documents.wfp.org/stellent/groups/public/documents/ena/wfp243024.pdf. Accessed 13 February 2013.
UN (United Nations) Population Division. 2012. *World Population Prospects: The 2010 Revision and World Urbanization Prospects: The 2011 Revision*. Population Division of the Department of Economic and Social Affairs of the United Nations Secretariat. http://esa.un.org/unpd/wup/unup/p2k0data.asp. Accessed 25 May 2012.
UNC (United Nations Command). 1953. *Military Armistice in Korea and Temporary Supplementary Agreement, Signed at Panmunjom, Korea, July 27, 1953, Entered into Force July 27, 1953*. Washington: U.S. Govt. Print. Off. http://www.ourdocuments.gov/doc.php?doc=85&page=transcript. Accessed 29 August 2012.
UNC (United Nations Command). 2012. Author interview and data provided by a United Nations Command Military Armistice Commission official. Seoul, South Korea. 20 September 2012.
UNCO (UN Command Official). 2012. Interview with author. 22 September 2012.
UNdata (United Nations Data). 2012. United Nations Official Data Website. http://data.un.org/Data.aspx?d=IFS&f=SeriesCode%3a99. Accessed 7 November 2012.
UNDP (United Nations Development Program). 1998. "Paper Presented at the Thematic Roundtable Meeting on Agricultural Recovery and Environmental Protection for the DPRK." Geneva, 28–29 May 1998.
UN FAIS (United Nations Food Aid Information System) World Food Program. 2013. World Food Program Website. http://www.wfp.org/fais/quantity-reporting. Accessed 23 January 2013.
UN WFP (United Nations World Food Program). 2011. "WFP/FAO/UNICEF Food Security Assessment Mission to the Democratic People's Republic of Korea." *United Nations FAO/WFP*. 25 November 2011.
United Nations Inter-agency Group for Child Mortality Estimation (IGME). 2012. http://www.childmortality.org/index.php?r=site/graph&ID=PRK_Korea%20DPR. Accessed 9 August 2012.
United Nations Office for Disarmament Affairs. "Treaty on the Non-Proliferation of Nuclear Weapons." http://www.un.org/disarmament/WMD/Nuclear/NPT.shtml. Accessed 29 October 2011.
UNSCR (United Nations Security Council). 1993. "Resolution 825 (1993)." *United Nations Website*. http://www.un.org/ga/search/view_doc.asp?symbol=S/RES/825(1993). Accessed 26 January 2013.
UNSCR (United Nations Security Council). 2006a. "Resolution 1695 (2006)." *United Nations Website*. http://www.un.org/ga/search/view_doc.asp?symbol=S/RES/1695(2006). Accessed 26 January 2013.
UNSCR (United Nations Security Council). 2006b. " Resolution 1718 (2006)." *United Nations Website*. http://www.un.org/ga/search/view_doc.asp?symbol=S/RES/1718(2006). Accessed 26 January 2013.
UNSC (United Nations Security Council). 2006c. "Security Council Condemns Nuclear Test by Democratic People's Republic of Korea, Unanimously Adopting Resolution 1718 (2006)." UN Security Council Press Release. 14 October 2006. http://www.un.org/News/Press/docs/2006/sc8853.doc.htm. Accessed 28 January 2013.
UNSCR (United Nations Security Council). 2009. "Resolution 1874 (2009)." *United*

Nations Website. http://www.un.org/en/sc/documents/resolutions/2009.shtml. Accessed 26 January 2013.

UNSC (United Nations Security Council). 2010. "Security Council Condemns Attack on Republic of Korea Naval Ship 'Cheonan.'" United Nations Security Council. 9 July 2010. http://www.un.org/News/Press/docs/2010/sc9975.doc.htm. Accessed 11 February 2013.

U.S. Army. 2009. "The Korean War 1950–1953." In *American Military History, Vol. 2, the United States Army in a Global Era, 1917–2008*, 221–254. Richard W. Stewart (ed). Washington, D.C.: U.S. Army Center of Military History.

U.S. Army. 2010. *FM 5-0: The Operations Process.* Washington, D.C., U.S. Government Printing Office.

U.S. Census Bureau. 2012. "International Programs." Online database. http://www.census.gov/population/international/data/idb/informationGateway.php. Accessed 20 May 2012

U.S. DoD (Department of Defense). 2011a. *Dictionary of Military and Associated Terms, Joint Publication 1-02*, Washington, D.C.: U.S. Government Printing Office.

U.S. DoD (Department of Defense). 2011b. *Joint Publication 3-0: Joint Operations.* Washington, D.C.: U.S. Joint Chiefs of Staff.

U.S. DoD (Department of Defense). 2011c. *Statistical Information Analysis Division (SAID) Web Site*, http://siadapp.dmdc.osd.mil/. Accessed 15 September 2011.

U.S. DoD (Department of Defense). 2012a. "Dod Personnel & Procurement Statistics: Personnel & Procurement Reports and Data Files." http://siadapp.dmdc.osd.mil/personnel/MILITARY/history/309hist.htm. Accessed 24 November 2012.

U.S. DoD (Department of Defense). 2012b. "Military Personnel Historical Reports: Active Duty Military Personnel by Regional Area and by Country." *DoD Personnel and Procurement Statistics Personnel and Procurement Reports and Data Files.* http://siadapp.dmdc.osd.mil/personnel/MILITARY/history/309hist.htm. Accessed 23 August 2012.

U.S. DoS (Department of State). 1979. *The Taiwan Relations Act,.* Washington, D.C.: U.S. Government Printing Office.

U.S. DoS (Department of State). 1994. "State Department Talking Points [Re the Agreed Framework]." November 1994. FOIA Release. *National Security Archive.* http://www.gwu.edu/~nsarchiv/NSAEBB/NSAEBB164/. Accessed 18 August 2012.

U.S. DoS (U.S. Department of State). 1996a. "North Korea's Food Situation." November 1994. FOIA Release. http://www.gwu.edu/~nsarchiv/NSAEBB/NSAEBB164/. Accessed 18 August 2012.

U.S. DoS (U.S. Department of State). 1996b. "Key Issue Papers for Secretary of State Madeleine Albright December 1996: Korea Peninsula Issues." December 1996. FOIA Release. http://www.gwu.edu/~nsarchiv/NSAEBB/NSAEBB164/EBB%20Doc%2012.pdf. Accessed 18 August 2012.

U.S. DoS (U.S. Department of State). 2005. *World Military Expenditures and Arms Transfers 2005.* U.S. Department of State Website. http://www.state.gov/t/avc/rls/rpt/wmeat/2005/index.htm. Accessed 23 August 2012.

U.S. DoS (U.S. Department of State). 2013. "Proliferation Security Initiative." U.S. *State Department Website.* http://www.state.gov/t/isn/c10390.htm. Accessed 10 February 2013.

U.S. Embassy. 1968. "Telegram from the Embassy in Korea to the Department of State/1/ Seoul, January 24, 1968, 2105Z." 28 January 1968. *Cold War International History Project.* http://www.wilsoncenter.org/document-collections. Accessed 14 January 2013.

The U.S. Misery Index. 2011. http://www.miseryindex.us/. Accessed 6 Sep 2011.

U.S. National Security Archives. 2003. "North Korea and the United States: Declassified Documents from the Bush I and Clinton Administrations." *National Security Archive Electronic Briefing Book No. 164*, Robert A. Wampler (ed.). http://www.gwu.edu/~nsarchiv/NSAEBB/NSAEBB164/. Accessed 7 August 2012

USAID (U.S. Agency for International Development). 1998. *Asia Obligations and Loan Authorizations FY 1946—FY 1997, U.S. Overseas Loans and Grants, Series of Yearly Data, Volume III.* Washington, D.C.: U.S. Agency for International Development. pdf.usaid.gov/pdf_docs/PNADL023.pdf. Accessed 18 December 2012.

USAID (U.S. Agency for International Development). 2011a. *U.S. Overseas Loans and Grants Series of Yearly Data, Volume III*, Asia Obligations and Loan Authorizations, FY 1946—FY 1997, http://pdf.usaid.gov/pdf_docs/PNADL023.pdf, accessed 20 June 2011

USAID (U.S. Agency for International Development). 2011b. *USAID: U.S. Military Assistance to South Korea.* http://gbk.eads.usaid

allnet.gov/query/do?_program=/eads/gbk/countryReport&submit=submit&output=2&unit=R&cocode=2KOR. Accessed 20 June 2011.

USAID (U.S. Agency for International Development) Bureau for Humanitarian Response. Office of U.S. Foreign Disaster Assistance. 1998. *BHR/OFDA Annual Report: FY 1998*. Washington, D.C.: Mitchell Group/Labat-Anderson.

USAPC (U.S. Asia-Pacific Center). 2008 "Interview with Michael Schiffer and Randall G. Schriver." *Asia-Pacific Center*. www.eastwestcenter.org/fileadmin/resources/washington/schiffer.schriver0908.pdf. Accessed 8 February 2013.

USFK (United States Forces Korea). 2012a. Author interview with USFK official. Seoul, South Korea. 25 September 2012.

USFK (United States Forces Korea). 2012b. "Combined Forces Command Announces ULCHI FREEDOM GUARDIAN 2012." United States Forces Korea Press Release. http://www.usfk.mil/usfk/press-release.combined.forces.command.announces.ulchi.freedom.guardian.2012.982. Accessed 17 January 2013.

USFK (United States Forces Korea). 2012c. "Mission of the ROK/U.S. Combined Forces Command." USFK Website. http://www.usfk.mil/usfk/. Accessed 24 August 2012.

USFK (United States Forces Korea). 2012d. "1953 Mutual Defense Treaty." *United States Forces Korea SOFA Documents*. http://www.usfk.mil/usfk/sofa.1953.mutual.defense.treaty.76. Accessed 25 November 2012.

USFK PAO (Public Affairs Office). 2010. "ULCHI FREEDOM GUARDIAN (UFG) 2010." 6 August 2010. *United States Forces Korea Public Affairs Office*. Seoul: USFK.

USG (U.S. Government)—Congressional-Executive Commission On China. 2005. *Annual Report: North Korean Refugees in China*, Washington, D.C.: U.S. Government Printing Office. http://www.cecc.gov/pages/annualRpt/annualRpt05/CECCannRpt2005.pdf. Accessed 28 June 2011.

USG (U.S. Government) 1951. *Security Treaty Between the United States and Japan; September 8, 1951*. The Avalon Project: Documents in Law, History and Diplomacy. Yale Law School Library. http://avalon.law.yale.edu/20th_century/japan001.asp. Accessed 8 January 2012.

USG (U.S. Government). 1953. *Mutual Defense Treaty Between the Republic of Korea and the United States of America*. URL: http://www.usfk.mil/org/fkdc-sa/sofa/mutdef.htm. Accessed 1 May 2008.

USG (U.S. Government) 1954. *Mutual Defense Treaty Between the United States and the Republic of Korea; October 1, 1953*. The Avalon Project: Documents in Law, History and Diplomacy. Yale Law School Library. http://avalon.law.yale.edu/20th_century/kor001.asp#1. Accessed 8 January 2012.

USG (U.S. Government). 2011a. "U.S.–China Joint Statement." 19 Jan 2011, http://www.whitehouse.gov/the-press-office/2011/01/19/us-china-joint-statement. Accessed 10 June 2011.

USG (U.S. Government). 2011b. *DOD Deployment of Military Personnel by Country*, http://siadapp.dmdc.osd.mil/personnel/MILITARY/history/309hist.htm, accessed 20 June 2011.

USG (U.S. Government). 2012. *DOD Deployment of Military Personnel by Country*. http://siadapp.dmdc.osd.mil/personnel/MILITARY/history/309hist.htm. Accessed 5 February 2013.

USITC (U.S. International Trade Commission). 1998. *Overview and Analysis of Current U.S. Unilateral Economic Sanctions*. U.S. International Trade Commission. Washington, D.C.: U.S. International Trade Commission.

Vance, Cyrus R. 1968. "Objectives of My Mission." Memorandum from Cyrus Vance to Lyndon B. Johnson. Foreign Relations of the United States, 1964–1968, Volume XXIX, Part 1, Korea, Document 181. http://history.state.gov/historicaldocuments/frus1964-68v29p1/d181. Accessed 7 November 2012.

Van Dyke, J. M., M. J. Valencia, and J. M. Garmendia. 2003. "The North/South Korea Boundary Dispute in the Yellow (West) Sea." *Marine Policy* 27(2): 143–158.

Vincent, Jack E. 1981. "Internal and External Conflict: Some Previous Operational Problems and Some New Findings." *The Journal of Politics* 43(1): 128–142.

Vincent, Jack E. 1983. "WEIS Vs. COPDAB: Correspondence Problems." *International Studies Quarterly* 27(2): 161–168.

VOA (Voice of America). 1998. "North Korea: Satellite Said to Be Transmitting Music." *BBC Worldwide Monitoring*. 14 September 1998. Accessed via LexisNexis, 5 September 2012.

VOA (Voice of America). 2005. "North Korean Succession Appears Uncertain." 3 February

2005. *VOA English Service*. Accessed via LexisNexis, 29 January 2013.

VOA (Voice of America). 2010a. "Sanctions Expected to Harm North Korean Economy." *Voice of America News*. 22 July 2010. http://www.voanews.com/content/sanctions-expected-to-harm-north-korean-economy-99090344/122462.html. Accessed 7 February 2013.

VOA (Voice of America). 2010b. "South Korea Formally Declares End to Sunshine Policy." *Voice of America News*. 17 November 2010. http://www.voanews.com/content/south-korea-formally-declares-end-to-sunshine-policy—108904544/130750.html. Accessed 7 February 2013.

VPA (Vietnam People's Army). 1966. "General Vo Nguyen Giap's Decision on North Korea's Request to Send a Number of Pilots to Fight in Vietnam." 21 September 1966. *Cold War International History Project*. http://www.wilsoncenter.org/program/cold-war-international-history-project. Accessed 10 January 2013.

Vreeland, Nena, and Rinn-Sup Shinn. 1976. *Area Handbook for North Korea*. Washington, D.C.: U.S. Government Printing Office.

Wakin, Daniel J. 2008. "North Koreans Welcome Symphonic Diplomacy." *New York Times*. 27 February 2008. http://www.Nytimes.com/2008/02/27/world/asia/27symphony.html. Accessed 28 February 2013.

Walder, David. 1974. *The Short Victorious War; the Russo-Japanese Conflict, 1904–5*. New York: Harper & Row.

Wallace, Robert Daniel. 2007. *Sustaining the Regime: North Korea's Quest for Financial Support*. Lanham, MD: University Press of America.

Wallace, Robert Daniel. 2014a. *The Determinants of Conflict: North Korea's Foreign Policy Choices, 1960–2011*. Dissertation, Kansas State University.

Wallace, Robert Daniel. 2014b. "North Korea and Diversion: A Quantitative Analysis (1997–2011)." *Communist and Post-Communist Studies* 47: 147–158.

Waltz, Kenneth N. 1954. *Man, the State, and War: A Theoretical Analysis*. New York: Columbia University Press.

Waltz, Kenneth N. 2000. "Structural Realism After the Cold War." *International Security* 25(1): 5–41.

Weathersby, Kathryn. 1993. *Soviet Aims in Korea and the Origins of the Korean War, 1945–1950: New Evidence from Russian Archives*. Washington, D.C.: *Cold War International History Project*, Woodrow Wilson International Center for Scholars.

Weeks, Jessica, 2011, "Strongmen and Straw Men: Authoritarian Regimes and the Initiation of International Conflict." Unpublished Working Paper. Cornell University. http://falcon.arts.cornell.edu.er.lib.k-state.edu/jlw338/index_files/Weeks-Strongmen.pdf. Accessed 15 August 2011.

Wendt, Alexander. 1992. "Anarchy Is What States Make of It: The Social Construction of Power Politics." *International Organization* 46(2): 391–425.

Westad, Odd Arne. 2007. *The Global Cold War: Third World Interventions and the Making of Our Times*. Cambridge: Cambridge University Press.

WFP (World Food Program). 2012. Food Information System. http://www.wfp.org/fais/quantity-reporting. Accessed 10 August 2012.

Whiting, Allen. 2001. "China's Use of Force, 1950–96, and Taiwan." *International Security* 26(2): 103–131.

Whymant, Robert, and David Watts. 1999. "Korean Dispute Ends in Sea Battle." *The Times*. London. 16 June 1999. Accessed via LexisNexis, 28 August 2012.

Wilkenfeld, Jonathan. 1972. "Models for the Analysis of Foreign Conflict Behavior of States." In *Peace, War, and Numbers*. Beverly Hills, CA: Sage, 275–298.

Wilkenfeld, Jonathan. 1974. "Conflict Linkages in the Domestic and Foreign Spheres." In *Quantitative Analysis of Political Data*, ed. S.A. Kirkpatrick. Columbus, OH: Merrill, 340–358

Wilkenfeld, Jonathan (ed.). 1973. *Conflict Behavior and Linkage Politics*. New York: McKay.

Wilkenfeld, Jonathan, Virginia L. Lussier, Dale Tahtinen. 1972. "Conflict Interactions in the Middle East, 1949–67" *The Journal of Conflict Resolution* 16(2): 135–154.

Williams, Victoria Claire. 2000. *Internal Woes, External Foes? Exploring the Theory of Diversionary War*. Dissertation, University of Kentucky.

Wilson, John B. 1998. *Maneuver and Firepower: The Evolution of Divisions and Separate Brigades*. Washington, D.C.: Center of Military History, U.S. Army.

Wilson Center. 2012. *Cold War International History Project*. http://www.wilsoncenter.org/program/cold-war-international-history-project. Accessed 17 November 2012.

Wit, Joel S. 2011. *Missile Negotiations with North Korea: A Strategy for the Future*. Washington, D.C.: US-Korea Institute at SAIS.

Wit, Joel S., Daniel Poneman, and Robert L. Gallucci. 2004. *Going Critical: The First North Korean Nuclear Crisis*. Washington, D.C.: Brookings Institution Press.

Witter, Willis. 1996. "Some Infiltrators Still Loose in South Korea; U.N. to Get Complaint About North." *The Washington Times*. 21 September 1996: A6. Accessed via LexisNexis, 7 September 2012.

Woo-Cumings, Meredith. 2002. *The Political Ecology of Famine: The North Korean Catastrophe and Its Lessons*. Tokyo, Japan: Asian Development Bank Institute.

Woods, Jackson S., and Bruce J. Dickson. 2012. "Victims and Patriots: Disaggregating Nationalism in China." Unpublished paper presented at the Comparative Politics Workshop, George Washington University. 2 November 2012.

Worden, Robert L., and Library of Congress Federal Research Division (eds.). 2008. *North Korea: A Country Study*. Washington, D.C.: U.S. Government Printing Office.

Worden, Robert L., Andrea Matles Savada, and Ronald E. Dolan. 1988. *China: A Country Study*. Washington, D.C.: Federal Research Division.

World Bank. 2012. "GHCN Station Temperature & Precipitation Variability Tool." http://iridl.ldeo.columbia.edu/maproom/.Global/.World_Bank/.Climate_ Variability/. Accessed 8 August 2012.

World dataBank. 2012. World Bank World Development Indicators and Global Development Finance. http://data.worldbank.org/indicator/SH.DYN.MORT?page=1. Accessed 9 August 2012.

World Trade Organization, 2010. *International Trade Statistics 2010* http://www.wto.org/english/res_e/statis_e/its2010_e/its10_toc_e.htm. Accessed 15 September 2011.

Wright, Quincy. 1971 [1942]. *A Study of War*. Chicago: University of Chicago Press.

Yi, Ki-baek. 1984. *A New History of Korea*. Cambridge, Mass: Harvard University Press.

Yomiuri (The Daily Yomiuri). 2006. "Tough U.S. Sanctions Triggered Launches." 6 July 2006: 2. *The Daily Yomiuri* (Japan). Accessed via LexisNexis, 26 January 2013.

Yomiuri Shimbun. 1993. "North Korea Missile Test Alarms Govt." *The Daily Yomiuri*. Tokyo. 13 June 1993: 2. Accessed via LexisNexis, 28 August 2012.

Yonhap News. 1994. "North Steps Up Subversion Against South." *Yonhap News*. Seoul. 4 October 1994. BBC Summary of World Broadcasts. Accessed via LexisNexis, 22 August 2012.

Yonhap News. 1996a. "Food Rationing Reportedly Suspended Until May.'" *Yonhap News Agency*. Seoul. 3 January 1996. BBC Summary of World Broadcasts. Accessed via LexisNexis, 7 September 2012.

Yonhap News. 1996b. "Recent Visitors to North Observe No Signs of Famine." *Yonhap News Agency*. Seoul. 28 June 1996. BBC Summary of World Broadcasts. Accessed via LexisNexis, 19 August 2012.

Yonhap News. 1996c. "South Korea Warns North Over 'Military Provocation.'" *Yonhap News Agency*. Seoul. 24 September 1996. BBC Summary of World Broadcasts. Accessed via LexisNexis, 22 August 2012.

Yonhap News. 1996d. "North Korean Family Defection Warns South Korea of Mass Exodus." *Yonhap News*. Seoul. 5 December 1996. Accessed via LexisNexis, 7 September 2012.

Yonhap News. 1996e. "Defector Says DPRK Beefing Up Border Guards, Checkpoints." *Yonhap News*. Seoul. 17 December 1996. Accessed via LexisNexis, 7 September 2012.

Yonhap News. 1997a. "DPRK Military Shows 'No Signs' of Lack of Food, Energy." *Yonhap News*. Seoul. 2 April 1997. Accessed via LexisNexis, 15 September 2012.

Yonhap News. 1997b. "JCS Reports on 10-Day DPRK Military-Civilian Exercises." *Yonhap News*. Seoul. 2 April 1997. Accessed via LexisNexis, 7 September 2012.

Yonhap News. 1997c. "NSP Announces Arrest of Spy Professor, Moles." *Yonhap News*. Seoul. 20 October 1997. Accessed via LexisNexis, 15 September 2012.

Yonhap News. 1998. "UN to More than Double DPRK Food Aid." *Yonhap News*. Seoul. 8 January 1998. Accessed via LexisNexis, 15 September 2012.

Yonhap News. 1999a. *Korea Annual 1999*. Seoul: Yonhap News Agency.

Yonhap News. 1999b. "Military Ordered to Boost Readiness Under 'Watch-Con 2.'" *Yonhap News Service*. Seoul. 15 June 1999.

Yonhap News. 1999c. "Roundup on DPRK-ROK Exchange of Fire in Yellow Sea." *Yonhap News Agency*. Seoul. 15 June 1999. Accessed via LexisNexis, 15 September 2012.

Yonhap News. 1999d. "DOD Finds No Signs of 'Heightened' Alert in DPRK." *Yonhap News Service*. Seoul. 16 June 1999.

Yonhap News. 2003. *North Korea Handbook.* Armonk, NY: M.E. Sharpe.

Yonhap News. 2009. "North Korea Extends Labor Drive by 100 Days Following '150-Day Battle.'" *North Korea Newsletter No. 73,* 24 September 2009. *Yonhap News* (Seoul). http://english.yonhapnews.co.kr/northkorea/2009/09/23/75/0401000000AEN20090923007500325F.HTML. Accessed 10 February 2013.

Yonhap News. 2010a. "Inter-Korean Relations: N. Korea Again Designates 'Naval Firing Zones' Along Sea Border." *North Korea Newsletter No. 95. Yonhap News Online.* 25 February 2010. http://english.yonhapnews.co.kr/northkorea/2010/02/24/9/0401000000AEN20100224009300325F.HTML. Accessed 11 February 2013.

Yonhap News. 2010b. "Kaesong Output Almost Unscathed by Soured Inter-Korean Ties: Report." *Yonhap News Online.* 4 October 2010. http://english.yonhapnews.co.kr/n_northkorea/2010/10/04/4301000000AEN20101004002300320.HTML. Accessed 11 February 2013.

Yonhap News. 2010c. "Military to Kick Off Annual Defense Drill Next Week."*Yonhap News* Agency (Seoul). 16 November 2010. *BBC Worldwide Monitoring.* Accessed via LexisNexis, 7 November 2011.

Yonhap News. 2010d. "Remaining Residents to Evacuate South Korean Shelled Island." *Yonhap News.* 25 November 2010. BBC Monitoring Asia Pacific—Political. Accessed via LexisNexis, 11 February 2013.

Yonhap News. 2011. "N. Korea Fired Short-Range Missile Off Its East Coast Monday." 19 December 2011. *Yonhap News.* Japan Economic Newswire. Accessed via LexisNexis, 13 February 2013.

Yonhap News. 2012. "China Decided on Food, Oil Aid for N. Korea After Kim's Death." 30 January 2012. *Yonhap News Online.* http://english.yonhapnews.co.kr/northkorea/2012/01/30/84/0401000000AEN20120130006800315F.HTML. Accessed 1 November 2013.

Yonhap News. 2013. " Seoul to Ramp Up Crackdown on Illegal Fishing in Yellow Sea." *Yonhap News* Online. 20 January 2013. http://english.yonhapnews.co.kr/national/2013/01/20/38/0301000000AEN20130120002600320F.HTML. Accessed 11 February 2013.

Yoo, J. 1999. "Korean Financial Crisis During 1997–1998 Causes and Challenges." *Journal of Asian Economics* 10(2): 263–277.

Yoon, Jeongwon. 2003. "Alliance Activities: Meetings, Exercises and CFC's Roles." In Donald W. Boose (ed.) *Recalibrating the U.S.-Republic of Korea Alliance.* Carlisle Barracks, PA: Strategic Studies Institute, U.S. Army War College.

Yoon, Jong-Han. 2011. "The Effect of U.S. Foreign Policy on the Relationship Between South and North Korea: Time Series Analysis of the Post-Cold War Era." *Journal of East Asian Studies* 11(2): 255–287.

Yoon, Sangwon. 2013. "N. Korea's 2011 China Trade Grew More than 60 Percent." *Bloomberg News.* 2 January 2013. http://www.businessweek.com/news/2012-12-26/north-korea-s-china-trade-expanded-more-than-60-percent-in-2011. Accessed 13 February 2013.

Youm, Kyu Ho 1994. "Press Freedom and Judicial Review in South Korea." *Stanford Journal of International Law* 30(1): 1–40.

Yu, Kun-chan. 1996. "'Changes' in U.S. DPRK Policy Seen as 'Reelection Strategy.'" *KBS (Korea Broadcasting System).* Seoul. 3 February 1996.

Yun, Duk-Min. 2004. "Long-Range Missiles." In *North Korea's Weapons of Mass Destruction: Problems and Prospects.* Ed. Kim Kyoung Soo, Elizabeth, NJ: Hollym, 121–148.

Yun, Tae-il. 2000. *The Inside Story of the State Security Department.* Seoul: Monthly Chosun Publications.

Yup, Paik Sun. 1999. *From Pusan to Panmunjom Wartime Memoirs of the Republic of Korea's First Four-Star General.* Dulles, VA: Potomac Books.

Zagoria Donald S., and Janet D. Zagoria. 1979. "Crisis on the Korean Peninsula." In Barry M. Blechman, Stephen S. Kaplan et al., *Diplomacy of Power: Soviet Armed Forces as a Political Instrument:* 9–1 to 9–95. Washington, D.C.: DARPA.

Zinser, Lynn. 2013. "Tensions Rising with North Korea, but Dennis Rodman Is There." *New York Times.* 26 February 2013. http://www.Nytimes.com/2013/02/27/sports/basketball/dennis-rodman-arrives-in-north-korea-for-tour.html?_r=0. Accessed 1 March 2013.

Zubok, V. M. 2007. *A Failed Empire: The Soviet Union in the Cold War from Stalin to Gorbachev.* Chapel Hill: University of North Carolina Press.

Index

Afghanistan 10, 129
Africa 85
Agreed Framework 78–79, 92, 94, 99; heavy fuel oil deliveries 75, 78, 160; light water reactor 78, 104
Albania 179
Azar, Edward 13, 45, 143, 147–148, 150–151, 153–155, 185, 202

Bell, B.B. 105–106
Blue House Attack 46–50, 63, 69–71, 122, 138
Bonesteel, Charles 66
Bulgaria 26, 198
Bush, George H.W. (Sr.) 199
Bush, George W. 129–130, 133

Carter, Jimmy 77–78
case study methods 5, 17, 35, 38–40, 44–46, 52, 61, 67, 70, 72–73, 75, 88, 91, 96, 103, 105–107, 119, 123, 131–134, 137–140, 142–144, 176–178, 180–181, 199, 201
Chang, Myon 65, 203
China (People's Republic of China) 9, 12, 14, 22–34, 36, 40–44, 50–56, 63, 65, 68, 71, 73–75, 79, 83, 86, 89, 106, 109–113, 115, 117, 119–120, 123–128, 143, 149, 159–161, 164–165, 171, 173–174, 179, 181–182, 197–198, 200–201; Chinese Communist Party 22; Great Leap Forward 75
Chinese Nationalists 22
Chosen Soren 57
Chung, Dong-young 128
Clinton, Bill 94–95, 101, 110, 112, 118, 127–128
Cold War 24, 26, 30, 65, 68, 97, 120, 138, 145, 154, 159–160, 164–166, 168–174, 181, 187, 197
Communist Bloc 26, 42, 68, 120
Composite Indicator of National Capabilities 16, 43, 50–51, 156–157, 169–172, 174, 187, 203
Conflict and Cooperation Scale (Azar) 8, 148
Conflict and Peace Databank (COPDAB) 147–148, 150, 154, 202
conflict theories (traditional) 4, 146, 180
Congo 52
control variable 12, 145, 152, 164–166, 170–172, 174
cross-sectional studies 6, 144
Cuba 129

deductive techniques 11, 143, 178
defectors *see* North Korea—defectors
Demilitarized Zone (DMZ) 4–5, 32, 44–46, 59–61, 65–66, 71, 81, 84, 101, 105, 113, 131, 144, 153, 155, 179, 198–200
dependent variable (DVAR) 12, 35, 38, 40, 142, 144, 146, 148–149, 152, 165–167, 169, 171–172, 174, 179
diverse case method 37
Dole, Robert 94

EC-121 Shootdown 49, 64, 69, 138, 198
Eisenhower, Dwight D. 30–32, 198; New Look Strategy 30

famine *see* North Korea—famine
foreign policy (definition) 13
France 201

GDP statistics 15–16, 52, 65, 87, 122, 153–154, 158, 169–170, 187–191, 193, 199, 201
Georgia 10
German Democratic Republic 198
Great Britain 201

hand coding of events 150–151

251

historians vs. political scientists 6–7, 10–11, 178, 183
Honest John nuclear systems 32, 77
hostile foreign policy: defined 13; scoring 146–147, 153, 185
Hungary 198
hypotheses 145–146, 174, 178

independent variable (IVAR) 12, 38, 40, 144–146, 152, 154–168, 170–172
India 201
Indonesia 52
inductive approach 10, 143, 178
infant mortality rates (IMR) *see* North Korea—child mortality rates
infantry engagements 45–46, 60–61
information warfare 182
International Atomic Energy Agency 77–78, 95
International Monetary Fund 93
Iran 129
Iraq 10, 129, 133
Israel 201

Jang, Sung-taek 117–118
Japan 10, 14, 19–22, 27, 29, 47–48, 55, 57–58, 62–63, 69–70, 73–74, 79–81, 83, 89, 91–92, 94, 102, 105, 107, 109–110, 115, 133, 140, 160–161, 197–200; occupation of Korea 19–21
Jenkins, Charles Robert 199
Johnson, Lyndon B. 61, 62, 66, 69, 71
juche 29, 34, 68, 72, 84, 126, 128
Jung, Sung-chul 5–6, 37, 40, 143, 179, 183, 203

Kaesong Industrial Complex 14, 113, 201
Kennan, George 69
Kennedy, John F. 37, 60–61, 71, 143
Khrushchev, Nikita 28, 33, 41, 51
Kim Dae-jung 60, 92–93, 96, 133, 200–201, 203
Kim Il-sung: background 19, 83; cult of personality 28, 83, 200; death 82–83; early years 20–23, 27–29; mutual defense treaties 41; NAM (relationship) 52; power consolidation 27–25, 50; PRC (relationship) 52; succession efforts 83–84; USSR (relationship) 51–52
Kim Jong-il: cult of personality 200; death 104, 119, 201; health concerns 104, 109, 116–117; rise to power 83–84; succession efforts 103, 109, 116–119, 137
Kim Jong-un 103, 109, 116–119, 137
Kim Yong-nam 117
Kim Young-sam 92–93, 96, 101, 150, 201
Korea: inter-Korean summits 96, 111, 128;

133; modern history 19–20, 197; special economic zones 12, 201
Korean Conflict Event database 45, 149–155, 168–174, 187–193
Korean War 23–26; armistice 26, 31–32, 66, 109, 112; casualties and cost 25–26; Chinese intervention 24–25; Inchon landings 24; instigator 23–24, 197

Laos 61, 63, 110
Lee, Hoi-chang 129
Lee, Myung-bak 115, 129, 133–134, 137–138
linear regression 142, 144, 146–147, 152, 167, 170, 177, 203; AR (1)—Cochrane and Orcutt 167, 170, 203; diagnostic tests 167–168, 203; longitudinal analysis 6, 143, 168, 183; models 164–166, 170

MacArthur, George 24
Mali 52
Mao Zedong 22–25, 28, 31, 33, 41, 52, 75, 197
Matador cruise missiles 32, 77
Mauritania 52
McCain, John 129–130
Michishita, Narushige 2, 4–5, 35, 37, 180, 203
Militarized Interstate Dispute (MID) data 147
military exercises 39, 62, 72, 95, 131, 141, 162; FOAL EAGLE 95, 132, 163; HOGUK 114; INVINCIBLE SPIRIT 131, 132; KEY RESOLVE 95, 112, 132, 162–163; RSOI 10, 162; TEAM SPIRIT 39, 92, 95–96, 99, 162–163; ULCHI FOCUS LENS 95, 162; ULCHI FREEDOM GUARDIAN 10, 113, 132, 162–163, 199
mixed-method approach 5–6, 10, 17, 142–143, 177–179, 197
Mount Kumgang 15, 110, 114–115, 130, 201

National Security Agency (US) 47
naval engagements 5, 12, 76, 82, 100, 111–112, 114, 116, 131–132, 137, 140, 163
Nixon, Richard 49, 61–62, 69, 71
Non-Aligned Movement (NAM) 52
Non-Proliferation Treaty (NPT) 9, 77–78, 86, 91–92, 95–96, 98, 101, 201
North Korea: agricultural practices 55, 73, 125; air defense 42, 49, 106; air forces 49, 57, 106; American journalists (detention) 110, 118, 127–128; artillery and artillery attacks 24, 31, 36, 60, 104–105, 112–114, 128, 131, 144, 163 (*see also* North Korea—Yeonpyeong Island shelling); assassination attempts 2, 61, 84, 95 162; black market

Index

activities 120–121, 123; bombings 25, 44, 84, 186; child mortality rates 88–90, 124, 154, 160, 169–170, 174, 202; Chinese troop labor assistance 27; citizen classification system 58, 88, 200; coup attempts 85; currency reform 84–85, 114, 116, 119–121, 136, 138, 180, 201; defectors (refugees) 16, 22, 25, 39, 56–57, 81, 85, 116, 125, 149, 159, 165–166, 169, 170, 172–174, 187–191, 193, 199–200, 202–203; defense spending 42, 50–55, 65, 86; donor fatigue 125; dual-track diplomacy 82, 95, 99, 101, 106, 141; early diplomatic relations 29–30; economy 33, 42–43, 52–55, 86–88, 119–124, 126, 143, 157–158, 197; energy assistance 73, 75, 78, 82, 87, 104–105, 125, 130, 160, 201; external debt 55, 120; famine 36, 72–102, 120, 124, 137–140, 149, 160, 164–165, 172–174, 179, 199–202; flooding 56, 73–75, 94, 101, 113–114, 123–124, 138; food aid 26, 72–76, 78, 80–82, 87–91, 96–97, 100, 105–106, 107, 110–111, 113–114, 120–125, 127, 130, 140–141, 160–161, 171; hijacking 32; industrial activities 14, 26–28, 30, 42, 50, 52, 55, 65, 86–87, 113, 122, 200–201; infiltration activities 14, 32, 60, 76, 80–81, 96, 100, 106, 140, 179, 198, 200; Korea People's Revolutionary Army 199; Korean People's Army 20, 45, 52, 83, 85, 121, 127; Korean Workers Party 200; malnutrition 89–90, 123–124; medical supply shortages 16, 75, 114, 123; Ministry of People's Security 58; missile programs 2, 4, 5, 10, 15, 36, 72, 76–88, 91–92, 96–100, 102–105, 107–109, 116, 121, 123, 126, 127, 129–130, 137–140, 144, 182, 198–200; naval forces 106, 111; New Year's Message 14, 110; nuclear program 15, 73, 77–78, 82, 86, 88, 96, 104, 108–110, 126–127, 129–130, 133, 138–139, 200; People's Provisional Committee 20; police state 58, 70, 200; prison camps 58, 84, 127, 159, 200–201; Public Distribution System (PDS) 74, 84, 88, 101, 123–125, 199; refugees see North Korea—defectors; repatriated Koreans 57–58; riots 84–85; societal collapse 27, 75, 111, 119, 133, 135, 137, 179; Songun military policy 100–101, 120; special operations forces 80–81, 85, 105–106, 111, 200–201; spy operations 81, 92, 93, 95, 111, 200; State Sponsors of Terrorism designation 130; submarine activities 81, 95, 106, 112–113, 201; turn-key plants 55; Winter Training Cycle training 100; Yeonpyeong Island shelling 113–116, 131–132, 138, 144, 163

Northern Limit Line 82, 106, 111–114, 195, 201

Obama, Barack 111, 129–131, 138
Okinawa 32, 61–62

Park Chung-hee 33, 44, 46, 60, 64–69, 71, 198, 201
Patriot anti-missile systems (US) 79
policy implications 17, 181–182
political shocks 35–37, 72, 83, 90, 99, 103; definition 35–36
presidential elections 39–40, 60–62, 67–68, 72, 84, 92–96, 98–99, 118, 128–131, 133–134, 143, 150, 161–162, 172, 175, 201–203
Proliferation Security Initiative 109, 113
Proposition 1 (Diversionary Theory) 145–146, 164–165, 168, 172, 174; defined 145
Proposition 2 (External Influences) 145–146, 164–165, 168, 172, 174; defined 145
proxy data 15, 56, 149, 155–156, 158–161, 175

qualitative analysis methods 10–11, 35–40
quantitative analsyis methods 10–11, 142–147

Red Cross 115
refugees see North Korea—defectors
Rhee, Syngman 20, 22–24, 26, 30–33, 64, 143, 198, 203
Ri, Young-ho 118
Rice, Condoleezza 109
Roh, Myoo-hung 133, 203
Roh, Tae-woo 92
Romania 26, 178–179
Russia 159, 201
Russo-Japanese War 10

sanctions 39, 91–92, 102, 104, 108–110, 112–113, 120, 126–128, 130, 147, 161, 181, 185, 202
Six Party Talks 110, 112, 127, 129–130, 133
soft power responses 182
South Korea: administration type 38, 96, 133, 139, 162–163, 170, 177; aid from the U.S. 43; artillery attack see North Korea—Yeonpyeong Island shelling; Cheonan (South Korean ship) 111–113, 115, 119, 121, 123, 128, 131–132, 134, 136, 138, 140, 144, 201; coup d'état (1961) 33, 34, 54, 60, 64; economic success 65; election cycles 202; media and press freedom 150; Ministry of Unification 129, 159, 201; navy 111, 132, 201; Sunshine Policy 96, 129, 133, 201; tourist incident 14–15, 130, 134

Stalin, Joseph 20–24, 28–29, 41, 58, 75, 197; de–Stalinization 28
Stata analysis program 168
structured, focused questions 37–38
Sudan 10
Syria 129

Taiwan 22, 63
theory (definition) 12
translation methods 151, 202
Truman, Harry 24, 26, 30

United Nations 10, 25, 30, 32, 39, 48, 59, 66, 104, 126, 127, 151, 158, 161, 198, 202; resolutions 39–40, 92, 103, 113, 128, 136, 139, 146, 165–166, 169–171, 174–175, 177, 187, 203; Security Council 38, 48, 49, 59, 67, 91, 98, 101, 108, 112, 126–127, 133, 136–138, 161, 200
United Nations Command (in Korea) 10, 48, 65–66, 151, 198, 202; World Food Program 76, 89, 107, 114, 123, 160–161
UN Commission on the Unification and Rehabilitation of Korea (UNCURK) 59
United States: Axe Murder incident 4–5, 84; 82nd Airborne Division 63; Fifth Air Force 48; leadership changes 38, 60, 94, 175; presence in East Asia 62; USS *Pueblo* 4, 5, 44, 46–49, 62–63, 69, 71, 138, 198; Seventh Fleet 47–48, 62–63; strategic-level exercises *see* military exercises; Trading with the Enemy Act 130
USSR 10, 20–24, 26–31, 33, 34, 36, 40–43, 48–56, 61–62, 64–65, 69, 71, 73, 75, 77, 79, 83, 86–87, 89, 95, 106, 119–120, 159, 164–165, 171, 173, 174, 182, 197, 198, 200, 203

Venezuela 129
Vietnam 5, 7, 47–49, 53, 60–64, 66, 69, 71, 129, 179, 197, 199
Vietnam War 47–49, 63

Wen, Jiabao 110
West Africa 202
Western bias 179
World Event/Interaction Survey (WEIS) 147, 149, 202
World Governance Indicators (WGI) 16, 155–156, 165–166, 169–171, 199–200, 203
World Vision International 74
World War I 197
World War II 19–21, 81, 200; post-war occupation of Korea 20–21

Yun, Bo-seon 203